ROGER
FEDERER

ROGER FEDERER

THE DEFINITIVE BIOGRAPHY

CHRIS BOWERS

jb

First published in the UK by John Blake Publishing
an imprint of Bonnier Books UK
4th Floor, Victoria House
Bloomsbury Square
London WC1B 4DA
England

Owned by Bonnier Books
Sveavägen 56, Stockholm, Sweden

www.facebook.com/johnblakebooks
twitter.com/jblakebooks

Parts of this book have previously been published in the author's *Fantastic Federer*,
Roger Federer – Spirit of a Champion and *Roger Federer – The Greatest*

First published in hardback, as *Fantastic Federer*, in 2006
Revised and updated hardback edition published in 2021
This revised and updated paperback edition published in 2023

Paperback ISBN: 978-1-78946-147-3
Hardback ISBN: 978-1-78946-366-8
Ebook ISBN: 978-1-78606-192-8

British Library Cataloguing-in-Publication Data:
A CIP catalogue record for this book is available from the British Library.

Design by www.envydesign.co.uk

Printed and bound in Great Britain by Clays Ltd, Elcograf S.p.A.

1 3 5 7 9 10 8 6 4 2

John Blake Publishing is an imprint of Bonnier Books UK
www.bonnierbooks.co.uk

CONTENTS

PART 4: THE BIG FOUR

PART 5: THE GLORIOUS TWILIGHT

ABOUT THE AUTHOR

CHRIS BOWERS is a freelance writer, broadcaster and tennis historian who has covered the global tennis circuit since 1992. After graduating in German with History, Linguistics and Music in 1983, he trained as a newspaper journalist, before moving into radio in 1986. Over the next two years, he worked for Switzerland's overseas service Swiss Radio International in Bern. During that time he played a year's Swiss league tennis for the Flamingo tennis club owned by František Kratochvil, whose son Michel became a touring professional; his doubles partner in that season was Severin Lüthi, a coach and close confidant of Roger Federer. After working for an environmental organisation for two years, he went full-time on the global tennis tour in 1992, working for newspapers, magazines, radio, television and internet media. He is best known as a commentator for various television stations and internet radio, but as a writer he has reported for a number of newspapers, magazines and websites and this is his eighth book about tennis. He also works in the environmental and political fields and has served as a councillor in English local government and stood for the British parliament four times. He lives with his daughter in East Sussex, England.

AUTHOR'S INTRODUCTION

The concept of 'greatness' is a superb subject for any discussion, because it can be interpreted in so many different ways. Does greatness just relate to performance? Or is it performance allied to a human dimension? Can 'greatness' only be for the benefit of humanity or can it be simply achieving excellence in a given discipline? And even: does 'greatness' exist at all, in the sense that we're all 'great' at something?

All these questions arise in different ways in assessing career and personality of the the remarkable Roger Federer. It would be hard to find a knowledgeable tennis fan who doesn't have him in their all-time five greatest tennis players; in fact he would make most aficionados' all-time three greatest players. And if he is not the greatest player ever, who would pip him? He will end up with fewer Grand Slam singles titles than Rafael Nadal or Novak Djokovic, but does that make them greater players? Would a player in an earlier era have a greater claim, in spite of all the difficulties in comparing one era with another? And what of Federer's standing beyond tennis? – and should that count for anything in the overall assessment?

Ultimately, everyone has to set their own criteria and come up with their own answer. This book sets out the evidence and starts the discussion. I do so with an implicit assumption that there is certainly a plausible case that Roger Federer is the greatest tennis player of all time, even if there may be counter cases to be made on behalf of other players. I also seek to broaden the discussion to Federer's status outside tennis. That includes overcoming certain misgivings to discuss, in the final chapter of this book, whether there is something saint-like about him– to flirt with such subject matter about a sportsman risks losing groundedness and perspective, and drifting into hyperbole, but certain aspects of his personality make airing the pros and cons legitimate. People can agree or disagree, and they will, but setting out the arguments is all part of the fun of discussing such subjects, whether over dinner, on a bus, or in the tennis club bar.

Because so much of a normal tennis year revolves around the four Grand Slam tournaments (Australian Open, French Open, Wimbledon and US Open), much of the heart of this book is about Federer's performances at those events. But I have done my best to ensure that it's not just an exercise in accountancy, with results and scores dictating the narrative. Some tournaments that he won warrant barely a paragraph, while others that he lost get a whole section to themselves. And I make no apology for blatantly slowing down the clock and describing some minute detail when it comes to the extraordinary twenty minutes in which he turned defeat into victory in the 2017 Australian Open final: surely the most dramatic moment of his career, if not the greatest. I have also been careful to ensure that what was going on behind the scenes gets prominence, because Federer has been far more than just a tennis player; even if one takes only his body of work within the sport into account, he has been a statesman of tennis for the past twenty years.

This book has evolved over a period of sixteen years. In 2005–6, I wrote the first English-language biography of Roger Federer, which was published under the title *Fantastic Federer*. At that time, he was still in his mid-twenties, so the book was very much a profile of him with speculation as to what he might go on to achieve. In the intervening years, that book has been revised, updated, reshaped and renamed, to the point where this is the tenth incarnation. Now Federer's playing career is over, we can get a true sense of the immensity of what he has achieved. In that sense it is now a true biography, where the early editions were really book-length profiles.

Some material from the original books has survived. After all, his childhood and early career haven't changed since 2006, but some events in the early years that seemed important sixteen years ago have been eclipsed by subsequent achievements. This book is therefore a new book making use of some old material, and not an old book with a couple of chapters tacked on to the end.

Some readers understandably want to know under what conditions it was written, though the question often used to ask this – 'is it an authorised biography?' – is a poor one to elicit a meaningful answer. It is not 'authorised' in the sense that Roger has not worked with me in giving me new material, revealing inside stories and checking facts. But I prefer to call it an 'independent' biography, as the word 'unauthorised' is often taken to mean inherently hostile. I first approached Federer in 2004 to discuss working on a book. Eighteen months later, I had a meeting with his agents, who passed on the message that Roger doesn't do anything that he doesn't put the required effort into, that he didn't have time to do a book to the standard he would feel happy with, and therefore he wasn't going to work with any author. That position hasn't changed in the years since, despite about a dozen approaches a year from publishers all wanting to write his 'inside story'. The Roger Federer inside story doesn't exist, and might never exist, such is the way he guards his privacy and information about the inner workings of Team Federer. And his consistency in giving the same response to any potential book author means that anyone who claims to have privileged access to him is almost certainly playing fast and loose with the truth.

Some who write about Federer claim to have privileged access to his family. This must also be taken with a pinch of salt. While invariably polite, the extended Federer family is as protective of their privacy as Roger and Mirka are. I therefore not only have no close knowledge of what goes on behind Roger's and Mirka's front door, but I don't seek any. This book is about Roger Federer, not about his children, and, while their presence and effect on his life are a small part of the story, they are entitled to a normal childhood away from the glare of publicity, and I am happy to respect that.

This is therefore an independent biography of Roger Federer; indeed my independence has given me a degree of freedom to write about him without constraints on what he or his advisers might have wanted me to say. I was able to speak freely with many of the people who have helped shape him, and paint a picture of him both as a person and as a tennis player. It is a largely positive picture, because I believe from twenty-five years dealing with him that he is a very special person, but I don't believe anyone is all good or all bad, and I don't shy away from criticising him when I feel it is warranted.

Some choose to view independent biographies as a good second-best holding option until the subject chooses to write their autobiography. That is a dangerous approach. It is true that the subject will know all the inside stories and be able to throw a different light on the background to certain events, but it is only his or her version of events, and may well be what they want the public to know, rather than what actually happened. If Roger Federer does one day write his own memoirs, they will add an interesting dimension to the Federer story, but they will not be the definitive work on their own. Biographies like this that draw on interviews done specifically for them plus various other pieces of information in the public domain are more likely to present a fair portrait of the person under discussion than that person's own account of what happened.

I am fortunate to be in a pretty much ideal situation to write about Federer. I've known him since he was sixteen – I first interviewed him after he'd won the boys' singles at Wimbledon in 1998 – and the fact that I have lived in Switzerland, speak German and French, can understand the Swiss-German dialects (that baffle many citizens of Germany), and know several people with whom he grew up puts me in a unique position among international tennis writers to write his biography. I believe this book is generally recognised as the definitive international biography of Federer, and I was gratified to learn that, after his shock first-round defeat at Wimbledon in 2019, a leading member of the millennium generation of male players, Stefanos Tsitsipas, admitted to reading it and finding it 'one really interesting book', after his agent had bought it for him as a way of lifting his morale out of a slump.

With Roger Federer's playing career now part of history, we are finally able to look back on a highly impressive body of work from a truly inspirational man. If this book helps people to understand the man behind the legend, it will have served its purpose.

CHRIS BOWERS
Lewes, 2023

ACKNOWLEDGEMENTS

This book could not have come to fruition without a lot of people helping me. Those who have assisted from the beginning include (in alphabetical order): Yves Allegro, Madeleine Bärlocher, Roger Brennwald, Darren Cahill, Beat Caspar, Marco Chiudinelli, Ashley Fisher, Roger Jaunin, Seppli Kacovski, Marco Mordasini, Francesco Ricci Bitti, Niki von Vary, Freddy Widmer and Thomas Wirz. I am also grateful for various bits of important help to: Faye Andrews, Nicola Arzani, Tim Curry, Richard Eaton, Mark Hodgkinson, Frank Hofen, Mitzi Ingram Evans, Annie Hammerton, Severin Lüthi, Ian McDermott, Konrad Meyer, Peter Miles, Jack Milner, Helen Mittwoch, Daniel Monnin, Claudia Moser, Andrew Rigby, Neil Robinson, Greg Sharko, Barbara Travers, Jürg Vogel, Michael Wehrle and Paul Zimmer. Special thanks to Beat Caspar, Richard Evans, Robert McNicol and Helen Scott-Smith for easing my work on the 2021 and 2023 editions. Thanks also to Lynette Federer and Tony Godsick for their help in discussing the original concept and for their willingness to do what they could within the constraints set by Roger. And finally massive thanks to John Blake and Michelle Signore of John Blake Publishing for having the original belief in me and the book, and for investing in keeping the book 'live' as Federer's career has developed. They have now moved on for Bonnier Books UK to take over this book, but one constant throughout has been Toby Buchan, the editor of this book, who has been a wonderful foil to my foibles, both on this work and on *Novak Djokovic: The Biography,* which I feel acts as a sister biography to this one.

THE FORMATIVE YEARS

THE STORY OF Roger Federer is no 'Williams story'. In fact, to those who hanker after an egalitarian tennis world where the economic circumstances of a child's background are no obstacle to them making it to the very top of the game, this will offer no supporting evidence. While Venus and Serena Williams were genuine products of the ghetto community of Los Angeles, and Jimmy Connors grew up in a blue-collar area of Illinois, encouraged to despise the rich kids who populated the established tennis clubs, Federer is a product of the affluent middle classes.

He is the second child of a modestly well-to-do but unremarkable family from Basel. He's certainly not had to defy social obstacles to reach the top, he's not even a middle-class rebel without a cause like John McEnroe was. He has never felt the need to turn his anger into on-court intensity, the way Connors, Lleyton Hewitt and even Pete Sampras could turn their opponents into deeply hated enemies, at least for the duration of a match. Nor has he ever resorted to the snide tactics of a McEnroe, Ion Tiriac or Ilie Nastase to derail an opponent's concentration. He's a well-spoken and well-behaved child without an apparent chip on his shoulder.

Yet the drive that underlies the phenomenal body of work he has created cannot be assembled without a steely deter-mination. Perhaps the lesson for tennis sociologists from the Roger Federer story is that such determination is classless – that it can burn as brightly in someone for whom everything was laid on as it can in someone who has had to fight for everything. Having said that, a little money to oil the wheels of junior coaching and a willing parental taxi service clearly helped, and Federer benefited considerably from both.

Roger Federer was born on 8 August 1981 in Switzerland's second-largest city, Basel, the second child and first son of Lynette and Robert Federer, who had lived there since their marriage in 1973.

Though hardly a destination for the trendy international jetsetter, Basel's location on the Rhine river at the junction of three countries – Switzerland, Germany and France – makes it a highly appropriate place of origin for a global sporting icon. In fact, the city's location at an international crossroads had something of a role in Federer today being conversant in three languages – or four, if you consider the fiercely independent guttural Swiss-German dialects as a language in their own right. Five languages are regularly visible in everyday life in Basel: the four Swiss languages – German, French, Italian, the original pure Swiss language of Romansh (now spoken only in the east but still in use on banknotes and some official signs) and English. The city's airport, sited on French territory, was for years known as Basel–Mulhouse but is today known as EuroAirport; cities in Germany, Switzerland and France all claim it as their own.

As the most European city in a country whose inhabitants are still very sceptical about joining the European Union, Basel has a mildly un-Swiss character and a sense of humour all of its own. It has its own variation of the German carnival called the *Morgestraich* (literally, 'morning roam through the streets'), a pagan procession held on the Monday after Ash Wednesday at 4am, at which time all the lights in the city go off to enhance the effect of a stream of candlelit torches. It's also one of Europe's oldest university cities and a centre of the European pharmaceuticals industry. It was in Basel in 1943 that a chemist, Professor Albert Hofmann, tested on himself a molecule he had devised and named LSD-25 – when he began having hallucinations, it became clear he had become the first man to experience the effects of the drug commonly known today as LSD.

Roger Federer's story begins in the Basel pharmaceuticals industry, though somewhat more prosaically. His father, Robert, was a laboratory assistant with the Basel-based chemicals giant Ciba-Geigy. As the 1960s ended, he decided to travel, threw in his job, and landed in South Africa, as much because it was easy to get into as for any other reason. Ironically, he then got a job with Ciba's main plant in South Africa, which was based in Isando, an industrial suburb on the east rand of Johannesburg. There in 1970 he met an eighteen-year-old secretary, Lynette Durand, who worked at Ciba and had lived all her life in the affluent nearby suburb of Kempton Park. They got to know each other outside work; he introduced her to tennis, she loved it, they played a lot, and began a romance, which led to marriage in 1973.

Robert Federer was born in 1946. The son of a textile worker, he grew up in eastern Switzerland near the town of Altstätten, and played tennis for fun, but never aspired to doing it particularly well. Lynette is six years his junior, born in 1952 to a family whose first language was Afrikaans. She went on to play tennis to a much higher level than her husband – according to Beat Caspar, the former sports editor of Basel's daily newspaper, the *Basler Zeitung*, 'She had a good sense of co-ordination, much better than Robert' – but, despite having a fair amount of ambition, she too never aspired to make a career of it.

In 1973, the couple moved to Switzerland – leaving Lynette 8,400 kilometres (5,200 miles) from 'home' – and settled in Riehen, a suburb of Basel near the German border. (Switzerland's second-largest city had an English spelling and pronunciation of its name – 'Basle', pronounced Barl – for many years, but as with many English variants of European city names it has largely died out. These days, the city is widely known by its Swiss-German name 'Basel', pronounced Barsl, which is the spelling used in this book. Basel also has a French language variant, 'Bâle', pronounced as in the English word 'balcony'.)

Robert went on to become a sales executive for Ciba while Lynette also secured a posting with the company in her new home city, and the two played tennis at the firm's multi-sports club, which had a handful of courts shaded by mature trees in the Basel suburb of Allschwil. Company sports and leisure grounds were a very cheap way for employees to practise their recreation; in fact some companies allowed their staff and their families to use the firm's facilities for free. That was fine for the bank balance but for anyone with a bit of ambition, the social nature and lack of competitive structure could become frustrating.

After a few years living in Basel, Lynette joined the 'Old Boys' Tennis Club, one of Basel's top two tennis clubs (the other being the equally Swiss-sounding 'Basel Lawn Tennis Club'), mainly to play competitive matches, and in 1995 she was a member of the Old Boys' women's team that became Swiss national inter-club champions in the 'Young Veterans' age group. She also actively supported local and regional tennis, serving on the board of the Basel regional subsection of the Swiss Tennis Association and taking on responsibility for developing young talent. In addition, for many years she worked at Basel's ATP tournament, the Swiss Indoors. As her adult years wore on, she largely traded tennis for golf, playing off a handicap of around fifteen.

The remarkable thing is that both Robbie and Lynette are very short. Neither is more than 1.7m (5ft 7in), and for a while it was feared that any offspring of theirs couldn't possibly grow tall enough to become a force on the tennis circuit. Yet, out of some genetic inheritance, Roger Federer grew to 1.85m (6ft 1in).

In late 1979, Lynette and Robbie's first child, Diana, was born. A much quieter person than her younger brother, she has quite deliberately kept out of the limelight, and has pursued her own career as a psychiatric nurse, working outside but not far from Basel. Like Roger, she too had twins.

Diana's childhood was inevitably strongly affected by Roger's exploits, but the Federers appear to have largely avoided the classic trap of having a gifted child whose interest needs to be serviced to such an extent that other offspring suffer. 'The family was always relatively harmonious,' says Thomas Wirz, a Basel journalist and tennis coach who on several occasions carried out interviews in the Federer family home. 'I have sometimes wondered what Diana did while Roger was being ferried from tournament to tournament, and she may well have certain misgivings about the tennis world, but she has always seemed very independent, pretty sure of herself and very polite. There certainly never seemed to be any sense of resentment.'

Diana, who enjoys skiing and snowboarding, was often approached by the *Basler Zeitung* for quotes. 'She never wanted to have an article about herself in the newspaper,' says Beat Caspar. 'I often asked her. I told her the people would be interested in her, especially when they see her sitting courtside watching Roger's matches, but she always said no. Lynette constantly made it clear that Diana wasn't to get the short straw from Roger's tennis. She always told Diana that she shouldn't be in any way bothered by the fact that people were always asking about Roger. And Diana has always kept her distance from tennis and the media, and has never wanted to talk publicly about her brother.'

Twenty months after Diana's birth, after the family had moved across the Rhine to Münchenstein, a suburb closer to Basel city centre, Roger was born. With no middle name, the birth register simply bears the entry: 'Roger Federer'. Because he's Swiss, and because French is the second language in Switzerland, many assume that his first name is pronounced the French way (eg as in *Roget's Thesaurus*), but, as he has often had to point out, it is pronounced the English way, and most French-speaking people who know this have developed their own pronunciation (as if written 'Roj-air'). The correct pronunciation of 'Federer' has the emphasis on the first syllable, with the vowel sound somewhere between the vowel in the English words 'fair' and 'fay' and the first 'r' flipped. The English-speaking world has settled into a pronunciation that resembles the English word 'federal', a pronunciation that Federer accepts as legitimate.

What was he like as a boy? Everyone who remembers him from that time talks about a happy and cheerful boy with seemingly limitless energy and a burning need to play sport, especially ball sports. In an interview in 2005, Lynette said, 'He wasn't a straightforward child. He was very, very lively, full of energy, and he was always trying out the boundaries with his parents – and, later, with his teachers – in sport, in school. He was always a bundle of energy and very emotional, not easy to be with. For a while, I was constantly worried about his concentration, but he later worked on that.'

The Swiss education system offers each Swiss canton (administrative region) a fair bit of freedom in its educational set-up. In Basel, then as now, children went to kindergarten at five, primary school at seven, secondary school at eleven or twelve and then on to various forms of further education at fifteen or sixteen, once the compulsory years were over.

Roger followed his sister Diana into the Neuewelt School, a state-run primary school in a quiet, leafy and affluent corner of Münchenstein – the name 'Neuewelt' literally means 'new world' but it is just the name of an area in Münchenstein and doesn't indicate any wider idealistic project. Although they could have afforded to send their children to private schools, Robbie and Lynette's decision to send Diana and Roger to the local state primary wasn't unusual, as that was very much what one did in Switzerland. There was little demand for private schools, especially in moderately well-off areas where facilities were good, and it was felt that parental support encouraged high standards of education. The Neuewelt School had a kindergarten as well as the primary school, and Diana and Roger went there from the ages of five to twelve.

Data-protection legislation and other privacy safeguards prevent Roger's teachers from saying too much about his schooling, but Theresa Fischbacher, who was head teacher for part of the time Roger was in his primary-school years, remembers him more from his time outside the classroom than in it. 'I was convinced he would become a footballer,' she recalled in 2005. 'You hardly ever saw him without a football at his feet, and he used to say, "I want to become a footballer!" For a long time, I had no idea he played tennis and, when I eventually found out, I assumed it had to be very much a secondary activity because of his passion for football. I have to admit that he was very good, and it wouldn't have surprised me to see him make it as a football player.'

A few years before Roger arrived at the Neuewelt School, two of its alumni, the brothers Murat and Hakan Yakin, had been as enthusiastic footballers in their primary-school days as Federer; they went on to become local icons for FC Basel, each playing more than fifty games for the Swiss national team. Their success created a culture at the school that it was cool to play football, and, with tennis at that time still a very limited sport in a country whose primary sporting passions were football, skiing and ice hockey, young Roger might well have felt more comfortable with the big ball at his feet than the small ball on his racket strings.

Fischbacher remembers one other thing about him: 'He was always moving. He was happy, had a lovely nature and was well brought up, in terms of his manners, but he had this constant need to be on the move. He was a fidget.' Yet she denies that this restlessness in any way made him a bad pupil. 'He was clearly bright, and I've known many restless, fidgety kids who were very bright.'

Federer himself has said of his primary-school days, 'I loved playing with balls, whatever sport they were from: ping-pong, tennis, basketball, football. I was always trying something.'

At twelve, he left to attend the Progymnasium, a form of secondary school specifically for children expected to go on to the full Gymnasium (literally 'grammar school', although not really comparable to the English grammar schools) at the age of fifteen. Although he never went on to the full Gymnasium, never excelled in academic pursuits and finished his schooling at Switzerland's National Tennis Centre, he wouldn't have been allowed into the Progymnasium if he hadn't been at least moderately bright academically.

One might expect there to be pictures of such inspirational alumni as the Yakin brothers and Roger Federer adorning the corridors of the Neuewelt School. In some countries, there might even have been a plaque, 'ROGER FEDERER WENT TO SCHOOL HERE, 1988–93'. But no. Switzerland just isn't that sort of country. For today's pupils, parents and staff at the school, Federer is just someone who went there a few decades ago. Perhaps this lack of ostentatious admiration provides a part-explanation for Federer's phenomenal normality and humanity in the face of the global admiration he enjoys today.

The Federers often holidayed in South Africa, but these trips largely dried up when both Roger and Diana were at school. In an interview with the South African *Sunday Times*, Lynette recalled, 'When the children were still young we used to come to South Africa more often, but when they went to school we couldn't return as often because the European summer holidays are in South Africa's winter, which isn't so appealing. But my kids love South Africa very, very much, especially the Garden Route [a popular tourist stretch of the south coast of South Africa between Cape Town and Port Elizabeth]. When Roger was still in his teens, we spent a holiday on the south coast. He loves the game and the wildlife.'

Federer began playing tennis at the age of three. That is not in doubt – there's even photographic evidence to confirm it – but throughout his playing career he was happy for one of the bibles of the global tennis circuit, *The Official Guide to Professional Tennis*, brought out by the ATP (Association of Tennis Professionals), to list him as having started playing tennis at the age of eight. It has to be assumed that Federer views his official start of playing tennis as age eight, even though he freely admitted to starting at three in a live Instagram chat with Rafael Nadal during the Covid-19 lockdown in April 2020.

There's a picture of him holding a wooden racket by the throat (it being too heavy for a three-year-old to wield by holding the grip), taken at the Ciba Club, his father's works club, in late 1984. Roger's story is like that of many players who go on to make it as professionals: his parents played as a hobby and at weekends took him along to their club, where he picked up a racket and was soon hooked. 'He loved the sport from the beginning,' his mother has said.

When he wasn't seeking out youngsters at the Ciba Club to mess around with, Federer would take his racket and hit ball after ball against the garage door of the family home. 'I remember always loving to play against the garage door,' he said in an interview in 2005, 'or even against the cupboard doors inside, with any kind of ball. My mum got fed up because it was bang, bang, bang, all day.'

He was taken to a handful of tennis clinics, and at the age of six or seven he attended a training course organised in the Basel suburb of Allschwil by the VBTU, the regional association of tennis clubs in greater Basel. The course involved a dozen under-tens receiving coaching on three full-length courts. It was there he met Marco Chiudinelli, a boy just thirty-three days his junior, who went on to become one of his best friends and a teammate in the victorious Swiss Davis Cup team of 2014.

By the time his eighth birthday came around, Federer was still playing at the Ciba Club. He had no rating, so by default was R9 (the lowest category in the system by which players are classified in Switzerland). His mother continued to play to a higher level at the TC Old Boys, but she was becoming aware of her son's talent, and also that her club had a framework in which Roger could prosper, one more suited to him than the Ciba Club's. One day, she approached Madeleine Bärlocher, who had taken over the dilapidated Old Boys' junior programme in 1980 and put some new life into it, and said, 'I have a son who plays tennis to a good level. You have a good junior programme. I would like you to take my son into your junior set-up.'

With that, Roger Federer became the new boy at Old Boys, and took the step that brought him into contact with the people who taught him how to play tennis.

2

THE TENNIS ENVIRONMENT into which Roger Federer was thrust at the age of eight was ready-made for a promising young talent. Madeleine Bärlocher, a secretary who had played in the Wimbledon juniors in 1959 in the days long before tennis was ever likely to offer career prospects, had a recipe that was hardly revolutionary – she just set in train fixed squads with a regime of private one-to-one coaching and group training, all at fixed times every week, some of it funded by money from youth sports foundations. And it worked. She brought in appropriate coaches and within a short time had vindicated her belief that, if you can attract one or two good people, a lot more good people will follow.

Although set in the affluent leafy suburbs of Binningen to the west of Basel city centre, the TC Old Boys was hardly a magnet for the rich. Founded in 1927, it was – and is – an outdoor club with just seven clay courts (now nine) and a modest clapperboard clubhouse. The only indoor facilities it has to this day are two courts covered by an inflatable bubble, and then only during the winter. If members want to play on a proper indoor court during the winter months, they find one elsewhere in Basel and pay by the hour.

In the 1980s, tennis was still very much a fringe sport in Switzerland. The country's main passions were football and winter sports. Advertising hoardings featuring sports stars were largely the preserve of Pirmin Zurbriggen, Maria Walliser and Vreni Schneider, a photogenic trio who headed a golden age in Swiss skiing, which itself followed on the heels of an earlier golden age headed by Bernhard Russi and Erika Hess.

In 1987, the Swiss tennis community was boosted when Switzerland finally qualified for the Davis Cup world group with a team featuring Jakob Hlasek, Claudio Mezzadri and the veteran doubles specialist Heinz Günthardt, who had won the Wimbledon men's doubles title in 1985. The Swiss chose to play their first world group tie in Basel in the St Jakobshalle, losing in February 1988 to the French team of Yannick Noah, Henri Leconte and Guy Forget. Hlasek had broken his wrist in a car accident a couple of months earlier and couldn't play, but he came back to post his best year on the tour, finishing in the top ten and finally putting Switzerland on the map as a tennis-playing nation.

In the mid-1990s, Old Boys had a promising player in Emmanuel Marmillod, a naturally gifted left-hander who might have blazed a trail for Federer to follow, but it was not to be. There are those who believe Marmillod was partly undone by a general lack of ambition in Swiss tennis. 'When a promising player came along,' recalls

Bärlocher, 'we tended to think of them as being potentially nationally ranked but never really world ranked. That was also the case when Roger arrived: we just didn't think in big terms because we had never had anyone who had reached those heights.'

Old Boys' connection with world tennis came via two channels: the annual Swiss Indoors tournament at Basel's St Jakobshalle, just twenty minutes' walk from the Neuewelt primary school, and the presence of a few professionals in the Swiss national inter-club league. There was a tradition of each of the top league clubs enlisting the services of one touring professional – usually in the twilight of his or her career – to come and play a few matches a year in the summer months. This arrangement gave the clubs the scope to make their team more attractive and increase their chances of winning, even though they were prevented from paying the players anything more than their expenses (at least officially – it's hard to see how it would have been financially viable for the players without some money changing hands under the table).

Old Boys had a national A-League team, and in the late 1970s they recruited the British player John Feaver, who reached ninety-eighth in the inaugural world rankings back in 1973, to play three seasons between 1979 and 1981. Feaver was so enamoured of the camaraderie and opportunities presented by inter-club leagues such as Switzerland's that he started a national league in Britain. 'The reasons we played were that you could get good, competitive clay-court matches,' he recalls. 'That was particularly attractive for the British players, as there were limited clay courts and no inter-club in the UK – and it was also really good fun. You had a nice evening after the match – a steak, a few beers. Sometimes they'd even ring the church bells. For some matches, we had a couple of hundred spectators, especially when you had teams each with a touring professional, so the singles match in which the two number ones played each other could be quite attractive. It was a great breeding ground for young players to get some good experience.'

Another touring pro who landed in Basel was Peter Carter, a shy Australian in his mid-twenties. And perhaps the single most beneficial thing Bärlocher did for Federer was to persuade Carter to do some junior-squad coaching.

Carter was a touring professional from Nuriootpa in the Barossa Valley, north of Adelaide, who reached 173rd in the ATP rankings in the 1980s. He was coached throughout his teens by Peter Smith, an inspirational Adelaide-based coach who played a part in the formative years of many Australian tennis players, including John Fitzgerald, Darren Cahill, Broderick Dyke, Roger Rasheed and Lleyton Hewitt, as well as Carter. Cahill and Carter were almost the same age (a year apart in terms of which junior year they fell into) and became good friends. Cahill recalls his envy at the fact that Carter not only always beat him but caught the eye of the opposite sex much more. 'He was a good-looking young man,' says Cahill of the man he called 'Carts'. 'Certainly I envied the attention he got from the women as we were growing up through the juniors – the blond hair, and the style and nature he had about him was very popular.' But while Cahill went on to reach the US Open semi-finals, Carter's career got bogged down below tour level. By 1989, he was approaching twenty-five, dogged by injury, and sliding down the rankings, so he accepted an offer to play a year's league tennis for Old Boys in the Swiss national A-league. He proved a hit there and enjoyed the experience, so he stayed for another year.

That second year, Madeleine Bärlocher asked him if he was willing to take a junior-squad coaching session. Carter was taken aback and had to fight off his initial instinct to say no. After giving the matter some thought, he agreed to try it. Despite having very little German, he found a way of communicating easily with the juniors, proved a natural at coaching and settled into a role looking after the club's squads that was to last until 1997. 'He had a sunny boy image,' recalls the Basel journalist and tennis coach Thomas Wirz about Carter, 'but underneath he was very serious. That combination really works for Roger. And he also played a very similar style to Roger: very classical strokes, especially the one-handed backhand.'

So when, in 1989, the eight-year-old Roger Federer arrived at Old Boys, he found not only a structure in place to meet all his needs but also an understated but highly disciplined character from an English-speaking southern-hemisphere country to guide him through squad training. Even though they didn't work together for a year or so, Federer had met one of the people who was to shape his career most profoundly. One night, a couple of years later, the Australian phoned home and told his dad, 'Oh, have I got a young boy here who looks promising. He's only about twelve or thirteen, but I think he's going to go places.'

But Federer also needed someone who could teach him to play tennis. He'd clearly demonstrated an aptitude for the sport at the Ciba Club and against his garage wall, but he needed someone to hone his strokes, to teach him footwork and general movement, and to give him the weapons that would one day conquer the world. That man was Seppli Kacovski.

Adolf Kacovski – 'Seppli' is a nickname he picked up in Switzerland – is a Czech who had the good fortune to be coaching in Tunisia when Soviet tanks rolled into Prague in August 1968 to crush what was known as the 'Prague Spring'. Once Alexander Dubcek, the Czechoslovak leader who had tried to practise what he called 'communism with a human face', had been deposed, it was virtually impossible for Czechoslovak citizens to travel abroad, a situation that lasted until the Velvet Revolution of 1989 swept away Soviet-controlled rule. Had he been at home, Kacovski might never have escaped the country and the Roger Federer story would have been somewhat different. But in 1969, Kacovski – by then an asylum seeker – was enticed to Basel to become the principal coach at the Old Boys club and given the priority of 'furthering the juniors and young talent in general'.

Kacovski, whose motto translates as 'we're going further', introduced a number of features to Old Boys. His main innovation was the introduction of a 'godfather' system of having a more experienced player assigned to youngsters as sparring partner and mentor. He also brought with him a strong sense of ambition.

When Federer arrived at Old Boys in 1989, it was Kacovski's job to give him one-to-one coaching. Of all the people who knew Federer there, Kacovski is the only one who claims to have seen the boy's potential from the start. 'When he came to me, after one or two days I knew this was a massive talent,' he recalled in 2005. 'I've been a tennis coach for more than forty years, and in that time you get to know who's got talent and who hasn't. After two days, I knew Roger was born with a racket in his hand. Everything about him suggested his talent: his speed off the mark, his footwork, his willingness to work hard – everything.'

Kacovski also recognised something else about Federer with which he personally identified: the fact that he was only half Swiss. 'I come from the East,' he says, 'and I have a very different attitude to sport. I'm much more ambitious, and at one stage I had to tone down my coaching because the Swiss weren't happy. Some of them complained that I was too ambitious for them. I believe Roger is more ambitious because he isn't one hundred per cent Swiss. His father is very Swiss, and the calmness that Roger has comes from his father, but the ambition and willpower come from his mother, who's not Swiss.'

Kacovski's theory is supported by others, including Niki von Vary, a teammate of Federer's in the 1990s who later became president of the Old Boys club. 'Here in Switzerland, sport isn't as accepted as it is in many other countries as a profession to go into,' he said. 'We're pretty keen on the security of a learned apprenticeship, and in that context sport is viewed somewhat suspiciously as a way to make your living.'

And Köbi Kuhn, the highly regarded former coach of the Swiss national football team, has said his job was made easier by the influx of Swiss players with dual nationality, especially those whose second nationality is from countries – many from south-eastern Europe – where football has a much higher priority than it does in Switzerland. He says it made more of his team keener to succeed than the all-Swiss national teams Kuhn himself was part of in his playing days.

Sadly, the story of the man who taught Roger Federer to play tennis had a somewhat messy ending. At the start of 2006, with Kacovski approaching his sixty-fifth birthday, the Old Boys committee told him they would have to end his employment when he reached sixty-five; this was largely for reasons of insurance, but there were also allegations of misappropriation that only came to light later. In March 2006, the club offered to throw a party to thank Kacovski for his thirty-seven years of service, but Kacovski declined, and settled for a small, low-key send-off. The following day he disappeared. For several weeks no one in Basel knew where he was, including his wife and daughter. Then it emerged he had returned to the Czech Republic, where he still lives now. It should really have been a triumphant homecoming for one of the victims of 1968, especially one who went on to play a crucial role in shaping the playing style of the world's best tennis player. Instead, it was all rather shabby, and Kacovski remains a rather sad figure in the country of his birth, largely detached from the scene of his greatest work. (His wife Irina and daughter Romana, or Romy, have remained in Basel, and Romana still teaches tennis there.)

For six years – from the ages of eight to fourteen – Seppli Kacovski and Peter Carter were Roger Federer's coaches. The two men were also linked off court, as Carter dated Romy Kacovski for a couple of years in an apparently tempestuous relationship. Kacovski, an ardent fan of the one-handed backhand, did the one-to-one work, Carter looked after squad coaching and refined some elements of Federer's game, and Madeleine Bärlocher ran the Old Boys' junior team for inter-club matches. Roger also had input from two other coaches, Haiggi Abt and Daniel Gerber, through the squads run by the VBTU, the regional association of tennis clubs in greater Basel, one of a dozen regional subsections of the national tennis association. It was a perfect environment for a talented, quick-to-learn and ambitious young tennis player.

But such ambition was not always his own. Bärlocher recalls an early practice session in which the young Roger wanted to play with his friends, even if they weren't the best players. 'His mother asked me to put him with the best,' she says, 'so I did, but his friends weren't the best, so Roger came to me and said, "I told you I wanted to play with my friends." He didn't have any fear of playing against the best, but it was more important to him to play with the people he liked. But his mother insisted I put him with the best, and that's where he ended up.'

Federer is sometimes asked by fan magazines and other publications who his idols were when he was growing up. The name he used to give most often was Boris Becker, with Stefan Edberg and Pete Sampras mentioned in close proximity, but after hiring Edberg as his coach at the end of 2013 Edberg assumed a greater prominence in the memory of his childhood idols! He admits that the fact that all three play with one-handed backhands was part of the attraction – although Federer always played his backhand the traditional way; Edberg and Sampras learned with two hands and switched to the one-hander in their teens. And Federer also stresses that admiration for a given player did not make him want to copy them – his playing style is his own.

Many of those who remember Federer from that time

describe him as a *Lausbub*, a Swiss-German word that best translates as a fun-loving rascal or rogue. There is certainly nothing malicious meant, and he clearly had a strong sense of fun. On one occasion, for example, at a team match at another Basel club, there weren't enough courts for everyone to play concurrently, so Federer had to wait his turn. Then, when a court finally became free, no one could find him – he had climbed a tree overlooking the club to observe what was going on, and to see how long it would take for people to find him.

Much of his sense of fun came as part of a double act with his friend Marco Chiudinelli, who proved something of a late developer, reaching a career-high ranking of fifty-two in February 2010 and lifting the Davis Cup as part of the victorious Swiss team of 2014. Both boys lived in the Basel suburb of Münchenstein, the Federers in Im Wasserhaus, the Chiudinellis 200m away in Pappelweg, and they frequently met up on their bikes and cycled to Old Boys, where they practised together before cycling home together again. 'We played a lot of sports,' recalls Chiudinelli. 'We were always pretty much on the same level, except for tennis which he always won. We also used to play squash together on the squash court with tennis rackets and a squash ball. It was pretty dangerous – certainly for the rackets!'

Another person who used the term *Lausbub* to describe Federer is Niki von Vary, who said, 'It was never boring with him around. He and Marco Chiudinelli were best friends – they're the same age and grew up with us at the club – and when those two were together, then we knew the crazy gang was around and the calm of the tennis club disappeared.'

Practice sessions were particularly difficult. 'We used to mess around in practice,' says Chiudinelli. 'We lost interest very quickly and used to talk a lot. There was a lot of unrest. Rackets used to fly around in all directions, which was probably the most dangerous thing that happened. We were frequently sent on training runs or just sent home. Peter Carter didn't have an easy time with us.'

While Marco and Roger engaged in typical boys' posturing, Bärlocher picked up on something that proved to be prophetic: 'Whenever Roger was messing around with his friends, he'd always say, "I'm going to be number one." He'd hit a great smash, and then he'd stop and say, "That's the shot I'm going to win Wimbledon with." It was obviously a joke – all boys do that – but that's what he used to say.'

The less agreeable side to the fun-loving personality was his temper, a far cry from the calm and composed figure Federer became known as. One of his coaches even referred to him as 'a little Satan' on court. He would throw his racket, scream and swear, and had great difficulty accepting defeat.

There was one notorious match when Federer was eleven. Whenever he played locally, he always seemed to come up against Dany Schnyder, the younger brother of Patty Schnyder, who went on to be ranked in the women's top ten. Dany was Roger's first nemesis. One year, the two played in the final of the Basel Junior Championships, Schnyder the Swiss number one and Federer the Swiss number two in the under-twelves age group. Thomas Wirz recalls, 'They played that match and threw their rackets and swore, and both of them got a warning from the supervisor. It was horrific, but also quite amusing.'

Madeleine Bärlocher says Federer could never stand it when an opponent played a really nice point against him. 'He'd often say, "Lucky!", and a couple of times I had to say to him, "Hang on. There are others who can play good tennis as well, you know." The fact is that he never liked to lose, and you could see that in the early years of his professional career in his attitude towards players who used to beat him regularly, like Agassi, Hewitt and Nalbandian.'

On one occasion after a defeat in an inter-club match, he was so angry that he cried his eyes out and hid under the umpire's chair; Bärlocher, his team supervisor, had a hard time persuading him to come out. Years later, she asked Federer if he remembered that scene. Federer said no. But he did remember another incident that also gives an insight into the youngster's character.

In one of his first Basel League inter-club matches, Old Boys were playing away at a club with only two courts and not a great reputation. At ten, Federer was the youngest and the smallest in the six-member team, and with a format of six singles and three doubles there was a lot of waiting around for matches to finish and courts to become free. Federer wasn't in one of the first two matches to go on court, and during the first matches it became clear that there was one player from the other team who kept screaming from the side, trying to influence line calls. Bärlocher intervened and some angry words were exchanged. Aware of the bad blood developing between the teams, she decided not to play Federer in the singles. 'He was the youngest, he would have been up against someone who wasn't playing fair on line calls, and I was worried that something would happen,' she recounts. 'And he was so angry with me because I wouldn't let him play singles, only doubles. He remembers that! I was concerned that they'd look at him and say, "Oh, that little kid. We can have some fun with him. We can call lines our way and he won't stand up to us." I knew that Roger was very fixated on the truth. He had a very powerful sense of fairness. He never took a call for himself that he felt wasn't absolutely right but, if someone on the other side of the net made a call that Roger knew was wrong, he'd be so angry that he'd start throwing his racket. That's why I didn't want to risk him. I wanted to protect him, but he was mad with me.'

Tears of frustration and ambition were a regular feature of Federer's junior matches, but he also had a charitable side to his nature. Marco Chiudinelli tells a story from the first time he played Federer in an official match. 'We were about eight or nine. He wasn't very good at losing, and I wasn't either. After about six games he'd opened up a considerable lead and I began to cry, so he came up to me at the change of ends and started consoling me, said, "It'll get better" – and it did. About five games later, I'd taken the lead, and then he began to cry, so I went up to him and said, "Take it easy," and he came back to win. In retrospect, it was a beautiful moment, because you can see that we were friends.'

Federer has admitted that there were times when he would be aware of his parents watching him from the Old Boys' terrace while he was losing his temper on court. Occasionally, they would call out for him to be quiet, and on one such occasion he shot back, 'Go and have a drink and leave me alone.' Federer said that the family would then drive home 'in a quiet car with no one speaking; I would carry on like an idiot.'

In general, the tightly wound bundle of emotion on the court was very polite and well mannered off it. Local journalists who dealt with him at that time speak of a happy and helpful boy, and Federer clearly recognised convincing authority figures when he saw them. Bärlocher says he seldom threw his racket when she was in charge, although his language could be colourful, which caused concern with his parents. 'I once had Lynette coming up to me, asking me to say something about his cursing,' she recalls, 'but I thought it was pretty harmless, and he always behaved pretty well with me. I had a lot of kids who behaved a lot worse than Roger. I was keen to enforce good standards of behaviour because I knew that anything bad [would reflect poorly] on the club.'

Seppli Kacovski noticed something else about Federer's on-court tantrums. 'I've known enough players who play a bad match,' he says. 'They scream at themselves, can't accept a defeat and say, "I'm giving up. I'm not playing tennis any more." Roger never said that. He got angry, he had difficulty accepting defeats, but he never once said, "I'm giving up".'

When Federer beat Gaston Gaudio 6–0, 6–0 in the semi-finals of the 2005 Tennis Masters Cup in Shanghai, he was asked whether it was true that he'd never until then won a match with that score. 'Yes, it is,' he said, before adding, 'I have lost one 6–0, 6–0, but that was in juniors.'

It was actually his first official match. Two weeks after his tenth birthday, the Basel regional championships took place. This was at the Grüssenhölzli tennis facility in Pratteln, an industrial area right by the motorway that takes traffic out of Basel towards Bern and Zurich.

As the rules state that you can play in an age group as long as you are below that age at the start of the year, Federer was eligible for the under-tens, but there were too few entrants, so he was put in the under-twelves event. In the first round he came up against Reto Schmidli, a powerfully built boy more than two years and eight months older than Federer. At that age, nearly three years can make a massive difference, and, with Federer one of the smaller boys in his year at that stage, it did. He didn't win a single game.

Asked about the defeat many years later, he replied, 'It's the only 6–0, 6–0 loss I've ever had, and I didn't play that badly!' Schmidli is today a police officer in the Basel region, and, since the first edition of this book revealed his name, he has become something of an occasional celebrity. 'I knew I'd beaten him 6–0, 6–0,' he says, 'but I had no idea I was the only one. Of course I was a bit lucky – I was so much stronger than him at that time, but given what he has done since, I'm proud of what I did.'

At eleven, Federer was ranked number two in his age group in Switzerland, and on 13 July 1992 he made his first few column centimetres in the local daily, the *Basler Zeitung*. He had lost in the final of a national under-twelves event for lower-rated players to the Geneva-based Japanese player Jun Kato, who later went on to play one Davis Cup match for Japan. A year later, however, Federer won the Swiss under-twelves national championship. But could anyone at that stage truly have said that this was a champion in the making?

To their credit, most people who remember him say no. 'There are plenty of people who like to think they saw it coming,' said Niki von Vary, 'but, as far as I can remember, no one ever seriously expected Roger to go as far as he went. Certainly not when he was eleven or twelve.'

Thomas Wirz remembers watching the twelve-year-old Federer at the time he won the national under-twelves championship, but he also remembers thinking the youngster's on-court temper tantrums might hold him back. 'You could see very early what good hands he had, but he'd play two or three good points and then do something wild, and he often threw his racket. He wasn't that disciplined, so it's hard to say that he was headed for greatness.'

Even in 1992, the year Marc Rosset won the gold medal for Switzerland at the Barcelona Summer Olympics and he and Jakob Hlasek steered the Swiss to their first Davis Cup final, there was still a lack of ambition in the Swiss ranks. 'At that time the Swiss level wasn't that high, so we didn't look that high,' says Madeleine Bärlocher. 'As a result, I can't say I or any of us ever thought Roger would go as far as he has. I always said to him, "Rogi, whatever it is you want to achieve in tennis, you have to decide for yourself. We can help you, but in principle you have to know what you want to achieve." We had a lot of good juniors, and he was always the youngest, so we knew he was good, but potentially world number one? I'd have to say no.'

What about those who knew him on court? 'I thought he'd make it on to the tour,' says Marco Chiudinelli, 'because from an early age he saw off his Swiss competition and did seem to have something special, but I don't think anyone at that time could have suggested he'd achieve what he's done.'

One person from outside Basel who saw Federer at thirteen or fourteen was Darren Cahill. He had accompanied his childhood friend Peter Carter to Basel when Carter had first gone to Old Boys and on one occasion got the chance to watch one of Federer's practice sessions. 'We had a laugh when he asked me what I thought of the kid,' recalls Cahill. 'I said I thought he was very good, that he looks all right but I reckon I've got someone a little bit better back in South Australia who I'm working with. That was Lleyton Hewitt. Roger struck me as being loose in everything. His forehand was really fast, he mis-hit a lot of balls, especially off the backhand, his footwork was a little bit all over the place, he was a little bit lazy with the feet. He looked like he played a French style of tennis: carefree, big-hitting and extremely loose. You could see he had beautiful hands and good hand–eye, and he tried to make a bit of magic happen on the court, even at that age, but he didn't hit the ball square all that often.'

The only member of the Basel contingent in direct contact with Federer in the early 1990s who claims to have seen the potential for greatness is Seppli Kacovski, the man who taught him his strokes. Interviewed for this book before his inglorious flight from Basel, Kacovski came across as a strict yet immensely likeable sexagenarian who oozed an enthusiasm for tennis that he managed to communicate to the youngsters he was coaching. It's easy to imagine him getting excited about the fluent strokes of a youngster, but he says it was Federer's ability to learn and bounce back from defeats that gave him such hope for the lad. 'The learning process went so quickly with him, and I never had to repeat anything. He had an enormous ability to grasp what I was telling him. I always say it's a long cable between the head and the racket to describe how long it takes most people to grasp what I'm coaching them, but Roger just got it straight away. I saw it; the coaches saw it; the club saw it.'

Kacovski also noticed that Federer's willingness to learn matched his ability to learn. 'Even back then he hated losing, but he had the ability to draw the conclusion that, "If I don't want to lose, I have to put in the work." If he won 6–1, 6–1, he'd often wonder how he could have won 6–0, 6–0. I was pretty hard with him, though in a friendly way. He was quite small – certainly smaller and physically less robust than everyone else – but then he played with such great technique, and that allowed him to win a lot of matches where he was physically inferior. But then, his father isn't tall, so we weren't sure how tall he'd end up.

'And he never had enough coaching,' Kacovski adds. 'We'd have a long coaching session, he'd work very hard, and then, when it was all over, he'd go to hit against the wall or seek out a sparring partner to hit some more. And he always used to say, "I'm going to be number one!" No one believed him. We could see that he had the potential to be a big star in Swiss tennis, but he was saying he was going to be *world* number one. He's not the only thirteen- or fourteen-year-old to have said that, but he had it in his head, and he worked towards achieving it.'

All of which may be true, but the *Basler Zeitung*'s former sports editor, Beat Caspar, remembers Kacovski having problems with Federer at the beginning. 'He might well have recognised his talent, but he also had to remove Federer from training sessions because Federer was, at times, impossible. For a long time he wasn't allowed to practise with the best because his head was always stuffed full of silly ideas.'

And there was a distraction: football. Federer's love of all sports, especially ball games, had made him a highly proficient footballer. He joined the club Concordia Basel and played as a striker. 'I'm personally convinced that, if he'd chosen football, he'd have made it to the Swiss national team,' recalls Seppli Kacovski. 'I only saw him twice, but he scored three goals in those two matches, and in one of them he took the ball in his own half, dribbled 60m with it and scored. He just had it.'

Federer has admitted that he thought he was 'pretty good, pretty skilful' at football, and he played the game with the same passion and competitiveness that he gave to tennis. His friend Marco Chiudinelli also played, having joined the FC Basel youth team, and on a few occasions the two came up against each other. 'We were both so determined to win,' Marco says. 'When we won, he cried. And when Concordia won, I cried. It meant a lot to us.'

Part of the Federer folklore is the claim that he was offered junior terms with FC Basel. This is almost certainly a myth, and he himself denies ever having received such an offer. Although it's true that today football clubs are showing an increasing interest in pre-teenage talent, in the early 1990s FC Basel had its own youth team, and Federer played for another club. (When asked about it in his twenties, Federer said, 'I wish I had had an offer!') After he became famous as a tennis player, there were offers for him to train with the FC Basel squad, but, while he was happy to be photographed with the club's players, he always turned down any chance to train with them, no doubt through fear of suffering an injury that could harm his tennis.

Once he'd become national under-twelves champion in

tennis, the question of which sport he should concentrate on became increasingly urgent. 'I was practising tennis and soccer in the week,' he says, 'but I was tending to favour tennis over soccer, so I couldn't attend all the soccer practice sessions. The coach eventually told me that if I didn't attend all the sessions he couldn't really put me in the team for matches at the weekend. And I couldn't make all the matches anyway because I was also trying to play tennis tournaments, even though I felt I was in one of the best soccer teams and playing in an age group above my own age. But I knew that I couldn't do both soccer and tennis until I die, that I would have had to improve my left foot – which was never a strength of mine back then – so I eventually made the decision to go for tennis.'

The fact that his parents were both into tennis – his mother seriously so – probably helped sway the decision and, although he occasionally wonders what would have happened had he opted for football, it's not a decision he's ever regretted. 'I like tennis more, and I like to be in control. In tennis, it's up to me – I can't blame defeats on goalies or something like that. So I'm happy I chose tennis. In the end, it wasn't a difficult decision.'

Having honed the strokes that Seppli Kacovski taught him, Federer by twelve was finding it was Peter Carter who was having a growing influence on his game. Although Carter was never Federer's personal coach at Old Boys (his main role was that of group trainer), his growing assurance as a coach brought on the games of many of those in his squads. 'If you had to define the attribute of calmness in a person, in whatever context, then Peter Carter was your perfect example,' says the Swiss journalist Marco Mordasini.

'He formed [Roger]. He took this bundle of energy, took the components and put them together, almost like taking a rough diamond and polishing it up.'

And Madeleine Bärlocher, who had brought Carter into the Old Boys' squad-coaching set-up, remembers, 'The training with Peter Carter was perfect, both in tennis terms and on a human level. Peter was very personable but very restrained; he never pushed himself into the foreground. If a youngster had problems, he'd always take them aside and talk with them. He could talk very well with the juniors, but, if someone behaved badly, he threw them out. Sometimes he sent Roger home.'

Marco Chiudinelli feels Carter had the great attribute of being able to tell each of his charges what they needed to do to improve. 'It was a great time with Peter Carter,' he says. 'There are three periods in my career when I was really able to raise my level, and the first of them was when I came to Old Boys and worked with Peter. I think Roger had the same thing, because, while Seppli was a very good teacher, Roger needed Peter to take him to the next level.'

There was still the unresolved issue of Federer's on-court outbursts. He would frequently go out on court, settle into a nice rhythm and then start having fun and lose his concentration. He later admitted, 'When I was ten, twelve, fourteen, I was definitely at my worst. It was horrible, even funny sometimes – a lot of throwing rackets, making comments on every shot, because I just couldn't accept to lose. I was very talented and I thought, How can it be that I'm not playing well?'

His mother, Lynette, later recalled in a newspaper interview, 'I used to say to Roger, "When you have these outbursts like this, you're just telling your opponent that you're ready for him to beat you. You're sending out invitations. Is that what you want?"' And on another occasion she said, 'This stage was part of his growing up but, when his behaviour was bad, we told him it was bad and that it upset us. We used to say, "Come on, Roger. Get control of yourself. Pull yourself together. Is it such a catastrophe if you lose a match?"'

There were some people at Old Boys who were concerned that their talented youngster might squander his talent in a whirl of joking around and losing his cool, but the combination of Peter Carter and Roger's parents was a very powerful one. While Carter kept Federer moving forwards in his game, Lynette and Robbie gave him a frame of reference for his behaviour. The Swiss tennis impresario Roger Brennwald, who met Federer for the first time when the boy was twelve, said, 'He has an awful lot to be grateful to his family for. He has parents who grew up with certain ideals and values, and he has been able to overcome the crises he has gone through, including crises with his results, because of those values.'

Federer had one other bit of exposure to top-level tennis: as a ballboy. In 1994, he and Marco Chiudinelli were ballboys at the Swiss Indoors ATP event, which gave them the opportunity to rub shoulders with some of the biggest names in the sport. He came away with an autograph from Pete Sampras, who at the time was his favourite player, and he received a medal from the beaten finalist Wayne Ferreira. It's a tradition at the Swiss Indoors that all ballkids receive a medal from one of the two singles finalists, and the family has a photo of Roger getting his medal from Ferreira.

Six years later the two men teamed up as doubles partners at the ATP event in Lyon; in fact they played four doubles events together, including reaching the third round at Wimbledon in 2001.

Lynette Federer believes the experience of being a ballboy at the Swiss Indoors shaped Roger's attitude towards ballpersons as a top professional. 'It was nice for him to know that his mum was always there in case he needed me,' she said in 2019, 'but he never did need me, which was a good sign. He just loved being around the players, and being together with boys of his own age. He had a great time, but unfortunately it was just for one year. I believe he treats the ballkids better having been in that position. It always strikes me that he's very respectful to them, even if he does sometimes challenge them because he knows it can become a little boring standing in the corner waiting for the balls. He's always very aware of the ballkids.'

Federer was also asked to ballboy at Old Boys for a women's satellite tournament the club staged every year until 2002. That was 1994, when the two finalists were Martina Hingis and Patty Schnyder, who along with Federer himself went on to become three of the eight most successful Swiss tennis players ever.

By the spring of 1995, Federer was classified R2 in the Swiss ratings scheme (effectively on the second tier at regional level), which wasn't bad for a thirteen-year-old but still a long way short of the national ratings to which he aspired. That year, he reached the quarter-finals of the Basel Championships, and was making steady progress. But there were worrying signs.

A note from an official Swiss tennis publication from the mid-1990s expresses concern about how the country's most promising youngsters were being handled. Referring to the Old Boys club's greatest prodigy pre-Federer, it reads, 'Emmanuel Marmillod is a glowing example of the lack of forward planning. Although the Basler has massive talent and was able to make his way easily to the age of eighteen, he has now suddenly become aware that without the necessary work he won't get anywhere, nationally or internationally.' Meanwhile, another note lists a group of youngsters (including Federer, ironically) and describes them as 'all talents who are prevented from unleashing their potential because the school system or society is not yet willing to accept this working together of education and top-level sport. Something has to happen!' (In fairness, Emmanuel Marmillod would probably never have made it as a top professional; he went on to study theology, worked in a prison, and those who know him say he lacked sufficient drive to make it as a tennis professional. But the structural weaknesses were probably there nonetheless.)

While Lynette Federer no doubt saw these notes, there's no evidence that the Federer family was in any way influenced by them. They were aware, however, that the 'Tennis Études' programme run at the Swiss National Tennis Centre in Ecublens, on the outskirts of Lausanne, offered a potential next step for their thirteen-year-old son. It offered the option of continuing his education in a tennis environment. For someone not keen on going to school, like Roger, it was certainly a possibility.

It was also a way to find out how good he really was at

that stage. He says now he had 'a horrible backhand' and, while there might be a bit of modesty in that statement, there was no doubt it was his worse side. After losing to Dany Schnyder at age twelve at a tournament in France, Federer had been so disgusted with his backhand that he'd started working on a double-hander, but that didn't work either. He says, 'I was thinking: you know what, I can't even do that, so I'll just stay with my bad one-hander. Thank God I did.' Darren Cahill, who first saw Federer at around thirteen, says, 'You could drive a truck through his backhand side. He was always really good about stepping to the left and getting round his backhand and hitting the forehand, but if you got it to his backhand you were in pretty good shape.'

So it was interesting that, when Federer took the three-day entry test to the National Tennis Centre in March 1995, he started to come over his backhand, to prove he could drive the shot as well as slice it. He was playing on a quick surface, and recognised that slice alone would not get him very far. And he passed the test with flying colours, clearly giving the coaches the impression that he really wanted to enrol on the programme. But going to Ecublens would mean leaving the tutelage of Peter Carter and, more importantly, leaving his family in Basel to live for at least five days a week in a different part of the country where he hardly spoke the language. And he had always professed himself to be very close to his family. He was chugging along nicely at Old Boys, so there was no need to uproot, was there?

His parents were happy to show him the tennis centre and investigate other possibilities for furthering his career, but Roger seemed set on staying in Basel. In the car on the way home from the entry test at the centre, he said to his parents, 'I'm never setting foot inside Ecublens again.'

3

FEDERER ARRIVED AT Ecublens just a few days after his fourteenth birthday and just a few months after vowing never to set foot in the Swiss National Tennis Centre again. While his decision to enrol on the Tennis Études programme seems to have developed a momentum of its own, it was probably a lot more intentional than that. Shortly after passing the entry test, he was asked by a journalist from the Swiss tennis magazine *Smash* whether he was thinking of taking up a place at Ecublens. 'Perhaps,' he replied, 'you never know.' That quote made it into print. On reading it, his parents – somewhat nonplussed after hearing his views in the car after first visiting the centre – questioned him about it, to which Roger replied, 'Well, it's written there, so I'm going.'

Lynette Federer says there was no parental pressure on him, and believes the fact that he took the big decisions himself helped him develop a sense of independence.

Asked in 2019 what advice she would give parents of talented teenagers, she told ATP Tennis Radio, 'I think what's very important is to let go, to give your child a certain amount of room to become independent, to stand on their own two feet. What they do need is your constant support, but you shouldn't concentrate on them day in day out. You need to give them a certain independence, you're there when they need you, but you mustn't be constantly around them, and you must let them make their own decisions. Once Roger had decided to leave home and go to Ecublens, which was two and a half hours from home, it was important that we respected that. But he knew that if he didn't manage it he could always come home again. It's important that the child knows you support them – you guide them, if necessary you can take certain steps like in our case speaking to the coaches. But to be constantly around the children, that's something we couldn't do. We were very much involved in Roger's career, we tried to guide him, to go with the flow, to support him, but nothing really changed for Robbie and me. We were working at Ciba-Geigy, and anyway Roger didn't need us so much once he moved to Swiss Tennis.'

By 1995, the Swiss National Tennis Centre was in something of an interim state. In 1992, the national association Swiss Tennis (the English name 'Swiss Tennis' has been used since the 1980s as a single brand to avoid the need to write the German, French and Italian versions of 'Swiss Tennis Association' on every official document) suffered a major internal schism over how best to structure the development of the country's top talent. The upshot was that, the following year, the four regional tennis centres were merged into one in Ecublens, a picturesque town on the shores of

Lake Geneva, just west of Lausanne, which would serve as a temporary arrangement until the organisation's brand-new purpose-built centre opened in Biel in 1997. Even the choice of Biel was politically sensitive; although its bid to host the new administrative and performance centre had its merits, part of the reason it was picked was its geographical location, right on the linguistic border between German- and French-speaking Switzerland (hence its frequent representation on maps as 'Biel/Bienne', 'Bienne' being its Francophone name).

The Tennis Études programme was inaugurated in 1993 and was intended to provide the most promising tennis players with the chance to make the most of their talent without neglecting their schooling. When Federer went there, his school lessons went down from thirty hours a week to twenty. The programme was set up by one of the most experienced coaches in European tennis, Georges Déniau, but he fell victim to the Swiss Tennis civil war of 1992, and, by the time Federer arrived, the centre was being run by Déniau's deputy, Christophe Freyss (responsible for the coaching), and Pierre Paganini (in charge of the fitness programme). After a troubled first year at Ecublens, the centre's reputation quickly grew among the Swiss tennis-playing community to the point where, in its third year, sixty young hopefuls applied for just four places. Those sixty were whittled down to sixteen who were allowed to take the entry test. This consisted of running, a fitness assessment course, demonstration of various strokes and a test match in which an applicant's technique and competitive temperament were analysed.

During his test, Federer so impressed the two heads of the

programme that he was offered a place on the spot. Freyss said of him, 'He shows a natural talent as well as a basic technique that has no significant weaknesses, but he will have to work hard physically in the next few months. But it was also an important criterion for selection that Roger left us with the impression that he really wants to come to Ecublens.' So much for never setting foot there again!

When Federer moved to Ecublens in 1995, the centre had a dozen or so youngsters (boys and girls). They couldn't accommodate more than about fifteen because the centre had access to only four indoor hard courts, four outdoor clay courts and a small gymnasium, all rented by Swiss Tennis. The students also had part-time use of a football pitch and a running track 100 metres from the tennis facilities. They had their own accommodation, generally in a studio or shared apartment for the older ones or lodgings with a family for those also attending a local school.

The average day for those based at the centre would begin with a wake-up call at something like 6.30, with school starting at 7.45 and lessons for those on the Tennis Études programme finishing no later than 1pm. The students would then head to the tennis centre for a two-hour practice session, followed by an hour's physical training, before going home for a quick dinner. At weekends, the centre was empty, the occupants either having gone home or – more often – participating in tournaments elsewhere in Switzerland, so any homework had to be done in the evenings during the week.

There were other coaches working at the centre besides Freyss and Paganini – Alexis Bernhard was one who worked with Federer – but Freyss had overall control not just of the programme but also of each player's tournament schedule. With one coach for every three or four players, when the students went to play tournaments, one coach would look after a handful of players. Everything at Ecublens was in the French language, not just the schooling and relations with host families, but French was also the house language of the tennis centre. So, while the handful of kids from the German-speaking part of Switzerland could speak German among themselves, they had to speak French to their coaches and officials.

In an article written by Thomas Wirz that appeared in the *Basler Zeitung* in March 1995 proudly announcing Federer as the first player from Basel to be accepted by the Tennis Études programme, his father Robbie made it clear that the school element was not to be neglected. 'Roger isn't the most hard-working in school,' he said, 'but thanks to the fact that he'll have access to one-to-one advice, and the centre has Annemarie Rüegg looking after the educational side of things, we're not expecting this to be a major problem.' (Another player to credit Rüegg with helping his educational development while he climbed the rungs of the junior ladder was Switzerland's promising player Dominic Stricker.) Wirz then ends the article with an interesting observation: 'Federer has now secured his place in the Tennis Études team, and after the summer holidays he will embark on the second stage of the apprenticeship that might soon lead to his becoming a very good tennis player.'

That Federer survived the first few months was something of an achievement. He had only limited French, was frequently homesick, and admits to being close on several occasions to packing his things and returning home.

'For me, the first half-year was very tough,' he has said in several interviews. 'I wanted to go home. I was not happy. I used to cry when I had to leave on Sunday nights to go back.' He told the Swiss journalist Roger Jaunin, 'I was the Swiss German who everyone liked to make fun of. People were mean to me and it was hard to leave for Ecublens on Sunday nights. Very hard.'

Piecing together tales emanating from that time, he was clearly the butt of numerous practical jokes, including frequent occasions when he entered his name on the massage list only to turn up for his appointment to find it had been erased by an older boy who then took his place. In short, it was bullying.

Federer found release for his frustration on court. Even so, while he was able to express himself through impressive forehands and backhands, the off-court stress hardly made him behave any better, and he became notorious for his racket-throwing. He had gone from being a big fish in a small pond – he had won the Swiss national under-fourteens title just a month before going to Ecublens – to being a small fish in a much bigger pond; 'small' in both size and standing.

One of the more senior players already at the centre when Federer arrived was Yves Allegro, a player three years older who went on to make it into the world's top fifty in doubles and partner Federer in the Davis Cup and the Olympic tennis event of 2004. He remembers Federer frequently reduced to tears of frustration at the difficulty of coming to terms with it all, phoning home at regular intervals and generally 'having a tough time'. Yet, through that difficult time, he developed a cussed will to stick it out and, while it might be a little far-fetched to attribute his determination to come back from seemingly hopeless match situations to those first few weeks in Ecublens, there's no doubt he learned several lessons that made him a stronger person for the somewhat strange life that was to follow on the global tennis circuit. His mother told the British journalist Mark Hodgkinson, 'It was a great lesson in life for him – that things don't always go your own way, and that you don't get anywhere in life with talent alone. You have to work at things. I know it wasn't always fun and games for Roger there, and that many days he wasn't that happy, but those struggles were good for him. Overcoming those ups and downs was a challenge, and it helped him develop as a person.'

Two things clearly helped Federer get through those first few weeks at Ecublens: tennis and his lodgings. However difficult he found speaking French, and however much he longed for his family and his friends in Basel, he could at least express himself on the court, and some of his former associates at Old Boys believe that the determination that Peter Carter had helped him unearth was instrumental in seeing him through the initial weeks. He also had a temporary family to go home to in the evenings, who clearly tried to make him feel like one of their own. While Allegro had his own studio apartment, Federer was housed with Cornelia and Jean-François Christinet, who had three children – Vanessa, Nicolas and Vincent. By August 1995, Vanessa and Nicolas had left home, and the Christinets agreed to take in a Tennis Études student, partly for the fourteen-year-old Vincent to have some domestic company of his own age. He and Federer became de facto brothers, and remain good friends to this day. 'Most evenings we used to mess about – fighting or playing basketball or table tennis,' Vincent later told Roger Jaunin. 'I remember his coaches reproaching him for his lack of punctuality, and he had no excuse. Even on the days when he had exams at school, you had to shake him three times to get him out of bed.'

Another factor that saw him through that time was a quiet realisation that the world didn't revolve entirely around him. He was not the only Swiss German with limited French to arrive at Ecublens in 1995; Sven Swinnen, another German-speaker who grew up near Bern, reminded Federer that he was not alone in his difficulties. 'I remember one episode when we were cycling home from our practice,' Swinnen recalled in an interview with ATP Tennis Radio, 'and he was really sick of it, he was like, "I've seen it here, I want to go back home to Basel and practise there." That was a tough time, but I told him, "Then I would be all alone here, that wouldn't be fun for me, so I hope you stick around." And I'm glad he did – we had a great two years there. After his first year when he struggled a lot, he really took off and never looked back." Swinnen pursued his career via the American college route, and went on to coach Switzerland's Dominic Stricker.

Federer understandably gets credit for battling through this time, when plenty of fourteen-year-olds with less determination might have thrown in the towel. But a crucial factor in those early months was the nightly phone call between Ecublens and Basel, many of them lasting an hour. When Lynette talks about her and Robbie having offered 'support' for Roger, this is perhaps its most practical manifestation.

Eventually, Roger settled down and became happy at the centre, but, until his tournament schedule became too heavy, he would come home every weekend to spend time with his family and his friend Marco Chiudinelli. 'We played very little tennis after he went to Ecublens, but we still used to hang out together,' Chiudinelli says. 'We'd play a lot of computer games, both at home and in arcades in the city. We both had a strong sense of competition, we both wanted to win. I look back on it as a wonderful time, and Roger was a big part of it.'

Federer also continued to be a part of the Old Boys set-up, turning up for inter-club matches until he became world junior champion at the end of 1998. The work he'd done at Ecublens became clear to his old sparring partners. 'There was one occasion,' recalls Niki von Vary, 'when he was fourteen. He'd just gone to Ecublens and had a national rating. Then he came back to play with us and I was up against him in practice for inter-club matches. He'd really improved, and we could see that he was going to be good. Even so, as good as he turned out, no one could have seen it at that time.'

Von Vary was also a witness to Federer and Chiudinelli's continuing demon double act. 'On one occasion, Old Boys staged the Basel championship,' he says, 'and during the event Roger, Marco, Reto Staubli [one of Roger's closest friends, who travelled with him in his early days on the full professional tour] and I were playing cards in the club restaurant. Roger and Marco were so loud that the tournament director stomped in and said that they were making so much noise that the players on the centre court couldn't concentrate. There are other stories about them, but that sums up who they were: spirited, funny and loud, yes, but never malicious. And you had to be on your guard, because they were always up for a prank or a practical joke.'

Looking back, Federer only really began seriously working on his tennis when he went to Ecublens, and again the question arises: were people aware at that time that they had a potential world-beater in their midst? Probably not, because by general standards Federer was something of a late developer. 'Up to the age of fourteen, he was what you might call a normally talented youngster, doing well in junior tournaments, winning some, but realistically not much more,' says the Basel journalist and coach Thomas Wirz. 'For example, at fourteen he lost in the quarter-finals of the Basel junior championships – a regional tournament – which isn't bad but doesn't indicate someone headed for the very top. He was a junior with a good game – no more, no less. Otherwise, he would have been more dominant. His biggest spurt, in terms of results and achievement, came between autumn 1996 and spring 1997, when he was fifteen.'

It was in 1996 that the first signs that people were getting excited about him began to emerge. In September that year, he made his international debut, representing Switzerland in the World Youth Cup, a team tournament organised by the International Tennis Federation, held that year in Zurich on outdoor clay. When Switzerland were drawn to play Australia, a number of media people showed up for the battle of the number ones: Federer against an exciting young Australian, Lleyton Hewitt.

It was a fascinating encounter in more ways than one. Hewitt was somewhat better known, having made more progress as a junior than Federer, and just four months later he was to announce his presence by winning the full ATP title in Adelaide at just sixteen. Although Federer wasn't working officially with Peter Carter at that time, he was in regular contact with him so was well aware that Hewitt was being coached by Darren Cahill, Carter's former stablemate from Peter Smith's set-up in Adelaide. There was a sense that this could be a meeting of players who would go on to great things, and the match lived up to the billing.

Cahill remembers 'a marathon match, a great match'. He had encouraged Hewitt to go for the backhand on the basis of having watched Federer practising in Basel two years earlier, but 'Roger had improved out of sight. I was kind of expecting Lleyton to run through the match, but the difference in Roger's game in those two years that I didn't see him was enormous.' It was also a fiery match: 'Roger was losing his temper, Lleyton was losing his temper, and you could tell already it was going to be an interesting rivalry between the two players,' says Cahill. Federer won it 4–6, 7–6(3), 6–4 after saving a match point, although Australia went on to win the tie on a deciding doubles.

The following year proved to be a pivotal one in Swiss tennis. In January, Martina Hingis became the first Swiss of either sex to win a Grand Slam singles title when she won the Australian Open. By the end of March, she was world number one, and she went on to win three of that year's four major singles titles, adding the Wimbledon and US Open trophies to her Australian success, and narrowly missing out on the French Open when she was beaten by Iva Majoli of Croatia in the final.

1997 was also the year Swiss Tennis opened up its new

performance and administrative centre in Biel. Finally, the political infighting of five years earlier could be laid to rest (well, partly; it's never far from the surface in Swiss Tennis) and the small Alpine country had a base devoted to training its top tennis talent, both juniors and touring professionals. With the opening of the new facility and Hingis's elevation to the status of sporting icon, tennis in Switzerland was appearing increasingly attractive, and soon a number of highly respected names were attracted to Biel, among them the Dutch coach Sven Groeneveld and the Swede Peter Lundgren, who was appointed 'National Trainer' there.

Another coach to arrive at Biel was Peter Carter, who had been lured away from the Old Boys club by Swiss Tennis in the summer of 1997, largely because of his links with Federer, who was being increasingly recognised as a prospect worth nurturing. After his eight years of service in Basel, the club held a large farewell party for him, and the collection raised for him went into four figures – a sign of how well liked and respected he was there.

Things were looking up for Federer, too. After two years at Ecublens, he could base himself much closer to home, having mastered French and overcome many of his other demons. And he had his most trusted coach back with him, with funding from Swiss Tennis. But where was he to live? He didn't want to lodge with another family, but at sixteen he wasn't ready to have his own place.

Enter Yves Allegro. Although he had finished his own schooling in Ecublens, when he turned professional Allegro decided to base himself in Biel and had taken an apartment there. When the Federer family heard about this, they asked him if Roger could share with him. Allegro agreed and the pair became flatmates for two years. 'We had a lot of fun,' Allegro said a few years later. 'We became very close friends. He was close to turning pro, so it wasn't very easy for him sometimes because he wasn't great at waking up at eight o'clock to go to practice and he was late a lot. He used to love playing PlayStation in the evening, and sometimes I had to stop him and say, "Come on, it's time to go to bed now." I was kind of like an elder brother to him.'

Given all the hassles with French that had plagued Federer when he first went to Ecublens, it may have been psychologically valuable for him to have developed a friendship in which the default language was French. 'We always speak French,' says Allegro, 'which is quite strange because by that point my Swiss German wasn't bad. Even today we speak more French than Swiss German together, although now we mix three languages: French, Swiss German and English.'

But what was Federer like to live with? Did he do his share of the washing-up? 'He was all right,' says his former flatmate. 'We weren't too bad. If I told him to do something, he did it. He probably wouldn't have done it by himself but, if I told him, he always did it.

'To be honest, we were away so much at tournaments that we weren't at home together very much, but in general I cooked and he played PlayStation. He was pretty lazy about clearing up and such things, and, if he ever tidied his room, within a couple of days it was as untidy as it was before. But he's always been someone who, when he decided to do something, he did it properly, and tidying up wasn't that important to him.'

Allegro also noted something else that everyone who had

observed the young Roger had noticed – he was so much better a player in matches than he ever was in practice. Most players, at all levels of tennis, can play some wonderful tennis in practice, but the moment they're in an official match, their level drops a little because of the pressure and the formality of the situation. With Federer it was the reverse. Many of his Old Boys friends can claim victories over him on the practice courts, but when it became official Federer's level rose. 'He was frequently late for practice,' recalls Allegro of their time in Biel, 'but then he was always more of a match player, and practice often bored him.'

Allegro carved out a moderately successful career for himself as a doubles player on the ATP tour. He had a succession of semi-regular partners, and for a while he enjoyed occasional high-profile appearances as Federer's doubles partner in Davis Cup ties, a few tournaments and the 2004 Olympics. So does he find it strange to be the former 'older brother' who became the junior on-court partner to one of the biggest names in world sport? 'No, it's not strange. In fact, I think it's a nice story. I'm not jealous at all. I'm very happy about what Roger's done. I'm doing my stuff and he's doing his stuff. It was nice to win two titles with him, and it's nice to play in the Davis Cup with him, just because it's a nice story.' Stan Wawrinka's rise to prominence as a singles and doubles player effectively ended Allegro's appearances alongside Federer.

1997 was also the year Federer gave up on his schooling. 'I told my parents, "I'm not in the mood to go to school any more and I want to focus on tennis,"' he said in an interview in 2004. 'They understood, but they said that if, in the next few years, I didn't have any results, I'd have to go back to school. It was a pretty big risk for me to stop school at sixteen because I didn't have an ATP ranking at that time. Maybe I was eight-hundredth or something, and in the juniors I was, like, sixtieth or something. But somehow I felt that school was disturbing me from being one hundred per cent focused on tennis. That's why I quit school, and then tennis went much better.'

Robbie Federer, who in 1997 turned down a plum job in Australia because he and Lynette felt it might hinder Roger's chances of becoming a top tennis player, later told the Swiss tennis journalist René Stauffer, 'Everyone kept telling us how talented Roger was, but we wanted to see deeds.' And Stauffer quotes Lynette as adding, 'We made it clear to Roger that we couldn't support him financially for ten years just so he could be ranked around 400 in the world.' She even increased her working hours to ensure the family remained financially secure, no doubt a sensible move at the time but one that, with hindsight, seems ludicrously overcautious.

By the time he left school, he had notched up his first international tournament success. In January 1997, he became the Swiss under-eighteens junior champion while still only fifteen. Then in May he won the international junior title in Prato, Italy, winning six matches in straight sets against some of the best juniors of the time. But that was to be the only title he won that year, and he still hadn't played in a junior Grand Slam.

So what kind of a player was Federer at sixteen? He has said his graceful style came naturally and didn't really emerge until his late teens, but under the guidance of Alexis

Bernhard, Christophe Freyss and Peter Carter he was clearly enhancing the efficiency of the smooth stroke-making Seppli Kacovski had taught him at Old Boys. Speaking in 2006, Thomas Wirz recalled of that time, 'I always had a little concern about his playing style. He always played a high-risk game, hitting very flat, clearing the net by very little, and that made me think at the time that he would never win the French Open. He's added some spin that allows him to play better on clay, but his game still isn't well suited to slow courts. But then, he's always had a very economical style, so he doesn't need the degree of musculature that some players need. He's a bit like Michael Stich in that respect, very efficient.'

And still the volatile temperament was there to haunt him. 'I was throwing around my racket like you can't imagine,' he said in an interview quoted by the website tennis-x. com. 'Helicopters were flying all over. I mean, I was getting kicked out of practice sessions when I was sixteen. I used to talk much more, too, and scream on court.'

His parents tell the story of driving home from a tournament through an Alpine pass. Federer was angry at the way he had played, and was becoming very hot-tempered in the car. His father tried ignoring him, but that didn't work, so he stopped the car, dragged Roger out and rubbed his head in the snow as a symbolic way of cooling him down. 'Roger never heard a bad word from us just because he had lost,' his mother said in an interview with Freddy Widmer of the *Basler Zeitung*, 'but when he misbehaved or when he just didn't make an effort, we weren't going to let that go.'

Lynette is convinced her son gained strength from his bad experiences because of her and her husband's attitude towards him. 'Our son was always allowed to be a bit wild, but he always had to take responsibility for the consequences. If he dug himself into a hole, he had to dig himself out of it.'

This same philosophy was adopted by the Swiss Tennis centre in Biel, where his temper soon landed him a punishment from hell. The new 'House of Tennis', as the centre was called, was newly fitted out, and one of its fittings was an expensive anti-noise drape. All players were warned that it had cost a lot of money and, if anyone damaged it, they would have to clean the toilets for a week. Federer later admitted he thought the drape was so thick you couldn't possibly damage it. But he was wrong. After missing a shot, he spun his racket out of his hand and it hit the drape and put a significant slit in it. 'He had to be in at seven in the morning to clean the toilets for a week,' says Allegro. 'For him it was the worst possible punishment. It was the middle of winter, so very cold, and he was hopeless at getting up even at eight o'clock, so getting up early enough to be at the courts by seven was a real nightmare for him.'

Yves Allegro certainly remembers the tantrums. 'He'd get pissed off very easily and throw rackets all over the place,' he recalls. 'Not very bad, but often. I think he was even worse in practice than in matches. He was very competitive in matches.' But Allegro also recognises that it was around that time, towards the end of 1997, that Federer began to make the most progress in his game. And, as the new year dawned, he was set to take the junior world by storm.

There are mixed opinions as to how to regard the official world junior champion. For some, the achievement is a stepping-stone to greatness, while for others it can be the opening chapter in a tale of unfulfilled promise. Since the first world junior champions were crowned in 1978, a number have gone on to top the rankings – Ivan Lendl, Stefan Edberg, Andy Roddick, Martina Hingis and Amélie Mauresmo, for instance – while others such as Brian Dunn, Federico Browne, Zdenka Malkova and Nino Louarsabishvili have disappeared with little trace. They might be the best in the world at under-eighteens level, but, if they're born in a year of few top players or many late developers, the honour might be of little ultimate meaning. The same goes for the Grand Slam junior championships: while they give young players a chance to rub shoulders with great players in the locker rooms and play on the courts they've recently vacated, winning a junior Grand Slam title doesn't always offer the greatest indication of likely champions of the future.

In 1998, Federer played a full year of the top junior events, which included the four Grand Slams and a series of colourfully named tournaments including the Coffee Bowl, the Banana Bowl and the culmination of the year: the Orange Bowl. He won the Victoria Junior Championships in Australia the week before the Australian Open, and then went on to reach the semi-finals at what was then still called Flinders Park (now Melbourne Park).

Playing his first Grand Slam event brought him into contact with the kind of regular media presence that would accompany him for the rest of his playing career. Marco Mordasini was a Swiss radio journalist, who was earning most of his money at the 1998 Australian Open reporting on Martina Hingis and Patty Schnyder, but – like most reporters – was keeping an eye out for any new home-grown talent in the junior events. He spoke to Federer several times during that tournament, most notably after the Swiss had lost a very close match in the semi-finals to Sweden's Andreas Vinciguerra 4–6, 7–5, 7–5.

'I'd asked to speak to him,' Mordasini recalls, 'so, a while after his match had finished, Mitzi Ingram Evans, the player liaison officer for the juniors, brought him into the radio room. At that moment, Hingis or Schnyder had just won and I had to go on air to give the result, so I asked Roger if he could wait a couple of minutes – I explained why – and he said yes. So I sat him down next to me and, as I was waiting to go on air, I heard a snuffling sound. I looked over and there he was, crying his eyes out. He cried for what seemed like about ten minutes about losing this match. I asked him what was up. As I'd seen it, he'd played a superb match; the other guy just happened to be one notch better. Roger explained that he wasn't sad because he'd lost but because he knew then that he'd had the chance to win and hadn't used his chances. He could see what he should have done differently, and it hit him hard. It was a powerful moment.'

Mordasini says Federer was easy to deal with on a personal level, although he needed some coaxing. 'He seemed shy,' said the journalist, 'at times very shy, but always very well mannered, said "Sie" [the more formal or deferential of the German pronouns for 'you'] to me, unlike most teenagers. He was very calm; he didn't speak in torrents. You had to encourage him to come out of himself a bit. It was like there were two people: one on the tennis court, where he knew what he was doing, and the other in the media area, where he was a bit restrained.

I told him the rules of my game – that I'd cut out anything he said which didn't come out right – and I think that encouraged him to develop something of a sense of trust with the media – at least with me. Over the years, he's genuinely come out of himself. It's not a PR act that he's learned.'

A third junior title, and the second of the year, came in the springtime in Florence, which helped to raise his profile in Switzerland. One of the many people who took note of his performance was Köbi Hermenjat, the tournament director in Gstaad whose Swiss Open clay court event used to take place the week after Wimbledon. Hermenjat judged that, if this young Swiss boy – still only sixteen – could win a junior title on clay, he was worth a wildcard. (The field for a professional tennis tournament is made up mostly of players who are the highest-ranked applicants, plus a handful of 'qualifiers' and 'wildcards'. A pre-tournament competition is held to work out who wins through 'qualifying', and a tournament director has a couple of invitations – 'wildcards' – to give to players who wouldn't qualify in terms of ranking but who would enhance the appeal of the tournament, eg local players or star names on a comeback after injury. Qualifying tournaments also have wildcards.)

Hermenjat offered Federer his wildcard, and Federer jumped at the chance. His opening on to the full ATP Tour had finally arrived, a milestone that helped him to decide that 1998 would be his last year on the junior circuit (even though he'd still be eligible in 1999). But, before the Gstaad tournament came round, he had another milestone to reach.

Although he bombed at Roland Garros, losing 6–4, 5–7, 9–7 to the Czech Jaroslav Levinsky, he found his feet on the grass in London. First, he reached the semi-finals at Roehampton, losing to Taylor Dent in three sets, and then went on to Wimbledon, where with barely a volley in sight he won the junior event, beating the Georgian Irakli Labadze 6–4, 6–4 in the final. Then he and the Belgian Olivier Rochus won the doubles title, beating Michaël Llodra and Andy Ram, also in a 6–4, 6–4 final. After all the fun in practice sessions at Old Boys in which he'd said, 'With this shot I'll win Wimbledon,' Federer was finally a Wimbledon champion, albeit in the junior events.

Permit me a personal recollection here. The day he won his Wimbledon junior title was the day I met him for the first time. During the 1990s, I talked to a lot of juniors. Some were cocky, some were shy, some were fiercely ambitious and some were coy about saying how far they could go. What struck me about Federer was a remarkable mixture of charm and ambition. He made instant connections with people, he certainly made me feel he was pleased to have chatted with me (and I know I'm not the only one to have felt this), and he had an arrogance that was in no way offensive. There's always quite a media interest surrounding junior Grand Slam champions – largely as an investment for the future, just in case they prove to be any good – and the clichéd question is always: do you think you'll win the full title one day? I regret I succumbed to the cliché; in response, Federer flashed his cheeky smile and said, 'Why not?'

I'd love to say that I saw there and then that he was destined for greatness, but I can't. I'd talked to too many juniors who saw their destiny in the world's top ten, if not beyond. What I can honestly say is that he made a bigger impression on me as a human being than any of the other juniors did.

Federer's two Wimbledon titles earned him an invitation to the black-tie Wimbledon champions' dinner at London's Savoy hotel, where he would have been fêted alongside the full singles champions that year, Pete Sampras and Jana Novotna. But he turned it down, after his coach Peter Carter persuaded him that concentrating on his ATP debut in Gstaad was more important than a social event in London.

Federer's ATP debut turned into a third successive 6–4, 6–4 match, but this time with him on the losing side. On a damp, overcast day, he was scheduled to face the German Tommy Haas, but, when Haas pulled out with a stomach upset, in stepped the Argentinian clay specialist Lucas Arnold. Arnold has one or two claims to fame, notably a courageous – and so far successful – battle against testicular cancer; on his return to the tour he added his mother's name, Ker, to his own in recognition of her role in his healing process. But his biggest claim is that he beat Roger Federer in Federer's first match at tour level, Arnold proving just too streetwise for the tour debutant. And yet Federer's reaction to his defeat wasn't one of disappointment but of excitement; he was buoyed up by the knowledge that he'd created enough opportunities and possessed the weapons to have perhaps even won the match. His confidence was building.

By now, like many other juniors embarking on the transition to the adult tennis scene, Federer was playing on two circuits: the junior and the lower ranks of the full tour. He was given a wildcard into the Geneva Challenger at the end of August, where again he lost in the first round, this time to Orlin Stanoytchev of Bulgaria, 6–4, 7–6.

In the first week of September, it was off to the US Open,

where he had the chance to go to the top of the junior rankings. He went to New York ranked fourth, and reached the final with wins over his doubles partner Olivier Rochus and the powerful Dane Kristian Pless (another junior world number one who felt he was headed for greatness but never made the top fifty), who had beaten three seeds en route to the semis: Aisam Qureshi, Taylor Dent and Fernando Gonzalez – all players who went on to enjoy good measures of success as professionals. If Federer had beaten David Nalbandian in the final, he would have gone to number one, but the sixteen-year-old Nalbandian – a year younger than Federer, which can make quite a difference at that age – worked out how to play the Swiss and beat him 6–3, 7–5.

Federer felt he was too negative in the whole tournament, saying after the final, 'I didn't play my best tennis, I didn't take enough chances.' Having shown his mastery of the useful but meaningless tennis player's answer, he gave a bigger indication of his determined mindset when asked what he could still improve in his game. 'I could improve everything,' he replied.

The Nalbandian defeat was one of the losses that Federer says taught him so much. 'I always learned more from losses, not wins, and losing the US Open junior final was one that made me wake up. I thought, "I've got to work harder," but it was only a few months after the US Open that I really decided to put in the work, and it paid off in results.'

The next pay-off came just a couple of weeks after his trip to New York. Offered a wildcard into the qualifying tournament for the ATP event in Toulouse, he came through three matches to make it to the main draw. A 6–2, 6–2 first-round win over the veteran Frenchman Guillaume Raoux meant Federer had opened his account on the full tour, and another straight-sets win over the Australian Richard Fromberg took him to the quarter-finals, where he was beaten by the eventual champion, Jan Siemerink. He had served notice that he had nothing to fear on the full tour.

Three days later, Federer was in his third ATP event and the one that really meant something to him: the Swiss Indoors, held at Basel's St Jakobshalle. The line-up for the event is normally impressive, and 1998 was no exception; the field featured four Grand Slam champions: Pete Sampras, Andre Agassi, Patrick Rafter and Yevgeny Kafelnikov. When the draw threw Federer into a first-round meeting with Agassi, the former ballboy was set up for his first encounter with one of the true greats of the sport. In front of a near-capacity 8,000 spectators on the first day of the event, he lost 6–3, 6–2, but he knew he'd arrived. 'The road is long,' he said after the match, 'but I've learned a lot in these past few months.' But, as he found out the following week, there was still plenty to learn.

After playing to the packed seats of one of the tour's most prestigious arenas, Federer went to Küblis, a picturesque resort near Klosters in eastern Switzerland, which was hosting the first event in a four-week autumn Swiss satellite tournament series. The town of Küblis was home to around 500 souls, and very few of them showed up to watch a few journeymen and budding tennis professionals plying their trade in the local indoor tennis centre, whose four carpet courts were out of bounds for the week. Such is the largely unseen reality of the supposedly glamorous pro tennis tour.

After his fêting in Basel, Federer struggled for motivation in Küblis. In the first round he came up against a low-ranked Swiss, Armando Brunold, and, instead of using the confidence of the Agassi match and his five Toulouse wins to sail through, he lost the first set on a tiebreak. When he went a break down early in the second set, he began just belting the ball, teeing off on every shot and missing most. He also threw in several listless double faults. This came to the attention of the tournament's referee, Claudio Grether, who came out to watch the last few games of Brunold's 7–6, 6–2 win. Grether judged Federer not to be giving his 'best efforts', as required by the tennis players' code of conduct, and fined the embryonic Swiss hero $100, $13 more than the first-round losers' prize money of $87.

The following day, Switzerland's mass-circulation daily *Blick* had a field day, printing large and colourful headlines to depict the shame of the boy who only the previous week had been portrayed as the future of Swiss tennis. 'It was tough,' says Yves Allegro, who played doubles and shared a room with Federer over the four-week series. 'It wasn't that he wasn't trying, but after Basel he lost the motivation a little. The next day he was in the paper, and he felt really bad about it.'

Yet you can't keep a good man down for long. Federer took his punishment on the chin, he and Allegro won the doubles in Küblis, and then Federer won the next singles tournament and reached the final in the one after that, finishing first – ahead of Allegro in second – in the satellite standings after the four weeks.

All that time, Federer had put on hold his unfinished business in juniors: the quest to finish the year as world junior champion. But he had three tournaments left, two of them with singles ranking points to collect. It started badly when he lost in the third round of the Eddie Herr Championships, but he then won his two matches in the Sunshine Cup team event (the first against Juan Carlos Ferrero, a junior contemporary who was to beat Federer to the top of the tree), and then went to the Orange Bowl in Miami, the most prestigious junior event outside the four Grand Slam junior tournaments.

On that trip, Federer did something that shocked his parents and many others who knew him: he dyed his hair blond. He says today of the decision, 'Actually, I wanted to change my hair colour many more times, but I just kept it to blond one time. I was on the point of colouring it red once, but that didn't go down too well with my parents. The next thing I wanted was long hair. I guess that's a little bit rebellious.'

Winning the Orange Bowl not only helped Federer to become world junior champion for 1998, but was also a significant psychological boost in helping him realise he could win when the odds were stacked against him. After his first match, he injured his foot while messing about in the gym, and feared he might have to withdraw. But he followed the medical advice he was given to the letter and, by the time he faced Nalbandian in the semi-finals, he was moving without hindrance. He then gained revenge for his US Open defeat, and went on to defeat Nalbandian's roommate Guillermo Coria, 7-5, 6-3, in the final for one of the most satisfying wins of his burgeoning career.

The champion's photos, which are somewhat comic anyway as the winner has to hoist a bowl of oranges overhead, testify to the glory (or horror, depending on your taste in hairstyles) of the blond rinse.

More importantly, Federer was guaranteed the year-end number-one ranking and with it the tag of world junior champion. His invitation to another black-tie dinner – the ITF World Champions' Dinner, during the second week of the following year's French Open – was guaranteed, but his passage into the higher echelons of the full ATP Tour was not. He'd made an impressive start but, with his junior career now over, the question was: would he join the ranks of Lendl, Edberg and Hingis to graduate from junior champion to world number one, or would he join Dunn, Browne and a host of other talented hopefuls who failed to make an impression as touring professionals? It was a question that took another four and a half years to answer.

TRANSITION TO THE TOUR

2

4

OBSERVING WHAT MAKES someone successful is both easy and difficult. On the one hand, everything they do contributes in some way to their success, while on the other it's often hard to pinpoint exactly what makes the difference between the top dog and the rest of the pack. It's therefore worth looking at the little changes Federer made as he left the junior circuit to join the ranks of the big boys, and how he dealt with some of the challenges that greeted him.

In his last days as a junior, he enlisted the help of a sports psychologist, Chris Marcolli, a former professional footballer. Although somewhat diffident today about recalling the help he sought and received, Federer said in one interview, 'I was getting too upset, so I needed some help on how to think about different things and how to get rid of the feelings of anger. That's why I worked with the psychologist. I think I've always been told the right things from the people around me – things like how to behave, how hard to work, what to do, what not to do – but in the end it's yourself who has to react and want to put in the effort, and thank God I realised that – probably a little bit late, but in time to change some things. So, after working with the psychologist, I kind of worked on it myself.'

Marcolli, who was just twenty-five when he began working with Federer, was pursuing a relatively new discipline known as performance psychology. As Dr Christian Marcolli, he went on to write a book, *More Life, Please!*, in which he admitted to having his own temper demons in his playing days. Professional ethics prevent Marcolli talking much about the work the two men did, but he said in an interview with the French sports daily *L'Équipe* that the main focus of their sessions was on how Federer could use his energy in the most constructive way to win matches, which sounds like a nice euphemism for overcoming his tantrums.

Yves Allegro, Federer's flatmate at the time he was seeing Marcolli, recalls, 'He didn't do it within Swiss Tennis; he went outside and found his own person and worked with him for a few months. I think it helped his tennis, certainly a little.'

Another thing that changed was a tiny gesture, but obviously a significant one. While playing at junior level, Federer had had a remarkable little routine before every point on his own serve, a routine the Swiss radio journalist Marco Mordasini remembers disappeared overnight. 'He would pick up the ball,' says Mordasini, 'take it with his left hand, throw it from behind his back, from back left to front right, then play it back with his racket between his legs before catching it behind his back, all with an amazing speed and precision. It became one of his trademarks, yet around that time it just stopped. When I asked him why, he just said, "That was junior time. This is now." He used to do it before every point, sometimes even while walking to the service line, and with a perfection that was incredible. But he obviously dropped it as part of a change in attitude, probably begun by Peter Carter and certainly continued by Peter Lundgren.'

With his tennis becoming increasingly disciplined, he needed an outlet for his sense of teenage fun, and that outlet seemed to be his hair. Having done the blond rinse on the Orange Bowl trip, he let that grow out and decided to go for the long look, growing it long enough to tie in a short ponytail, supplemented with a bandanna. That became the trademark Federer look, and he kept it until the second half of 2004. Often in the early days, he was asked why he was growing it long, to which he tended to reply, 'I like it this way. Why should I have it cut?'

Most players coming into their rookie professional year end up working their way up a three-tier progression. The lowest level of pro tournaments are the satellites; then there are the Challengers, which generally attract those ranked around 100–250 but can feature players ranked as high as fifty; and then there are the tournaments on the full tour. It's a mark of how quickly Federer rose up the lower rungs of the ladder that he played just eight Challenger events in his entire career.

Part of the reason is that, as a marked man in terms of potential, there was no shortage of wildcards being offered by tournament directors who wanted to showcase one of the big names of the future. One of those wildcards came in February 1999 in Marseille, where in the first round he beat Carlos Moya, who was only six weeks away from being world number one. Then, having qualified for the main draw in Rotterdam, he reached his second successive quarter-final.

Such was the reputation he was creating on the tour that he was given another wildcard, this time into the Ericsson Open in Key Biscayne, his first Masters series event (the series was still known at that time as the 'Super Nine'). Although he lost in the first round, he was knocking on the door of the world's top 100 just four months into his first full year on the tour.

Then, in April 1999, Federer made his Davis Cup debut. Normally, a seventeen-year-old playing his first Davis Cup tie will attract some attention but is by and large viewed as one to watch for the future. Not so with Federer's debut. Switzerland were at home to the previous year's runners-up, Italy, in a first-round tie played in Neuchâtel. The former International Tennis Federation president Francesco Ricci Bitti – then president of the Italian Tennis Association – recalls, 'I saw the line-up and thought, "Oh dear, we're in trouble." His results didn't surprise me, because he had amazing talent, but from 1999 to 2003 he was a guy lacking in concentration. It was so easy for him to play that he didn't work on his concentration. He was really up and down, except in the Davis Cup, when he played wonderfully well, because the responsibility for the country gave him more reason to concentrate.'

By April 1999, Italy were in trouble, and for reasons other than having to face the young Roger Federer. The nation that had won the Davis Cup in 1976, at the height of the career of the charismatic Adriano Panatta, had never been outside the competition's sixteen-nation world group, but by the late 1990s the Italians were in serious decline in world tennis. They seemed to use up all their luck in getting to the 1998 final, which they lost heavily at home to Sweden, and by the following April they'd lost two of their mainstays, Andrea Gaudenzi and Diego Nargiso. Nonetheless, they still paraded as their top player the experienced Davide Sanguinetti, who Federer had to face after Marc Rosset had won the opening rubber against Gianluca Pozzi.

In Federer's first best-of-five-sets match, he despatched the greying Italian 6–4, 6–7, 6–3, 6–4 in a remarkable display of maturity that backed up what Ricci Bitti had feared. 'I was nervous at the start,' Federer said later. 'It was just so different. You're not playing for ranking points but for your country.'

With Rosset and Lorenzo Manta beating Italy's Stefano Pescosolido and Laurence Tieleman in the doubles to seal Switzerland's passage inside two days, Federer suddenly found himself part of a team fancied to go a long way.

With the veteran Rosset, the increasingly confident doubles specialist Manta, who in June 1999 reached the fourth round of the Wimbledon singles, and the emerging talents of Federer and George Bastl, Switzerland had the makings of a useful team. Suddenly, an away quarter-final against Belgium two weeks after Wimbledon seemed not only winnable but a passport to a home semi-final against France.

With Rosset recovering from a viral infection, Federer was promoted to number-one Swiss player for the quarter-final at the Primrose Club in Brussels, with Manta playing second singles. The Belgians themselves had a rising star in Xavier Malisse, who took Manta apart in the opening match. In the second, Federer was favoured to beat Christophe Van Garsse, but Van Garsse was one of those low-ranked players who seem to find at least two extra gears when playing for their country. A left-hander with a somewhat unorthodox playing style, he'd previously posted a handful of ranking-defying results in the Davis Cup, and added another five-set victory on 16 July 1999 against the still seventeen-year-old Federer. In the fourth set, with Federer leading by two sets to one, Van Garsse needed treatment for cramps, but then Federer also ended up by cramping as Belgium took a 2–0 lead.

Aware that the Belgians had a tradition of being chronically unable to win doubles matches, the Swiss knew they still had a chance, and they took the doubles to narrow the deficit to 1–2. But all hope rested on the Federer–Malisse match that Sunday. As the American journalist Christopher Clarey wrote of the match, 'Though it is undeniably risky, in this era of egalitarianism and injuries, to predict the future in men's tennis, it was tempting to view the match as the first of many between these two in the game's major events.' As it turned out, that view – shared by many others at the time – did not bear fruit, for, while Federer went on to great things, Malisse was unable to capitalise on his unquestioned talent, posting just one Wimbledon semi-final compared with Federer's tally of twenty Grand Slam titles. But on that summer Sunday on the clay of Brussels, Malisse had the edge and won 4–6, 6–3, 7–5, 7–6, to end Swiss involvement in the Davis Cup in the twentieth century.

Although the Swiss team had performed creditably, the fallout from their defeat was bitter. Always a patchwork of linguistic and political factions, the Swiss tennis scene can at times be vulnerable to descending into internecine fighting, and the result in Belgium unleashed a period of infighting that took a good two years to work through. In the debriefings that followed, it was noted that Rosset's viral infection – which some clearly didn't feel was that debilitating – had probably cost Switzerland a home semi-final against France. Rosset's devotion to the national cause suggests he would only have refused to play if he really was physically unable to, and suggestions that he might not have been as ill as he made out say more about the civil war in the Swiss camp than about Rosset himself. The captain, Claudio Mezzadri, came in for criticism – he had only come in as captain for the tie against Italy three months before, after his predecessor, Stéphane Oberer, had been forced to resign because Rosset had fired him as his personal coach. In November 1999, Mezzadri was himself fired, only to be replaced by his former Davis Cup teammate Jakob Hlasek, a man hardly likely to usher in harmony. Hlasek was on record as saying he couldn't see a reconciliation between himself and Marc Rosset. In other words, the Swiss national tennis association had picked a captain whose relationship with the country's top player was decidedly rocky.

Worse still, the association hadn't consulted the players. In sports with large teams, such as football or rugby, a national governing body would find it impractical – and probably unfair – to consult the leading players formally about their preferred choice of coach. But in tennis, where two players – or one outstanding player and a doubles partner – can take a team a long way, failing to speak with the leading players before deciding on a captain can be suicidal. In fact, in most teams, the captain is *in situ* by the grace of the players.

Swiss Tennis's announcement provoked a display of solidarity among the players and elicited the threat of a strike over Switzerland's first Davis Cup tie of 2000 against the newly crowned champions, Australia. That match in February 2000 was first scheduled to take place at Geneva's Palexpo Arena, a venue that can hold over 18,000 spectators. Through fears that no noteworthy players would end up playing for Switzerland, the venue was switched to Zürich's Saalsporthalle, a venue that could just about clear 4,000.

As it happened, the tie against the Australians proved to be a superb spectacle. Federer found himself forced to play, despite his solidarity with those who were threatening to strike, because he was under contract to Swiss Tennis and was receiving financial help from them. As expected, Hlasek opted not to pick Rosset, which upset Federer, who made it clear he wasn't happy with the choice of Hlasek as captain. Hlasek managed to persuade Bastl and Manta to play, but Manta made it clear he was playing under protest. Not a happy team!

And yet, on the opening day of the tie, Federer beat Mark Philippoussis in four sets to cancel out Lleyton Hewitt's win over Bastl. Then, when he and Manta beat Wayne Arthurs and Sandon Stolle in the doubles, the feuding nation was on the point of bundling out the champions just two months after the Aussies had triumphed in the 1999 final in Nice. But Hewitt – no doubt mindful of his World Youth Cup defeat to Federer in that same city four years earlier – stormed back to beat his former junior rival in four sets in the first reverse singles, and Bastl couldn't quite overcome Philippoussis, the Australian winning the fifth rubber 6–4 in the fifth set.

To have come so close to victory amid such unrest must have given the Swiss hope, but it was a blow to Hlasek's already under-fire captaincy and sowed the seeds for further trouble fourteen months later.

Back on the tour, Federer's rapid rise of early 1999 came to a bit of a standstill for a few months. Six successive tour events all ended in first-round defeats, including his main draw debut at Roland Garros and Wimbledon. He lost at the French to Patrick Rafter, and at Wimbledon to Byron Black. His best results had come in indoor tournaments, and, when the circuit allowed him to play indoors again, he picked up his rise. He lost a three-setter to Lleyton Hewitt in Lyon in their first match at tour level (a match characterised by the unusual spectacle of their coaches, Peter Carter and Darren Cahill, sitting next to each other in the stands and chatting away happily). He beat Cédric Pioline – a top ten player that year – in Tashkent in September and Rainer Schüttler in Toulouse the following week. Those results took him from being a player knocking on the door of the top 100 to breaking into it.

He closed 1999 by returning to the Challenger circuit, winning his first and only Challenger title in Brest to end the year ranked sixty-fourth, a rise of 238 places from his start-of-year position of 302.

At the start of 2000, winning two rounds at the Australian

Open boosted Federer's ranking further, and he reached his first tour final in Marseille in mid-February, the week after the politically charged Davis Cup tie against Australia. And who should he meet in that final but the man he'd sided with throughout the tussles: Marc Rosset. It was a highly respectful final, decided in Rosset's favour on a 7–5 third-set tiebreak. Whether Federer wasn't quite ready for his first title is open to question; the chances are that, had he been facing someone he was less close to than Rosset, his will to win might have been a little sharper. Rosset later joked that he'd thanked Federer for letting him win, which clearly hadn't been the case, although Federer was particularly pleased that Rosset had won another tournament, the fourteenth of his career and his third in Marseille.

If any period marks Federer's coming-of-age, it has to be the early part of 2000, as he took several decisions then that defined his independence. He finished with the sports psychologist Chris Marcolli after working with him for over a year. Late in 2002, Marcolli told the Swiss newspaper *Neue Zürcher Zeitung* that the sports psychologist's job is 'to offer the client help so he can help himself', and that by the early part of 2000, Federer had reached the necessary state of autonomy so there was no need to continue working together. Then in April, he announced he would be leaving Swiss Tennis later in the year.

A successful feature of many national tennis programmes is the help offered to players in their first couple of post-junior years. The Swedes in the 1970s and the Germans in the 1980s learned that many a promising junior career was wrecked because of insufficient help to ease the transition from the junior ranks to the full tour. So, while Federer had turned professional in 1998, he had remained under contract to Swiss Tennis, a situation that enabled him to practise at the new performance centre in Biel and receive financial assistance from the organisation. But it also gave Swiss Tennis the final say on who coached him, and meant he'd had to play in the Davis Cup even though he'd objected to the association's choice of captain. While he might have left under his own steam, the fact that he was obligated to the national association in the Australia Davis Cup tie probably focused his mind.

Deciding to leave Swiss Tennis was one thing, but who would then coach him? Peter Carter had been lured to the national performance centre in Biel largely because of his links with Federer from Old Boys Basel, but little by little the National Trainer Peter Lundgren came to share the job of coaching Federer with Carter. The arrangement worked perfectly well but, with Federer now breaking free, he wanted someone to travel with him, and there were three names in the frame: Peter Carter, Peter Lundgren and Sven Groeneveld. Groeneveld is quoted in Christopher Clarey's book *The Master* as saying he was offered the job first but turned it down. He was clearly sounded out, but how firm the offer was remains part of the confidentiality that covers much of Federer's business dealings. However strong the offer, it meant the job would go to Carter or Lundgren.

Biblically, the name Peter comes from the Hebrew for 'rock', and Federer was certainly caught between a rock and a hard place. It was a difficult decision for him because, while Carter was reluctant to travel full-time, having a fiancée who was battling against cancer, he was also reluctant to let Federer go. Besides, the bond between

Federer and Carter was much stronger – having been built up over ten years – than the three-year-old bond between Federer and Lundgren.

'It was a decision where everyone was sure he was going to take Carter,' recalls Yves Allegro, 'and then he decided to take Lundgren. I was surprised too. It was a tough decision for Roger, and tough for Peter Carter to take.'

Darren Cahill spent a lot of time with Carter around the time of Federer's decision (Carter was one of the three-man 'wedding party' when Cahill got married that year), and says his friend was very disappointed. 'He was disappointed to the point of being somewhat upset, because he really believed he could help him go all the way. We used to sit down and talk for hours about the two guys we were coaching. We'd talk about how we could become better people for these players, how we would deal with the emotional side of tennis, how we could deal with something that happens on court. Of course deciding on a coach is a personal choice. Peter Lundgren is a great coach, and he also had a close relationship with Roger. Maybe Roger was looking at it that Carts had got him to a certain level and he needed someone of Lundgren's experience to take him to the next level, and maybe he was right. But Carts had invested heavily in Roger's career, being a friend to Roger as well, so when he went that direction Peter outwardly didn't show much emotion and supported it and was right behind it. But inwardly it hurt him.'

Federer says he made the decision on the basis of 'feeling'. Much was said about Carter not wanting to travel, and that was certainly a silver lining for the Australian, who was needed at his fiancée's bedside over the next year and a half.

But Cahill believes Carter would have 'done it in a flash' if Federer had asked him to be his travelling coach. Once the decision was made, Carter backed off gracefully without ever showing any sense of being aggrieved, and moved on. That quietly impressed Federer, and played a part in his strong push for Carter to become Switzerland's Davis Cup captain in 2001 and 2002. Cahill adds, 'Peter becoming part of the Swiss Davis Cup set-up was really Roger saying "this guy needs to be a part of my life and my career, I need him by my side, even if it's not in the prime role".'

Lundgren wasn't everybody's embodiment of a typical coach. He'd enjoyed modest success as a player, reaching twenty-fifth in the world rankings at the age of twenty and making it to the fourth round at Wimbledon and the Australian Open doubles final. But he'd earned his reputation more as the player who always toured with a guitar and who loved his hard rock as much as his soft backhand. After his playing days ended in the early 1990s, Lundgren filled out to take on the shape of someone not normally associated with top-level sport, and with his long hair and goatee beard he looked like someone more at home on the Australian beaches than coaching a tennis player aspiring to be the best in the world.

Nevertheless, Lundgren was of great value for Federer, just as he had been for Marcelo Rios and would be for Marat Safin. It's impossible to say exactly what a coach should be – every player needs something different, and only the players themselves know if they're getting what they need from their coach. But Federer clearly felt good in the laidback company of Lundgren; Lundgren had the tactical acumen to allow his charge to construct game plans, and he helped him to work on what still lingered of his volatile temperament. With Federer's hair down to his shoulders by early 2000, he and Lundgren frequently gave the impression of being, if not quite elder and younger brothers, then certainly some kind of soul mates.

By the end of 2000, there was a third 'rock' in the picture. Pierre Paganini had been at the Swiss Tennis national centre since before Federer went there in 1995. Mindful of the rigours of the global tennis tour, Federer appointed Paganini as his personal fitness trainer, working with a physiotherapist, initially Thierry Marcante and subsequently several others – the need to tour with Federer means most of his physios lasted about eighteen months before returning to their families or day jobs.

Born in 1957, Paganini is a shaven-headed fitness fanatic who doesn't go in for shouting from the sidelines but instead enjoys sweating with his charges. He and Christophe Freyss ran the Tennis Études programme that Federer joined as a fourteen-year-old, so it was a natural progression for Paganini to become Federer's personal fitness guru, working with him about 100 days a year. Paganini, who was of vital but underestimated importance, made it clear he had to be involved in planning Federer's tournament schedule as well as his diet and physical training. Out of this arose a structure to Federer's year that evolved somewhat over the years, especially as his body began to show signs of wear and tear, but which remained largely intact. In the early years, it included three three-week blocks of physical work – one in December, one in February and one in July – with shorter, more intensive blocks worked in between. This gave a general cycle of tournaments followed by recovery, followed by fitness training, then tennis training, and then back to tournaments, recovery etc. The physical work was based around a five-point plan Paganini worked out for Federer. It involved general fitness training (gym work to improve stamina, strength, speed and agility), specific fitness work (a mixture of gym work and on-court work concentrating on specific aspects, one at a time), integrated fitness work (various on-court exercises based on general fitness and tennis work), specific fitness training (tennis-playing with clear physical goals) and preventative training (involving physiotherapeutic exercises designed to prevent injuries). Over the years, Paganini made a few alterations to the routine, but the regime stayed largely the same.

Paganini, a former footballer and decathlete, shuns the limelight. He seldom appeared in Federer's courtside entourage, and has always been reluctant to give interviews, even when Federer signalled he did not object. The couple of times he has spoken publicly have been in specialist interviews, notably with the Swiss journalist René Stauffer and the American writer Christopher Clarey. Stauffer quotes Paganini as saying Federer's problem was 'his extreme talent, as that allowed him to compensate for physical shortcomings.' And to Clarey he said, 'I think we underestimate all the work Roger does, and it's a beautiful problem he has. We underestimate it, because when we see Roger play, we see the artist who expresses himself. We forget almost that he has to work to get there, like watching a ballet dancer. You see the beauty, but you forget the work behind it. You have to work very, very hard to be that beautiful a dancer.'

Paganini's value to Federer was that he kept the player

in peak physical condition – and largely injury-free until the latter years of his playing career – without turning him into a machine or a bodybuilder. The most crucial factor was that Paganini recognised early that physical training was not near the top of Federer's wishlist of activities, so he always had to make the gym work fun. The exercises were seldom the same two days running, and that mixture of fun and variety, coupled with a recognition that he felt in better shape as long matches wore on, allowed Federer to embrace the physical side without which no tennis professional can flourish these days.

With Lundgren as his personal coach and Paganini as his fitness trainer, Federer had the team in place for his assault on the top level of professional tennis.

5

I T'S EASY TO make the mistake of thinking that, because Federer went on to win twenty Grand Slam titles, his transition from junior player to tour professional was a rapid one. It was, in fact, a more measured learning process, and, because his Wimbledon junior victory at sixteen had raised expectations and made him something of a marked man, many of the lessons he had to learn as part of his professional apprenticeship were learned in the full glare of publicity.

In fact, the four-and-a-half years between him abandoning the junior circuit and winning his first Grand Slam title were characterised by slow but inexorable progress. The new Lundgren–Paganini regime took a few weeks to bring results, and he lost some matches that seem baffling in retrospect. For example, by June 2000, Michael Chang was a spent force in men's tennis – and he had never been at his best on grass – but the veteran American still contrived to beat Federer on the green stuff of Halle. And a strange grass-court defeat came in Nottingham at the hands of Richard Fromberg, another veteran whose best surface was clay. Perhaps the defeat at this time that hit Federer the hardest came in September 2000 at the Sydney Olympics.

The Olympic format allows all four semi-finalists two bites at a medal, with the losers playing off for the bronze. Federer sailed into the last four without dropping a set, but then lost his semi-final 6–3, 6–2 to Tommy Haas. He hadn't shown his best tennis but certainly hadn't disgraced himself, and he was strongly favoured to beat Arnaud Di Pasquale in the bronze-medal playoff.

Di Pasquale was Federer's predecessor as world junior champion, but the two couldn't have been more contrasting. A flamboyant player, the Frenchman was let down by flawed technique and a body that wouldn't stand up to the rigours of life on the modern tennis tour. He'd beaten three seeded players to reach the last four, but had been stopped by Yevgeny Kafelnikov in the semis and came into the play-off against Federer with several niggling injuries and little gas left in the tank.

Somehow, Di Pasquale eked out the first set on a 7–5 tiebreak, yet still Federer seemed to be in charge. He sailed close to the wind in the second set, but, once he'd levelled on a second tiebreak, the medal seemed to be his. Yet he was broken early in the final set, and Di Pasquale claimed the bronze – and the biggest smile on the podium – with a 7–6, 6–7, 6–3 win. The International Tennis Federation's then president Francesco Ricci Bitti, an unashamed Federer fan despite the requirement of his position for a semblance of neutrality, said, 'It was one of the most frustrating matches as a Federer fan. He was the better player and Di Pasquale was injured, but Federer still somehow managed to lose.' The frustration Ricci Bitti felt was to be magnified three years later as Federer seemed to many to be on the verge of squandering his immense talent, and it was to take another eight years for Federer to get his hands on an Olympic medal.

Yet it would be wrong to say Federer came away from the Sydney Olympics empty-handed. An open-minded citizen of the world, he thrived in the Olympic environment and enjoyed meeting other athletes. And yet it was a member of the Swiss tennis team who made the greatest impression on him.

Miroslava Vavrinec, known for short as 'Mirka', had a history resembling Martina Hingis more than Roger Federer. Born in the Slovak part of Czechoslovakia in 1978, she had moved to Switzerland when she was two. Originally a dancer, she moved into tennis, with Martina Navratilova playing a role in encouraging her to pursue the sport, though accounts vary as to exactly how big that role was. There appears to have been contact between Vavrinec's family and Navratilova's stepfather (her de facto father) before a nine-year-old Mirka met Navratilova at the Filderstadt tournament of 1987. By fifteen, Vavrinec was the Swiss national under-eighteen champion, and by 2000 she had bounced back from a serious ankle injury to be included in the Swiss squad for the Sydney Olympics.

Roger and Mirka had first met at Biel, shortly after the 'House of Tennis' opened in 1997, so they already knew each other a little when they met again in Sydney. While Federer was powering to the semi-finals, Vavrinec lost two first-round matches; in the women's singles, she went out 6–1, 6–1 to the eventual silver medallist Elena Dementieva, and partnering Emmanuelle Gagliardi, she crashed out of the women's doubles 6–2, 7–5 to the Venezuelan pairing Milagros Sequera and Maria Vento. Vavrinec lost something else in Sydney as well: her heart.

It seems Federer did most of the chasing. 'I couldn't work out why he wanted to talk to me so much,' Vavrinec said later, 'and then, near the end of the Games, he kissed me.'

Just before the end of the Olympics, Federer ran into Mitzi Ingram Evans, an International Tennis Federation player–media liaison officer who had been in charge of liaising between the juniors and the media when Federer was a junior. Federer said, 'Mitzi, wait there, I have someone very special to introduce to you.' He disappeared, and returned a few minutes later with delight and pride. 'This is Mirka,' he said.

The Sydney Olympics signalled the start of a relationship that has been of both personal and practical nourishment for Federer, and that culminated in marriage on 11 April 2009 as the couple were preparing for the birth of what turned out to be twin girls.

Vavrinec wasn't his first love (he'd had a steady girlfriend earlier in his teens), but it soon became clear that this was more than a fleeting romance. She went on to become his diary secretary and the force behind the development of his RF fragrance, but she insisted that the two of them knew the difference between personal and commercial matters. For a while, they had an understanding with the Swiss media that they were not to be photographed together. That was inevitably broken, yet the Swiss media have generally recognised that the public's right to know stops at the front door of wherever they happen to be living. 'We now allow ourselves to be photographed together,' Vavrinec told the Swiss journalist Roger Jaunin in 2004, 'but you will never read in a newspaper or magazine what goes on in our house.' It was a demarcation that was adhered to by pretty much everyone in the Federer team.

The Swiss Indoors event in Basel is one of the regular features on the global tennis calendar. First staged in 1970, making it older than most events on today's tour, it grew from being a gathering largely of Swiss players held in a school sports hall to a highly regarded title in a modern-day indoor sports stadium. These days, its budget makes it the biggest annual sports event in Switzerland, though still relatively small in the global sporting market place. For many years it marked the opening of the European indoor season. In 2000 it was given a later slot, sandwiched between the second-last and last Masters Series tournaments of the year, and it continued to survive as a prestigious and financially healthy event. That prestige was rewarded in 2009 when it was granted '500' status, making it just one level below Masters or '1000'.

The tournament was part of the Federer family's annual routine well before Roger showed promise with a racket in his hand. In the 1980s, Lynette had approached a fellow member of the Ciba Club asking if there was a small job she might be able to do at the Swiss Indoors. 'He said "Oh yes, the badges",' she recalled in an interview in 2019. As a result of that approach, she ended up working for the accreditation office for ten years: 'I knew just about everyone in the tournament, because everyone involved – VIPs, media, ballkids, linesmen – they all need a badge, so everyone passed through our office. It was interesting for me to see what the organisation of a tournament involves.' That thorough knowledge of what it takes to run a professional tennis event, that it doesn't just happen when tennis players walk through the gates, has been key to Federer's understanding of the full picture, which in turn helped him keep a sense of perspective in his six years as president of the ATP Player Council.

The tournament is the baby of Roger Brennwald, the Basel tennis impresario, who founded it as a precocious twenty-four-year-old entrepreneur and is still its driving force half a century later. Brennwald's first experience with Roger Federer came when Federer was twelve and Brennwald had to present him with the Most Talented Young Player in Switzerland award. Before the ceremony, Brennwald learned that he should pronounce the boy's first name the English way, not the French way as he does with his own name. Brennwald has built the Swiss Indoors into an event that is so established he was able to boast for many years that Federer was 'a bonus rather than the foundation stone of the tournament', and indeed it survived several isolated years when Federer didn't play. Relations between the two became somewhat strained after Brennwald brushed off Federer's casual expression of interest in buying the tournament in 2010, but Federer always put playing in Basel ahead of differences with Brennwald and turned up at the St Jakobshalle every year he was fit, even if he felt he was being remunerated well below his market value. How well the tournament fares in the post-Federer years remains to be seen. There are some in the Basel tennis scene who feel it is perhaps too much of a social event, with the well-dressed, cigar-smoking visitors appearing to outnumber the genuine tennis aficionados. While there is some truth in that, there is barely a tournament on the planet that doesn't have this problem to some degree.

The Swiss Indoors was Federer's introduction to tour tennis: through his mother's work in the accreditation office, through his own experience as a ballboy rubbing shoulders with the likes of Jim Courier, Boris Becker and Pete Sampras, and through it being the event that brought the international circus to his town. By the time he was a professional, Basel was one of just two Swiss cities to have a tour-level men's tournament. The other was Gstaad, one of the most picturesque venues on the global tennis circuit, nestling in the Bernese Oberland, where Federer had made his tour debut. Both events have special meaning for Federer, but Basel more so, given his home-town history.

On the morning of 29 October 2000, everything seemed set for the Swiss Indoors to be the first title in Federer's portfolio. In one of his best performances as a professional, he'd beaten Lleyton Hewitt the previous day to reach the Basel final, a result that seemed to be another small turning point in his career. Strange, then, that it took another six years for him to lift his home trophy, despite his domination of world tennis.

Federer's semi-final win against Hewitt in 2000 was one of the outstanding matches of his early professional career. Just five and a half months separate the two players in age, they had played against each other in juniors, they were both spurred on by coaches from Hewitt's home city of Adelaide, and both were very much standard-bearers for their generation. Had Hewitt not matured vastly more quickly than Federer, it's possible he would never have got to number one in the world rankings. But, by the time they met in Basel, Hewitt had won all three of their post-juniors matches, including the four-sets Davis Cup win earlier in the year that had helped Australia to beat Switzerland by the narrowest of margins.

That allowed everyone in Basel to build up the Hewitt–Federer semi-final into the match of the week – and it was, a classic clash of the home underdog, ranked thirty-second, against the visiting celebrity favourite, ranked seventh. The two players played an outstanding match, which Federer won 6–4, 5–7, 7–6 (8–6 in the tiebreak). The Saturday faithful in the St Jakobshalle stood in admiration of both men, especially their local hero who had vanquished his opponent.

But the effort nearly broke him. The following day, Federer turned out for a best-of-five-sets final against the Swede Thomas Enqvist, who was in the twilight of his career but still ranked ninth and was still very much able to grind out victories against opponents not steady enough to match his relentlessness. Federer dug deep, and took the match to five sets, but he lost 6–2, 4–6, 7–6, 1–6, 6–1.

The expectation that, at nineteen, he might win his home-town title clearly made his failure to beat Enqvist into a crushing blow. Twenty years later, his mother described that lost final as 'nearly a disaster, and it happened again a year later', which speaks volumes for how much winning Basel meant to Federer. Yet individual setbacks notwithstanding, the trend was still inexorably upwards. By the end of his third full year on the tour, he had broken into the top thirty – he finished 2000 ranked twenty-ninth – thanks to the ranking points gleaned from reaching the Marseille and Basel finals and the Olympic semi-finals.

If timing is everything in terms of tennis stroke-making, the timing of Federer's rise to prominence during Switzerland's tennis adolescence was also perfect. A country with a reluctance to embrace sports that don't thrive on its own territory, it was forced to sit up and take notice when Martina Hingis became world number one in 1997. But Hingis wasn't Swiss-born and, while her immigration at the age of seven came early enough for her to speak fluent Swiss German, she never spoke in a way that made her sound born-and-bred Swiss, and the man and woman in the Swiss street seemed to find it hard to truly embrace her. One of the country's most experienced tennis journalists, the *Neue Zürcher Zeitung*'s long-standing tennis correspondent Jürg Vogel, once described her as 'the somewhat different Swiss'.

There was no such reservation about the Basel-born Federer. Just a week after Hingis lost in the Australian Open final to Jennifer Capriati, narrowly failing to add to her five Grand Slam singles titles, Federer finally won a tour title. The milestone came in Milan, when he beat Julien Boutter in the final to become an ATP champion. Boutter was hardly a player to instil fear into a still teenaged Federer, but the real work had been done in the previous two rounds. In the quarter-finals, he beat Goran

Ivanisevic (who would win Wimbledon later that year) 6–4, 6–4, and in the semis he saw off the former world number one Yevgeny Kafelnikov 6–2, 6–7, 6–3.

And what better place to celebrate than in Basel, where just five days later the Swiss team played the USA in the Davis Cup.

That year, the Americans were a team in transition. Patrick McEnroe had picked up the captaincy after his elder brother, John, had given up the job after one eventful year in which he'd enticed Pete Sampras and Andre Agassi back into the Davis Cup fold, only for both to cry off from a semi-final in Spain that the Americans went on to lose 5–0. The American recovery, which was to culminate in winning the Davis Cup in 2007, began in Basel.

That weekend in February 2001 was to be Federer's. With his surging confidence, he made short work of the often brittle but immensely loyal Todd Martin – by then thirty and with creaking joints, yet still dangerous on his day – who he beat in four sets before wrapping up Switzerland's victory with another four-set victory over Jan-Michael Gambill. Sandwiched between the two singles was a win in the doubles with Lorenzo Manto over Gambill and Justin Gimelstob. Perhaps symbolically, it took five minutes for the Swiss team to get the cork out of the celebratory champagne, and it was Federer who eventually prised it from the bottle.

With Switzerland 3–1 up in the five-match tie, Patrick McEnroe gave a Davis Cup debut in the dead rubber to Andy Roddick, who was clearly enthused about competing in the tournament – something that couldn't be said for the good burghers of Basel. The stadium was nowhere near sold out for the weekend, despite the distinct possibility that McEnroe might pick his illustrious forty-one-year-old brother to play in the doubles. The empty seats created a lacklustre atmosphere, and no Davis Cup tie has been staged in Basel since 2001 (although in fairness this was partly due to the unavailability of the St Jakobshalle, and partly to Swiss Tennis never being sure whether Federer would actually play in a Davis Cup tie). It seemed that, while Federer might have won the admiration of his home folk, he hadn't entirely won their willingness to support him.

The next Davis Cup tie – a home quarter-final in Neuchâtel against the French in April 2001 – proved a significant moment in Federer's emotional development. 'That was the first time that Federer showed that he wasn't everybody's darling,' recalls the Swiss radio journalist Marco Mordasini. 'After his first match on the Friday, he stood before the press – it was nearly midnight – and said, "I will not, I cannot play Davis Cup as long as Jakob Hlasek continues in the captain's chair."'

Like many disputes, the background of the falling out between Federer and Hlasek is somewhat complicated, but the fact is that the player never got on with the captain. Why this should be so is unclear. Although they are very different characters and players – Hlasek achieved what he did through discipline and sheer hard work while Federer relied much more on natural talent – they have a lot more in common in terms of mentality and approach to life than Federer does with Marc Rosset, with whom he got on fairly well. Whatever the reason, it was hard going for both parties, as well as those around them. Hlasek brought Peter Lundgren into the Swiss entourage in the hope of understanding Federer better, and by the time they got to Neuchâtel he said Lundgren had indeed been a great help.

Hlasek had also made some sort of peace – more of a ceasefire, really – with Rosset, and both tried to put their differences behind them. When the team gathered for the week, everything seemed to be happy in the Swiss camp – but, as Roger Jaunin wrote in his 2004 booklet *Roger Federer*, signs of discontent were visible to the sharp eye: 'A team photo was taken in front of the hotel they were all staying at and, while almost everyone had broad smiles, Federer's face wore a very sombre expression. Was he just tired, or was it the sign of a deeper malaise? Behind the scenes, the talk was of Hlasek and Federer no longer getting on – in fact, not getting on at all. The tension was palpable, and the smiles were fake.'

As with the tie in Zurich fourteen months earlier, the unrest bubbling within the Swiss camp contributed to a truly magnificent sporting spectacle. The tie not only went to a live fifth rubber but in total had twenty-three sets featuring 275 games in twenty-one hours and two minutes of play. On the opening day, France's Arnaud Clément beat Rosset 15–13 in the fifth set of a match that lasted five hours and forty-six minutes. Rosset saved eight match points but succumbed on the ninth.

Federer then stepped up against Nicolas Escudé before a packed house in the Littoral Arena. The crowd might have been behind him, but he played probably the worst Davis Cup match of his career. By then, the sight of Hlasek repelled Federer; photos from the match show Federer staring into the distance as Hlasek spoke to him at changes of ends.

Although Escudé was to become the Davis Cup's player of the year – going unbeaten in five singles and a doubles, and winning the cup for France on a live fifth rubber in the final in Melbourne – and had beaten Federer in the Rotterdam final six weeks earlier, the match was decided by Federer's disappointing showing. Escudé won 6–4, 6–7, 6–3, 6–4, leaving Federer facing the media at around midnight with eyes betraying the signs of recently shed tears.

If Federer feels he can't do a task properly, he doesn't want to do it at all. That explains his statement, 'I can't go on like this. I've been saying for months that I have no pleasure at all in playing while *he* [Hlasek] is there. To lose a match like this, and to lose it in the way I did, is destroying me. It's my career that's on the line here.'

Something had to give, and Hlasek – a pioneer of Swiss tennis who had put Switzerland on the map by reaching the top ten in 1988 and steering his country to the 1992 Davis Cup final – was always going to be the casualty. He fell on his sword in the aftermath of what, despite Switzerland's 0–2 deficit after that first day, still proved to be a highly dramatic quarter-final.

That night, Rosset and Federer had a fervent discussion in the team hotel. Rosset was physically exhausted after his marathon match, but both he and Federer decided that they had to play on for the sake of the fans and their teammates. Dealing with Hlasek could come later. For now, they resolved to embark on a salvage operation, one that was to come within one point of being spectacularly successful.

Despite having had little sleep, Federer partnered Lorenzo Manta in the doubles on the Saturday afternoon. No doubt pleased to have Federer alongside him after the fireworks of

Friday night, Manta played one of his best ever Davis Cup matches, the Swiss pair beating Cédric Pioline and Fabrice Santoro in a 9–7 final set that took the match time to four hours and thirty-one minutes.

When Federer beat Arnaud Clément 6–4, 3–6, 7–6, 6–4 to level the match at 2–2, a phenomenal Swiss comeback was a real possibility. However, the talismanic Rosset was still too battered from his match on the Friday, so George Bastl, who had lost his only previous live fifth rubber 6–4 in the fifth to Mark Philippoussis at the start of Hlasek's reign fourteen months earlier, was thrown in again. And again it went to a deciding fifth set.

At 5–6, 30–40 on the Escudé serve, Bastl had match point. A rally developed. Escudé went for a big forehand that ended up landing close to the baseline. Someone shouted, 'Out!' and Bastl began to raise his arms in triumph – but then realised it might not have been the line umpire who'd called. He played the shot but had been knocked off balance by the call and spooned his forehand over Escudé's baseline. Deuce.

Whether that 'call' beat Bastl will never be known, but Escudé won the next two points to hold serve, and in the next game Bastl was broken. Minutes later, France were triumphant.

After the match, the disappointment in the Swiss camp was obviously great, though tempered by the fact that they had salvaged some pride from the horrors of Friday. They just needed the turmoil to end.

Not that the weekend in Neuchâtel could be said to have drained Federer; a week later, he won three matches in Monte Carlo, and then two more in Rome in early May – giving an early sign of his ability to bounce back from heartfelt defeats. He had now joined the ranks of the world's top ten. But for all his talent, he still hadn't found the right way to channel his nervous energy and, as he went to Hamburg for the final Masters Series tournament before the French Open, the safety valve that was keeping his on-court emotions under control was reaching bursting point.

6

IT WOULD BE wrong to view any single event in Roger Federer's career as the defining moment. His rise to prominence was a gradual one, and there are several highs from the peak years. But what happened in Hamburg on 14 May 2001 was one of the most significant stepping-stones in his entire career.

The record reads that Franco Squillari beat Roger Federer 6–3, 6–4 in the first round of the Hamburg Masters. But it was what happened at the end of the match – and the lessons that Federer drew from it – that had the most profound effect.

Hamburg's Rothenbaum is a tennis venue that oozes prestige and tradition. Set amid the imposing architecture of the grand Rothenbaumchaussee boulevard, it is the venerable home of German tennis, where one of the oldest tournaments in the world is played. Until 2009, it was known as the Hamburg Masters, but then lost its Masters

Series status when Madrid's megabucks proved mightier than Teutonic tradition. In 2001, neither Federer nor Squillari were names that cut a lot of ice with either German fans or global television broadcasters, so their first-round match took place on the Rothenbaum's Court 1, a concrete-laden mini-arena in the shadow of the main stadium. Its location in something of a wind tunnel means it always seems to attract the worst of the Hamburg weather, and, as a result, few people witnessed the conclusion of the match.

The match summed up where Federer was in his career. He was clearly the more talented player, but he delivered a patchy performance in a match that was always finely balanced but forever tipping Squillari's way. At 5–4 in the second set, Squillari worked his way to match point. In the ensuing rally, Federer pushed the wily Argentinian left-hander back well behind his baseline and rushed to the net. It should have been an easy volley for him. Squillari played the ball with as much topspin as he could in an attempt to force Federer to play a low volley. Federer lost sight of the ball, and suddenly realised it was jammed between his racket and the heavy clay. In the background, the umpire called, 'Game, set and match Squillari, 6–3, 6–4.'

Federer shook Squillari's hand at the net, acknowledged the umpire, and then smashed his racket in a rage under the umpire's chair.

That smashed racket was perhaps one of the most valuable he has ever played with. The reaction to his defeat made him take a long, hard look at himself. 'What made me upset was not just losing the match but my attitude,' he said several years later. 'I said there that I needed an attitude change. I remember thinking, "I never smash my racket after matches, only during matches." And then I said, "That's it, I'm not getting pissed off any more. I'm acting too bad."'

He was as good as his word. The attitude did change, almost too much at first. His on-court composure was almost Buddhist-like in the next handful of tournaments – he would hit great shots or make horrendous errors and show absolutely no reaction, merely stroll into position for the next point. 'I almost had a problem with being too quiet,' he remembers. 'I had motivation and fire, but I couldn't express it any more, so I was struggling with my behaviour. Maybe I lost some time but, looking back now, it was probably very important for me.'

It was important, but so was the fact that his new attitude was rewarded with results. Within seven weeks of his rattle-throwing in Hamburg, he had reached his first two Grand Slam quarter-finals, thanks to the result that really announced his potential to the tennis world at large.

The four victories that took him to the quarter-finals of the French Open restored some confidence and then, on the grass of Halle, he looked supremely confident for two rounds before falling to one of the top grass-court players of the time, Patrick Rafter, in the quarter-finals. Wanting more practice on grass, he opted to play the Dutch event in 's-Hertogenbosch, notching up three wins there before running into his old nemesis Lleyton Hewitt in the semi-finals.

While Federer was in the Netherlands, the Wimbledon draw was made, with the name P Sampras at the top. There was nothing unusual in this – Sampras had won seven of the previous eight men's singles titles – but by June 2001 the grandmaster of Wimbledon had been looking increasingly vulnerable. He hadn't won a tournament all year after losing to Todd Martin in the fourth round at the Australian Open and to Hewitt in the semi-finals of his favourite grass-court warm-up event at London's Queen's Club. In fact, Sampras's last title had been won on the final day of Wimbledon 2000, when he'd come back from a poor start to beat Pat Rafter in four sets in the last vestiges of daylight. It seemed he was ready to be toppled.

That year, the British were too fixated on Tim Henman to look seriously in anyone else's direction. With Sampras on the wane, it seemed that the great hope of British tennis might finally have found his moment. The projected quarter-final between Sampras and Henman was the talk of the Wimbledon build-up, and the flames were only fanned by Sampras's unimpressive showing in his second-round match, during which he dropped two sets against the unfancied British player Barry Cowan, whose ultimate defeat in five sets proved the high-water mark of his career.

When Henman beat Sjeng Schalken and Sampras beat Sargis Sargsian to reach the fourth round, the Sampras–Henman clash was still on. But, unbeknown to anyone at the time, Sargsian, a likeable Armenian who had come through the American college system to carve out a living on the professional tennis tour, was to be the last man to lose to Sampras at Wimbledon that year, and the second-last ever.

On an overcast Monday on which all remaining singles players of both sexes were in action, Federer walked out on to Wimbledon's Centre Court for the first time. As well as preparing to face Sampras, he'd had to become acquainted with certain Centre Court traditions, including bowing to the Royal Box if a member of the British royal family was seated there (a practice since abolished). As the fifteenth seed, he was still thought by most tennis watchers to be too much of a work in progress to beat the reigning champion, and it was generally felt this would be a match he'd end up having to chalk up to experience. And to most British watchers the contest was just a stepping-stone to a Sampras v Henman quarter-final.

Yet enough people close to Federer had expressed their faith in the nineteen-year-old's ability to beat Sampras, and after taking a first-set tiebreak with some good fortune (a dubious serve was called in his favour, and he profited from a lucky net cord) his confidence began to grow. Federer could have been two sets up but missed six break points in the second set, which Sampras took 7–5. A poor smash from Sampras gave Federer the third set, but Sampras stormed through the fourth-set tiebreak to make it two sets all. The fifth set went with serve until the twelfth game, when Federer had Sampras at 15–40. The Swiss guessed that Sampras would serve wide to his forehand side – and he was right. Federer struck a winning forehand return and promptly fell to the ground. After three hours and forty-one minutes, he'd won 7–6, 5–7, 6–4, 6–7, 7–5 to end the great man's run of thirty-one successive Wimbledon wins, dating back to the start of the 1997 event. It was to prove the only time Federer and Sampras ever played each other in an official match.

Ever the conservative statesman, Sampras paid tribute to a man he recognised as having many of the attributes that had taken himself so far. 'There are a lot of young guys coming up, but Roger is a bit extra-special,' he observed.

'He has a great all-round game, like me doesn't get too emotional, and is a great athlete.'

The last person to have beaten Sampras at Wimbledon – Richard Krajicek in 1996 – had gone on to win the title, and on that Monday night of 2 July 2001 there were many who were tipping Federer to do the same. But the British had got it right – this was the best year for Henman to win. With Sampras out of the way, Henman played one of his best ever matches to bundle Federer out in the quarter-finals 7–5, 7–6, 2–6, 7–6. The win over Sampras had taken its toll on the young Swiss. Although he refused to use it as an excuse, or even mention it at his post-match press conference, Federer had strained an adductor muscle in his third-round match against Jonas Björkman, an injury that had got worse in his match with Sampras. That kind of injury needs a few days to heal. At some Wimbledons, the rain gives players that kind of time, but not Federer in 2001. He played on – understandably given that it was Wimbledon – but the muscle strain hampered him in his match against Henman and later caused him to miss several weeks of the American hard-court season.

All the same, by beating Sampras at Wimbledon, Federer had announced his presence to the wider tennis world, and, although Henman had beaten him, the message for the British was clear: if Henman doesn't win Wimbledon this year, it might be too late for him, because the interregnum between the Sampras and Federer eras looked like being very short.

And so it proved. 2001 was Henman's best chance, but he lost to the astonishingly revitalised Goran Ivanisevic in the semi-finals in a five-set match played over three days.

Ivanisevic's win over Rafter in a raucous Monday final is one of the great romantic tales in modern tennis folklore, so it was perhaps a good year for Federer to garner useful experience, rather than win the title that would have created expectations he was probably not yet ready to handle.

Despite the win over Sampras, Federer felt there was still work to do on getting his emotional balance right. 'I felt like I was walking on a tightrope,' he said in an interview that appeared in Melbourne's daily newspaper *The Age* in January 2004. 'When I was getting upset, I was right away called "the bad boy", and then when I wasn't showing anything I was "the guy tanking" ['to tank' is a verb used in tennis to denote the supposedly non-existent practice of a player deliberately losing a match while giving the impression of trying to win it]. So I really had to watch what I was doing, and... I had to find the way I wanted to be and feel on the court. Maybe I can still show more emotions or still show less, but the right balance will come in the next few years.'

The adductor injury meant the only tournament he played on the American summer hard-court circuit in 2001 was the US Open. As the guy who had beaten Sampras at Wimbledon, Federer was suddenly a marked man. He cruised through his first three matches, winning all in straight sets, and then came up against Andre Agassi in the fourth round.

Federer was eventually to get the better of Agassi, but, in their clash at the 2001 US Open, Agassi gave a masterclass, showing some of the best form of his career, making Federer pay for every small error and eventually crushing him 6–1, 6–2, 6–4. At one stage, he had the crowd purring with a drop shot dripping with so much backspin that the ball bounced back to his side of the net, leaving Federer stranded.

That US Open was also notable for the coming-of-age performance of Lleyton Hewitt, who crushed Pete Sampras in the final in a shock result. Hewitt had continued his quicker development to beat Federer to the Grand Slam roll of honour by twenty-two months. The feisty Australian was to beat Federer to the number-one ranking by twenty-six months.

From the high of his win over Sampras, Federer had been brought down to earth. After beating the great man at Wimbledon, he'd had good reason to hope for enough subsequent wins to enable him to qualify for the Tennis Masters Cup, the eight-man year-ending elite tournament (these days known as the ATP Finals) that took place that year in Sydney. But his defeat to Henman and the groin injury had left him with just five matches in two months, and, when he lost to Nicolas Kiefer on a final-set tiebreak in the first round of the Moscow indoor event in the first week of October, his year was fizzling out.

But there was still Basel. As the beaten finalist in 2000, Federer was hoping to improve on his previous year's performance for the third successive year and, when he beat Andy Roddick 3–6, 6–3, 7–6 in the quarter-finals, his route to victory looked clear. A straight-sets win over Julien Boutter in the semi-finals then set him up for his first meeting with Tim Henman since Wimbledon three months earlier. With his groin strain now healed, with the Swiss public behind him, and without the kind of strength-sapping semi-final that had wrecked his chances the previous year, this was surely his moment.

Henman had other ideas. He'd won Basel three years earlier, taking Agassi apart in the final, and once again he showed his comfort in the Swiss metropolis by turning Federer's dream into a nightmare. The Briton won 6–3, 6–4, 6–2 in a one-sided match that took the sting out of the Basel crowd and left Federer numb. 'I just wasn't there,' he said afterwards. 'I played a bad match. I think I just put too much pressure on myself.' More than that, he was building up a complex about Henman, who had now beaten him in all of their four encounters on the tour.

Federer finished 2001 ranked thirteenth and having won his first ATP tournament – a respectable achievement, and an improvement on his 2000 year-end ranking of twenty-ninth. He was making gradual progress, but it could have been so much better.

Having witnessed Federer beating Pete Sampras at Wimbledon, the tennis world was expecting him to press on in 2002, and the Australian Open seemed the ideal venue. He arrived in Melbourne fresh from his second tour title in Sydney the previous week – the arena in which he'd been so frustrated at missing out on a medal at the 2000 Olympics proved a happier hunting ground sixteen months on. The draw fell kindly for him, but what happened seemed to add more weight to the growing bank of evidence that this was a great talent who just couldn't hack it at the highest level of the sport.

After straight-sets wins over Michael Chang, Attila Savolt and Rainer Schüttler, the eleventh-seeded Federer came up against Tommy Haas in the round of the last sixteen. Although the German was enjoying the spectacular run of form that would take him to number two in the rankings by mid-May, Federer should still have beaten him that day. In fact, he had Haas beaten – only to let his fish off the hook. He had the advantage of serving first in the fifth set, in which both men were increasingly battling fatigue. At 6–5, Federer had Haas at 30–40, but then made five consecutive errors to turn match point for him into a 6–7 deficit. Haas – at seventh the highest remaining seed left in the tournament after a first week of carnage among the big names – served out an 8–6 final-set victory. A golden opportunity for Federer had gone begging.

And a week later, he failed to defend his title in Milan. He went all the way to the final, but lost to Italy's Davide Sanguinetti, seriously folding in the final set to lose it 6–1. It was an emotional win for the twenty-nine-year-old Italian, who posted his first career title, and in his home country.

Then came a week that, in retrospect, proved to have massive emotional value to Federer.

Switzerland hadn't played a Davis Cup tie since that turbulent weekend ten months earlier in which he said he just couldn't play under the Swiss captain Jakob Hlasek. With the threat of losing not just his best player but the one who single-handedly carried Swiss hopes in tennis's top team competition, Hlasek had no option but to step down in the interests of team unity.

Federer then made it clear he wanted his former coach Peter Carter to become the Swiss Davis Cup captain, but there was a problem: Carter wasn't a Swiss national, and according to Davis Cup rules the captain of each team has to be a citizen of the country he or she is captaining. In 2001, however, Carter had married his Swiss fiancée and was in the process of applying for Swiss citizenship, so a deal was struck by which he became the head of the Swiss team (under the term 'Teamchef', literally team boss) while Ivo Heuberger – the fifth member of the four-man playing staff – was nominated as captain, with the sole responsibility of sitting on the bench and chatting to the players at changes of ends. This model proved sufficiently successful that the Swiss used it for many years, until Severin Lüthi became sufficiently established to play the roles of both 'Teamchef' and captain.

Switzerland were drawn away to Russia in the 2002 first round. For the trip to Moscow, Federer's personal coach Peter Lundgren was allowed to be part of the Swiss entourage. By some accounts, not everyone was happy with Federer's influence on team affairs. The Swiss journalist Roger Jaunin says Michel Kratochvil – Switzerland's number-two player by a long way – felt he was denied any such privilege, though it should perhaps be pointed out that Kratchovil was never the most popular member of the Swiss team and was less crucial to its success than Federer. Be that as it may, with Carter pulling the strings off the court and Marc Rosset still offering an option in the doubles, the Swiss had a more powerful team than they'd presented for some time.

In Moscow's indoor Olympic Stadium, the Swiss were up against a Russian team desperate to win the Davis Cup. Well, Yevgeny Kafelnikov was desperate to win it, in what looked like being his last year on the tour, and in Marat Safin he had a partner who – if he was on his game and sufficiently motivated – could beat anyone on any surface, other than grass. The Russians chose to play on clay and, when Russia plays at home on clay, the clay is frequently very damp and heavy. So it proved for this tie, but Federer played superbly on the first day to beat Safin 7–5, 6–1, 6–2 to win in one hour and thirty-six minutes.

When Kratochvil took a two-sets-to-one lead against Kafelnikov in the second singles and then served for the match at 6–5 in the fourth set, the Russian plan to play on clay looked to have backfired miserably. But beautiful ball-striker that he was, Kratochvil often had difficulty finishing off big matches, and so it proved on this occasion. 'I didn't play defensively or afraid,' he said after the match. 'I went for my shots, but I just lost them.' Kafelnikov won the fourth set on a tiebreak and took the fifth 6–2.

A crowd of 8,000 surged into the stadium for the doubles, and they were rewarded with one of the best displays of teamwork Kafelnikov and Safin ever put together. Federer and Rosset didn't play their best on that occasion; indeed Rosset had a particularly bad day and felt he was to blame for the Russians' 6–2, 7–6, 6–7, 6–2 victory, which was also Federer's first-ever defeat in a Davis Cup doubles rubber. They almost got back into the match after saving four match points in the third set, but then lost it in four. It was no disgrace, but it meant Switzerland's fate was now out of Federer's hands.

All he could do was win his second singles and hope for an unlikely Swiss victory in the deciding rubber. The next day, he played his part, putting in his second outstanding display of the weekend to crush Kafelnikov 7–6, 6–1, 6–1, which threw the initiative back to Kratochvil, but he squandered an impressive second-set lead, and Safin took Russia into the quarter-finals with a 6–1, 7–6, 6–4 win.

After the final match, Federer observed, 'For myself and my singles matches, there was some great tennis from me this weekend. I couldn't have expected much more. I would have loved to win the doubles, but they played very well. In the end it was just tough that we lost the tie.' One can, of course, read too much into casual comments made in post-match press conferences, where emotions often run high, but the impression these words leave behind is that Federer fully expected that, in order for Switzerland to win, he had to win all his three matches. As the British journalist Neil Harman had written in the Davis Cup yearbook about Switzerland's win over the USA the previous year, 'The result might just as well have read, "Federer 3, USA 2."' It seemed that, at least in terms of the Davis Cup, Switzerland *was* Federer – even if Kratochvil would have a solitary moment of glory the following year.

Impressive though Federer's wins over Safin and Kafelnikov were, the man was still being formed from the remnants of the boy. One salutary lesson came in Dubai, where Federer lost 6–3, 6–1 to the German Rainer Schüttler in the second round. It was not that he lost, rather the manner in which he lost, that caused concern. To those watching the match, he hardly seemed to care in the second set. Most tournaments below Masters level tend to pay either appearance fees or minimum prize money guarantees to their bigger names – it's a practice no tournament likes to talk about, but it's recognised as part of what oils the wheels of the global tennis machine. Federer had been offered an appearance fee for Dubai, but such was his slapdash showing against Schüttler that the tournament threatened not to pay it. After lots of to-ing and fro-ing with Federer and his agents, the tournament agreed to hold the agreed fee, to be paid if he turned up the following year and made the appropriate effort. Federer did turn up the following year and did make the effort, winning the first of three back-to-back Dubai titles. He had clearly profited from Dubai's lesson.

At the end of March 2002, he finally did play a consistent tournament from start to finish: the Nasdaq-100 Open in Miami. As well as being one of the nine Masters-1000 tournaments (ie the level of men's event immediately below the four Grand Slams), it was also then arguably the most prestigious. Back in the 1980s, its organisers even hoped it would take over from the Australian Open as the fourth Grand Slam. Although that plan was foiled and the event now lags well behind the four majors, the year-end ATP Finals, and the Indian Wells tournament, in prestige terms, it is still an event all the major top players turn out for.

That year, Federer had to face two of his bogeymen, Tim Henman and Lleyton Hewitt. Henman was dispatched in the third round (albeit on a retirement), while Hewitt was beaten majestically in the semi-finals. This second victory was something of a prized scalp for Federer. Not only was Hewitt the world number one at the time – and Federer had never beaten a number one before – but he was also on a winning streak of twenty-three matches on American hard courts. Yet Hewitt was stretched to his limit in his first four matches, and looked tired as Federer beat him 6–3, 6–4 to secure his passage into his first Masters Series final.

After the match, Hewitt offered his own thoughts on

Federer's form. 'I think this could be a breakthrough year for him,' he predicted, 'but whether he's going to get up to the top four or five, that's another question.'

Hewitt, whose bullish on-court manner often hid a highly perceptive tennis brain, knew Federer's strengths and weaknesses, and the remark proved highly accurate: Federer did improve, but he finished the year just short of the top five.

With the jinx players Hewitt and Henman vanquished, Federer found himself up against Andre Agassi in the final. It looked to be heading for a fifth set when Federer served at 4–3 in the fourth. Until the final, he hadn't dropped serve all tournament and, after being broken three times in the first two sets, he seemed to have steadied the ship. But then Agassi – by then just four weeks short of his thirty-second birthday – showed why he was one of the sport's greatest-ever returners. He broke Federer's serve twice in succession to take his fifth Key Biscayne title in his 700th full tour win.

It's worth taking stock here. Federer was just fifteen months away from winning Wimbledon and starting his era of dominance, yet here he was still to win one of the nine Masters tournaments. In April 2002, a good tournament for him was playing consistently throughout and losing to a big name in the final. In this respect he is more in the category of Ivan Lendl, Andre Agassi and Andy Murray in being recognised as a great talent but having to serve something of an apprenticeship before winning his first major, as opposed to players such as Björn Borg, Mats Wilander, Pete Sampras and Novak Djokovic, who all won their first Slam quite early, even though some of them struggled before they could win a second. But the next spurt for the twenty-year-old Swiss was just around the corner.

When Federer speaks of the matches that served as turning points in his career, he often mentions one that few might consider: his win over Marat Safin in Hamburg in May 2002. Perhaps it signified coming full circle after his ill-disciplined outburst in the German city the previous year. 'It was my first Masters Series win,' he says, 'and probably my second-biggest breakthrough after the Sampras match.'

It had always been something of an oddity that a player who'd learned his tennis on clay was thought to be so vulnerable on the red stuff. A little relativity is called for here. For a start, Federer was not alone in this: both Boris Becker and Stefan Edberg had honed their skills on clay (though also on fast indoor courts during the winter months) and it always proved their least favourite and least effective surface. More importantly, by his going on to reach five successive French Open finals and lifting the trophy, nobody could possibly claim that Federer had a weakness on clay. Had it not been for the presence of Rafael Nadal, who is without question the greatest clay-court player ever, it is highly likely that Federer would have won the French Open several times, and it is only his superb achievements on grass and hard courts that make his clay achievements pale in comparison.

However, from the vantage point of mid-2002, Federer did seem vulnerable on the principal European tennis surface. He had lost his first dozen or so tour matches on clay, and by May 2002 he needed a tournament at which he could show that he did have the game for the underfoot conditions that demand so much patience and fitness. The Hamburg Masters was to be that tournament.

His first four wins – the first three in straight sets – were against players of proven clay-court pedigree: Nicolas Lapentti, Bohdan Ulihrach, Adrian Voinea and Gustavo Kuerten. He then saw off the big-serving Max Mirnyi in the semi-finals to set up a final against Marat Safin, the man who had just gone to the top of the 2002 'Race'. (The 'Race' is similar to the rankings but is based solely on results since 1 January of each year, so it gives a fairly reliable indication of recent form in the first few months of the year.) Two years earlier, Safin had lost a fifth-set tiebreak to Kuerten in the Hamburg final, and the mercurial Russian seemed well set to avenge his defeat to Federer in the Davis Cup three months earlier. But it was to be Federer's day, and one of the best of his year.

'It was definitely the best match of my career,' Federer enthused after his 6–1, 6–3, 6–4 win in barely two hours. 'I thought it would be much tougher, but I played unbelievable tennis. I could risk a lot and the balls went in. It was just incredible. I always had the feeling I could break him.' Even Safin said, 'I thought he played the best match of his life.'

Winning the Hamburg Masters revolutionised Federer's clay-court status. He was suddenly installed as one of the favourites for the French Open. But he had yet to learn to deal with the pressure of expectation, and in Paris he froze in the first round against the highly gifted but frustratingly erratic Moroccan Hicham Arazi. Twice a quarter-finalist at Roland Garros, Arazi went into every match knowing he was probably ahead of his opponent on natural ability, even if he let himself down on discipline. Against Federer he was arguably only equal on natural ability and inferior on discipline, but he still ran out a 6–3, 6–2, 6–4 winner. 'I was hoping for so much from this tournament,' Federer said sadly after his defeat, 'but I put too much pressure on myself.'

At least there were still the grass-court tournaments to come. Federer put in his usual appearance in Halle, and looked best placed to win the title, but he came up short over the finals weekend, this time to Nicolas Kiefer, 6–4 in the third set of their semi-final. He then managed to get three more batches of match practice on grass before losing in the quarter-finals of 's-Hertogenbosch to Sjeng Schalken.

Next stop was Wimbledon, to which Federer returned in 2002 with the confidence of the previous year's win over Sampras still ringing in his ears. When he was put on Centre Court for his first-round match against the Grand Slam debutant Mario Ancic, he looked set for a comfortable win, but the big-serving eighteen-year-old from Croatia showed phenomenal composure to deliver a stunning 6–3, 7–6, 6–3 defeat that sent Federer home when he'd barely finished unpacking. Ancic later revealed that his tactics had come from the reigning champion Goran Ivanisevic – they had been merely to avoid the big Federer forehand and attack the second serve. So simple.

'It was a shocker,' said Federer pithily, scarcely concealing his anger. Had he known it would be his last defeat at Wimbledon for six years it would no doubt have been easier to take, but such things seem scarcely plausible in the immediate aftermath of such a frustrating defeat. Instead of Federer, it was his Davis Cup colleague George Bastl who made the Swiss tennis headlines at that Wimbledon, stunning Pete Sampras in the second round in five sets to draw a somewhat ignominious close to the American's glorious Wimbledon years.

Back on the clay in Gstaad, Federer showed how easy it should have been in Paris by dispatching Hicham Arazi 6–4, 6–3 in the first round, but the following day he was again inconsistent against another gifted but erratic player, Radek Stepanek. It was time for a holiday and some fitness work before the American summer hard-court swing. But that season began badly, and swiftly got worse.

On 1 August 2002, Switzerland's national day, Federer lost 7–6, 7–5 in the first round of the Toronto Masters to the muscular Argentinian Guillermo Cañas, who went on to win the tournament. But the disappointment of defeat was as nothing compared to the news that greeted him when he arrived back in the locker room after the match: Peter Carter had been killed in a car crash while on his honeymoon in South Africa.

7

PETER CARTER HAD met his wife, Sylvia von Arx, in Basel. She was a receptionist at the Paradies indoor tennis facility owned by the Basel sports and entertainment impresario Roger Brennwald. Shortly after they'd got to know each other, she had been diagnosed with a brain tumour. For a long time the prognosis didn't look good, but in 2001 her condition began to improve. That year they got married, but decided to delay their honeymoon until she was fully fit and they could have the holiday of a lifetime.

In late 2001, Sylvia was finally given a clean bill of health, and the pair arranged a trip to South Africa the following summer, as a combined honeymoon and celebration of her recovery. They were touring in the Kruger National Park in separate four-wheel-drive cars when the driver of the one Carter was in swerved to avoid an on-coming minibus and then had to veer back onto the road to avoid hitting a bridge near the township of Gravelotte. The soft-topped car overturned and landed on its roof, which caved in, crushing Carter and the driver.

When Federer came off court in Toronto, his coach Peter Lundgren – the man he had opted for ahead of Carter when he had to choose between them in early 2000 – rang him to break the news. For a while, Federer couldn't believe it. 'I'm very shocked and very sad,' he said in his first public statement. 'He was a very close friend. This is the first time a close friend of mine has died. He wasn't my first coach, but he was my real coach. He knew me and my game, and he was always thinking of what was good for me.'

Eventually, he and Lundgren decided Federer should play the following week's Masters Series event in Cincinnati, and then fly back to Switzerland for the funeral. Needless to say, he was in no fit state of mind for Cincinnati, and crashed out against Ivan Ljubicic in the first round. 'When something like that happens,' he said after the match, 'you see how unimportant tennis is.' Unlike in Toronto the week before, where he had played doubles the day after Carter's death, Federer withdrew from the Cincinnati doubles and headed for home.

In his book *Das Tennisgenie,* 'The Tennis Genius', René Stauffer gives a very sensitive account of Carter's moving funeral in St Leonard's Church in Basel. Around 200 people turned up, among them Andre Agassi's coach Darren Cahill, who had been Carter's stablemate at Peter Smith's set-up in Adelaide. The priest conducting the funeral had married Carter and Silvia just a year earlier. Silvia made a short and moving speech, as did three others. As well as Roger, Lynette and Robbie Federer were also inconsolable – as

Stauffer points out, they had lost the man who had been such a vital channel of communication for them as Roger had gradually asserted his independence during his teenage years. A week after the funeral, Federer said, 'Compared with a moment like that, losing a tennis match is nothing. I normally try to avoid sad events, and it was my first funeral. I can't say it did me good, but I was very close to Peter in my thoughts and feel I've said goodbye in a dignified setting. Now I feel a bit better, especially in terms of tennis. The motivation that I felt I'd lost after the event is back.'

Cahill believes Carter's death left a deep scar on Federer. 'I know he's never been the same since,' the Australian says. 'I think it's the type of person he is, on the court especially. He's gone from being a young kid who could lose his temper pretty quickly because it was all about the tennis, to going, "You know what, life's all about being a good person, treating people the right way, being respectful and doing the right thing" because that's the way Carts lived his life. It's the way he reacted even when Roger chose Lundgren. Maybe if Peter hadn't passed away, when the Lundgren–Federer thing finished, maybe Carts would have stepped into that role again. Maybe Roger would have played more Davis Cup ties – there are a lot of "what ifs". What's certain is that Roger learned a lot from Peter, in fact I think we all learned from him that there's much more to life than just a sport that we're involved in, and that's been the premise for the way Roger has lived his life ever since. He's a better man for it, both inside and outside the lines.'

Speaking several years later, Federer said of Carter, 'He was a very important man in my tennis career, if not the most important. I had been with him from ten to fourteen years old, and then again from sixteen till twenty, so I knew him very well. He gave me a lot in terms of his personality, in terms of technique and on the court. It was a hard loss. In those weeks after he died, everything went very quickly. I decided that I would compete in the US Open because I guessed that that was what Peter would have liked to see me do, not just to sit around. I don't know if it was for good or for bad... It was also a very influential moment in my career. It certainly marked me, and there was a reaction in terms of how I look at life now. It was a hard moment, and I think of him very often still.'

In the months that followed, Federer frequently had to suppress tears. But the grief made him stronger. In an interview with the Melbourne newspaper *The Age* in January 2004, he said the period pulling himself together after the shock of Carter's death was one of the most crucial in his tennis maturity. 'I guess it made me strong mentally, and I started thinking,' he said. 'I suddenly had time to ask myself, "What do I need to do to get to the next level?"'

Federer's first commitment after the US Open had a poignancy about it that could have brought his grief-blighted tennis right back. But the opposite happened – he played three of his best matches of the year.

After losing to Russia in the Davis Cup earlier that year, Switzerland were drawn away to Morocco in a tie they had to win in order to maintain their membership of the sixteen-nation elite world group. At the time of his death, Swiss Tennis had been confident Carter would be granted his Swiss citizenship in time for the trip to Casablanca; that would have enabled him to assume the role of Swiss captain and thus sit on the bench coaching his players at changes of ends. But, with Peter Lundgren acting as temporary team supremo and Marc Rosset now promoted to captain, the tie became something of a homage to Carter. The Swiss team was united as never before, any unrest put aside for the tough assignment on clay in the heat of North Africa. At the official ceremony, all the Swiss players had their names on the backs of their shirts, but Federer and Rosset had Carter's name as well as their own. As the Swiss national anthem was played before play on the Saturday, Federer's eyes were moist with emotion. It was that kind of occasion.

When Younes El Aynaoui beat Michel Kratochvil in straight sets in the first rubber, the spotlight was on Federer, who faced Hicham Arazi, the man who had bundled him out of the French Open. On his least effective surface, it could have proved too much for the still just twenty-one-year-old Swiss. But if he froze under the pressure of expectation in Paris, he flourished under the opportunity to make a statement for his deceased friend in Casablanca. He crushed Arazi for the loss of just six games, playing as if in a trance.

The trance continued into the doubles, in which Federer and George Bastl conceded just nine games in beating Younes El Aynaoui and Karim Alami, and in the first reverse singles el Aynaoui achieved no more against Federer than the six games his teammate had posted two days earlier. It was awesome stuff and, as the Swiss journalist Roger Jaunin reported, El Aynaoui recognised it as such. One of the game's most humane characters, the Moroccan gatecrashed the Swiss celebration party on the Sunday night to say to Federer, 'What you have done this weekend no one else but you could have done.'

Federer dedicated his first victory and his first tournament title after Carter's death to his former coach and mentor. The first victory was a four-sets passage to the second round of the US Open against Jiri Vanek, while the first title came in early October in Vienna. The weekend in Casablanca had restored the on-court confidence that now went with the off-court lessons in life Federer had learned since 1 August.

The Vienna title helped Federer qualify for the first time for the elite eight-man Tennis Masters Cup, that year staged in Shanghai, but both that event and his home tournament went to players who continued to exercise something of a hold over him.

In his fifth assault on the Swiss Indoors, Federer managed to reach the semi-finals, again beating Andy Roddick in the quarter-finals. Everything seemed set for a final featuring the local boy and the French Open runner-up Juan Carlos Ferrero, but neither made it to the final; Federer was taken out in the semis by David Nalbandian, who had yet to lose to Federer since their junior days, while Ferrero lost to another alumnus of the 1998 junior year, Fernando Gonzalez. Nalbandian's win over Gonzalez in the final cut very little ice with the aficionados in the St Jakobshalle!

And then, having battled through the round-robin stage of the Tennis Masters Cup, with wins over Ferrero, Jiri Novak and Thomas Johansson, Federer lost a high-quality semi-final to Lleyton Hewitt, the Australian winning 7–5 in the third set as he became only the fourth man since computer rankings began in 1973 to go a full calendar year in the number-one slot.

Federer finished the year ranked fifth, another advance on the previous year, but still in the 'flattering to deceive' category. When he again stumbled against Nalbandian in the fourth round of the Australian Open in another mid-tournament five-setter, he had played the first Grand Slam of the year four times and got stuck at the halfway stage all four times (twice in the third round, twice in the fourth). After his five-sets defeat to Tommy Haas the previous year, Nalbandian took the fifth set 6–3, to make his record against Federer three wins in three tour-level matches. Federer was an acknowledged colossus on the tour, but still unproven in the tournaments that really mattered.

Roger Federer's Davis Cup career can be broken down into three phases. The first covered his first six years from 1999 to 2004, when he played every tie Switzerland contested. The second phase covers the years 2005–2013, when he declined to play in the first round but was by and large available for Switzerland's playoff-round tie in September (the Swiss never won a first-round tie without Federer). And the third phase was his glory year of 2014, when he announced very late that he would play in the first round, and continued to leave open whether he would play subsequent matches until it was clear he couldn't back out. There were a couple of blips in this approach to the Davis Cup – after winning the Olympic doubles gold medal with Stan Wawrinka in 2008, he seemed so inspired with the team ethic that he appeared to commit to more Davis Cup in 2009, but he pulled out of Switzerland's first-round tie in March 2009 citing back problems, though concerns over Mirka's pregnancy were a bigger factor. And he played in the 2012 first round, but the Swiss lost a tetchy tie at home to the Americans, a weekend that saw Wawrinka fail to turn up on the final day because he felt slighted by comments Federer had made on the opening day.

Federer's attitude towards the Davis Cup is discussed in Chapter 17, but the nine years in which he seemed distinctly half-hearted towards the team competition should not dilute the tremendous commitment he had shown towards playing for his country in the first phase. The pinnacle came in 2003, when Switzerland reached the semi-finals, its most successful run since the two-man team of Marc Rosset and Jakob Hlasek took the Alpine nation to its first Davis Cup final in 1992. Indeed there were many who felt that, having come so close in the 2003 semi-final, Federer was emotionally scarred and lost some of his enthusiasm for the competition. There was more to it than that, but Federer's leading role in Switzerland's third-best Davis Cup year is worth documenting.

To reach the semis in Australia, Switzerland had to win two ties, and the first of them suggested that the Swiss team of 2003 might be more than a one-man band.

The Swiss were drawn away to the Netherlands, and the Royal Dutch Lawn Tennis Association opted to play the tie in a corner of the GelreDome football stadium used by the top Dutch football club Vitesse Arnhem. The stadium not only had a retractable roof, but its grass pitch was on wheels, so it could be rolled out of the stadium for non-football events, or for a bit of fresh air during the week. When the grass was in the stadium, the venue had an extra car park.

To history scholars, the city of Arnhem is best known for being the site of one of the bloodiest battles of the Second World War, when British troops looking to set up a bridgehead on the Rhine were shot down in their thousands in 1944. And the Davis Cup tie played there in February 2003 was one of the bloodiest in the then 103-year history of tennis's premier team competition.

Before Federer had taken to the court, there was uproar in the stadium, and Rosset – who had been confirmed as Switzerland's captain after the emotions of Peter Carter's death had died down – had kicked a refrigerator in frustration. The Swiss number two, Michel Kratochvil, had battled impressively to come back from two sets down against the solid Dutch number one, Sjeng Schalken, but in the final set a small band of Dutch supporters unused to Davis Cup etiquette became increasingly loud and unruly. When Schalken had match point at 5–4, some of them threw celebration balls on to the court, only to find their hero hadn't yet won. Kratochvil saved a second match point, but on the third one of the troublesome supporters screamed during Kratochvil's second-serve ball toss, causing the Swiss to double-fault the match away. The visitors were furious. Rosset and Kratochvil railed at the umpire, Javier Moreno, and the referee, Brian Earley. As Rosset vented his spleen by delivering a massive kick to the courtside drinks fridge, the atmosphere became decidedly tense.

Into it stepped the man who as a boy had been unable to control his temper. But not any more. Federer kept his head down between points, and kept the points to a minimum in a 6–2, 6–1, 6–3 win over the dangerous though inconsistent Raemon Sluiter. It was his sixth successive Davis Cup singles win and his third consecutive victory for the loss of just six games.

But Federer and Bastl lost the doubles against the veteran Paul Haarhuis and the Davis Cup debutant Martin Verkerk.

Once again, the Swiss squad were in a position where their fate no longer hung entirely in Federer's hands. He certainly wasn't expected to lose to Sjeng Schalken in his next match and, while the match was no formality, his 7–6, 6–4, 7–5 victory was a fair reflection of the two players. 'I played better and better,' said Schalken after the match, 'but Roger does that to me – he brings out the best in me. But then he proved himself even more.'

Federer had done his bit, but now he had to watch as Kratochvil again held Switzerland's fate in the decisive rubber. This was his sixth live Davis Cup match, and he had yet to win one. After Verkerk's impressive showing in the doubles, he came in for the final match. It looked a good choice when Verkerk had set points at 5–0 after less than twenty minutes of play, and Kratochvil looked a fish out of water. But the Bernese son of Czech immigrants, who had grown up at a tennis centre run by his dad called TC Flamingo, put both feet on the ground to score the biggest single win of his career in one of the most raucous environments ever seen for a tennis match. The culmination of the third set was played like a basketball match, with fans screaming while the ball was in play, but Kratochvil kept his cool and won in four sets.

What Federer thought of it as he sat by the court watching is anyone's guess. He made all the right noises afterwards; two months later he was to say Rosset had fostered 'a wonderful team spirit', and he was obviously pleased to have another chance of glory, one he was to seize in spectacular fashion in the quarter-finals. But it's never easy for someone used to being the undisputed hero to sit back and let a lesser teammate take the applause, even someone as balanced and OK with himself as Roger Federer. He certainly didn't exude much obvious joy as the Swiss team spoke to the media afterwards. Whatever his inherent good manners and sense of team unity had taught him to say that night, there must have been a tiny bit of discomfort in the realisation that this was someone else's moment.

There was no question that Federer was the undisputed hero of Switzerland's quarter-final win away to France. Some veteran tennis watchers even described it as the most remarkable individual performance in the Davis Cup – high praise indeed from those who had seen Björn Borg and Boris Becker take Sweden and West Germany to team triumphs largely single-handedly. In the aptly named Zenith Stadium in Toulouse, Federer reached one of the early peaks of his career, beating Nicolas Escudé and Fabrice Santoro in the singles, and teaming up with Rosset to scoop victory in the doubles.

In the aftermath of Peter Carter's death, the Swiss and Australian tennis associations had taken up a suggestion made by Australia's captain John Fitzgerald that, when the two nations met each other in the Davis Cup, they would play for the Peter Carter Trophy. Fitzgerald had a personal interest, having known Carter from their time together as boys at Peter Smith's academy in Adelaide. The first opportunity to play for the new trophy came in September 2003, when Australia hosted Switzerland in the semi-finals. Tennis Australia chose to stage the tie in the Rod Laver Arena in Melbourne and, with the previous two Wimbledon champions spearheading their teams, the stage was set for a cracker of a tie.

At that time, however, there were large question marks

hanging over both teams. Federer came to Melbourne having made no obvious progress since Wimbledon. Switzerland welcomed back Michel Kratochvil as its second player, but he was woefully short of match practice. The same could also be said of Australia's number two, Mark Philippoussis, and even their number one, Lleyton Hewitt, hardly came into the tie with the best of records. He'd lost his Wimbledon title on the first day to Ivo Karlovic, he'd lost in the quarter-finals of the US Open to Juan Carlos Ferrero, he'd lost his number-one ranking, he'd lost his coach, Jason Stoltenberg (and people weren't at that stage sure whether his replacement, Roger Rasheed, was a mate standing in or a genuine coach – he proved to be the latter by working with Hewitt for well over three years), and there was speculation about whether he was spending too much time with his girlfriend, Kim Clijsters, rather than concentrating on his tennis. It meant that all five rubbers of the semi-final seemed up for grabs.

After Hewitt had crushed a disappointing Kratochvil, Federer and Philippoussis faced each other for the first time since their Wimbledon final eleven weeks earlier. The Australian claimed to have learned a lesson from the Wimbledon final, but what it was nobody could quite work out as Federer won 6–3, 6–4, 7–6.

When Australia's Todd Woodbridge and Wayne Arthurs beat Federer and Rosset in five sets in the doubles, the pressure was on Federer in the first reverse singles against Hewitt. When he won the first set 7–5, Federer equalled John McEnroe's record of thirty successive sets won in Davis Cup singles rubbers. When he won the second 6–2, he beat it. When he led Hewitt by two sets and 5–3 in the third, it seemed the formbook was holding firm and a live fifth rubber was imminent. But two things remained in Hewitt's favour: he had a good record against Federer (he'd won six of their eight matches as professionals) and he became even more passionate than normal when playing for his country. This is the man who, when his clothing company (the same as Federer's at that time) refused him permission to put the name of his country on the back of his shirts and wouldn't give him any in Australia's colours, got up early one morning to dye some white shirts yellow and some white shorts green. He is a patriotic Australian to the core, and that day he showed it.

The British tennis journalist Neil Harman described the match as 'the indomitable will against the extravagant talent'. On the point of victory for the talent, the will took over. Federer was within two points of levelling the tie, but Hewitt was determined not to be beaten in front of his own people and, when Federer gave him a couple of cheap points, the tide turned. After Hewitt had taken the third-set tiebreak 7–4, Federer took a breather; it's called a 'bathroom break', and no doubt there was a genuine call of nature, but he was clearly hoping to take the opportunity to regroup. He did for a while, but it didn't last. At 5–6 in the fourth set, he served a double fault to give Hewitt a set point. Hewitt then lunged at a volley to claim the set, and with it effectively break Federer's spirit. The final score read 5–7, 2–6, 7–6, 7–5, 6–1, and Hewitt enjoyed one of the biggest adrenalin rushes of his life. 'You can take your Wimbledons and your US Opens,' he said in an on-court interview. 'This means more to me than anything.'

Even if Federer had won, Switzerland would still have

had to rely on Kratochvil to beat Philippoussis. Kratochvil would have been the underdog in a match few would have felt confident about. In theory, Philippoussis, the man who had reached two Grand Slam finals and beaten a world number one (Pete Sampras in 1996) should have had the edge against a player with a fragile match temperament and on the rebound from knee surgery. But having won a live fifth rubber in his previous Davis Cup tie, Kratochvil might well have risen to the occasion against the flaky 'Flip'. We will never know.

At the end of the tie, Federer was in tears as the Peter Carter Trophy was presented to Australia's captain, John Fitzgerald. He knew his great run in Davis Cup singles would one day come to an end, but for it to do so in the crucial rubber of the tie for the trophy named after his mentor was hard. He restated his wish to have another go in 2004, and he duly turned out for Switzerland's first and second ties. But maybe something of the Davis Cup magic died in Federer that September night in Melbourne, at least for a few years. Turning out for his country certainly slipped down his priority list after April 2004, and didn't come back until several years later. It was interesting that, while he always said he was happy carrying the load single-handedly, he only redeveloped an interest in the competition when he had a quality second player alongside him and Switzerland had a genuine chance of winning the trophy.

The dignified Fitzgerald was no doubt trying to be consoling, though in no way untruthful, when he said after the Hewitt–Federer match, 'They're going to have some battles over the years and, goodness, what a talent Roger is! What he can do with the ball – it's like a magic wand in his hand.' 'Fitzy' was right about Federer's talent, but proved totally wrong about the future battles. Though no one could know it at the time, Hewitt was a largely spent force, and was soon to lose his status as a serious challenger to Federer.

In sport and other disciplines such as music and dance, there is a phenomenon whereby some highly gifted players find it tough to reach the very top – footballers who are giants in the club game but can't get comfortable in the national team, or runners who beat the best in Grand Prix meetings but who freeze at the Olympics and world championships, and golfers who on the tour hit round after round below par but who miss the crucial chips and putts in the majors. Similarly, numerous musicians and dancers offer scintillating performances in unpressured situations but can then lose something of their lustre on the biggest stages. Why this should be so is an academic field of its own. For example, the Swedish psychologist Anders Ericsson, who did a lot of research into sporting and artistic excellence, said natural talent is overrated, and hard work allied to good coaching and 'purposeful practice' is the key, so performers who find things come easy to them often don't put in the hard yards that can help in moments of pressure (Ericsson's work has been brought to a wider audience via the fascinating book *Bounce* by the former British table tennis champion, Matthew Syed). As a result, many such gifted performers all too easily join the ranks of the nearly-men and nearly-women who look like getting to the top but never quite make it.

That was the prospect facing Roger Federer after the first few months of 2003. His form on the tour had gone up to another level, landing him titles in Marseille, Dubai and Munich – none of them are massively prestigious events on their own but, thanks to those wins, together with reaching the semi-finals in Rotterdam and the fourth round in Miami, he'd climbed into the world's top five. Among those who ply their trade writing and broadcasting about tennis, the general view was that he was probably heading for the top but one couldn't be sure, and he was taking a long time getting there.

A little irritation – understandably – seeped out at a press conference when he was once again asked about getting to number one. 'I believe I will get there one day,' he said politely yet through somewhat gritted teeth, 'and, when I do, I'm a bit concerned that I won't get the credit for it, because people will have said for so long that I'm going to get there.'

As it happened, he needn't have worried; such was the elegance of his play and the dominance he showed when he finally made it to the top of the rankings that people couldn't help but give him the credit. And the fact that he had appeared to stumble so much en route to the pinnacle probably added to the public's appreciation of his success.

There was another unofficial school of thought at that time, which can best be summed up as 'he'd be better if he wasn't so good'. Behind the obvious illogicality of the statement lay a belief among some that he was so gifted and had so many options on the tennis court that he couldn't work out the right options at the right time. Federer himself said in early 2010, 'I always knew I had it in my hand – the question was: do I have it in my mind and my legs? That's something I had to work extremely hard at.' That is not only a fair assessment, but seasoned tennis watchers know that gifted and all-court players take longer to mature, often because it takes them longer to assemble the experience of putting more components together, unlike baseliners, who have fewer options and so are surer of what they should be doing. But then many gifted all-court players never quite put it all together, and this was the quiet fear behind where Federer stood approaching the mid-point of 2003.

A fourth title of 2003, and a second clay-court Masters trophy shield, seemed on the cards when Federer reached the final in Rome in May, beating some quality clay-courters en route. In that final he came up against the revitalised Felix Mantilla, a twenty-nine-year-old former French Open semi-finalist whose best days were behind him, and who later fought a successful battle against skin cancer (one of the few touring professionals to be afflicted by a disease they are all very vulnerable to). It seemed a formality that Federer would win. But the old demons returned.

Mixing the pace of his groundstrokes, Federer made all the early running but then failed to convert his seven break points and lost the first set. In the third he had three set points but ended up losing the tiebreak 12–10 and, with it, the two-hour-and-forty-one-minute final. It left the unseeded Mantilla somewhat astonished and tearful, having won 7–5, 6–2, 7–6. Federer had created seventeen break points but had converted just three of them.

A defeat in a tournament final offers no immediate escape – no rushing off court, no quick exit to dodge the cameras and seek sanctuary in the locker room. While the winner cavorts around the stadium in his or her moment of triumph, the loser has to sit there, waiting for the presentation ceremony, working out what nice things to say through the disappointment of a big match that has just got away.

When Federer finally got back on to the court, he found himself at the end of a long line of dignitaries, the last of whom was Francesco Ricci Bitti, the International Tennis Federation's president and one of Federer's greatest fans. 'I found myself standing next to Roger,' recalls Ricci Bitti, 'so I took the liberty of saying a few words to him. I said, "Roger, I don't think you should be losing this kind of match. You have to start winning this kind of match, or this is going to become sad for you and sad for tennis." It was totally the wrong moment to say something to him, but I am such a fan of his that I couldn't control myself saying something. Some players would have thought it very bad, but Roger was polite enough to accept it, and that restrained reaction impressed me greatly. He's a very sensitive guy but very controlled.'

Mantilla made a comment after the match that to some seemed to sum up where Federer might be failing. 'I believe I won today because I had the hunger,' he said. 'I played with heart and courage and everything I had.' Was that what Federer wasn't doing? In truth, no. Federer was working very hard away from the public gaze, and was to a certain extent suffering from the curse of the gifted performer: it always looks so easy that the hard work put in behind the scenes doesn't show.

The following week was the Hamburg leg of the Masters Series, and Federer proved somewhat touchy when asked if he thought he was playing too much tennis and thereby jeopardising his chances at the French Open. Even after losing in the third round to Mark Philippoussis, he declined to take any comfort in the fact that his defeat effectively gave him ten days rather than seven in which to prepare for Paris. Hamburg, it seemed, was becoming a place of contrasting emotions for him, with his smashed racket in 2001, his victory in 2002, and now a slightly edgy run-up to Roland Garros 2003.

In most people's eyes, after his first-round defeat in 2002 to Hicham Arazi, he was due a reasonable run at the French. And the draw was kind to him, or so it seemed. Seeded fifth, in the first round he came up against the sixty-seventh-ranked Luis Horna, a player who attracts that unkind and dishonest epithet of the 'tennis journeyman'. The match was scheduled for the main Philippe Chatrier arena at the start of the first day. A couple of hours beforehand, Federer had been given the customary chance to hit on the greatest clay-court arena in the world, but instead of grooving his strokes he flicked the ball casually around and never looked fully focused. Not that this seemed to matter when he led by a break early in the first set. But Horna broke back, Federer's angst set in as the first set wore on and, once he had lost it on a tiebreak, his self-belief ebbed away. Though a hardened clay-courter from Peru, Horna was making his Roland Garros debut, and playing his first match since becoming a father a couple of weeks earlier. Surely Federer would come back. But the second set rattled past and, while Federer made a better fist of it in the third set, he lost another tiebreak, allowing Horna to walk away victorious after just 131 minutes of play by almost exactly the same score by which Mantilla had beaten Federer in Rome.

'I played a poor match and he played well,' was Federer's

assessment through the disappointment. 'And, when those two combine, it doesn't help my cause.'

For the second year running, Federer had fallen at the first hurdle in Paris. Was he the real deal, or was the great Swiss talent flattering to deceive?

THE GOLDEN YEARS **3**

8

FEDERER'S GRAND SLAM period began at the time when people were seriously beginning to question whether he might ever get there. With the benefit of hindsight, it's hard to imagine that he was still very much an unproven quantity as he arrived at Wimbledon in 2003. His victory over Pete Sampras was two years back, he had lost to Mario Ancic in the first round the year before, and for the second year running he was coming to south-west London fresh from a first-round defeat at the French Open. Since beating Sampras in 2001, he hadn't got past the fourth round of any of the four Grand Slam events.

At least he'd notched up his first grass-court title. That came in Halle, but even there he'd come very close to losing his semi-final against Mikhail Youzhny, and in the ten previous stagings of Germany's top grass event the best the Halle champion had done at Wimbledon was the fourth round. According to Gerhard Weber, the women's clothing magnate who launched the Halle tournament in 1993, the idea was that 'Wimbledon starts in Halle', and his press officer Frank Hofen had even cajoled a couple of local radio journalists into using the term 'Kleinwimbledon' (Little Wimbledon) to describe the tournament. Yet the failure of those who had done well in Halle to go on and do well at Wimbledon was beginning to undermine the reliability of the Halle event to offer valid Wimbledon preparation. By 2003, Weber was becoming desperate for the champion of his tournament to go on to win Wimbledon – and in his 2003 champion, he finally seemed to have someone with the potential to do so. With Sampras announcing his retirement a few weeks before Wimbledon and the reigning champion, Lleyton Hewitt, struggling for form, the way seemed open for a new name on the Wimbledon roll of honour.

The British thought they knew what that name would be – and it wasn't Roger Federer.

Andy Roddick had begun working with Andre Agassi's former coach Brad Gilbert just five weeks earlier. Like Federer, Roddick had been the-next-big-thing-waiting-to-happen since becoming the Swiss's next-but-one successor as the world junior champion in 2000. He needed something to take him to the next level, and in Gilbert he found it.

The effect of Roddick bringing Gilbert on board was instantaneous. In their first event together, Roddick stormed through the pre-Wimbledon tournament at London's Queen's Club, beating Andre Agassi in a glorious semi-final and humbling Sébastien Grosjean in less than an hour to claim the title.

The British press went mad about him, nominating him as the favourite for Wimbledon, even though he was seeded fifth behind Hewitt, Agassi, Juan Carlos Ferrero and Federer. Of course, the locals still harboured hopes that Tim Henman might finally win their event, but the serious money was on Roddick. And the dramatic events of the first day hardly slowed the Roddick bandwagon.

The Centre Court programme at Wimbledon is always opened on the first day by the defending champion, and the match is normally something of a formality. Not so in 2003. For the first time since the 1966 champion Manolo Santana lost in the first round in 1967, the champion was struck down at the first hurdle, Hewitt losing in four sets to the big-serving giant from Croatia, Ivo Karlovic.

More fuel was added to the Roddick fire in the second round, when the American kept his cool while Greg Rusedski lost his. Roddick played a much more assured match than the indignant Brits were willing to acknowledge in beating Rusedski in straight sets. Rusedski led 5–2 in the third set, but then at 5–3 he let a ball go when he heard the call of 'out'. The call proved to have come from the crowd rather than the line umpire and, with his serve under threat, Rusedski went wild. With several million people watching at teatime on British terrestrial television, Rusedski let fly a tirade of expletives towards the match umpire, Lars Graff, who had been one hundred per cent correct in his application of the rules. Rusedski lost the match shortly after the outburst, and he was the talk of Wimbledon until the following day.

Meanwhile, Federer cruised comfortably through his first couple of matches, beating Hyung Taik-Lee and Stefan Koubek each in straight sets, and then in his third match he beat Mardy Fish in four. Although no one could have guessed at the time, the thirtieth-ranked Fish was to be the only person to win a set against Federer in the whole tournament. But, after three rounds, nothing had been proved – yet. After all, Federer had never been beyond the quarter-finals, and his next opponent was Feliciano López, a Spaniard with a passion for fast courts who had reached the fourth round the previous year and whose big left-handed serve was particularly effective on grass. Yet, with Hewitt gone and Agassi, Henman, Nalbandian and Ferrero all in the bottom half of the draw, anticipation about the projected Federer–Roddick semi-final was growing.

A personal recollection perhaps illustrates this sense of anticipation. Over the middle weekend of that year's tourna-ment, London's oldest Sunday newspaper, the *Observer*, asked me to write a preview of the likely semi-final between Roddick and Federer. The brief I was given was 'to look at the two players' strengths and weaknesses, explain why it should be a great match, and why Roddick should win'. 'But I don't think he *will* win,' I replied. I was allowed to make my case for Federer, although this was very much against the tide of opinion in the British media.

Fifteen minutes into Federer's match against López, the prospect of a Roddick–Federer semi-final was receding rapidly. On a cold, overcast June Monday, the two players walked out on to what was then Court 2, the showcourt nicknamed 'the graveyard of the seeds'. After the first game, Federer called for the trainer, and after three he took an injury timeout. His back had seized up. 'I felt a twinge in my upper back,' he said later. 'I told the trainer what I was feeling and he massaged it but couldn't tell me what it was, so I just went on playing.'

Federer doesn't know for certain what went wrong with

his back that day. The likeliest explanation is a pinched nerve, but the fact that he had no further problems with it (the back problems he suffered from over a period dating from late 2008 to 2012 were not the same injury) suggests it was the nerves getting to him. Was the perennial prodigy about to flop again and fuel the growing suspicion that he was a little flaky in the big tournaments?

No, he wasn't. In fact, the injury may have been the best thing that happened to him. Fearing he might have to retire, he relaxed, and, while he trailed for most of the set, a run of López errors helped Federer to break back to level at 5–5. Once he had taken the first set on a 7–5 tiebreak, he was never in trouble again.

That day, Roddick dropped his first set of the tournament, beating Paradorn Srichaphan in four and adding to the aura of the seemingly phenomenal effect Gilbert was having on his game. Nine matches the two had had together: nine wins, just three sets dropped.

Another man on a run of nine successive victories was Sjeng Schalken. The Dutchman had won the pre-Wimbledon grass-court tournament in 's-Hertogenbosch, and must have hoped Federer's back problem would help redress the balance from when the pair had played in Arnhem earlier that year when Federer had won in straight sets. But a break in each set sufficed for Federer to sail through. With Roddick beating the Swede Jonas Björkman, also in straight sets, the match all the neutrals wanted to see had been secured. Having a Roddick–Federer semi-final was also some minor comfort for the home fans, who that day had to endure another Tim Henman defeat, this time in the quarter-finals to Sébastien Grosjean.

If the hype surrounding the Roddick–Federer match had turned the semi-final into a spectacle that threatened to eclipse the final, it wasn't a sentiment shared by Federer. 'I expected to win it,' he said later. 'It was just the media that was hyping up everything, that he was the big favourite to win the tournament. I – how shall I say this? – I wasn't of the same opinion. Because he won Queen's and I won Halle, and because Queen's is in England, everybody was talking about him more, for about a month. But I knew that if I played my game correctly I should beat him.'

The word 'correctly' doesn't seem sufficient to describe one of the most emphatic performances of Federer's career. Even if his passage to his first Grand Slam final wasn't as big a breakthrough for him as certain other matches had been, it was the one at which he effectively announced to the tennis world that, if he was on his game, it was virtually impossible for anyone else to beat him. Roddick's comment 'I got my butt kicked' was short and to the point, but doesn't give sufficient credit to the sublime display his opponent offered on what was America's national day. Writing in a British newspaper, Boris Becker said of Federer's display, 'A video cassette of this should be sent to every tennis coach in the world.'

One point in particular stays in the memory: the point with which Federer reached set point in the second set. Rallying from the baseline, he came in to the net on a late decision and found himself having to play a low volley. To experienced tennis watchers, he appeared to have made a tactical error that left him stranded in no-man's land. But playing the kind of shot he would normally attempt only in the last few minutes of a practice session when the fun and artistry takes over from the hard work, he flicked the low ball cross-court, driving it ferociously into the forehand corner of Roddick's baseline. Federer himself couldn't suppress a wry smile. Even he knew it was sheer brilliance.

'I know I played a fantastic match with fantastic points,' he says today of the 7–6, 6–3, 6–3 win that took him into his first Grand Slam final, 'but that made it all the more necessary for me to settle down in the final. I got praised like crazy for beating Andy, because people had seen him playing so well, but I'd already beaten him before. It was the final I had to get up for, and that was the real breakthrough.'

Facing Federer in the final was Mark Philippoussis, the big-serving but injury-prone Australian whose five-sets victory over Andre Agassi in the tournament's fourth round seemed to have relaunched his career. Philippoussis had two advantages over Federer: he had the bigger serve and he'd been in one previous Grand Slam final, the 1998 US Open decider, which he'd lost in four sets to his compatriot Patrick Rafter. For those reasons, he had a chance – theoretically, at least.

Federer, however, had the momentum. After beating Roddick so convincingly, he could probably have lost the final and still claimed to have exorcised his demons. But, with the wind in his sails, he wasn't going to let himself be blown off course.

In the final, he out-aced Philippoussis by 21 to 14 in notching up a 7–6, 6–2, 7–6 win that was effectively decided in the first-set tiebreak. At 6–2 in the third-set tiebreak, Federer had four championship points. On the first, Philippoussis delivered a big serve: 6–3. On the second, the Australian netted a return, and Federer fell to his knees.

It was what happened in the moments after Federer became Wimbledon champion that really sold him to the British public. Tears in the moment of winning a major sporting event are nothing new, even in a country like England where men crying openly is still not something many are comfortable with. By the time Federer faced a live on-court interview that was broadcast around the world, it was assumed he had 'regained his composure', as the British like to call it. He had already answered a couple of questions from the former French Open champion Sue Barker, when he described how he was finally living one of his childhood dreams. As he uttered the words 'And now I'm here!' his voice cracked with emotion, the tears of joy flowed, and he captured the hearts of a lot more than the 13,800 people in the venerable arena that day.

'There's no rule about how you should conduct yourself in the moment when you win or when you lose,' he said the following morning. 'The only thing you mustn't do is throw your racket into the crowd and injure someone. There are people who don't smile when they win, and there are people who smile for weeks afterwards. I'm the kind of guy who lets the tears flow, and I think that goes down pretty well, especially when people see this is the realisation of my biggest dream and that it's just amazing for me. I got a lot of feedback that people in the crowd also cried and enjoyed it, and it's nice to share this with a lot of people.'

One of the photographs taken immediately after the final that frequently gets reprinted shows a fan in a Swiss shirt with tears streaming down his face. That man was Michael Purek, a member at Old Boys Basel, who had been a sparring partner of Federer's in his teenage days.

While Purek was lucky enough to watch his old mate's performance courtside, most of the rest of the Old Boys fraternity were glued to the television set in the Old Boys' cramped clubhouse. 'That was a great day at the club,' said Seppli Kacovski, the man who'd taught the Wimbledon champion to play tennis. 'I was OK at the beginning, but I got so nervous that I could hardly watch in the tiebreak, and then I got so nervous I uncorked the champagne too early. It was his first match point, and suddenly there was champagne everywhere, and then Philippoussis saved it. Everyone was laughing at me, but only for one point, because Roger then won it. We drank and cried. We sang. We toasted Roger. We were so proud.'

Lots of people were proud of Federer that night, among them Peter Carter's parents, Diana and Bob, who watched the match in the South Australian town of Nuriootpa and shed their own tears at Roger's victory. It was still less than a year after Peter's death, but Bob admitted in a television interview around this time that Federer's success had helped ease the pain of their loss. 'I feel really good about it,' he said of Federer's title. 'It's a wonderful feeling, really, because Peter had such an influence on his career, and to watch Roger play you can sort of see a little of Peter there.'

Although keen not to praise any single person's contribution to his success when he faced the media after the final, Federer was happy to acknowledge Carter's role in his moment of triumph. 'Peter was one of the most important people in my career. We would have had a big party together if he was still here. I'm sure he was watching it from somewhere.'

That night, Federer was invited for the second time to

the Wimbledon champions' dinner at London's Savoy hotel, and this time he accepted. The dinner always takes place very late because all champions and finalists are invited, including those from the junior events, and some don't finish playing their finals until well into the evening. The tradition of the men's and women's singles champions having the first dance with each other has long since gone (in fact, there's no dancing at the Wimbledon champions' dinner, although Novak Djokovic briefly revived the tradition in 2015 by inviting the women's champion Serena Williams to dance with him, an invitation she gleefully accepted), but both singles champions are asked to make a small speech, and the moment normally falls sometime after midnight. In his, Federer said, 'This is the first time I've attended this event. Five years ago, when I won the junior title, I declined your invitation because the following day I was playing in Gstaad. I now realise I made a mistake. I'm really proud to be here and to have earned my membership of the All England Club. I look forward to dropping by to hit a few balls at Wimbledon just for fun. If anyone wants to hit with me, give me a ring.'

Sitting close to Federer at the dinner was Francesco Ricci Bitti, the president of the International Tennis Federation. Referring back to their on-court conversation at the Rome prize-giving ceremony eight weeks earlier, when Ricci Bitti had chided Federer for the way he had lost to Felix Mantilla, Federer looked into the Italian's eyes and said, 'You see, Mr President, I *can* win these kinds of matches. Aren't you proud of me?'

Luckily for both the media and himself, Roger Federer is a good communicator. For any tennis player who does not enjoy chatting with journalists and television crews, winning a Grand Slam singles title is a serious health hazard.

As well as the obligatory post-match press conference and interview with the host television broadcaster, there are usually at least half a dozen one-on-one interview requests, often a dozen, with everyone considering it their moral right to have at least three minutes with the new champion. And that's just for the English-speakers; for someone who has their own language, you can double the time. And for someone from Switzerland, where trilingualism is nothing special, the process can take even longer. As a result, Federer has become accustomed to allowing at least an hour and sometimes much more for his media obligations after Grand Slam quarter- and semi-finals, while, for finals, it's normally about two hours, plus time for photo-shoots with whichever trophy he's won.

After winning Wimbledon in 2003, Federer duly discharged his two hours of media responsibilities before heading back to the family house in Wimbledon he'd rented for the fortnight, where he showered, shaved and quickly changed into his dinner jacket and Swiss-red bow tie. Then he was off to the Savoy, before returning home in the small hours of the morning. After a few hours' sleep, there was another round of media appointments, starting with radio and television appearances, followed by breakfast with first the British press and then any journalist wanting to converse in French, High German and Swiss German. He could have said no and enjoyed a lie-in; indeed, many champions do just that. But this wasn't just Federer's first Grand Slam title where the novelty was something to be enjoyed, he is also someone who understood early the responsibilities of promoting his sport that come with being one of its high-profile figures.

That morning, the papers had glowing accounts of Federer's success, and he continued to charm them. There was no hint of irritation, or even the tired autopilot of answering the same questions over and over. He listened to every one, thought about his answers and allowed his simple humanity to shine through. 'Life will change in some ways,' he said when asked how his victory would affect him. 'I'm more famous now, a celebrity. Before, I was just a good tennis player. I don't know how that's going to be. My star sign is Leo, and Leos like to be the centre of attention, but I'll do the same work on court because, if you don't work, people will catch you.'

A bit of context is needed here. At the time that Federer won his first Wimbledon, the ATP was publicly fighting the four Grand Slam tournaments for the players to receive a bigger share of the majors' profits. In addition, a list of tennis grandees was calling for the permissible dimensions of rackets to be reduced because, they said, tennis was getting 'tedious'. And the previous August, Lleyton Hewitt became embroiled in a dispute with the ATP that seemed to sum up tennis's problems.

At the time the undisputed world number one, Hewitt was asked to do an interview with an American television station. Both the station and the ATP had been chasing him on the matter for some time, and at the Cincinnati Masters the patience of both the ATP's communications managers and Hewitt himself snapped. Astonishing as it might seem, the matter escalated to such a degree that the Australian took out a $1.5 million lawsuit against the organising body of the men's professional tennis tour. Irrespective of the arguments on both sides, the case seemed a metaphor for an epidemic of ills at the top of world tennis.

Into this tense environment steps a striking twenty-one-year-old man, with a personality of open emotions, considerable decency and the ability to express himself with great eloquence in three languages. And he wins the most prestigious prize in tennis! Federer was the kind of ambassador tennis could only dream of; the PR folk couldn't have staged it better. No wonder the sport felt good at that Wimbledon champions' dinner.

The message Federer was giving out was summed up in one sentence from his post-match press conference: 'There was big pressure from all sides, also from myself. I've proved myself to everybody. It's a big relief.' Now the real part of his career could begin.

It began with a flight on a private jet from London to Saanen, a tiny airfield high in the Swiss Alps and a few kilometres from arguably the most picturesque venue on the tennis tour: the small town of Gstaad, set amid the stunning splendour of the Bernese Oberland. The small club that hosts the tournament builds plenty of temporary seating for its week in the spotlight, but breathtaking vistas of chocolate-box scenery are always in the players' and spectators' peripheral vision, as is the fairy-tale castle towering over the town that looks like a drawing from a children's storybook. Gstaad is home (or second home) to many big names of the stage and screen, as well as sport (including the twelve-times Grand Slam champion Roy Emerson) and other celebrity walks of life, and the tournament would have featured more prominently on the tennis map if it hadn't for many years had a graveyard slot the week after Wimbledon. The calendar was re-jigged in 2009 to put a couple of weeks between the end of Wimbledon and the start of Gstaad, but that was still not enough to fit into Federer's tournament schedule, nor to change the unfortunate but understandable fact that Gstaad attracts only the hardened clay-courters for whom Wimbledon is an interruption – albeit a lucrative one – from the European red-clay season.

But in 2003 and 2004, Gstaad had the Wimbledon champion, an almost unheard-of occurrence. And it has the legacy of its decision taken back in 1998 to thank for that.

All tournament directors like to look for promising youngsters, on the basis that promising youngsters are looking for tournament opportunities, so, if a tournament director offers a player a chance to play while the player is on the way up, that same player might look favourably on the tournament when he or she is at the top.

In 1998, the Gstaad tournament director Köbi Hermenjat had offered Switzerland's promising junior Roger Federer his first-ever match at ATP tour level and, although Federer had lost in straight sets to Lucas Arnold, he never forgot the gesture of assistance. So, instead of feeling an imaginary twinge of pain in his left calf that might have emerged during the second and third sets of the Wimbledon final and thus forced him to withdraw from a tournament that made no sense from a tennis or physical point of view, Federer honoured his commitment to Gstaad and showed up. He might also have been forgiven for tanking his first or second match, knowing that he would have turned out for the fans and could always say the tiredness from Wimbledon or his becoming reaccustomed to clay had been his undoing. But Federer isn't like that. The tennis verb 'to tank' is barely in his vocabulary, and it's certainly not in his mentality; if he's out on a tennis court, he plays to win. Besides, he had given his word to Hermenjat that he would be there, and anyway this was the chance to celebrate. He knew his countryfolk wanted to see him, and he was determined to oblige them.

There was always going to be some sort of token present in Gstaad for the returning hero, but what a present the tournament in Gstaad hit on! After Federer's opening-round win over Marc López in three sets, his gift was brought on to the centre court. Her name was Juliette, and she was a tan-and-white Bernese Oberländer milk cow weighing something close to 800kg. She was presented to Federer decked out in a garland of sunflowers and wearing a traditional Swiss cowbell.

For a while on court, Federer looked nonplussed, but then he entered into the spirit of the gesture. Asked later by the media where he would keep her, he questioned whether she would really be happy either touring with him around the world or watching the trams go by in the streets of Basel, so he agreed to leave her to graze on the slopes of the Oberland mountains. She clearly did more than grazing; when asked at Wimbledon the following year how she was, Federer replied, 'She's doing well, and she has a calf now.'

As for the tournament at Gstaad, it was almost a phenomenal victory to follow Federer's heroics at Wimbledon. He beat the quality clay-courter Gaston Gaudio in the semi-finals in straight sets, before losing a five-set final to Jiri Novak, a Czech whose best year was the one before and whose star was beginning to fade. There would have been yodelling in the streets of Gstaad that night if Federer had won, but he'd still performed heroically; after his efforts at Wimbledon, he had not only shown up but had played all matches asked of him and fought to the end. 'I really wanted to win this for you,' he told the crowd after the final, 'because the way you have received me here has touched me greatly.'

After giving his all at Wimbledon and Gstaad, Federer admitted to being 'dead on my feet'. It was almost time for a holiday, but there was one more obligation.

Six months earlier, back in January 2003, his old friend and flatmate Yves Allegro had asked Federer if he would come to his home town of Grône, near Sion, to put in an appearance as part of the Grône tennis club's twenty-fifth anniversary celebrations. Federer had agreed to appear, telling Allegro in March that the evening of Tuesday 15 July would be the best time to appear. 'Gstaad finishes on the Sunday, we're off on holiday on Wednesday, so we'll fit it in on Tuesday,' he had said.

When Federer won Wimbledon, the folks at Grône thought he'd now be too big to spare an evening to play a set at their club. And when he got to the final in Gstaad, they all but gave up hope. Only one person was sure Federer would show, and that was Allegro. 'I know Roger,' he says today, 'and I knew that, once he'd said he'd come, he would come unless there was really something unavoidable that would prevent it. Everyone at the club was convinced he would cancel, but I knew he wouldn't.'

Federer did indeed show up at Grône as promised and provided a memorable night for the townspeople, playing three sets against Allegro, signing autographs and posing for the camera – all without even the mention of a fee. He saw at first hand how much it means to people to have him around, and his appearance allowed the club to raise enough money to wipe out debts that were threatening to close it down.

The following morning, it was off to Sardinia for a hard-earned holiday, but off court the sweet smell of success took a different form.

In the months after she became his girlfriend, Mirka Vavrinec persuaded Federer to launch his own range of cosmetics. Ever open to new ideas, Federer agreed, and the resulting RF cosmetics line became Vavrinec's project. She developed the logo, which featured Federer's autograph, and worked on the development of the range's four products: eau de toilette spray, aftershave balm, body wash and deodorant stick, plus special sets – all made in Switzerland and marketed under the slogan 'Feel the touch'. The advertising blurb described the range as 'fulfilling the highest demands of modern sports-oriented men'.

'It's something we've done all ourselves,' said Federer proudly in an interview with the tennis-x.com website. 'It's the Roger Federer fragrance. I helped a lot with it, including the selection and refinement of the fragrances. It's something that means a lot to me. We'll see what happens.'

One can only hope Federer wasn't involved in drafting the RF advertising literature, which in places puts the most pseudo of art critics and wine writers in the shade. The eau de toilette spray, with its 'elegantly sporty fragrance', is described as having 'citrus chords and ozone elements… with a hint of green tea'. The blurb goes on: 'Transparent floral themes, noble woody notes and sensuous ambergris tones create a lingering background to round off an unmistakable, sophisticated fragrance image.' The fragrance image may have been unmistakable and sophisticated, but it clearly wasn't particularly marketable, as it was withdrawn from sale a couple of years later.

Another significant off-court development in the weeks after Wimbledon was Federer's declaration of independence from his former management, a decision that sat well with his sense of self-determination.

Most tennis players – indeed, most top athletes – are 'managed' by a player agency. Such agencies look after advertising deals, contracts with clothing and racket suppliers, media appearances and in a few cases some of the minutiae of everyday life. Until about fifteen years ago, the vast majority of players were with one of three big player management companies: the International Management Group (IMG), set up by the pioneering Mark McCormack in the 1960s when he turned Arnold Palmer from a successful golfer into a highly lucrative brand; Octagon Worldwide (formerly Advantage International); and SFx (originally ProServ, now Live Nation).

Since 1998, Federer had been with IMG, but by mid-2003 he had come to the conclusion that he wanted control of his affairs closer to home. There were murmurings that he was unhappy about the way IMG had handled the renegotiation of a contract and Federer would not have been the first player on the rise to feel his management company may not have appreciated what an asset he was. Whatever the reason, he ended his relationship with IMG and set up Roger Federer Management. Federer himself and the people close to him were in a better position than many on the tennis circuit to take matters into their own hands. And take them they did.

Roger Federer Management had a number of high-profile officers, notably Mirka Vavrinec as Roger's diary secretary and Lynette Federer, Roger's mother, as a secretary for bigger projects. The Basel lawyer Bernhard Christen had a prominent position, and even Federer's coach Peter Lundgren was part of the team, giving him an air of permanence that proved to be illusory. The company was based in the offices of the law firm that Christen worked at in Bottmingen (the same suburb of Basel to which Lynette and Robbie Federer had relocated; 2003 was the year Roger first moved in with Mirka in the neighbouring suburb of Oberwil), while publicity was handled by a communications firm in Germany. Chairman and chief executive was Roger Federer – and anyone assuming this was nothing more than a figurehead position misunderstands him; he might be willing to listen to advice, but he makes his own decisions.

Many people criticised the arrangement, notably those from other player-management companies who saw it as setting a precedent that didn't augur well for their own credibility. Others suggested there was a risk that in-house management would take up too much of Federer's time and distract him from tennis. His results in 2004 safely scotched that fear, and, if there was a risk of becoming distracted from his tennis, that probably came more from the generous way in which he gave his time to the media, sponsors, tennis politics and outside initiatives than from any internal management issues. In retrospect, Federer's entrepreneurism was ahead of the times. He was not the only player to opt for a smaller-scale private arrangement over one of the big three management companies; other players – notably the Spanish friends Albert Costa and Alex Corretja – had split from recognised agencies and put their trust in friends and family. But it was against the trend of the time. Two years later, Federer went back to IMG, but it did not prove a long-term relationship, and in 2013 he became part of the growing trend towards smaller, 'boutique' player representation agencies with his Team8 initiative (see page 349).

The Wimbledon honeymoon lasted well into August. Federer came within a point of reaching the final of the Montreal Masters, losing his semi-final to Andy Roddick on a final-set tiebreak. Had Federer won that match, he would have gone to the top of the rankings, but somehow he didn't seem ready for it and the result didn't feel altogether wrong. After all, Roddick was on the best roll of his career, one that would see him take the US Open and finish the year ranked number one. Nonetheless, Federer still had a match point, and the match remained Roddick's only win against him until March 2008.

Despite a second-round defeat to David Nalbandian in Cincinnati, Federer's Wimbledon boost could be said to have lasted until the US Open, but it was there that it certainly ended. In fact, the next two months were to prove particularly troublesome for the young Swiss.

Although no one had done the Wimbledon and US Open double since Pete Sampras in 1995, Federer looked a reasonable bet to do so at a tournament without any obvious favourite. But, as the weather worsened, Nalbandian again showed up to spoil the party.

Federer cruised through his first three rounds without dropping a set, but then had to sit by as fine drizzle held up play for three days. Although the tournament was now in its seventh year in the 'new' Arthur Ashe Stadium, the US Tennis Association had apparently not foreseen the problem of mild drizzle affecting the playing surface. The dark-green concrete court was fine, but at the slightest hint of moisture the white lines became as slippery as ice and play had to stop (a problem that, remarkably, has still not been solved, though is less likely to interrupt play now the main two courts at Flushing Meadows both have retractable roofs). The skies were grey for three solid days during that year's US Open and, while play seemed always on the point of starting, it never really did.

On the fourth day, the skies were still grey, but it was finally dry, and Federer took to the Arthur Ashe Stadium against Nalbandian for a place in the quarter-finals. He won the first set, but, once he'd lost the second on a tiebreak, his face took on the colour of the sky, and after that there was no way back. Asked after his 3–6, 7–6, 6–4, 6–3 defeat why he hadn't managed to beat the Argentinian in five previous meetings, Federer replied, 'I've never had a great day playing against him. I guess I'm struggling against him. I don't know how to comment on this. I'm trying to figure out how to beat him. He likes my game; that's all I can say about it.'

Nalbandian was scarcely more illuminating, 'I like playing against him,' he said. 'What more can I say? I like his game. I don't know exactly why, but I think I know him.' If such comments sound a bit shallow, they also testify to a feature of tennis that's not widely understood, namely that the way two players' games match up with each other can deliver some freakish results. Some players find the game of a certain opponent just suits them, or gives them problems they would never have foreseen, even if the rankings suggest otherwise. The best example is Federer's 'match-up' with Rafael Nadal, in which Nadal troubled Federer yet Federer seldom troubled Nadal, at least until 2017. In the early days, Nalbandian found Federer's game well suited to his own, and the results showed it.

If Federer's defeat in New York against Nalbandian was demoralising, another was to follow against another nemesis in another Grand Slam arena that was more demoralising, more dramatic, and certainly more emotional.

From the disappointment under the ashen skies of New York, Federer went to the disappointment of his defeat to Hewitt under the bright lights of Melbourne Park (pages 134–6), and thereafter began to look tired. Many a breakthrough player plans his/her schedule on the basis of an expected average of matches per tournament, and, having won five titles in the first six months of the year, he had gone beyond whatever average he had anticipated at the start of 2003. As a result, he began to look like a teenager who hasn't had enough sleep. He won the title in Vienna and reached the semi-finals of the Madrid Masters, but he bombed out of Basel in the second round and was unimpressive at the Paris Masters. There he even talked about not wanting to go to the year-ending Tennis Masters Cup, which that year moved to Houston, and he certainly left observers in Paris with doubts about whether he would make the trip to Texas.

He probably always intended to go and, after the event,

he was more than glad he did. For out of the tiredness of the year that had seen him inscribe his name on the Grand Slam roll of honour, he summoned a breakthrough that eventually enabled him to move from being a member of the elite with a Grand Slam title to the all-conquering undisputed world number one.

Federer actually turned his fortunes round in the first of his three round-robin matches. He was never going to lack motivation against Andre Agassi, but he was helped in finding a little more pep in his game. The 2003 and 2004 Tennis Masters Cups were staged more by an individual than a club or organisation, and the individual in question – a larger-than-life home furniture magnate called Jim McIngvale, known in his locality as 'Mattress Mack' – was not hot on his tennis etiquette; the fact that McIngvale quite brazenly favoured the two Americans in the field, Agassi and Roddick, in the build-up to the tournament irked the other six players and made them all keen to beat an American. Federer edged out Agassi on a 9–7 final-set tiebreak after saving three match points, one of them in a marathon rally. Although the round-robin format meant both men could still qualify for the knockout stages – and both did – Federer had the wind back in his sails, and was never to lose to Agassi again.

In his next match he notched up his first tour-level win over David Nalbandian with an emphatic 6–3, 6–0 victory. In the semi-finals he dispatched Andy Roddick in straight sets to make something of a mockery of the fact that Roddick had secured the year-end number-one ranking. And in the final he was irresistible in beating Agassi for the second time in the week, this time 6–3, 6–0, 6–4.

After the event, Federer talked about having found something within himself, but it was an observation by Agassi that stayed in the memory. In the on-court presentation ceremony, the American congratulated Federer on the way he'd played all that week and added, 'It's a pleasure to watch you play.'

Federer's Wimbledon triumph back in July had turned something that had until then been only a trickle into a deluge. The Federer family had been hatching the idea of establishing a charitable foundation and, when the handful of requests for money from good causes suddenly multiplied after Federer had become a Grand Slam champion, it provided the impetus the Federers needed to turn intent into action.

The result was the launch of the Roger Federer Foundation in December 2003, its trustees being Lynette, Robert and Roger Federer, the lawyer Bernhard Christen and Urs Wüthrich, a member of the Basel-Land cantonal council. The foundation's mission statement was to fund projects that benefit disadvantaged children and to promote sport for young people. There was also a wish to make the most of the family's connection with South Africa, so in June 2004 the foundation joined forces with a Swiss–South African initiative called Imbewu-Suisse, the name meaning 'seed' in the Xhosa language. Founded in 2001, Imbewu's mission was to improve social conditions for children and young people in the New Brighton township on the edge of Port Elizabeth, one of the most impoverished areas in the country.

Since 2003, the foundation has supported a number of initiatives, and no longer works with Imbewu, but

Imbewu's status as the first beneficiary of the foundation was significant. Its work was based out of a somewhat ramshackle operation in New Brighton, so the Roger Federer Foundation agreed to fund improvements to Imbewu's administrative infrastructure so it could be more effective in its work. In early 2005, three schools attended by children helped by the foundation held a competition to find a motto to accompany the children through their school years, and the winner was 'I'm tomorrow's future', a slogan that neatly sums up what Federer was trying to achieve through his charitable work.

In March 2005, Federer used his absence from the Swiss Davis Cup team to travel to New Brighton to visit the results of the funding that the foundation had provided, taking with him a consignment of T-shirts, emblazoned with 'I'M TOMORROW'S FUTURE', produced by his clothing supplier. As the Swiss journalist Freddy Widmer wrote, 'The children don't know that the young man visiting them is a world-famous sportsman. They only know that the Federer Foundation will allow them what it says on their T-shirts: a future.'

Cynics might wonder if the foundation is little more than a convenient financial arrangement. Doubtless Federer does reduce his tax liability when he contributes to the foundation, but his record of putting his hand in his pocket over the years for humanitarian causes – from the 2004 Indian Ocean tsunami to the 2020 coronavirus outbreak – means no one should seriously doubt that his primary motivation behind setting up the venture is a genuine concern to divert some of his riches to the benefit of those at the bottom of the financial ladder. At the launch of the initiative, he said, 'I chose a project in South Africa because my mother grew up there, which means that I have always had a close affinity to the country. But to me South Africa is also a shining example of a country that has overcome hatred and oppression, making it a potential source of inspiration for other crisis regions around the world.'

On 20 December 2003, when most people were thinking more of Christmas than tennis, Federer dropped a bombshell. The Swiss media were summoned to a hastily arranged press conference in the premises of Christen Rickli Partners, the official home of Roger Federer Management, to hear that Federer had parted company from his coach, Peter Lundgren. Federer sat there looking grim as Bernhard Christen made the official announcement. He said the Federer team had hoped to have a news conference with Lundgren present to show that it was a mutual and amicable decision, but a rumour had leaked out and had been printed in the *Neue Zürcher Zeitung* newspaper, so the announcement had to be made now.

The split would have taken no one by surprise had it happened in the first half of 2003. At that stage, Federer's game seemed to have got stuck, and tennis observers found themselves wondering – certainly before Wimbledon – whether he needed a new coach to take him to new levels. Although he was highly experienced as a player and coach, Lundgren's corpulent figure never quite fitted with the image of the highest sporting aspirations and, while his laidback approach might have suited Federer away from the court, was it really the right thing for him as a player? So went the whispers on the tour.

But the decision to part company after Federer's most successful year to date – when he was Wimbledon champion, had just finished the year as Tennis Masters Cup champion, and was within striking distance of the world number one Andy Roddick – took the tennis world by surprise. In Houston four weeks earlier, he'd said he had no intention of changing coaches, and indeed Lundgren had briefed the Swiss media on how he was intending to get Federer into shape for 2004, when he hoped his charge would take over the number-one ranking. But, as Federer and Vavrinec departed for a holiday in Mauritius, Federer phoned Lundgren to say their four-year professional relationship was over.

In the news conference, Federer said he'd made the decision himself. It was the result of a long process, he said, after he'd come to the conclusion that his working relationship with Lundgren had become 'everyday' and that he needed 'new impulses'. He said he was sure that he and Lundgren would remain friends.

On the day that the parting became public, Lundgren, at home in Gothenburg, declined to comment. Later, he said he felt it was a move that was always likely to happen at some stage. 'This is what happens with the kind of relationship we had,' he said in an interview shortly afterwards. 'We were so close; we did everything together. We ate together. We went out together. We even played PlayStation together. Now it's good for him to carry on with someone else, and I'm happy to be doing something else.'

Several months later, when Lundgren had developed a fruitful working relationship with Marat Safin, he said Safin was easier to coach than Federer because he generally took

Lundgren's advice, whereas his predecessor had listened politely but normally done his own thing anyway. While this remark might add an extra brushstroke to a picture of Federer's character, it should probably be viewed with a degree of caution, as any coach is likely to say the most positive things about the player they happen to be coaching at that moment, even if it's to the relative detriment of those they've coached in the past.

There are some with reasonably close access to Federer who believe Mirka was strongly behind the decision to part with Lundgren, and she did play an underappreciated role as a sounding board for her boyfriend during 2004. Whatever her influence over the Lundgren decision, Federer still took responsibility for it. Ultimately there are arguments that can justify almost any decision, but Federer had just contradicted the sporting proverb: 'Never change a winning team'. He had ended 2003 on the unexpected high of Houston that gave all his followers hope for 2004, but had suddenly parted with one of the cornerstones of his 2003 success. Moreover, he had not appointed a successor. Suddenly, Federer looked a shade vulnerable again as 2004 approached.

9

DESPITE THE UNCERTAINTIES with which Federer went into 2004, this was the start of a four-year period in which he stood splendidly at the peak of the game of tennis, monopolising its major prizes like no one had done before him. Until Pete Sampras won Wimbledon in 2000, no male player had won more than twelve Grand Slam singles titles in a career. Yet between 2004 and 2007, Federer won eleven of the sixteen majors on offer, and of those he missed three were in Paris at the hands of the man now recognised as the greatest clay-courter of all time, and in one of the other two he had a match point in the semi-finals. Quite simply, in this period it was a shock when Federer lost a match.

Some argue that there was a lack of competition at the time, that the likes of Roddick, Ferrero, Safin, Hewitt and Ljubicic were such a class below Federer that his dominance speaks more for a lull in the strength of men's tennis than for Federer's brilliance. The alternative viewpoint is that, if Federer hadn't played at the same time as two other all-time greats (Nadal and Djokovic), he would have finished his career with around thirty major titles. That is subject matter for conversations at tennis club bars and café terraces. In terms of the log of Federer's career, 2004–7 were quite simply the golden years.

His first task in January 2004 was to capture the world number-one ranking, something he would achieve if he won the Australian Open, or even if he didn't win it and other results went his way. Because of what he went on to accomplish over the subsequent four years, it's easy to see the 2004 Australian Open as an easy win, yet his draw was far from straightforward. In fact, anyone with an urge to create an obstacle course designed to test whether or not he had dealt with his demons could hardly have done any better than create his run-in in Melbourne that year. Having never been beyond the fourth round in the first major of the year, his passage from there looked like being Hewitt, Nalbandian, Roddick and Agassi – three of his bogeymen plus the reigning world number one.

After the shockwaves of parting from Lundgren, the world wanted to know who was going to be in Federer's corner henceforth. Federer took full responsibility for the decision and said he was in no hurry to appoint a successor to Lundgren. 'Maybe it's good to be on my own for a bit,' he'd said before the 2004 Australian Open. 'I've been given good advice for most of my life, so maybe there's something good about looking after myself for a time.' Although no one could argue with that sentiment, nor the logic of not rushing into a new coaching arrangement, for the number-two player in the world to be without a coach was generally perceived as a weakness. At least it was at the start of the year – by the end, things looked a little different.

Having opted not to play a tournament before the Australian Open, he took the opportunity to acclimatise himself to conditions in Melbourne by playing at an exhibition event held the week before the Australian Open at the Kooyong Club, the tournament's former home. There he spoke to a number of journalists, granting almost every interview request. Then, on the Saturday before the Open, he did a little more media work at Melbourne Park, before telling the media liaison people he wanted Sunday off. The following day, the majority of the Swiss press showed up and were most put out to discover that their crown jewel was doing no media that day. When it was put to Federer that the Swiss press were not happy, Federer told the International Tennis Federation's on-duty player–media liaison officer that he would deal with it himself.

And he did. At the first available opportunity, he explained to the Swiss journalists that he felt that he'd done more than his fair share of media work, told them that he really did want a day off and asked them to respect that. Barbara Travers, at the time the ITF's head of communications, said, 'It's only the second time in the twenty-plus years I've worked with tennis players that a player has said, "Leave it to me." The other was Ivan Lendl. To me, it showed an unusual but refreshing sense of taking responsibility.'

The tournament began with Federer posting three straight-sets wins against modest opposition, but then the stakes were suddenly and theatrically raised. On 26 January, Australia's national day, he came up against Lleyton Hewitt for the first time – and on the same court – since he'd lost so dramatically to the Australian from being two sets and 5–3 up in the Davis Cup semi-final four months earlier. The two shouldn't really have met so early in a Grand Slam event, but Hewitt had deliberately stayed off the tour after the US Open until the end of the year, using the time to have a bunion removed and concentrating solely on the Davis Cup. His ranking had therefore slipped to fifteenth, and he landed in Federer's eighth of the draw. As the match started, Hewitt was quick off the blocks, winning the first set to suggest that he still had Federer's number. But then something changed.

A little luck is often needed at a crucial moment, and Federer got his luck in the sixth game when Hewitt was foot-faulted after serving an ace. It wasn't a major incident, but Hewitt was seldom called for foot-faults, and players who seldom infringe the foot-fault rule generally feel mightily aggrieved when it happens, especially when – as in this case – the serve in question would have been a winner. Had Hewitt been trailing in the match, it would probably have fuelled him with the necessary aggression to bounce back, but, with everything going swimmingly for the Australian, the baseline umpire's call threw him momentarily off balance, Federer seized his opportunity to break, and the match turned. And, as it turned out, the destiny of the tournament too.

From then on, Federer was unstoppable. As he closed in on victory, the night skies were lit up with the traditional Australia Day fireworks display over the Melbourne skyline, adding a theatrical audio-visual backdrop to the on-court tension. But it didn't distract the champion-in-waiting. He later admitted to being a little nervous when he served for victory, the memories of the Davis Cup semi-final coming back to pose a psychological question, and when Hewitt saved two match points there was a frisson around the Rod Laver Arena, the electrified crowds daring to hope that maybe their streetfighter was to stage another comeback. But Federer was not to be denied, and converted his third match point.

After dispatching the somewhat match-rusty Hewitt to win 4–6, 6–3, 6–0, 6–4, Federer had brushed aside one jinx player – only to be greeted by another in the next round. In the quarter-finals, he found himself up against Nalbandian.

Looking at the players who did most damage to Federer in the early part of his career (mainly Nalbandian, Hewitt, Henman, Agassi and Nadal), the one thing they all had in common was their use of the full width of the court. Federer tended to dominate when he was able to stay mostly within the width of the 36ft (10.97m) doubles court, but like all players he became somewhat less effective when driven wide by angled and heavily kicked shots. It was therefore crucial for him to assert control from the outset against such players. And against Nalbandian in that quarter-final he did so almost to perfection, surviving a lapse at the end of the third set to win 7–5, 6–4, 5–7, 6–3.

Joining Nalbandian among the quarter-final casualties was the world number one, Andy Roddick, who was beaten in five sets by the mercurial Marat Safin. Safin's win meant Roddick would lose the top spot after the tournament, and either Federer or Juan Carlos Ferrero would take it from him.

By a twist of fate, Ferrero and Federer were up against each other in the semi-finals. It wasn't quite a straight eliminator – had Ferrero won, he would have had to win the final to return to the top – but it felt like one. And there was no question who the better player was. If Federer had wobbled in sight of the number-one spot against Roddick in Toronto five months earlier, there was no wobble now. He was ready to rise to the pinnacle of his profession, and he did so with a crushing 6–4, 6–1, 6–4 victory (although in fairness, Ferrero was carrying an injury that restricted his movement). Irrespective of the outcome of the final, Federer would become the twenty-third man to top the world rankings since the computerised system was introduced in 1973.

Not that there was any doubt that he wanted to ascend to the throne as a newly crowned Grand Slam champion, and few gave his final opponent, Safin, much of a chance. He'd reached the final after four successive five-set wins over Todd Martin, James Blake, Andy Roddick and the defending champion, Andre Agassi, spending nearly twenty hours on court, and, although he said his body would recover in time for the final, it was clear that he had to get off to a good start to have any chance.

He didn't. The first set went to the tiebreak, Federer took it 7–3, and, after that, the strength drained from Safin's limbs. Just over an hour later, Federer had claimed his second major title, taking the final 7–6, 6–4, 6–2.

'It's really nice,' he said later of his success, with his typical brand of understatement. 'It just gets me all emotional inside. To win the Australian Open and become number one in the world is a dream come true.' Then, when asked if he felt himself to be the best player on the planet, he replied, 'I feel I'm maybe the most natural ball-striker.

I'm not going to start praising myself, but, for me, my game feels natural. I feel like I'm living the game when I'm out there. When a guy is going to hit the ball, I know exactly the angles and the spins. I just feel I've got that figured out.'

Now Federer had climbed to the top of the tree, his tournament schedule started to look a little out of alignment with the requirements of staying at the top. As world number one, each match is the opponent's cup final, and, while he couldn't have been expected to win every time, he had to reckon on playing in every round of every tournament he entered. The ranking system that made eight of the nine Masters tournaments obligatory (in the sense that failure to show up would have led to zero ranking points in one of the eighteen events that counted towards a player's ranking) meant much of his schedule was pre-programmed, so the challenge was to decide which were the highest priorities among the events outside the majors and Masters. And this is where his commitment to the Davis Cup started to make less sense.

At that time, the Davis Cup involved four weekends a year – effectively four weeks. This was a reduction from the six or seven that was the case in the 1970s; in 1981 a new format was introduced to reduce the demands on the players, but it was still a heavy burden for the top names. In addition, the International Tennis Federation had carried out a survey of players that found that most of them preferred Davis Cup weekends to be the week after a Grand Slam tournament. That makes sense for those who don't expect to get beyond the quarter-finals of a Slam, but for those who make the semis and final it can be a brutal turnaround, especially if they have to fly round the globe to play on a different surface. And that was the reality that faced Federer after winning the Australian Open.

As it was his first triumph in Melbourne, everyone wanted a piece of him. He did several hours of media interviews and photo-shoots, and then got up early to do another round of breakfast shows on the Monday morning. By the time he reached Melbourne's Tullamarine airport that afternoon, it was barely four days before he was due on court again on clay in Bucharest. He spent some of Tuesday being fêted at a civic reception in Basel that included an appearance on the balcony of the 'Roothuus', Basel's striking sixteenth-century Gothic city hall with its deep-red sandstone and gilded pagan figures, and then jetted off to Bucharest for Switzerland's first-round tie against Romania.

Sheer class overcame jetlag in the opening day's singles when he crushed Victor Hanescu, and another straight-sets win on the Sunday over Andrei Pavel saw Switzerland through to the quarter-finals. Sandwiched between was a personal milestone for the former flatmates, as Federer and Yves Allegro teamed up for the first time for their country, and won the crucial doubles 10–8 in the fifth set. Federer was all smiles but, while he never said this out loud, he was aware that it would make sense to avoid such a mad travel schedule in future.

Perhaps the biggest benefit from the win in Bucharest was that Federer had the chance of a proper celebration of his achievements on home soil. That came in April when Switzerland hosted France in the quarter-finals, and the reception Federer received in the Prilly suburb of Lausanne when he stepped out on court to open the tie against Nicolas

Escudé gave even the neutrals and French supporters goosebumps. The predominantly Swiss crowd – all clad in scarlet T-shirts, creating a striking visual tableau – were treating the match as their hero's festive homecoming following his ascent to the top of the rankings in Australia. An emotional character such as Federer could have been forgiven for taking a few games to get into his tennis after such a heartfelt welcome, but his start was anything but slow. He rode the tide of emotion to win the first four games, conceding just ten in total in a highly emphatic 6–2, 6–4, 6–4 victory.

Yet Switzerland's dependence on Federer was shown up in the second singles match. Ivo Heuberger made no impression on Arnaud Clément, falling to a 6–3, 6–2, 6–2 defeat. It was clear that Federer and Allegro needed to win the doubles if a home victory was a realistic possibility. Hence the delight of the French pair, Escudé and Michaël Llodra, when they won it in four sets.

Once again, Switzerland's fate was no longer solely in Federer's hands, and once again Michel Kratochvil had to play a live fifth rubber after Federer's 6–2, 7–5, 6–4 drubbing of Clément. Persistent knee problems had reduced Kratochvil's ranking to 194th, and against the sixty-eighth-ranked Escudé he lacked both confidence and nerve. Although Escudé too had been off the tour for the last six months of 2003 with a hip injury, the Frenchman had too much nous for Kratochvil, and even came back from being 3–6 down in the third-set tiebreak to beat Kratochvil 7–6, 6–3, 7–6. Once again, Switzerland's reliance on Federer was just a bit too great.

At the Swiss team's post-tie press conference, Kratochvil

got visibly irritated with one of Federer's off-the-cuff comments. Some of the things Federer said in interviews that day suggested the Davis Cup was losing its appeal. 'At least I now know where I stand in terms of tournament planning for the rest of the year,' he said with some relief. 'Last year I didn't know whether I'd be needed during the off season, but now I know I won't have to play Davis Cup for another ten months.'

As it transpired, he didn't play for Switzerland again for another seventeen months, and henceforth the Davis Cup weekends ceased to be one of the first entries in his schedule when he and his entourage began planning his itinerary.

Any defeat for a world number one is going to be news-worthy, and especially when it's against a seventeen-year-old being touted as a big name of the future. On 28 March 2004, Federer walked on court for his third-round match of the Masters event in Miami nursing something of a cold, which made the task of facing someone he had never played before additionally challenging. In retrospect, the cold seems immaterial. The seventeen-year-old challenger went about his business without fear and in a way that made everyone sit up and take note. He won the match 6–3, 6–3, inflicting only the second defeat of the year on Federer. While no one knew it at the time, this kid was the real deal. His name was Rafael Nadal.

A worrying stress fracture in his foot meant Nadal couldn't make his debut at Roland Garros, where Federer was seeking his third Grand Slam title. The latter travelled to Paris having again won one of the clay-court Masters tournaments in the build-up, taking Hamburg for the second time in three years. Wins over Kristof Vliegen and Nicolas Kiefer took him into the third round of the French Open, where he faced the three-times former champion Gustavo Kuerten in an appetising clash.

The Brazilian, known affectionately as 'Guga', had been Paris's darling since his first shock title in 1997 when he took the tennis world by storm by winning with a ranking of 66. The combination of a winning smile and years of caring for a severely disabled brother had given the down-to-earth Kuerten a likeability rating as high as most celebrities enjoy, whatever their discipline. In 2001, his relationship with the Paris public intensified when, after winning his third title there, he chalked into the clay a heart, in the centre of which he lay flat on his back. The Roland Garros crowd, so hard to please if a player once crosses them, just adored him, and he loved them back. By 2004, however, a troubled recovery from a complicated hip operation in 2002 had taken its toll on the affable beach boy, and it was widely assumed that time and Federer would have caught up with him. By and large, that was the case, but, as with many greats who know their best is behind them, they can still summon themselves for the odd great match, even if they're no longer capable of winning a great tournament. That's what Kuerten did in the feature match of the first Saturday.

Playing some of the tennis that saw him top the rankings for forty weeks in 2000–1, Kuerten took Federer apart, winning 6–4, 6–4, 6–4. He took Federer's first two service games, broke early in the second and third sets and, apart from one dropped service game at the beginning, he was never broken. 'It's like a love affair between me and the crowd,' he said afterwards. 'If it wasn't for this tournament, I wouldn't be here. I'm just happy I can play here, given the way my physical condition has been. Any other tournament and I'd have pulled out.'

No doubt Federer wished he had. He clearly still had something to learn about dealing with true clay-court specialists. 'I tried but he didn't give me much of a chance,' he said afterwards. 'Usually I can control these kinds of matches, but today that wasn't the case. Guga deserved to win. Now I'm just looking forward to getting out on the grass.'

That third-round defeat has since acquired an element of Federer folklore, because it proved to be the last time he lost before the semi-finals of a Grand Slam until Robin Söderling beat him in the quarter-finals of the 2010 French Open. It also remained his earliest defeat at a Slam until Sergiy Stakhovsky beat him in the second round of Wimbledon in 2013. After losing to Kuerten in 2004, Federer went on to reach the semis or better in twenty-three successive majors, failing to reach the final on only three of those occasions. Given that the next-best run of consecutive Grand Slam semi-final appearances was at that point Ivan Lendl's ten, no one could have suspected the streak that was about to begin following that Parisian Saturday afternoon in 2004.

Federer's second Wimbledon triumph has ended up as one of his less memorable major wins, but it drove another stake through the confidence of his rivals.

He again warmed up by playing in Halle, defending his Gerry Weber Open title without dropping a set and cutting the entertainment in the final to less than an hour in a clinical demolition of Mardy Fish. Then at Wimbledon, he again dropped just one set en route to the final, where he faced Roddick.

With a number of Wimbledon's spectators being very much occasional tennis fans (there are still a few Britons who wonder what the players do during the forty-eight weeks of the year when the tennis circuit isn't in England), the final between Federer and Roddick was billed as a great rematch from the previous year's semi-final. It was in fact their seventh match, and Federer had won five of the previous six, but Roddick seemed focused and determined to make the most of his one advantage over the Swiss: his sheer power. While he'd lost his number-one ranking in Australia, Roddick was still the world number two and saw himself as the principal threat to the reigning champion. And with the fastest serve in tennis, Wimbledon was the place to make it pay.

On a showery day, Roddick came out fastest. He looked the better player before rain held up play after just five games. Rain breaks can turn matches, often because they allow players to consult their coaches in the locker room, but Federer had no coach, at least no one formally in that role. When the players came back on court, he looked subdued, and Roddick stormed to the first set.

Roddick couldn't hold his level, though, and Federer raced to a 4–0 lead in the second set without ever looking totally convincing. He'd created such a dominating reputation for himself that the set was as good as gone, but his curious display continued as Roddick got both breaks back and levelled at 4–4. Then, with Roddick serving at 5–6, Federer profited from a lucky net cord that gave him set point and, when he then hit a running forehand down Roddick's backhand wing to level the match, he screamed and punched the air with real emotion. The real Federer, it seemed, was back.

Or was he? In the third game of the third set, it was the passive Federer who dropped his serve, and at 2–4 he was in serious trouble. Then it rained again. Roddick walked off to talk to his coach, Brad Gilbert, while Federer went off to talk to... well, himself. During that period of introspection, he worked out that he had to be a little more pro-active to counter Roddick's aggression. And, when he came back out on court, it was a different match.

When Federer took the third-set tiebreak 7–3, Roddick could have folded, but the combination of his conviction that his power would win out and Federer's inconsistent display gave the American good reason to hope. Early in the fourth set he created six break points but converted none of them. That failure proved costly, for at 3–3 Federer broke, and the game was up for the American, Federer running out a 4–6, 7–5, 7–6, 6–4 winner.

The Reuters news agency tennis writer, Ossian Shine, used a nice analogy in his report of the match. 'Certainly,' he wrote, 'there was a moral in there somewhere, one of which Aesop would have been proud, regarding the Swiss's steady, deliberate progress overcoming Roddick's whizzbang fireworks and general uproar.'

'I got lucky, for sure,' was Federer's more modest verdict. 'I was down a break in the third set, and if Andy had served a few better games it would have been two sets.'

After the match, Sue Barker came on court to conduct brief interviews with the two players. Roddick must have felt sick about having let Federer get away, but he still managed to muster enough wit to charm the British public. 'I threw the kitchen sink at him,' he said, 'but he went to the bathroom and got the tub.'

Yet it was another bit of Roddick wit that told the truer story. Barker asked Roddick about the 'great rivalry' he had with Federer, to which Roddick replied, 'I'm going to have to start winning some of these matches if we're to call it a rivalry.' The crowd loved Roddick's humility, but his response had summed up what Federer's third Grand Slam title meant to the tennis world in general: while he had challengers, he certainly had no rivals based on equality of expectation, except perhaps on clay.

In the eyes of many tennis watchers, what Federer achieved over the four weeks after Wimbledon in 2004 enhances his claim to greatness. Not since Björn Borg in 1979 had a player won three successive tournaments on clay, grass and hard courts, but Federer did just that.

Arriving in Gstaad the day after Wimbledon, Federer made the often difficult transition from grass to clay in a matter of hours and, six days later, Gstaad had its home-grown champion. Although the list of people Federer beat that week hardly reads like a who's who of clay-court tennis, it was still a momentous achievement when he beat Igor Andreev in a four-set final to finally win a title on Swiss soil. Although he didn't say so at the time, he'd come to the conclusion that Gstaad's position in the tennis calendar was too impractical for him, and in early 2005 he announced it would no longer have a place in his annual tournament schedule.

A short holiday followed, before he took to the court again on the concrete of Toronto. Again, Roddick awaited him in the final, and again Roddick's weapons weren't accurate enough to stop the Swiss clock. It was Federer's nineteenth tour title and his fourth Masters Series shield – and he wasn't even twenty-three.

Wimbledon, Gstaad and Toronto, and a twenty-three-match winning streak. Not even Novak Djokovic has emulated the feat of three successive tournaments on three different surfaces, although Nadal won successive titles on clay, grass, grass and hard in 2008, which one could say is as good as or even a greater achievement (Ivan Lendl twice won successive tournaments on clay, hard and indoor carpet, but the difference between carpet and hard was small enough not to require different footwork, so the absence of grass is significant). But all the matches meant Federer was starting to run on empty, and a first-round defeat to Dominik Hrbaty in Cincinnati was probably the best thing for him, as it allowed him a bit of much-needed time off.

During those days off, the Federer look began to change. At first, the changes were subtle, and the complete new look wasn't unveiled until the Tennis Masters Cup in November, but after Cincinnati he had a haircut that looked as if it hadn't quite worked, for when he turned up at the Olympics in Athens his hair was held in place not just by the usual bandanna and ponytail but by a set of hairpins, too. When he was on court, his hair didn't look that different, but when he appeared without the bandanna the layering effect was somewhat unusual.

The Athens Olympics gave him the chance of an honour he was to appreciate to the full. Having put Switzerland not just on the tennis map but the general sporting map too, he was asked to carry the Swiss flag in the opening ceremony. But his bigger goal – in fact his main goal of 2004, he said – was to win an Olympic gold medal, either in singles or doubles.

His first match in Athens, a stuttering 6–3, 5–7, 6–1 win over Russia's Nikolay Davydenko, serves to emphasise that the volatile Federer hadn't disappeared; he'd merely hidden it from view, and occasionally a safety valve had to be released. Federer served for the match in the second set, but when he played a poor game and was broken he belted a loose ball on to the roof of the centre court and earned a code violation from the umpire. 'It's a long time since I got my last warning,' he said after the match. 'For me, it was a sign. I just needed to show a reaction because I was unhappy with the way I played in the second set. I got frustrated. But the important thing is that I won, not how I acted on court.' The hidden meaning behind that assessment can be found in his analysis of the outburst in Hamburg in 2001, when he felt that by learning to control his temper he risked becoming too passive. In other words: while he'd learned to keep his composure on court, even the cool, calm and collected Roger Federer needed to vent his spleen on occasion.

He also admitted he'd have to play a lot better in his next match, against a player he had never faced before, a tall eighteen-year-old Czech, Tomas Berdych. With his mop of tied-back ginger hair, Berdych had become known on the circuit as a promising prospect but was still ranked only seventy-fourth coming into the Olympics. On a windy day, on an outside court, he was to make his introductory statement to the tennis world. Why the world number one and gold medal favourite was on an outside court is perhaps another question (then again, why shouldn't the very best also play on the lesser courts as long as their safety isn't compromised?), but it clearly added to the effect of the swirling wind. And when, after the match, Andy Roddick walked into the locker room, having saved three match points in a thriller against Tommy Haas, saw Federer and threw him the casual question, 'How'd you get on?', he was astonished to hear Federer reply, 'I lost.'

Against Berdych, Federer looked sluggish, even in taking the first set, but a single break and adequate serving proved to be enough. Then, from 3–4 in the second set, Berdych took control. With the wind acting as a leveller and Berdych doing some tremendous retrieving, Federer began to lose confidence in his serve in the final set. It just about saw him through to 5–5, but he had had to save two match points at 4–5. Then, at 5–6, he hit a double fault and made three unforced errors to give Berdych the breakthrough win of his career, 4–6, 7–5, 7–5.

'It's hard to play these big players on centre court because they have more practice there,' said Berdych in the post-match press conference. 'It's easier on the outside courts, where they haven't been practising or playing.'

Federer didn't do his own press conference until much later. Immediately after his defeat, he sat motionless for several minutes in the locker room, not knowing how to take it in. And by the time he faced the media, he was even more demoralised, for by then he and Yves Allegro had lost 6–2, 7–6 in the doubles to the Indian pair of Mahesh Bhupathi and Leander Paes. 'It's a terrible day for me, losing singles and doubles,' he said. 'I've been playing non-stop, you know, and it's obvious it's going to catch up with me eventually. Unfortunately, it's during the Olympics.'

Hindsight is a wonderful thing, but, if Federer had known that day that it would be more than five months before his next defeat, he would probably have felt a lot better.

The US Open is more than just a tennis tournament. It reflects the city of New York, with all its brashness. As a tournament, it's a little less brash today than it was between 1978 and 1996, when the main stadium was a hurriedly rehashed version of an open-air concert venue used by the jazz musician Louis Armstrong during the World's Fair of 1964–5, but it still takes a certain mentality to get used to the environment, especially for non-Americans. In the late 1980s, when playing on the outside courts meant inhaling the aroma of barbecued spare ribs from the chaotic food court, the Swedish champion Stefan Edberg got so fazed by the atmosphere that he threatened never to return there, until his coach, Tony Pickard, suggested that he stay in a family house on Long Island to give him a little peace. (It did the trick; Edberg won the US Open twice and played his best match there in the 1991 final.) Even Jim Courier, an American who made it to number one in the rankings, suggested the site at Flushing Meadows should be 'nuked'.

Although he always professed to enjoy his trips to New York, Federer does not have the natural personality to thrive in New York conditions. And having failed to make any in-roads against Nalbandian in the 2004 US Open, there was a question mark hanging over his capacity to win the top American tournament, certainly at the age of just twenty-three. But it was in New York that he was to make one of the most emphatic statements of his career.

He didn't look totally comfortable in his second-round match against the smiling Cypriot Marcos Baghdatis, nor in his third-round outing against the wily Frenchman Fabrice Santoro, but he raised his game when he needed to and qualified for the second week. A walkover against the injured Andrei Pavel meant Federer could conserve a little energy for his quarter-final, in which he had to go to five sets to beat Andre Agassi in a match played in quite ridiculous wind. With much calmer conditions for his semi-final, he showed that he'd worked out how to play Tim Henman, beating the Brit for the loss of eleven games. Those eleven games looked a massive achievement for Henman in the light of Federer's superb display in the final.

On 12 September 2004, Federer stepped out to face another old nemesis, Lleyton Hewitt. At that time, the Australian was the man of the moment, and in some people's eyes was the favourite for the Open title, having won it three years earlier. More pertinently, he'd won four titles on the 2004 North American summer hard-court swing and was clearly the form player coming into both the tournament and the final. Yet Hewitt was humbled by one of the most impressive displays of sporting prowess of modern times. Only once did Federer wobble, towards the end of the second set, when Hewitt had a couple of chances, but, once the Swiss had taken the tiebreak 7–3, he was irresistible, storming to a 6–0, 7–6, 6–0 victory. The US Open – or US nationals, as it was called before 1968 – dates back to 1881, yet you had to go back to 1884 to find the last time there had been two 'bagels' (6–0 sets) in a final.

After taking out his hairpins prior to the trophy-presentation ceremony, Federer did an on-court interview with the veteran CBS sports broadcaster Dick Enberg, who had just commentated on the final. Enberg tried to do justice to Federer's performance by asking him, 'Roger, I don't know where to start. We're up in the television booth, raving about your forehand, then it's your backhand, and then all of a sudden you go to the net and you made all but four of thirty-two points at the net. What else do we have to look forward to in the future?'

To which Federer replied, 'That's all I've got!'

Federer held three of the four Grand Slam titles, which had allowed him to erase the Olympic disappointment. The world was on his racket strings, and he picked up another title in Bangkok. As he returned to Switzerland, surely this was the year for him finally to win his home-town title. But a pulled thigh muscle meant he couldn't even play his first-round match, and the Swiss Indoors slipped away for another year.

Missing Basel and Paris meant there was a question mark over his form as he went back to Houston for the 2004 Tennis Masters Cup, sporting the post-ponytail look for the first time. His fans needn't have worried. He eased through his round-robin group with wins over Gaston Gaudio, Lleyton Hewitt and Carlos Moya – this was the tournament where there are supposed to be no easy matches because only the year's top eight players compete, yet Federer was making mincemeat of them. 'I respect everybody but fear nobody' was his neat soundbite, but his passage to the semi-finals looked effortless.

But then came one of those moments of theatre that make all the run-of-the-mill 6–1, 6–2 early-round scorelines worth tolerating. Federer's match against Marat Safin was always going to have a poignancy about it, because since May Safin had been working with Federer's former coach, Peter Lundgren. Here were the two players facing each other for the first time since Safin began working with Lundgren, and at the tournament that, a year earlier, had been the last in the Federer–Lundgren partnership.

There was just one break of serve in the whole match, and that allowed Federer to take the first set. But the key statistic was the tiebreak score with which he took the second set in his 6–3, 7–6 win: 20–18. The tiebreak lasted twenty-six minutes. Safin saved seven match points, Federer saved six set points – and the tennis was outstanding, pure drama. And when Federer converted his eighth match point to move through to the final, the two men had equalled the record for the longest ever tiebreak (measured in points) set by Goran Ivanisevic and Daniel Nestor at the US Open eleven years earlier.

After such a match, Federer might have been mentally exhausted, but he did an hour-and-a-half's media work, accepting every interview request handed in. Admirable though that was, such generosity of time and spirit created a rod for his own back and could never be sustained in the long run with the on-court success rate he was to have over the next three years. As he began to cut down on his media time, reporters and broadcasters felt unfairly rebuffed when he refused them an interview they had previously become accustomed to expect, but even they had to accept that his time was not limitless. Quite rightly, he saw his dealings with the media as part of his duty to the sport that had nourished his bank account so well, but, as he subsequently learned, even the generous Roger Federer has to say no on occasion.

After such drama, the final couldn't hope to live up to the same standards – and it didn't. This was through no fault of Federer and Hewitt, who were facing each other for the sixth time that year and the third time in nine weeks. Heavy rain reduced the match to a best-of-three-sets contest (and ensured that the event will never be awarded to an outdoor venue again), and the rain meant it was played late at night, by which time many television stations had cancelled their coverage. Although Hewitt battled bravely, the match served only to show what the previous two had done: that, when Federer was on his game, Hewitt no longer had a chance against him.

So ended a year in which Federer had become the first man since Mats Wilander sixteen years earlier to win three of the four major titles in the same year (although, in fairness, Pete Sampras held three of the four titles for much of 1994 but had won them across two calendar years). He'd won seventy-four of the eighty matches he'd contested, a ratio not seen since Ivan Lendl's most consistent year of 1986. He was clearly the tennis player of the year, but he was more than that. The World Sports Academy awarded him its Laureus Award as the 2004 world sportsman of the year, arguably the most prestigious honour in world sport, despite a rather notable bias towards tennis.

And all without a coach.

10

WHEN MATS WILANDER won three of the four major titles in 1988, the effort just about killed him. His victory over Ivan Lendl in the US Open final, in what was a direct eliminator for the world number-one ranking, allowed him to achieve what he had struggled all his life for. He freely admits that, after his *annus mirabilis*, motivation became hard to find, and his ensuing downward slide proved to be swift.

Although the same age at the end of 2004 (twenty-three), Federer was not at the same point in his career as Wilander had been when he ended 1988. The US Open title that saw Wilander to the top of the rankings was his seventh Grand Slam in a haul spanning six years, starting with his breakthrough French Open at just seventeen. No one seriously expected Federer to have peaked after 2004 the way Wilander had done after 1988. And yet few could have expected him to have had as lustrous a year in 2005.

It would have been no disgrace for Federer to have had a quieter year than 2004 – but if anything, he scaled even greater heights in 2005, certainly in terms of consistency.

He set out his stall before hitting his first ball of the new year by hiring the former Australian great Tony Roche as his part-time coach. Born in Wagga-Wagga, the wily, self-effacing but somewhat inscrutable Roche, a former French Open champion and thirteen-times Grand Slam doubles winner, made his name as a coach in the 1980s with Ivan Lendl. He'd taken on the task after Lendl had had a succession of coaches who'd led him to Grand Slam success just once, despite his immense potential. Had Federer signed up Roche in the second half of 2003, the circumstances would have been similar to those in which Roche began working with Lendl. In the 1990s, the Australian had worked as a casual coach to Patrick Rafter, escorting him to two US Open titles and a week at the top of the rankings. And he was also Australia's Davis Cup coach, under the captaincy of his former doubles partner John Newcombe, which allowed him to play a leading role in the development of the young Lleyton Hewitt.

Federer had first approached Roche in February 2004. The Australian – then fifty-eight and increasingly reluctant to travel both for personal reasons and because of a hip problem – turned him down, but did travel with Federer on two occasions. In mid-December 2004, Federer flew to Sydney, ostensibly to acclimatise for the Australian Open, but, as he was playing the Qatar Open in the first week of January, the trip had a different justification. He went to Roche's home to discuss the Australian becoming his coach. Roche again said he didn't want to do much travelling, so Federer worked out a part-time deal that would commit the Aussie to just ten weeks' travelling per year.

On 5 January, after beating David Ferrer in the first round in Doha, Qatar, Federer told the media of his new signing. 'It's good to know that there is help there, because I need someone to analyse and help improve my game.'

When the news was reported in Australia, the former doubles champion turned television pundit and politician John Alexander said, 'It's a great shame for Australian tennis.' Alexander's comment reflected not only the esteem in which Roche was held down under, but also the fact that one of Australia's top coaches was working not with Australia's top player Hewitt, but with Hewitt's principal rival. Roche did eventually work as Hewitt's personal coach but not until 2008, by which time Hewitt was a spent force, certainly at the very top of the game.

Despite the impressiveness of Federer's total of twenty Grand Slam singles titles, there were enough near-misses for that total to look shorter than what it could – perhaps should – have been. There are at least three contenders for majors Federer ought to have won but didn't – Wimbledon in 2019 when he had two match points in the final is an obvious one, as is the 2009 US Open when he came within two points of winning the title. And the 2005 Australian Open is arguably another that was just waiting for Federer to walk off with the trophy, only for it to slip out of his grasp in a moment of remarkable drama.

Federer arrived in Melbourne fresh from winning the title in Doha, and teamed up with Roche for the first time since their new working relationship had been announced.

There, playing what seemed effortless tennis, Federer breezed through to the quarter-finals for an eagerly awaited clash with Andre Agassi.

Although the American was fast approaching his thirty-fifth birthday, Agassi was still a factor in Australia, having won the title on four previous occasions, most recently in 2003, and had only lost in 2004 in a five-set semi-final to Marat Safin. If there was anywhere Agassi still had a chance against Federer, it seemed to be on the high-bouncing Rebound Ace courts of Melbourne. The theory might well have been valid, but on a balmy late summer's evening Federer won before the last of the daylight had disappeared, notching up a 6–3, 6–4, 6–4 victory over the popular American in what proved to be Agassi's last-ever match in the Rod Laver Arena.

But he picked up an injury in the course of the win. He said nothing about it afterwards, but it was to hamper him in his eagerly awaited semi-final against Safin, their first match since the epic 20–18 tiebreak in Houston two months earlier.

The 2005 Australian Open was the tournament's centenary event, made up of its six decades of being staged as an amateur event prior to 1969 and four as an 'open' tournament. And going into the final four days it had already been blessed with four matches of the kind of quality and drama that most tournaments would normally be glad to have one of – Hewitt–Nadal, Molik–Davenport, Hewitt–Nalbandian and Serena Williams–Sharapova – so drama was in the air when Federer and Safin entered the arena on the Russian's twenty-fifth birthday. The first of the men's semi-finals was a mouth-watering prospect, and the reality lived up to the promise.

When tennis watchers are asked for a list of their all-time most memorable matches, their responses are obviously many and varied. A truly great match normally has an off-court element alongside the actual tennis, like Jimmy Connors suing the ATP's president Arthur Ashe at the time the two met in the Wimbledon final of 1975, or Pete Sampras learning that his coach Tim Gullikson had an inoperable brain tumour just before his five-sets quarter-final against Jim Courier at the 1995 Australian Open (a match in which Sampras played – and won – the final set with tears streaming down his face). If an out-of-tennis element is a criterion for greatness, then the Federer–Safin semi-final of 2005 falls slightly short of the all-time great category, but it was nevertheless the most enthralling and entertaining match of the 2005 tennis year.

What had most people on the edge of their seats was the fact that Federer was clearly unsettled in the early stages of the match. Although hardly as volatile as he had been in his junior days, he was growling about the court as Safin matched him shot for shot. He won the first set, but then Safin came back to level. Federer won the third set 7–5 – the same score with which he'd won the first – and when the fourth set came to a tiebreak he looked set to edge through to what would have been the first leg of a dream final for the organisers. For waiting in the wings was Lleyton Hewitt, who was all set to become the first Aussie finalist at the Australian Open in seventeen years if he beat Andy Roddick in the semi-final the next day – which he did. In the centenary Australian Open, marketed under the banner '100 years in the making', the semi-final line-up offered the prospect of a home player contesting the final against the defending champion and world number one.

Back in the fourth-set tiebreak of the Federer–Safin match, neither player ever had a significant lead, but then Federer got to match point at 6–5. He served and volleyed on his second serve, Safin tried to pass him on his backhand side and Federer stretched for an exquisite backhand volley that just cleared the net. Surely that was good enough to win the point? But no. Safin raced forward and got the ball back. Federer played a second volley at Safin. Safin played the only shot he could: a lob. Federer chased it back. He seemed to have the option of playing a high defensive lob or an audacious attempted pass – either would have made sense. Instead, the controlled, disciplined Federer – the man who'd supposedly put his junior tricks behind him – had a rush of blood and attempted a 'tweener', the flamboyant but highly risky shot through the legs with the player's back to the net. He netted it, and Safin levelled the tiebreak at 6–6. It was to prove Federer's only match point.

When asked after the match what he'd thought he was doing playing a shot like that, he seemed slightly nonplussed by the question. 'Well, the point was already lost, so I tried it,' he said. Maybe he believed it at the time, but more likely he felt very silly about choosing such an ambitious shot at such a crucial stage of the match and just wanted to keep the attention away from it. There are plenty of tennis watchers who love to see Federer attempt a tweener and a few other showy shots, but they expect it in the early part of an early set, not at match point in the fourth-set tiebreak of a Grand Slam semi-final!

Being Federer, he might still have won the match, but

from that point on the momentum changed. Safin won the next two points to take the match into a fifth set, at which point Federer called for the physio. The trapped nerve he'd sustained during his match against Agassi was sending pain right down his playing arm. The match, it seemed, was now Safin's, and several years later he said he was convinced the match was his after that missed Federer 'tweener'.

It seemed even more Safin's when the Russian opened up a 5–2 lead in the fifth set. Federer was obviously in pain but hanging in there. He saved a handful of match points, broke back in the ninth game and hauled the set level at 5–5. Then, at 6–6, with Safin serving, Federer led 0–30, but the Russian snuffed out the danger.

Because he was serving second, Federer was always under more pressure than his opponent, and, at 7–8, it told. Safin worked his way to match point – his seventh in total. Federer couldn't gain an advantage with his serve, Safin hit a big backhand and Federer lunged for the ball, got it back but dropped his racket in the process. The court was then open for Safin, who might have been put off by Federer's loose racket, but he wasn't – his volley crashed into an unguarded court with Federer stranded. Thus, the Russian claimed the second-greatest victory of his career after his win over Pete Sampras in the 2000 US Open final.

The match had lasted four hours and twenty-eight minutes and was another triumph for the Australian Open in its centenary year. It was also a considerable triumph for Peter Lundgren, who had coached his charge to a win over the man he'd helped to make pretty much unbeatable in the first place. Little wonder the Swede was mildly tearful at the end.

Whatever injury he was carrying, the fact that Federer was able to play four and a half hours suggests that, had he converted his match point in the fourth set, he would have dealt easily with Hewitt and defended his title. Hewitt had ridden the wave of Australian emotion to get him to the final, but he was fighting the tide of the top players starting to leave him behind, and Safin didn't need to be at his best to run out a four-sets winner. Federer's twenty-seven-match winning streak dating back to his defeat to Berdych at the Olympics had been broken, leaving a sense that this was one title that had got away.

Having engraved his name on the Grand Slam roll of honour, added three more major titles, and cemented his place at the top of the world rankings, Federer augmented his growing reputation as a global statesman in 2005. It began with giving $20,000 to relief efforts following the Indian Ocean tsunami on 26 December 2004. One could argue that $20,000 is small change to someone of Federer's earning power, but the fact is that, while other players donated rackets and souvenirs for auctions to raise money for tsunami victims, Federer dipped straight into his pocket. Having been in Sydney discussing terms with Tony Roche when the tidal wave struck, he flew over many of the worst-hit areas on his way to Qatar for the Doha Open. He was apparently very affected by the carnage. The Swiss tennis journalist René Stauffer quotes a conversation he (Stauffer) had with Federer's partner, Mirka Vavrinec, at the time, in which she said, 'The whole thing has consumed him [Federer] like hardly anything else before.'

Federer went on to organise several initiatives to raise

funds for the appeals co-ordinated by the United Nations children's fund, Unicef. The most high-profile was a tennis exhibition featuring a galaxy of top names, both men and women, which took place in California in March 2005. That event also saw the launch of a programme between the ATP and Unicef called 'Ace' ('Assisting children everywhere'), aimed at using tennis to help the world's children; it featured a teddy bear called the 'Feder-Bear' modelled on Federer, which sold for $8, of which $5 were profits (it's doubtful Federer ever imagined having a lookalike teddy bear as a trapping of fame when, as a boy, he dreamed of winning Wimbledon).

In April 2006, Unicef formalised the relationship by appointing Federer a Unicef Goodwill Ambassador. It prompted one journalist to ask him jocularly, 'What's the proper way to address you now – is it Mr Ambassador, Your Honour, or what?', to which Federer replied, 'You decide, and you can also call me Roger, it's OK!' In December 2006 he visited Tamil Nadu, the Indian state hardest hit by the tsunami, to see the results of rebuilding work and to help earn those efforts some international exposure. The trip included meeting children whose school facilities were being rebuilt to a higher standard than had existed before the disaster; he chatted with orphans and psychological support staff, and met teenagers being educated about HIV and AIDS.

In March 2005, he used his time that would otherwise have been spent playing Davis Cup to travel to South Africa to visit the Roger Federer Foundation-funded Imbewu project. He also used the visit to discuss developing an investment he had made the previous year in a plot of land on the Pezula private golf estate near Knysna, a resort in the Cape just north of South Africa's much-promoted Garden Route. Having spent several holidays in South Africa in his youth, and having a South African passport by dint of his mother's nationality, there was much speculation about whether he would set up a base there, but he never did develop his Pezula plot, and ended up selling it in 2010.

In July 2005 he also made a decision that seemed at the time an admission of failure, but it was somewhat more nuanced than that. Having sent the International Management Group (IMG) packing two years earlier in order to run his own business and marketing affairs, he re-signed with IMG. The word at the time was that IMG would look after his international commercial interests, while Roger Federer Management would look after the Swiss side of things. In fact, IMG took on the whole lot, leaving Roger Federer Management effectively running just the Roger Federer Foundation.

So, had the Roger Federer Management model failed? Up to a point yes, because if he wanted to exploit his full economic potential, he couldn't rely on a management model that was heavily dependent on two retired people (his parents) and a lawyer who had other clients. But he learned some valuable lessons from his 2003 declaration of independence, and the return to IMG actually ended up sowing the seeds for his second breakaway, in 2013, when he set up his own management agency, Team8.

A little context is necessary here. It was widely reported in Switzerland at the time that Federer's earnings were lagging behind other global sporting names, such as his fellow tennis stars Andre Agassi and Maria Sharapova. To some, that wouldn't matter; to others, it would represent underexploited potential – it all depends on how much value one attaches to judging someone by their monetary worth.

The fact is that, even in a league behind the likes of Agassi and Sharapova, Federer was still earning the kind of money well beyond what most people can imagine ever earning. As such, the decision to look to maximise his international value meant he was effectively entering a new table of comparison based solely on marketable value. To that extent, he was arguably no different from the bankers and senior corporate executives who insist on certain salaries, not because they need the money, but because their earning potential is the marker of their professional esteem. Should one condemn him for that? Probably not. The point is only worth making given that the widely held perception of Roger Federer is that he is a down-to-earth guy who understands the human values that money cannot buy; this may be an accurate perception, but it seems clear that the lure of mammon had attracted Federer at this stage of his career, even if he remained largely immune to the ostentatious displays of what money can buy.

But why IMG? There were the two other major player management companies at that time (Octagon and SFx), plus numerous smaller ones, and they certainly courted him. But he went back to the firm he had jettisoned in 2005 and entered a deal in which IMG would be responsible for marketing him. On a personal level, he was assigned the IMG agent Tony Godsick, the husband of the former Australian and French Open finalist Mary-Joe Fernandez, whose other clients included another popular and eloquent world number one, Lindsay Davenport. He clearly developed a very good relationship with Godsick, to the point where they both left IMG together in 2012 and set up their own agency in 2013 (see page 349). But in 2005 Federer threw in his lot with IMG, a somewhat risky move in a global economy showing signs of the jitters. Subsequent developments showed IMG as being more resilient in the global economic downturn of 2008–9 than some of its rivals. But the suspicion abounds that Federer was tempted by a very lucrative offer, probably in person from IMG's then-new chairman, the financier Teddy Forstmann, whose company Forstmann-Little had bought IMG in 2004. Forstmann, a keen golfer with no lack of appreciation for his own ability to spot talent, conducted the personal negotiations with Federer that led to the player returning to IMG.

It would be wrong to read too much into the moanings of those who had had massive access to the young Roger who then had to make do with crumbs from the master's table when Federer hit the heights. But it is interesting to hear the comments of Beat Caspar, the former sports editor of the *Basler Zeitung*, who observed, 'In 2002, Lynette made it clear that the *BaZ* had helped Roger in his rise to prominence, that Roger would never forget that, and whenever we wanted an interview we could have one. Not only did that assurance disappear after 2003, but it gradually became clear that his media time was to be spent on publications and television programmes that linked up with his marketing goals. He was still interested in Basel, but in commercial terms he wanted world exposure, and we couldn't give him that.'

Federer's gradual divorce – or at least amicable separation

– from Basel was to culminate in him slipping away to live in a more tax-friendly Swiss canton in the spring of 2008.

Despite all this off-court activity, his tennis remained on a very high level. He won the hard-court tournaments in Rotterdam, Dubai, Indian Wells and Miami, and in two of those finals he was taken to deciding sets by Ivan Ljubicic, the cerebral Croat who had emerged as a refugee from the bloodshed of the Yugoslav civil wars and was in the best form of his life. Though a much more naturally gifted player than Ljubicic, Federer was clearly impressed by the Croat's ability to think his way through matches, and ten years later was to make the smart move of appointing Ljubicic to his coaching staff.

On his visit to Dubai, he found himself playing Andre Agassi in the most bizarre and spectacular setting for a tennis 'match'. Dubai is home to the world's only seven-star hotel, the Burj al-Arab. Built on a man-made island in the Gulf of Arabia just off the main settlement of Dubai, the hotel was designed to resemble a graceful sailing boat from a distance. Near the top, at 211m (692ft) above sea level, it boasts its own helipad, a plate-like addition to the structure measuring 415sq/m (1361sq/ft) – almost big enough for a tennis court.

Almost? Why let a few missing metres stop the fun? On this plate, someone had the idea of laying a temporary tennis court and inviting Roger Federer and Andre Agassi to play on it.

And so, on 22 February 2005, Federer and Agassi played a gentle set on the makeshift court. It was a little shorter than a regular tennis court, but the length of the court wasn't of primary concern. It was billed by many in the media as the highest tennis court in the world, which isn't entirely true; Alpine resorts that host tournaments, such as Gstaad and Kitzbühel, are considerably higher above sea level than 211m, but, with no ground immediately beneath the helipad, it would have felt high enough.

'When I was asked to do this [play tennis on the helipad], I didn't know what to expect,' Federer said. 'The view is absolutely amazing. I've been in Dubai many times and have stayed at the Burj al-Arab before, but this was an absolute treat. To play tennis with Andre on top of such an amazing hotel and overlooking the whole of Dubai was absolutely spectacular.'

The two players were so taken by the experience that they wanted to continue playing, but the hotel had to chase them off because a guest was about to arrive via helicopter and the 'court' had to be cleared.

Despite missing Switzerland's Davis Cup tie against the Netherlands, Federer still had the awareness to put in a quick 'good luck' phone call to the man replacing him in the Swiss team, who, in a nice twist, was his childhood friend Marco Chiudinelli. After expecting to play tennis just for fun and go to university, Chiudinelli had suddenly found himself with a spurt in form in his mid-teens, which prompted him to put his study plans on hold and try to make it as a tennis professional; several years later, here was his Davis Cup call-up. 'Roger phoned me a few days before the tie,' the eloquent Chiudinelli recalls, 'but we didn't speak much, only for about three minutes. He didn't want to give much input as we had coaches in the team and the captain, but he sent me a message from South Africa on the day of the tie.' The Swiss very nearly pulled off a remarkable win, Chiudinelli and Stan Wawrinka both taking the top Dutch player Sjeng Schalken to five sets (Wawrinka had three match points), and Allegro and Bastl winning the doubles.

Interestingly, when in the aftermath of the tie the Swiss players felt the captain Marc Rosset no longer fitted with their idea of how the team should be run, they sounded out Federer before going to Swiss Tennis to request a change of captain. 'We were all in favour,' says Chiudinelli. 'If Roger had been completely against it, Marc would have remained captain.' With Federer happy to go along with the change of personnel – albeit keen not to be the instigator – Rosset was removed from the captaincy. His replacement, Severin Lüthi, was also tactically calculated to keep Federer on board. Little-known outside Swiss tennis circles at the time, Lüthi was a studious boy from a village near Bern who had been a promising junior but had never quite broken into the world's top 600; he then became a part-time coach and part-time businessman with a firm selling merchandise at tennis events. He had been brought in by Peter Lundgren as part of the backroom staff at the Davis Cup tie in Morocco in 2002, and had proved popular with the team. As he was becoming a regular in the Federer camp, appointing a close confidant of Federer to run a more businesslike Davis Cup set-up was a way of keeping Federer in the loop, and ultimately contributed to Federer never cutting his ties with the Davis Cup team until after Switzerland had won the competition nine years later.

With just one defeat since the start of the year (against Safin in Melbourne), Federer went into his 2005 clay-court season as the man to beat, especially as he only suffered one loss in the run-in to Roland Garros, and even that was one of the more bizarre matches of his career.

When Federer beat Fernando Gonzalez to reach the quarter-finals of the Monte Carlo Masters, he'd gone twenty-five matches unbeaten and had lost just once in his previous fifty-three. But the streak came to an end against Richard Gasquet in a very strange atmosphere for a high-level tennis match.

Nine days earlier, Prince Rainier III, the monarch and ruler of the principality of Monaco, had died. His funeral was scheduled for the Friday of the Monte Carlo Masters. With dozens of heads of state and government in town, security was tight and a curfew was imposed from breakfast time until mid-afternoon, which meant anyone wanting to go to the Monte Carlo Country Club – the site of the tournament (half of which is actually on French territory) – had to get there early. And, while the view across the Mediterranean from the clubhouse is one of the most spectacular in world tennis, there isn't a lot to do on site, so all the players were somewhat at a loose end. With the overall ambience in Monaco very subdued, it created an eerie atmosphere seldom witnessed at a top-level tennis tournament.

That atmosphere was heightened by a minute's silence before play began. And, although Federer's two-hour-eighteen-minute match against the still teenaged Gasquet was a cliffhanger, it was characterised more by nerves and errors than by the glorious aestheticism of both men's elegant strokes.

For Gasquet, that quarter-final provided the potential of a coming-out party. Three years earlier, he'd become the youngest player ever to win a main-draw match at a Masters Series tournament, a success that seemed to justify years of being hyped by the press after first appearing as a nine-year-old on the cover of France's principal tennis magazine, which had hailed him as the future of French tennis. Yet a series of injuries, coupled with a belief that advancing up the rankings would be easier than it is in reality, saw him slide out of public view. By now approaching his nineteenth birthday, he was finally working his way back, and in Monte Carlo he had the chance to measure his progress against the best in the world.

Federer took the first set on the tiebreak, but Gasquet broke early in the second and levelled the match. When he led 5–3 in the final set, a shock result was on the cards. Gasquet then had a match point that he should have won but, having opened up the court for an easy volley, he fluffed it. When Federer then broke back for 4–5, Gasquet's chance looked to have gone. He had a second match point in that tenth game, but Federer saved it.

The tiebreak they played in that third set was full of drama and tension, with neither man able to finish the job. Federer had three match points but missed them all; Gasquet then had his third match point at 9–8, Federer came to the net, and Gasquet ripped a backhand down the line to win the match 7–6, 6–2, 7–6. The shock result suggested to the world that Gasquet was likely to become a factor at the top of men's tennis. It also prevented Federer from becoming the first man to win three successive Masters Series tournaments.

But it had been a subdued Federer and, with his energy levels back to normal four weeks later, he showed the true balance of power between him and Gasquet by beating the Frenchman 6–3, 7–5, 7–6 in the Hamburg final, a tournament he won without dropping a set.

Before heading to the French Open, Federer had another appointment. He had been nominated for the top 'Laureus' award, that of world sportsman of the year, for 2004. At the awards ceremony he beat off the competition of Lance Armstrong (cycling), Hicham el Guerrouj (athletics), Michael Phelps (swimming), Valentino Rossi (motor cycling) and Michael Schumacher (motor racing) to earn arguably the highest honour in overall world sport. (An interesting footnote is that the world sportsman of the year couldn't quite manage to win the Basel sportsman of the year award! A committee of sports journalists from his home city decided that naming Federer, the winner in 2003, would be boring, so they gave the award to Marcel Fischer, who had won a gold medal in fencing at the Athens Olympics.)

Federer therefore approached the high point of the clay-court season, the French Open in Paris, as the undisputed world number one and one of the front-line favourites for the title. But the tennis headlines in the weeks leading up to the 2005 French had been made less by him than by a phenomenal eighteen-year-old who was to play a defining role in Federer's career.

11

IT WOULD BE easy to see Rafael Nadal as bad news for Federer. After all, the Spaniard was a threat, and ultimately it was he who, in August 2008, finally ousted the Swiss from the top of the rankings after more than three years spent as world number two. But Nadal was actually very good news for Federer, and the 2005–10 period in tennis history should be known as the Federer–Nadal era – or alliteratively, the 'Roger–Rafa' era – rather than the Federer era.

Much as people admire a master craftsman, what gets the pulses racing in sport is a rivalry. People never sickened of the Borg–McEnroe and Evert–Navratilova rivalries of the 1980s, and the ATP and the media tried their best to build up clashes between Pete Sampras and Andre Agassi into a rivalry in the 1990s (which it was for short periods). The exuberant and ebullient topspin-heavy Nadal – with his pirate-like appearance in sleeveless shirt, plus-four-length shorts and shoulder-length hair – provided a wonderful counterfoil to the calm, flatter-hitting, neat Federer. The rivalry Nadal generated with Federer played a vital role, not just in lifting Federer's level of play, but in bolstering Federer's standing when the historians debate his place in tennis history.

The emergence of Novak Djokovic as a genuine rival to Federer and Nadal in 2011 means the Nadal–Djokovic and Federer–Djokovic rivalries can also compare with Federer–Nadal, but what makes the Federer–Nadal clash stand out is not just that it came first, but that most of their matches were played while the two were ranked one and two in the world. Nadal ascended to the number-two ranking on 25 July 2005 and, with the exception of four weeks in August 2009 when Andy Murray briefly broke the duopoly as Nadal recovered from tendinitis in his knees, the pair occupied the top two positions uninterrupted for more than four-and-a half-years until 1 February 2010 and ended 2010 in the top two slots for the sixth successive year. Federer held the top spot for most of that time, Nadal taking over for just under a year from the 2008 Olympics to the 2009 Wimbledon, and then again after the 2010 French Open (Nadal had subsequent spells at the top of the rankings, but, apart from in early 2018, Djokovic was his main rival after 2010).

No other pair of players has ever dominated the rankings to such an extent, not even Chris Evert and Martina Navratilova, who had the greatest rivalry in the women's game. The computer rankings have only existed since 1973, but it is hard to think of anyone who had such an enduring rivalry before then. One thinks of Rod Laver and Ken Rosewall, who played countless times on the professional circuit after Laver turned professional in 1963, and then in the early 1970s, culminating in a superb WCT final in Dallas in 1972 in which Rosewall won the fifth-set tiebreak 7–5. Or of Bill Tilden, whose battles with Henri Cochet and René Lacoste in the late 1920s caught the imagination of the tennis world. But the tennis world was much smaller then, and Federer and Nadal have surely eclipsed them.

Rafael Nadal Parera (in Spain the mother's maiden name is often used as a second surname) was born into a sporting family based in Manacor, the second city in Spain's Balearic island of Mallorca. He is the elder of two children, but has a large extended family. His uncle, Miguel-Angel, played football for both Barcelona and the Spanish national team, and the rest of the family had greater or lesser sporting involvement.

When young Rafa showed an aptitude for tennis, another uncle, Toni Nadal, became his coach. One of his first acts was to get the youngster to stop playing his forehand with two hands, and many expected the left hand to come off to leave a right-handed forehand – after all, he writes right-handed and kicks a football with his right foot. But the right hand came off, leaving a left-hander who has developed a fluency of stroke with immense power and, in latter years, a very effective serve and one-handed sliced backhand.

Federer first played Nadal in Miami in March 2004, when Nadal took advantage of a Federer head cold to win in straight sets. Their second match was again in Miami, in the 2005 final. Nadal had been long known as a great prospect, beating his fellow Mallorcan Carlos Moya in his Masters Series debut in Hamburg in 2003, and proving the find of the 2004 Davis Cup year. At eighteen, he beat Andy Roddick in the final to help Spain earn their second title. But, as Roddick correctly observed at the time, while the youngster had played some great individual matches, he had yet to string them together. Three months later, the string was about to begin.

In a superb best-of-five-sets final, Nadal won the first two sets, and then led 4–1 in the third. Federer pegged him back but, when Nadal led 5–3 in the third-set tiebreak, he was just two points from a famous win. But then his lack of experience allowed Federer to win four points on the run, and the Swiss raced away with the fourth and fifth sets for a 2–6, 6–7, 7–6, 6–3, 6–1 victory. Nonetheless, the eighteen-year-old left-hander had served notice that he was ready for an assault on the top level of the sport and, by the time he and Federer next met two months later, he was ready to win on a bigger stage.

The defeat in the Miami final proved Nadal's last for a while. He arrived in Paris on a phenomenal run of twenty-nine wins in his last thirty clay-court matches, the previous seventeen having brought him the titles in Monte Carlo, Barcelona and Rome. Yet he had never played in the Roland Garros main draw, injuries having prevented him from competing there in 2003 and 2004.

So tennis fans were licking their lips at the prospect of a Federer–Nadal final, but the Spaniard still wasn't ranked high enough to be seeded second, the position that would have guaranteed he would be kept apart from Federer until the final. Instead, he was seeded fourth, and the draw wasn't in a mood to co-operate – he came out of the hat in the same half as Federer, which meant the two were projected to meet in the semi-finals. That seemed to play into Nadal's hands;

Federer had after all won his previous nineteen finals, so most of his main challengers felt the best chance of beating him came in the semis or earlier.

Meanwhile, the draw was also unkind to Federer, who looked like he'd have to face Carlos Moya, David Nalbandian and Nadal before reaching the final. Moya he beat in straight sets in the fourth round, on the same day as the neat but unremarkable Romanian Victor Hanescu beat Nalbandian. Freed from having to face his Argentinian nemesis, Federer beat Hanescu comfortably to reach the semis without having dropped a set since losing to Richard Gasquet in Monte Carlo. As expected, Nadal awaited him.

On the night of his victory over Hanescu, Federer went to the ITF's champions' dinner, an annual black-tie bash staged on the second Tuesday of the French Open to honour the singles, doubles, junior and wheelchair world champions of the previous year. It was his second champions' dinner – he and Jelena Dokic had been the best juniors of 1998 and had received their award at Paris's Hôtel de Ville in June 1999.

It was a slightly off-colour Federer who showed up after beating Hanescu. Nothing of substance can be held against him – he turned up on time, carried out all his obligations, and, when all the speeches and ceremonies were over, he asked the ITF president Francesco Ricci Bitti if he was now free to go. That showed a sense of co-operation and responsibility not shared by some of his predecessors as world champion. And yet something didn't seem to be quite right. He showed up on his own, without his partner, Mirka Vavrinec, despite her having told an ITF official three hours earlier that she'd be there; he turned up unshaven; and, while his dinner jacket was immaculate and his black shoes brightly polished, he had omitted to wear a bow tie, and the top three buttons of his shirt were undone. It might have been just a fashion statement, but it contrasted with his two previous appearances at the Wimbledon champions' dinner at London's Savoy hotel, when he had shaved beforehand and had worn his bow tie.

Two days later, he walked out on to the Philippe Chatrier Arena at Roland Garros looking somewhat ashen-faced to play his semi-final against Nadal. He was entitled to be a little frustrated, given that the most eagerly awaited match of the tournament had been delayed until 6.29pm due to rain and the fact that the first semi-final had gone to five sets. If the Federer–Nadal match had gone to five, it would not have been completed that evening. There was also an omen in Nadal's favour; the Spaniard was celebrating his nineteenth birthday that day, and four months earlier Federer had been defeated in the semi-finals of the Australian Open by another birthday boy, Marat Safin.

Both men were nervous in the early stages, and neither found serving an advantage. In fact, six of the nine games in the first sent went against the serve, with Federer losing a remarkable four out of five, as both men tried to sound each other out. Federer found his form in the second set and, at one set all, looked the stronger player. But Nadal's heavy topspin and use of angles – especially his looped left-handed forehand, which drove Federer well wide of his comfort zone on the backhand wing – was undermining Federer's confidence in his game, which in turn led to him serving poorly and committing an uncharacteristically large number of errors with his normally deadly forehand.

Nadal took the third set, but Federer came out with an early break in the fourth and led 3–1. Yet still he didn't seem comfortable. At 3–2 he was broken back, and when Nadal held serve to lead 4–3, with the clock striking nine, Federer had a word with the umpire about the light. Had he won the fourth set, they would have had to come back the next day, and maybe Federer would have been more on his game. But Nadal held firm, broke again and won the match 6–3, 4–6, 6–4, 6–3 on Federer's thirty-fifth forehand error of the match.

Later that night, Federer said, 'I had too many highs and lows. He was much more consistent. I started bad and finished bad. I was good in the middle, but it wasn't good enough.'

Federer is adamant he wasn't beaten by anything going on off court. Asked about it six months later, he said, 'There was no problem, and also during the match there were no problems whatsoever. I was even being pushed by the fans, which was exciting. I would have wished that things went better, but there was nothing upsetting me incredibly much, except that I thought they should have stopped the match because of darkness, but they didn't. But again, what can I say as a player? I could have addressed that later to the supervisor, but I didn't do that because the match is over and that's it. I don't want to make a scene here. No, there were no problems leading up to that match.'

Nadal had actually made his Wimbledon debut well before he played in Paris and, while Paris was to become his fortress, Wimbledon was always his biggest dream. Forever keen for a challenge, Nadal had worked out that a Spaniard winning Roland Garros would not get the same recognition as a Spaniard winning Wimbledon, so Wimbledon became the target. But in 2005, he was still too inexperienced on grass. He went to Halle to get some practice, but lost in the first round to the passionate but unsubtle Alexander Waske, and then succumbed in the second round at Wimbledon to Gilles Müller, the only male player of note to have come from Luxembourg.

Given another year, Nadal and Federer might have met in the Halle final, for they were both in the starting line-up in the impressive but slightly incongruous northern German stadium. By the time another year had elapsed, they were so entrenched at the top that they had become rival attractions in the biggest grass-court events leading up to Wimbledon – Federer in Halle, Nadal at London's Queen's Club. Though he was not to know it at the time, 2005 was Federer's last year on grass unencumbered by the challenge of his Spanish nemesis.

Federer won Halle, in a little gem of a final in which he beat Marat Safin in three sets. Many hoped the match would be a sign that Safin could play on grass, but the Russian's results on the surface continued to be patchy, peaking in a Wimbledon semi-final in 2008.

Halle had done its job for Federer. He had regained his confidence after the Nadal defeat in Paris, and went on to claim a third Wimbledon title – his fifth Grand Slam – for the loss of just one set. In the final he again came up against Andy Roddick, but a match that promised much ended with Federer winning 6–2, 7–6, 6–4. With refreshing frankness, Roddick said after the match, 'I'm a better player than I was two years ago and last year, but I have nothing to show for it. It's frustrating, but he's better too – head and shoulders better than the rest of us.'

The veteran American journalist Bud Collins, writing a Wimbledon Diary, used typically colourful phrasing to describe Federer's dominance: 'Federer was playing a game called run-sheep-run with Roddick as the scrambling lamb eventually getting shorn, just as Lleyton Hewitt had been in the semi-finals. Roger, constantly varying his farm tools, has so many ways to hit a tennis ball in so many directions, with so many shifting spins and speeds, that the best Roddick could hope for was to catch up with some of them. But far from enough.'

And still Federer continued to charm the tennis world in three languages. At the end of a long press conference at Wimbledon, when someone shouted to him across the departing journalists, 'Roger, are there any more languages you speak?' he replied, 'If I did I wouldn't tell you, or my press conferences would take even longer.'

With his Wimbledon victory in 2005, Federer had gone thirty-six matches unbeaten on grass, putting him within striking distance of Björn Borg's run of forty-one, posted between 1976 and 1981. Perhaps more significantly, he had reached the same stage Pete Sampras got to around 1998 – he had become so good that some of his major titles were becoming less memorable. In winning the Wimbledon final that year, he said he felt his display against Roddick was better than the way he'd played against Lleyton Hewitt in the 2004 US Open final, which was viewed by many at the time as his greatest single match. He was beginning to transcend the excellence barrier and enter that realm where many people don't really appreciate the heights a player is scaling simply because he or she scales them so often. It was a problem he was to run into with his compatriots later in the year.

When tennis fans discuss who the greatest-ever player was, a pastime that will probably go on as long as tennis is played, Andre Agassi's comments after the US Open final of 2005 should always be among the evidence cited. It proved to be Agassi's final hurrah as a player, and his sheer persistence in getting to the final of a Grand Slam tournament at thirty-five years old (and carrying a hip injury) seemed at the time an age-defying achievement. The fact that Federer, Nadal and Djokovic have all won majors after their thirty-fifth birthdays has slightly rewritten the way a tennis player's age is viewed, but Agassi's feats in New York that year added to his own legend. And yet on 11 September 2005 he added more to Federer's.

Although Agassi had missed Wimbledon with a back injury, he returned in great shape at the US Open to pick up the pieces of the shattered hopes of American tennis after Andy Roddick's shock first-round exit to Gilles Müller. Roddick had been hyped in the weeks leading up to the Open, and his defeat silenced not only the American public but also the reams of advertising material in which Roddick had appeared in the run-up to the tournament. While Federer was nonchalantly disposing of Kiefer, Nalbandian and Hewitt to reach the final, Agassi had a run-in of three five-set matches, including a quarter-final against James Blake decided on a final-set tiebreak and a semi-final against Robby Ginepri. Fortunately, none of them was particularly long, and the charismatic Las Vegan

Above: First steps – playing at the Ciba Club in late 1984, aged three.
(Copyright © Roger Federer Management)

Below: International appearance – an eleven-year-old Roger represented the Old Boys Basel club at the Preussen Adler Cup in Duisburg, Germany in 1993.
(Copyright © Basel Old Boys)

Above: Grand Slam
Junior Champion.
Federer won both the
singles and doubles at
the 1998 Wimbledon
Junior Championships.
He is pictured here with
his doubles partner
Olivier Rochus.

Right: Made it at
last! The smile that
accompanied Federer's
first Grand Slam title,
Wimbledon 2003.

Above left: Federer cited carrying the Swiss flag in the opening ceremony at the 2004 Olympics in Athens as one of the proudest moments of his life . . .
(Copyright © Tommy Hindley Professional Sport)

Above right: . . . and he was to carry it again at another Olympics, this time in Beijing on his twenty-seventh birthday in 2008. *(Copyright © PCN Photography/Alamy)*

Below and inset: Simply the best. In May 2005 Federer was crowned World Champion for 2004. Two days later he played the first of six matches against Rafael Nadal at Roland Garros, losing a rain-affected semi-final. It would be another four years before he finally won the French Open. *(Copyright © Paul Zimmer)*

Above: A phenomenal comeback! After missing the second half of the 2016 season with a knee-injury, Federer bounced back spectacularly to win the 2017 Australian Open at the age of thirty-five. The final against Nadal included making good a 1–3 deficit in the fifth set. *(Copyright © Recep Sakar/Anadolu Agency/Getty Images)*

Below: A stroke of beauty. Federer shapes up for his trademark one-handed backhand, a stroke universally admired, even if he himself questions whether he would teach it to his children. *(Copyright © Tim Clayton/Corbis via Getty Images)*

Above: So near and yet so far. Three weeks before his thirty-eighth birthday, Federer came within a point of a twenty-first Grand Slam title but lost the 2019 Wimbledon final to his long-standing rival Novak Djokovic. *(Copyright © Ben Stansall/AFP via Getty Images)*

Below: Too good! Andy Murray acknowledges Federer's quality in a match in 2017. Despite Murray's beating Federer in tour-level matches, Federer lost just once to the Scot in their Grand Slam meetings. *(Copyright © Michael Buholzer/AFP via Getty Images)*

Above: The Great Rivalry. Rafael Nadal comforts a tearful Federer on the podium after winning a five-set Australian Open final in 2009. *(Copyright © Victor Fraile/Corbis via Getty Images)*

Below: Match in Africa. Nadal and Federer play an exhibition match in Cape Town to raise money for educating African children, probably setting a world record for the most people ever to attend a tennis match. *(Copyright © Justin Tallis/WPA Pool/Getty Images)*

Above: Don't write off a champion! Five years after winning his seventh Wimbledon title, Federer held aloft the trophy for an eighth time in 2017.

Below: Social occasion. Federer and his wife Mirka attend the wedding of Pippa Middleton and James Matthews near Windsor, England, in May 2017.

Left: Not a mannequin! After a video went viral showing two Italian girls, Vittoria (*left*) and Carola, hitting tennis balls from the roof of one residential block to the roof of another, Federer agreed to surprise them by ambushing an interview and hitting balls with them. Vittoria was so shocked she said 'It's Federer, he's not a mannequin!'

(Copyright © Barilla Group)

Right: Tennis in a pandemic. A masked Roger Federer keeps his social distance while scouting a match in Doha, Qatar, in March 2021.

(Copyright © Mohamed Farag/ Getty Images)

Left: One of the most memorable sporting images of 2022: Roger Federer and Rafael Nadal in tears during the Laver Cup in London, 23 September 2022. It was Federer's last professional match.

(© Ella Ling/Shutterstock)

was sustained by steadily rising hype and anticipation of his final against the great Federer.

Though there was less than twenty-four hours between the end of the semi-finals and the first point of the final, the match was the talk of New York. When they finally began playing at 4.30pm on a sunny September Sunday, Federer struck first. He won the first set, but Agassi broke in the second game of the second set to signal his intention to make a fight of it. When the American levelled at a set all, the crowd was right into the match. When Agassi broke to lead 4–2 in the third set, the crowd was going wild at the prospect of a sentimental victory for their thirty-five-year-old hero. An upset was a genuine possibility.

But that was Federer's cue to find some of his best form of the tournament. He broke straight back, almost broke in the eleventh game and then stormed through the tiebreak 7–1.

From then on, Agassi was a beaten man, and when at 5–0 in the fourth set Federer played a slack game, one could be forgiven for suspecting that a sense of charity had crept quietly into his mind, so Agassi's last set of the tournament – and at the time it felt as if it might be his last set ever at the US Open – wouldn't end 6–0. It made the final score 6–3, 2–6, 7–6, 6–1 to Federer.

Agassi's parting words to the Flushing Meadows crowd were: 'Thank you, New York. It's been a great twenty years.' But it's what he said in his post-match press conference that carries most weight.

By winning his sixth Grand Slam title, Federer had equalled the number of majors won by Boris Becker and Stefan Edberg. 'That's fantastic,' he said, 'tying your idols.

Isn't that great? It's every boy's dream, and I made it come true today in a memorable final.'

But Agassi was not talking about equality. 'There's only so long you can go on denying it: he's the best player I've ever played against,' he said. 'Pete [Sampras] was great, no question, but there was a place to get to with Pete. You knew what you had to do. If you did it, it could be on your terms. There's no such place like that with Roger. There's a sense of urgency on every point, on every shot. If you do what you're supposed to do, you feel like it gives you a *chance* to win the point. That's just too good. He plays the game in a very special way that I haven't seen before.'

Agassi has since suggested Novak Djokovic is the best player he has seen. To be clear, he was quoted by an economic magazine in 2019 as saying, 'The highest standard of tennis I have ever seen is when Novak [Djokovic] is playing his best tennis … I think [Roger] Federer has made more of his career than anybody else, he's more versatile than anybody.' None of which undermines Agassi's statement that Federer is the best player he ever played against, because he never played against Djokovic in a tour-level match.

Federer felt the American's praise was a little over the top. 'The best player of this generation, yes,' he accepted when Agassi's comments were put to him, 'but nowhere close to the best ever. Just look at the records that some guys have. I'm a little cookie.'

Modesty as a polite shield for immense self-belief is central to the Federer make-up. He knew, of course, that he was more than a little cookie; he was resorting to statistics, when what Agassi was saying was that statistics cannot do justice to what Federer was bringing to a tennis court.

More was added to the Federer legend in the last tour match of the year, the Tennis Masters Cup final. But this time it was a defeat, or at least the nature of it, that stood out in the memory.

Pete Sampras found at the height of his career that defeats were so rare that if he lost a match narrowly he would often get immense credit for it. His dignified loss to Federer at Wimbledon in 2001 was one example; a better one was his defeat to the diminutive Peruvian Jaime Yzaga at the 1994 US Open, when he battled against dwindling energy and poor fitness following an injury lay-off to put up a magnificent fight, only to lose 7–5 in the fifth set.

Federer's defeat to David Nalbandian in the 2005 Tennis Masters Cup final falls into a similar category. The background to it began several weeks earlier when he was practising at the Paradies club owned by the Swiss Indoors' impresario Roger Brennwald. He was hitting with Michael Lammer, a contemporary from junior days and later Davis Cup-winning teammate who had just had his breakthrough by qualifying for the US Open and reaching the second round. As the *Basler Zeitung* journalist Freddy Widmer reported in his short book *Moments '05*, on that occasion Federer had tried to book a court, only to find they'd all been taken. But then genial octogenarian Ernst Schneider – the lifelong driving force behind the cigar and luxury-goods company Davidoff, which sponsored the Swiss Indoors for many years – offered to give up the court he'd booked to allow Federer to practise. During that practice session,

Federer felt a stinging pain in his right foot while running for a forehand, and landed on the ground in agony. A subsequent X-ray revealed he'd torn a tendon in his right foot and needed a plaster cast.

Three weeks later, Brennwald was faced with the same unpopular task he'd had a year earlier: he had to tell his loyal public that the man they really wanted to see in Basel wouldn't be competing for the second year running.

Following the X-ray, Federer's entourage began a race to get him ready for the Tennis Masters Cup, which in 2005 returned to Shanghai. Federer has always had a soft spot for Asia, and had gone to Shanghai after winning the title in Bangkok to take part in the official opening of the Qi Zhong Stadium, a purpose-built 15,000-seater state-of-the-art arena with a beautiful retractable roof made of eight interlocking petals. Now there was a serious danger that he wouldn't be able to compete in the event the stadium was built for.

Less than three weeks before the Tennis Masters Cup was due to begin, Federer was still on crutches, but some careful yet intensive rehabilitation work with Pierre Paganini got him healthy just in time to take part. It was the same as in 2004: he was fit, but was he match-fit?

The organisers desperately hoped he was. In the run-up to the elite event reserved for the best eight players of the year, there were three high-profile withdrawals: Lleyton Hewitt, Andy Roddick and Marat Safin. Rafael Nadal came to Shanghai with a recurrence of the injury to his left foot that had caused him to miss Roland Garros twice as a teenager, and concluded after practising that it would be pointless for him to take to the court, and then Andre Agassi withdrew with an injury after losing his first match. After working so hard to get the tournament, and building a brand-new stadium for it, the Shanghai officials clearly felt they had lost face, and one of them made a stinging attack on Agassi that would have ensured the American never played in China again, had Agassi not retired anyway the following year. Losing face is a serious embarrassment in China; and in the absence of five of the six most illustrious names in tennis, Federer was effectively carrying the responsibility for the public credibility of the tournament.

He took to the court wearing a protective brace around his right ankle – a precaution, he said, more a comfort blanket than a real need – but came through his group matches, two of them going to three sets. That set up a semi-final against Gaston Gaudio, the Argentinian who had said the day before that he didn't really know how he could beat Federer – and promptly proved himself more than right by failing to win a game! Federer notched up the first 6–0, 6–0 victory of his career, the hapless Gaudio having lost heart early in the second set of what was only a fifty-minute match.

By reaching the final, Federer had done what the organisers in Shanghai had hoped: he had appeared in a maximum five matches, and had helped deflect attention from the five high-profile withdrawals. And he then ensured that the 2005 Tennis Masters Cup would forever be remembered for its best-of-five-sets final rather than for those who didn't show up.

When Federer led his opponent, David Nalbandian, by two sets to love, the match seemed to have been won, but it had taken him two hours and twenty minutes, the second-set tiebreak had been 13–11, and both players had done a lot of running. Instead of building on the momentum of winning the second-set tiebreak to plough home to victory, Federer suddenly began to feel very tired. The ankle wasn't a problem – or so he said – but the six weeks of practice and match time he'd missed while convalescing were beginning to take their toll. The turnaround was dramatic – Nalbandian took sixteen of the next nineteen games to open up a 4–0 lead in the final set. Federer looked beaten.

Federer has often said people didn't give him the credit for his talent until he showed that he could fight. 'It wasn't until I showed more grit when the going got tough that they started to respect me,' he said in a newspaper interview at the end of 2009. 'Then it was "Well, this guy is not just a wonderful shotmaker, he can also fight".' And faced with a 0–4 deficit in the Shanghai final, Federer fought. He fought his way back to 4–4, and when he broke to lead 6–5 he was serving for a third successive Masters Cup title. At 30–0 it seemed all over. Asked what he was thinking at that point, Nalbandian said, 'I can't go home like this!' And he wouldn't. He played four great points to break back and force a final-set tiebreak, and after a couple of points he was never behind, winning the tiebreak 7–3 to post the biggest win of his career.

That defeat meant that Federer was denied the opportunity to share a remarkable statistic with John McEnroe. In 1984, McEnroe so dominated world tennis that he lost just three matches out of the eighty-five he played that year. The final in Shanghai was Federer's eighty-fifth match of the year, and he went into it having won eighty-one and lost three; a victory would have meant tying McEnroe's phenomenal record. As it was, he finished on eighty-one

wins and four losses, but with possible extraneous circumstances surrounding all four of his defeats in 2005.
Nevertheless, it was a truly phenomenal year for Federer, in
which he showed a consistency that outshines the fact that
he 'only' won two Grand Slam titles, compared with the
three he won in 2004, 2006 and 2007.

Yet such subtleties aren't always appreciated by the
person in the street. And the Swiss can be a tough people
to please.

After his heroics of 2004, those of 2005 probably
seemed no better, or even slightly worse. When it came to
the poll for the Swiss sportsperson of the year, Federer was
beaten by Tom Lüthi, Switzerland's world motorcycling
champion. Half of the poll is voted for by Switzerland's
sports journalists in advance, while the other half is
determined by the public via telephone voting during a
televised awards gala.

Federer had won the award in 2003 and 2004, so in
2005 was going for his third in a row. In a three-way battle
between himself, Lüthi and the ice-skating world champion
Stéphane Lambiel, Federer led with forty-two per cent of the
ballots after the journalists had made their choice. But the
spectacle of Lüthi – who in 2004 was known more for his
crashes, but who kept his bike upright in 2005 to claim the
125cc world championship at the age of nineteen – swayed
many members of the public, and he edged out Federer.
It was clearly no snub to Federer, who took it well.

If there was a minor consolation, it came not in his third
successive nomination for the Laureus Award – although
that in itself must have been immensely satisfying, and he
went on to win the principal Laureus honour for the second

year running – but in being named as one of 'the twenty sexiest men alive' by *People* magazine. When that particular accolade was announced during the Tennis Masters Cup, Federer was more amused by it than anything else, but, for a man who had won the highest honours the sporting world can bestow, having the attractiveness of his masculinity recognised was probably a more meaningful award than being Swiss sportsperson of the year would have been.

Federer's second Australian Open title in 2006, his seventh in the Grand Slams, is remembered more for his emotional response to lifting the trophy than for much of his tennis. After receiving the Norman Brookes Trophy from Rod Laver, the only man to win all four majors in a calendar year with everyone eligible to play, Federer walked up to the microphone, said to the crowd 'I think you know how much this means to me,' and promptly burst into tears. Although he managed to finish his speech, in which he thanked the necessary dignitaries and sponsors, he did so with a quivering voice that clearly endeared him to the Melbourne faithful, just the way it had won over the Wimbledon crowd two and a half years earlier.

After breezing through the early rounds, his game went off a little, but he was still the clear favourite in the final against the twenty-one-year-old Cypriot Marcos Baghdatis, for whom that Australian Open appeared to be a breakthrough event but proved the high-water mark of his career. Federer was in serious trouble until he struck a rich vein of form late in the second set, running out a 5-7, 7-5, 6-0, 6-2 winner. Then at the ceremony came the tears, which took most people by surprise, despite Federer being well known in the tennis world for displays of emotion once matches were won.

There is no obvious explanation for the tears he shed on the podium. Federer's appreciation of tennis's history means Laver's presence alongside him could have tugged at the heart strings. Peter Carter's parents Bob and Diana were in the Melbourne crowd that day as Federer's guests, which might also have been an explanation. Federer has been asked on several occasions but has never really offered an explanation, certainly not a convincing one. Maybe it was simply a release: that, for a man like him who had subverted many of his boyhood emotions in the quest to be the best in the world and who consequently gave little away during matches, no one should be really surprised if the emotions run free when the discipline is allowed to fall.

Federer passed up the opportunity of a home celebration when he declined to play for Switzerland in a Davis Cup tie in Geneva starting eleven days after his Australian Open triumph. He was prioritising the Grand Slams, and his health and fitness regime didn't allow for even just three days of competition after his seventh major title. He also said he had set himself the goal for 2005 and 2006 of 'remaining number one', which meant chasing ranking points. By the time Nadal came back on the tour having taken time off to manage his persistent foot injury, Federer's hold on the number-one ranking was pretty much impregnable. But Nadal was to bounce back with a bang.

12

THE FEDERER–NADAL head-to-head record goes back to March 2004, when they first played in Miami. But the rivalry really took off in the four months between early March and early July 2006, when the two played each other five times. Nadal won the first four, leaving Federer in the strange position of having lost the same number of matches by early June that he had lost in the whole of 2005, and all to the same man. He was a runaway world number one who just couldn't beat the world number two.

With Nadal thought to be Federer's inferior on all surfaces other than clay, the Spaniard made a lot of people sit up and take notice when he came back from being a clear second-best in the final in Dubai to beat Federer 2–6, 6–4, 6–4. It was Federer's first defeat in Dubai since his ignominious capitulation to Rainer Schüttler in 2002.

Any suspicions that Nadal's win in Dubai was something of an aberration were brushed aside when Nadal beat

Federer in two clay-court finals, still played in those days over the best of five sets. The Spaniard won in four sets at the Monte Carlo Masters, and then inflicted probably the greatest psychological blow of the year on Federer by winning a quite superb final in the Rome Masters. It allowed him to equal Guillermo Vilas's record, set in the late 1970s, of fifty-three successive clay-court victories, a record he went on to break at the French Open. But that statistic was an incidental detail. What Nadal did at the Foro Italico was what Federer does to most of his opponents – makes them play their best yet find that it still isn't good enough.

Federer played near perfect tennis to take the first set on a 7–0 tiebreak, and seemed the dominant player in the second. But Nadal hung on, and took the set on a 7–5 tiebreak. That gave Nadal the momentum to take the third; Federer bounced back to take the fourth and open up a 4–2 lead in the fifth. Federer's moment to beat Nadal on clay had surely arrived. Nadal levelled at 4–4, only for Federer to have two match points at 6–5. Remarkably, he missed both by making errors on his biggest weapon, the forehand. Still Federer should have won; he led the final-set tiebreak 5–3 but mis-hit another forehand that would have given him a 6–3 lead. He didn't win another point, as Nadal wrapped up the glorious five-hour final on his first match point, the score reading 6–7, 7–6, 6–4, 2–6, 7–6.

A sign of the frustration Federer was feeling towards Nadal came with a slightly biting aside. At one stage in the match, Federer slipped out of his normally rock-solid focus and said to a person in the crowd 'All right, Toni?' Many thought he was talking to his IMG agent Tony Godsick, but it was an ironic quip directed towards Nadal's camp made to highlight what Federer perceived as unauthorised coaching Nadal was receiving from his uncle Toni. There was a feeling on the circuit that Nadal got away with more than he should, notably over the issues of mid-match coaching and taking too long between service points, and it could get under the skin of fair-minded players like Federer.

Perhaps that match holds the secret of Federer's some-what listless display in the French Open final. The scene was set for him to hold all four Grand Slam titles. When he beat David Nalbandian on a third-set retirement in their semi-final, he had made it to the final of all four majors. There were many respected pundits who were willing to say, even then, that if he won the final he could be considered the greatest-ever tennis player. And when he won the first set 6–1 on the warmest day of the fortnight, he was just two sets away.

Nadal came back to win the second as Federer played a couple of sloppy games, but Federer looked to have regrouped early in the third. In the fourth game he had Nadal at 0–40, and seemed to have shrugged off the lull and regained control of the match. What happened next may never be fully explained.

Federer seemed to lose his intensity. He couldn't convert his break points, and in the following game Nadal broke. Federer's face suddenly took on the ashen look that had characterised his defeat to Nadal in the semi-finals the previous year. It was almost as if he didn't quite know what to do, as if Nadal's constant ability to make use of every conceivable angle, and thus make Federer use more of the court than he needed to against any other opponent, had finally ground the Swiss down. It was as if the Rome final had been the act of hypnosis, and the events of the fourth and fifth games of the third set had merely reintroduced the hypnotic effect. Perhaps this was where the seeds of Nadal's phenomenal psychological hold over Federer were sown. One can look at the way Nadal's heavy topspin played well against Federer's flatter hitting (although Federer's forehand has plenty of topspin on it) and other aspects of their respective games, and those who have played Nadal say the way his heavy topspin explodes off the court surface grinds down opponents, especially those who start matches against him with a lot of confidence. But the discrepancy in their head-to-head has to have a psychological element, and the Rome and Paris finals of 2006 may well be where the doubts got deep into the Federer psyche.

Federer held his own during the fourth set, but never looked like seriously threatening the defending champion. And when Nadal won the final on a 7–4 tiebreak, it seemed a natural conclusion to what had gone on in the previous four-and-a-half months.

Post-match press conferences are not always the best places to find the most telling analysis of how a match was won and lost – the players are often too close to the event and still emotionally involved. Yet there was something uncharacteristically incoherent about the way Federer was flailing about in trying to explain his collapse after the 6–1 first set. He first suggested it was because the conditions were slower than in Rome, then that he couldn't get to the net, he wondered if the heat might have been a factor, and ended up by saying he just didn't play the match he wanted to. 'I mean, I tried,' he said, 'I can't do more than try. Obviously it's a pity, but it goes on, right.'

There was no faulting Federer's attitude or sense of how a single defeat in a final – his first French Open final – was hardly a tragedy. But the impression he gave after that final was that he still hadn't worked out how to play Nadal, at least not on clay.

There was no question of Nadal challenging Federer for the number-one ranking. Federer left Paris nearly 3,000 ranking points (6,000 points by the ranking points system introduced in 2009) ahead of the Spaniard, the kind of deficit that could only have been erased during the remainder of 2006 if Federer had suffered a serious injury requiring a break of several months. But by the mid-point of the tennis year, Federer had lost four matches – and all to the same man. The anomaly was clear to everyone in the game: the phenomenally dominant world number one had a head-to-head record against a young pretender (Nadal turned twenty during the French Open) of six defeats in their seven matches, and even the sole victory had been snatched from the jaws of defeat. Was the writing on the wall for the great man as he approached his twenty-fifth birthday?

Not yet. Roger Federer still reigned supreme at Wimbledon and, if anywhere was to be a Nadal-free zone for Roger Federer, Wimbledon seemed the most likely place. Even though Nadal had signalled at the age of seventeen his intention of breaking with the Spanish mantra that 'grass is for cows' (a casual remark attributed to the godfather of Spanish tennis, Manolo Santana, which came to characterise Spanish players' dislike of playing on grass courts), it was thought that, at twenty, he still lacked the necessary know-how, and that a realistic challenge to Federer's Wimbledon dominance was a long way off. But the Nadal challenge was for real, even on grass.

Federer came to Wimbledon on the verge of a piece of history he was trying very hard to play down. By winning the Gerry Weber Open in Halle for the fourth year running, he had equalled Björn Borg's record of forty-one successive wins on grass, set between 1976 and 1981, when the Swede won Wimbledon five times and reached a sixth final. Federer clearly wasn't that bothered by the record, choosing to view it partly as just another trick with numbers, and partly as being unfair on Borg, who had won all his forty-one matches at Wimbledon, whereas twenty of Federer's had come at the tour-level event in Halle, which only attracted a sample of big names. Trick with numbers or not, it was further testimony to Federer's remarkable dominance of grass-court tennis. But then the streak very nearly snapped before Borg's record had been broken.

Barring some unforeseen catastrophe, the record was always going to fall on 26 June when Federer played his first match at Wimbledon, but bigger headlines that day were made by what he wore to walk on court.

Although Federer doesn't use the terms 'class' and 'classy' as much as Pete Sampras did in his playing days, he shares Sampras's appreciation for the classic traditions of the game. So it seemed entirely appropriate when he strode onto the hallowed turf of Wimbledon's Centre Court wearing a white blazer. On the left breast pocket was a crest made up of various symbols relevant to him, the whole lot in gold weave. The symbols included three rackets, one for each of his Wimbledon titles, and below the crest the name 'Federer' appeared in capital letters. There were a few suggestions that his clothing company, Nike, had come up with the idea in an attempt to steal the scene from its rival, Ralph Lauren, which was introducing its new collection of clothing for Wimbledon's ballkids and umpires that same day. But, by and large, Federer's jacket was acclaimed and helped add a modicum of fashion interest to the single-mindedness of the greatest tennis player on earth. It became his leitmotif for the 2006 Wimbledon championships: seven times he walked on court in it, seven times he walked off victorious in it, and he even wore it to the Wimbledon champions' dinner in place of a dinner jacket, complemented by a purple and green All England Club tie. By then the crest was out of date, Federer having won a fourth title, so the quick-thinking curator of the Wimbledon Museum, Honor Godfrey, asked him if he would donate it to the museum's collection. Federer agreed, and for the next three years the jacket was on show throughout the year to tennis tourists visiting the Wimbledon Museum, before it was replaced by the waistcoat/cardigan he wore at Wimbledon in 2009.

Federer swept into the final without dropping a set. But awaiting him there was the man from Manacor: Rafael Nadal.

By his own admission, Nadal had a lot to learn about playing on grass when he arrived at Wimbledon in 2006. But good learners are often fast learners and, with a little luck, Nadal learned fast. He was two points from losing to the American Robert Kendrick in the second round; he showed up Andre Agassi's dwindling movement in the third in the match that ended Agassi's Wimbledon career; and by the time he faced Marcos Baghdatis in the semis, he had worked out how to play on tennis's most idiosyncratic surface.

Now came Federer. It was a mouth-watering final, because of Nadal's hold over the world number one. The clay results could be dismissed as being merely a reflection of Nadal's best surface and Federer's worst. But the Nadal victory in Dubai, coupled with the two Key Biscayne results from 2004 and 2005, suggested Nadal could get under Federer's skin on any court. It wasn't quite in the 'make or break' league for Federer, but a defeat to Nadal on the surface on which he was supposedly impregnable would have been hard to take.

When Federer took the first set 6–0, he seemed to be making an emphatic statement. But there was a lot about that set that suggested Nadal was still adjusting to his first major final outside Paris. Once the Spaniard got going in the second-set, it was suddenly a match. In retrospect, the second-set tiebreak, which Federer won 7–5, decided the final, because, while Nadal came back to take the third on a 7–2 tiebreak, the task was by then too much. Yet the fact that he had become the first man to take a set off Federer at that year's Wimbledon put down a marker, and, with Nadal having recovered one of two breaks he conceded early in the fourth set, the feeling at the end was that the finish line had come just a little too soon for the twenty-year-old. Federer had won his fourth Wimbledon title, which seemed appropriate, but Nadal had made his point.

Tennis finally had the rivalry at the top that it craved. Nadal had proved himself on hard and grass courts, to go alongside his unofficial epithet of 'king of clay'. Federer and Nadal were so far ahead that they had reduced the title of world number three – which oscillated in 2006 between David Nalbandian, Ivan Ljubicic and Nikolay Davydenko – to denoting merely the best of the rest. Yet Nadal's challenge fell away in the second half of the year; he was to play Federer only once more in 2006. Despite Nadal's ability to trouble Federer, the gap between them was to widen before it narrowed.

One of the things that marks out the rivalry between Roger Federer and Rafael Nadal is the fact that, for all their contrasts, they are two incredibly decent human beings. There are a lot of good things that can be said about the great names of tennis history, but in many cases the good sides emerged as the competitive days waned. By contrast, for Federer and Nadal, it is almost as if the generous naïvety of youth was never crushed by the trappings of riches and fame, but has merely been modified to allow them to keep the worst excesses of mass adoration at arm's length.

As Nadal started to become Federer's equal in tennis terms, he managed to maintain his respect for Federer's achievements without being in awe of them. On beating Federer he was frequently asked whether he felt he should be number one, regardless what the rankings said. He always replied in the negative, saying Federer's achieve-ments spoke for themselves and he wasn't going to let one match distort the big picture. Such respect, coupled with a modesty that was in no way false, allowed the two men to develop a friendship that, if not quite on the level of bosom buddies, stands out in marked contrast to several previous rivalries that included an element of personal dislike, whether real or manufactured.

John McEnroe has gone on record as saying that he is surprised at the friendship between Federer and Nadal, and Federer has some sympathy. In a candid 2009 interview with Paul Kimmage (a cyclist turned journalist) for the British *Sunday Times* newspaper he said, 'I'm surprised myself by the degree to which we actually get along, because we've had a very intense rivalry and you could say he has hurt my career and that I've hurt his career. But we've actually helped each other become the players we are today, and the rivalry has helped the game. It's nice that the two greatest players in tennis, or any sport, actually get along well, because normally there is all this hate and it's so negative – I don't like that. We've had enough controversy in recent years, so it's a welcome change. At the end of the day we are also role models for a lot of children, and sometimes that gets forgotten.'

All of which is very nice and admirable, but there are some who feel it's a shade phoney and would like to see more obvious passion in the rivalries. Whether it would be good for tennis to go back to the days when Pat Cash growled at Boris Becker at changes of ends during a Wimbledon quarter-final, or Andre Agassi suggested Pete Sampras was barely more developed than a monkey because of Sampras's habit of letting his lower jaw hang down during tense phases of matches, is uncertain. It would garner interest off the back of nervous tension, but at the cost of what tennis gains from being a generally clean-cut sport. But there are some who would like to feel there's a middle way in which the top players are more openly competitive, whatever that actually means in practice.

Anyone who wonders whether tennis is lacking something

because Federer and co. are too nice to each other should look at the economics. Throughout his playing career, Federer was quite simply a massive draw. He sold more tickets than anyone else, his matches boosted television and radio ratings in a way that no other players do, and his manager Tony Godsick could sell Federer for megabucks every week of the year. Perhaps one of the legacies Federer will leave is that nice guys don't always come last, and that human decency can be economically marketable.

Another sign of Federer's 'diplomatic' work is his membership of the International Club. The IC is a club originally established to allow tennis players who have represented their country to remain competitive, but it has also taken on a more pastoral role alongside its central aims of promoting fair play and good sportsmanship.

Federer also became more politically involved in his own sport. Initially reluctant to express much of an opinion on tennis matters, he began to be less reticent in 2005 and 2006.

His views on electronic line-calling were well known by March 2006, when the Miami Masters tournament became the first tour-level event to use electronic review of line calls. The breakthrough had come in late 2005 when the British 'Hawk-Eye' system had its accuracy approved by the tennis authorities and was given the green light to be used in official competition. By the end of 2006, electronic review was an established feature of top-level tennis, and, while it still has a few detractors, it is now hard to imagine a serious tennis event without it.

Yet Federer was never a fan. Before it became accepted, he said it should not be used, and since it has been introduced he has left many with the strong impression that he doubts the accuracy of the system. It's possible that the system is accurate and Federer isn't entirely wrong – one of the central doubts about electronic review is that tennis is played to the human eye and, if a ball looks out but a tiny fraction of it did in fact catch the line, then electronic review will call a ball 'in' when no one would have questioned a human call of 'out' if the facility to review it hadn't been there. But it is with us, and Federer knows he would be deluding himself if he felt he could somehow wish it out of existence.

Perhaps his attitude towards its legitimacy goes a long way to explaining his curious body language when it came to calling for electronic reviews, especially in the first two or three years after the system was introduced. When he challenged a call, he seemed highly dismissive – some would say arrogant – in the way he raised his arm like an ill-tempered diner in a restaurant who believes the waiters are beneath him. At the time he also had a habit of barely looking at an umpire during a match, almost as if he was chronically shy or feared eye contact – he went on to largely remedy this and generally spoke very respectfully to umpires, but in the early days of electronic review his manner gave his challenges an additional air of contempt. Interestingly, he had an appalling record on challenges in the early years, frequently going a whole match without getting one right, but eventually assimilated challenges more comfortably into his game.

Federer's growing comfort with tennis-political issues culminated in him agreeing to run for the ATP Player Council, the advisory body made up of players and elected by players that feeds views and suggestions to the ATP's board of directors. He was elected to a two-year term in June 2008, and four months later voted in as president; he was re-elected to both offices in 2010. The ATP Player Council has four players from the top fifty, plus lower-ranked and doubles players. In the past it has at times struggled to get top-ranked players to stand, but not in 2008! For the first time ever, the intake included the world's top three players (Federer, Nadal and Djokovic) plus Fernando Gonzalez, with Federer and Nadal elected president and vice-president respectively. Not only were they the two players and personalities setting the tone in the player lounges, they actually held the leading administrative positions in the players' parliament.

One of the doubles players also elected to the ATP Player Council in 2008, the Australian Ashley Fisher, said at the time of President Federer, 'Roger's leadership style in the meetings is very respectful and diplomatic. Although he is the president, he recognises that every member should have an equal say and makes a point of ensuring that everyone is satisfied with a decision.'

Such involvement in tennis-political issues made Federer a harder person for the top ATP executives to deal with than he had been earlier in this career. The South African Etienne de Villiers, who ran the ATP as chairman and chief executive from late 2005 to the end of 2008, began on good terms with the world's top player, but some see Federer's public statements as playing a quiet but key role in de Villiers' departure after just three years in charge.

De Villiers, a South African who came to tennis management after a career of some success at the Disney Corporation, was an instant hit with the players and with other tennis officials, and his South African background added a further sense of solidarity with Federer.

Yet despite the two men being on the same wavelength in the early days, Federer was opposed to de Villiers' plans to demote Monte Carlo and Hamburg from Masters Series status to general tour level once the majestic Caja Mágica ('Magic Box') tennis complex opened in Madrid in early 2009. As world number one, Federer found himself as an impromptu shop steward, joining Nadal, the veteran Carlos Moya and the eloquent Ivan Ljubicic in a four-man delegation to see de Villiers. They were partially successful, winning the battle to keep Monte Carlo in the elite, but losing Hamburg.

A bona fide disagreement alone would not have turned Federer against the executive chairman, but the two men had differing personalities and, in an environment where the administrators need to ensure they don't upstage the stars, de Villiers always seemed to be seeking the limelight more than many top players (not just Federer) were comfortable with. Suffice it to say, de Villiers' relations with many in the tennis world seemed decidedly more strained at the end of his ATP time than they were after his initial round of introductions.

And it was a single line from Federer that perhaps did most damage to de Villiers. De Villiers had pushed hard for an experiment in which the traditional knockout format was replaced in the early rounds by round-robin matches in some lower-ranking ATP tournaments. Inevitably with an experiment, there was some learning as they went along, but the format hit crisis one Thursday night in Las Vegas in March 2007. A farcical situation developed in which one of the quarter-final places seemed to be in the gift of an ailing player (Juan Martin del Potro), who could have played his final round-robin match to a conclusion to allow James Blake to go through, or could have retired injured to allow Evgeny Korolev to advance. No doubt unaware of his power, del Potro retired hurt. De Villiers got involved by telephone and ordered Blake to be put into the quarter-finals in place of Korolev, only to be reprimanded by his board for unjustifiably overruling an ATP supervisor who had followed the rules correctly. To a certain extent, de Villiers was the victim of unfortunate circumstances – he had been woken late at night and could justifiably claim to have acted in good faith. Federer was several thousand miles away in Dubai and could legitimately have declined to comment, but, never a fan of the round-robin format, he said of de Villiers, 'He's got his fingers burned.' Federer's subsequent comment that 'He's doing his best' was largely overlooked or dismissed as faint praise, and the round-robin experiment was abandoned three weeks later.

The influence of the world number one is remarkably potent, both in terms of the mood in the locker room and players' lounge, and also in how the players feel about certain developments – it is as if they take their lead from the best player. With de Villiers clearly having a different view for the future of tennis from a number of key professionals including Federer, the South African's days were numbered, and one-by-one his supporters were voted off the ATP Player Council during 2007 and 2008. De Villiers was gone by the end of the year.

*

Despite Nadal's obvious progress, the Roger–Rafa rivalry was at this stage largely an early-year phenomenon. In his first few years on the tour, Nadal seemed to have run out of gas by the build-up to the US Open, and the last man standing between Federer and his ninth major title was Andy Roddick.

After losing in the third round of Wimbledon to the little-known but promising Andy Murray, Roddick announced that he was teaming up with the former world number one and streetfighter par excellence Jimmy Connors. Connors had little experience of coaching at the highest level and didn't need the money, but Roddick clearly felt Connors had something that could help him stem the tide of his ebbing ranking. And when Roddick captured his first Masters-1000 title for two and a half years by winning in Cincinnati, there was a buzz around him again, especially in the US.

When Roddick followed up that Cincinnati title with a run to the US Open final, his meeting with Federer was the most eagerly anticipated match of the American hard court season. In many ways it was a repeat of the Federer–Agassi final of a year earlier. On that occasion, the excitement and anticipation meant people had rather turned a blind eye to the fact that Federer came into the final much fresher than Agassi, and the same happened again. The champion had dropped just one set and had played more than an hour less in his semi-final against Nikolay Davydenko than Roddick had done in beating Mikhail Youzhny in a four-setter that came close to three hours.

A year earlier, Federer had beaten Agassi 6–3, 2–6, 7–6, 6–1 to seal Grand Slam title number six. Grand Slam number nine was achieved by the remarkably similar scoreline of 6–2, 4–6, 7–5, 6–1, and the match followed a near-identical pattern. Just as Agassi – who ended his illustrious career at that US Open after losing in the third round – had led 4–2 in the third set, Roddick led 3–2 and had Federer at 0–40. Federer got back to deuce, saving all three break points with some sublime shot-making, but Roddick had a fourth, which he seemed destined to win, only to miss with a forehand. It was to prove his last chance. When Federer broke in the eleventh game and then served out to take the third set, he was unstoppable. 'At that stage of the match,' Federer said of the fourth set, 'I felt almost invincible.' As with Agassi a year earlier, Federer won the first five games, before Roddick picked up a lone consolation game to avoid the indignity of a 'bagel' in a US Open final.

History records Roddick as something akin to cannon fodder for Federer, though that is a little unfair on the American. A strange mix of class act and immature teenager, he made absolutely the most of his talent, in particular a serve that was the mainstay of his game and for a couple of years held the record as the fastest-ever measured in an official match. In retrospect, Roddick was a shade fortunate to catch the interregnum between the Sampras and Federer eras, in that he had a game that was distinctly limited by the standards of the formidable trio he counted as his contemporaries. But he deserves credit for being up there at all, and he was a colossus in the Davis Cup, where the pressure of expectation is often greater than anywhere else on the tennis circuit. He has since gone on to become a very natural broadcaster, and was deservedly inducted into the International Tennis Hall of Fame in 2017. He just had the misfortune to find that his game suited Federer down to the ground, a circumstance that allowed for some pretty brutal scorelines when the two played each other and which often made Roddick look ordinary.

Roddick came within a point of beating Federer at the 2006 Tennis Masters Cup in Shanghai, but even that seemed to emphasise Federer's unreachability for the big-serving American. As it was a round-robin match, Federer could have afforded to lose and still win the tournament – a feat he achieved the following year – but Roddick was desperate to beat his long-time nemesis. When he failed to do so, the wind went out of his sails, and he didn't make it to the semi-finals.

Roddick had another shot at Federer at the Australian Open two months later. It was also at the semi-final stage, and in the build-up to the match he had expressed the view that he was 'getting closer' to the Swiss. It seemed an entirely reasonable statement at the time – Roddick had shown superb focus in beating Marat Safin in the third round, and had out-hit the big-hitting Croat Mario Ancic in the fourth. With Jimmy Connors now in Melbourne after the death of his mother, and Nadal out of the tournament, everything seemed set for Roddick to present a significant challenge to Federer.

How hollow those words 'getting closer' seemed after eighty-three minutes of play! Federer had won 6–4, 6–0, 6–2, taking eleven games on the run from 4–4 in the first set. It's easy for people to rush to superlatives when they have just witnessed a devastating display of sporting prowess, often forgetting that the passing of time offers a more realistic context, but there were many experienced tennis watchers not given to hyperbole who found themselves wondering whether they had ever seen a display of tennis quite so magnificent.

Roddick, who had been ticked off by Connors for overpraising Federer after the US Open final four months earlier, took the defeat well. A man for whom a five-second answer counted as long, he warmed up from a monosyllabic start to his press conference to offer the assessment, 'I've just got to keep doing what I do. I wake up every morning, I put in as much work as I can every day. You do your best not to get discouraged, you try to take it like a man. I caught an absolute beating tonight, there's no doubt about it. But you deal with it and you go back to the drawing board. You act like a professional, and you try to keep working hard.' Brave words, and realistic ones, but they hid the wreckage of hopes built up over several months that were destroyed in an evening.

During the Federer–Roddick match, a placard appeared in the stands bearing the words 'Quiet, genius at work'. It was not the first time it had appeared, but it seemed most appropriate that night.

A somewhat different side of Federer's character was on display in September 2006, when he faced Novak Djokovic for only the second time. Djokovic, still only nineteen, was highly regarded as a prospect for the future, but his reputation included a slightly unsavoury side, and the normally mild-mannered Federer wasted no time in pointing it out when he saw evidence of it, even going so far as to exercise the full weight of his office as world number one by branding the upstart 'a joke'.

When Switzerland were drawn at home against Serbia & Montenegro in the playoff round for the 2007 Davis Cup world group, it was to be a closer tie than many might have thought. The Serbian team (and it was all Serb – the 'Montenegro' was only a formality, and that for the last time) that travelled to Geneva had not only one of the world's top doubles players in Nenad Zimonjic, but in Djokovic it also had one of the most promising names in world tennis.

Djokovic was very much grouped with Andy Murray. The Serb is just seven days younger than the Scot, and tennis watchers considered them prospects of equal promise. If Murray could beat Federer (as he had in Cincinnati a few weeks earlier), the logic went, so could Djokovic. But Djokovic's first couple of years on the tour had been punctuated by a breathing problem that frequently caused him to call for the trainer mid-match, and there were those who wondered whether he had come to rely too much on his mid-match breaks. So when he called for the trainer to have his legs massaged, after going two-sets-to-one down on the opening day against Switzerland's second player, Stan Wawrinka, there were no doubt some who felt that there may have been a tactical element to the inquiry.

Djokovic denied there was, but Federer clearly felt otherwise. He became convinced that Djokovic's leg massages threw his teammate off his game and, without the treatment, Switzerland would have ended the first day two-up. Wawrinka felt the same, but chose to view it as a failure on his part to remain focused rather than blame it on anything approaching gamesmanship by his opponent. Whatever the interpretation, the first day score was 1–1, which meant the Federer–Djokovic match on the final day would be live. By the time the players took to the court, the Swiss were 2–1 ahead, and Federer was playing with a little venom in his veins. His 6–3, 6–2, 6–3 win was nothing unexpected, but his post-match comments took many by surprise.

When Federer said of Djokovic, 'I don't trust his injuries,' during his main post-match press conference, it drew a few nervous laughs from the audience. 'No, it's not funny,' he added admonishingly, 'I'm serious. I think he's a joke when it comes to his injuries. The rules are there to be used, but not abused. But it's what he's been doing many times, so I wasn't happy to see him doing it and then running around like a rabbit again. It was a good handshake for me, I was happy to beat him.' Later, Federer had an informal chat with the Swiss-German press, at which he added: 'I got irritated on Friday when he put on this show in his match against Wawrinka. Ninety-five per cent of players use these breaks fairly, but this isn't fair, and the rules need to be changed.'

Djokovic later admitted that he and Federer had chatted privately at the Madrid Masters three weeks later and cleared the air. The Serb claimed many of his withdrawals came from positions of strength, thus undermining the idea that his injuries and ailments had been psychosomatic responses to hopeless situations. A look through Djokovic's matches doesn't entirely bolster his argument, but he did appear to learn from it. His calls for the trainer and premature retirements became fewer and further between after that spat with Federer and, when the two men met in the fourth round of the Australian Open three months after their Madrid chat, there wasn't a hint of a timeout in another Federer straight-sets win. In hindsight, Djokovic probably profited from Federer's outburst – while it would be another three years before Djokovic identified the underlying cause of his health issues, he clearly learned a lot about how to deal with it. Whether it also set the two men off on a relationship that has been mutually respectful but also silently suspicious is another matter.

When a player wins as many tournaments as Federer has, the currency gets devalued, and the smaller events get largely forgotten. Even some of the bigger ones can get forgotten too – not many among even the most ardent Federer fans could recite all his Grand Slam finals. So tour titles seem of peripheral importance; but there was one in the autumn of 2006 that counted for a lot more.

As Federer made his annual pilgrimage to the still-barren venue of the St Jakobshalle in his home city of Basel, his battle was against the ill-fortune that had thwarted him in previous years as much as against any opponent in the 32-man field. Surely this year nothing could stop him!

Paradorn Srichaphan very nearly did. The likeable Thai delivered a dream performance in the semi-finals. Twice he led Federer by a minibreak in the final-set tiebreak, but Federer just did enough to win. 'I obviously got a bit lucky in the end,' said the relieved local hero afterwards. In his third Basel final, he faced Fernando Gonzalez, the Chilean who had begun a rise up the rankings under the guidance of the experienced American coach Larry Stefanki, which was to see him reach the Australian Open final three months later. But he matched Federer for just one set, as Federer took his home-town title 6–3, 6–2, 7–6 at the seventh time of asking. Had he known that, fourteen years later, Basel would be one of the tournaments he would win ten times, the long wait would have seemed incidental. But the wait made the win over Gonzalez very emotional as Federer completed the journey from Basel ballboy to Basel champion.

'It's one of the most beautiful moments of my career,' he said, 'and also one of the most important to me after Wimbledon. Although I always wanted to be a professional tennis player, I never dreamed that I would one day be the champion here. It's also my one thousandth day as world number one, so a very fitting day for this to happen, and one of those moments I'll never forget.'

Federer ended his 2006 season with a third Tennis Masters Cup title, brushing aside the cerebral James Blake in the Shanghai final with tennis that at times bordered on perfection. In the semi-finals he had beaten Nadal in straight sets; it was an oddity for the world's top two players to meet before a final, but the round-robin format means it can happen at the ATP Finals. It's interesting to note that, after Federer's 6-4, 7-5 win, the American tennis journalist Christopher Clarey, writing in the *International Herald Tribune*, offered this analysis: 'It was hardly the best Federer–Nadal duel, nor the most significant. But the match in Shanghai intrigues because of its relatively lopsided nature, and because of what it said about Federer's drive and focus at the end of a globe-trotting, glad-handing year that would have drained many a top athlete of his energy and ambition. Instead, the Artful Roger (the best of Federer's several sobriquets) was in something like full flight in late November: swooping around the indoor, medium-speed court and giving a hint to his closest pursuer in the rankings, and frequent conqueror in head-to-head matches, that something fundamental had changed between them.'

It was a legitimate point to make at the time, but it was to take another ten years before anything fundamental changed between Federer and Nadal. All that match proved was that Nadal had still not learned how to spread his blistering tennis of the first half of the year throughout an entire season, whereas Federer had.

As such, Federer kept up his remarkable level of form from the start in Melbourne to the close in Shanghai. Across 2006, Federer won another three major titles, became the first man in the 'open' era of tennis to win ten or more titles in three consecutive seasons, became the first professional tennis player to earn $8 million in prize money in a single season, and won ninety-two of the ninety-seven matches he contested.

But to most people, his single greatest achievement was in falling just one match – or two sets – short of doing a pure, calendar-year Grand Slam. Until Federer's ascent to the summit, it was generally believed that men's tennis was too competitive for anyone to win all four major titles in the same year. Yet here he was, the first man since Rod Laver did the only 'open' Grand Slam in 1969 to reach all four finals in the same year. But for the disappointing display in the Roland Garros final against the man now generally recognised as the greatest-ever clay-court player, he would probably have emulated Laver's achievement.

13

HE CAME EQUALLY close in 2007, which proved to be the fourth of the golden quartet of years (2004–07) that mark the peak of the Federer career. Again three Slams, again falling just two sets short of the fourth, and again Nadal standing in his way. And yet it was to be the last of the years of Federer dominance, with the seeds of the subsequent period of tennis being ruled by 'the big four' growing into very clear green shoots.

Not that there was any absence of quality in Federer's tenth Grand Slam title and third Australian Open. Where his emotional response to victory had been the defining feature of his title a year earlier, unbridled excellence was the leitmotif in 2007. The fact that he didn't have to face Nadal no doubt helped: the Spaniard emerged from an exhilarating five-sets victory over Andy Murray in the fourth round with an injury that made him dead meat against the big-hitting Fernando Gonzalez in the quarter-finals. But Federer did play two outstanding matches in Melbourne that year, and it's possible Murray and Gonzalez saved Nadal from a drubbing, such was the form Federer was in.

The bald statistics can record that he became the first man since Björn Borg at the 1980 French Open to win a Grand Slam singles title without dropping a set, and the first since Ken Rosewall in 1971 to win the Australian Open with the same distinction. But statistics don't do justice to the way Federer dismissed Novak Djokovic in the fourth round and Andy Roddick in the semis.

The match against Djokovic was their first meeting since the ill-tempered Davis Cup tie in Geneva four months earlier. Since then, Djokovic's stock had risen, and he came to Melbourne having won the tour event in Adelaide two weeks earlier. As the tennis world geared itself up for a classic, Federer simply raised his game, and beat Djokovic 6–2, 7–5, 6–3. The handshake at the net was unusually perfunctory by Federer's standards, despite Djokovic's smile and clear wish to impart a compliment or two. The sting from their spat appeared not to have been entirely eradicated by their *tête à tête* in Madrid.

The other outstanding display was against Andy Roddick, the American being made to pay for his seemingly legitimate comment that he was 'getting closer' to Federer (see pages 252–3).

Despite his aversion to electronic line-calling, Federer used one call to great effect in the final against Gonzalez, in which he delivered a performance not quite worthy of the 'genius at work' placard that again appeared in the stadium, but still more than good enough to snuff out the Chilean's challenge. Federer needed to save two set points on Gonzalez's serve at 4–5 in the first set, and a challenge to the electronic adjudication system that he got right gave him a decisive advantage at the start of the first-set tiebreak. But the aura Federer had built up meant that Gonzalez was playing the reputation as well as the man. As the match wore on, the mental fatigue wore the challenger down as Federer ran out a 7–6, 6–4, 6–4 champion.

There is a school of thought that has the 2007 Australian Open – Federer's forty-sixth tour title and tenth Grand Slam – as the high point in terms of quality in his entire career. There are some, including Federer himself, who believe the tennis he played at the 2010 Australian Open was better, and in certain matches it probably was. But he had slip-ups in his matches against Igor Andreev and Nikolay Davydenko, dropping sets in both, whereas in Melbourne in 2007 he was consistently majestic from start to finish. It was as close to perfection as a tennis player can reasonably expect to get.

Yet where do you go after achieving perfection? What was to sustain Federer's motivation after a tenth major title? His oft-cited love of the game was in evidence, but was that enough to see him through the grind of the tour?

Signs that he might have been having difficulty motivating himself for events other than the Grand Slams were spotted when he lost twice in successive tournaments to Guillermo Cañas, a quality player on the comeback trail after a fifteen-month ban for taking a prohibited diuretic, but there was no doubt he was up for it when he resumed battle with Nadal on Nadal's favourite surface.

The rivals met in the finals of two of the three big

lead-up tournaments to the French Open, Monte Carlo and Hamburg, yet there was something missing from both matches as a spectacle. Instead of celebrating the wonder of the best-of-five-sets format for the finals of its top tier of tournaments, the ATP decided that the risk of playing a very long match fairly close to a Grand Slam tournament was greater than the benefits of the drama that comes from epic five-set contests, so decided to abolish best-of-five-sets finals in all its tournaments. It meant that when Nadal beat Federer in Monte Carlo and Federer then beat Nadal in Hamburg, it seemed to have less significance for the up-coming French Open than the Rome final of 2006, which undermined Federer's confidence in his ability to win three sets on clay against his great rival. Many were happy to read into Federer's 2–6, 6–2, 6–0 victory in Hamburg proof that he had worked out how to play Nadal on clay, but in truth there were mitigating circumstances. Hamburg's clay is always somewhat lower-bouncing than that of Rome and Paris, and Nadal was particularly tired after winning the titles in Indian Wells, Monte Carlo, Barcelona and Rome. In fact, had the two men not been in the vanguard of the players' attempts to show solidarity with Hamburg (the event threatened with the loss of its Masters Series status), it's possible neither might have played the tournament, and by the end Nadal was in serious need of some recuperation before the French Open.

Another interesting factor was that Federer's off-court set-up was in something of an upheaval. His coaching arrangement with Tony Roche, which had seen him win six Grand Slam titles, had slipped into a state of disrepair by the time the clay court season of 2007 came round, and, when

Federer committed 44 unforced errors to lose his second match in Rome 6–2, 6–4 to Filippo Volandri, a competent Italian who would never normally have threatened a player of Federer's class, even on clay, he promptly parted company with the respected Australian.

How much Federer ever needed a coach is a question that must always be asked before getting into a discussion of a specific coaching relationship. Since he had won three Grand Slam titles in 2004 without a coach, and three more in 2007–8 with only informal support, it would be wrong to read too much into the demise of any individual coach of his. But what was interesting about Roche was that Federer was on record as saying he was looking for input for winning on clay, and Roche had encouraged him to slice more and go to the net to avoid the baseline wars of attrition that Nadal was always going to win. So for Federer to part company with a man he clearly respected just two weeks before the biggest clay court tournament in the world, having seldom ventured to the net in his defeat to Volandri, suggested that the two were no longer on the same wavelength, and those who saw the pair at close quarters during the Rome tournament were not surprised to see the parting of the ways.

Shortly afterwards, Federer asked his long-time friend Severin Lüthi to travel with him. There was no announcement of Lüthi's appointment as a coach, but the low-key decision began a fifteen-year tenure for the unassuming Bernese, who was five years older than Federer and remained a fixture in his coaching set-up until Federer's retirement in 2022, often as co-coach alongside a more illustrious name. Speaking over the weekend of Federer's final match, Lüthi told the

ATP podcast, 'People always think that a player like Roger doesn't need any coaching, but he wants to hear every day what our opinion is about what he should do. He always gave us the possibility to say our opinion, and I think this is important. Sometimes, when I worked alongside another coach, we had different opinions on tactics, and we saw details a little bit different, but he was very good, he always saw that as the basis of an interesting discussion. So we argued why we thought our solution is the best one, and Roger made his decision.'

The significance of the Hamburg final was to let the tennis world know that Roche's departure did not amount to Federer hitting the panic button. In fact some even saw it as a form of liberation, especially when he reached a second successive French Open final for the loss of just one set. But while Nadal had forced Federer to improve his clay-court game, the reverse had also happened, and the match was to be decided by Nadal's ability to raise his game when danger threatened.

Federer arguably came closer in 2007 than he had in 2006. Although he was never ahead, he took the match to Nadal, attacking with his returns of serve, and created seventeen break points in the four-set final. Yet he converted just one of them, the other sixteen being largely saved by Nadal's burgeoning ability to play perfect tennis on the points that really mattered. By contrast, Nadal was brutal when he had break points on the Federer serve. The crucial break was the one in the second game of the third set, which wiped out all the momentum Federer had worked so hard to build up by taking the second set with a late break that momentarily ended Nadal's dominance. Federer had a break point in the second game of the fourth set but, once Nadal had saved it, he dropped just two more points on his serve in a 6–3, 4–6, 6–3, 6–4 victory.

Speculation about how much that victory had taken out of Federer, both mentally and physically, was fuelled by his decision to skip his hitherto traditional Wimbledon warm-up tournament in Halle. For a man known for sticking to his word, his withdrawal was something of a shock and it earned him a fine because there was no question of his being injured. Federer returned to Basel to undergo medical tests (he was later to say of this period, 'I couldn't move for a week', so there was some sort of fatigue at play), but he was never going to dress these up as a reason for evading the fine that players incur when they miss without good reason a tournament they have committed to.

The Halle personnel, who were glued to the French Open final despite having the final round of their qualifying tournament to deal with, say they began to fear Federer might withdraw when he lost the first set. Frank Hofen, Halle's long-standing media manager, said, 'It was during our qualifying tournament party late on Sunday night that Ralf Weber [the Halle tournament director] took a call on his mobile. It was from Roger, and he said he was just not able to play and he needed time to himself if he was to mount a realistic challenge for a fifth Wimbledon title.

A small detail to note is that Federer phoned Weber himself. Many players get their agent or someone else to pass on the message, but Federer carried his own responsibility. As a tournament director of fifteen years' standing, Weber will have known that the only response in such circumstances is to show complete understanding, as anything else will only worsen the chances of getting the player back the following year. But it's easier to show such understanding when the player has the decency to make his own call, and Weber's response was well rewarded, for not only did Federer sign a three-year deal to play at Halle from 2008 to 2010 (a commitment he honoured in 2008 and 2010) but Weber, a competent club player, got to hit with Federer for half an hour on the Halle centre court during the 2008 event.

The break clearly did Federer good, because he returned to Wimbledon refreshed, and dropped just one set en route to his thirteenth meeting with Nadal. The Spaniard had dropped four in successive back-to-back matches against Robin Söderling and Mikhail Youzhny, and his subsequent performances on grass make it easy to forget that there were many who felt he was vulnerable in 2007, and that his run to the 2006 final had not delivered proof that he was the finished article on grass. The final he played against Federer put an end to any such thoughts.

With Björn Borg sitting in the front row of the Royal Box ready to witness Federer's equalling of his record of five successive Wimbledon titles, the two men played one of the great matches of recent times. It was in one way also unique, because the venerable stadium dating from 1922 was a completely open bowl, the previous roof having been removed but the new structure not yet in place – it gave the arena a most un-Wimbledon-like feel. Like the previous year, Nadal was slow to get going, but this time he got his act together early enough to make his mark, and Federer was taken to five sets for the first time at Wimbledon since he had beaten Pete Sampras in the 2001 fourth round. Many felt Nadal should have won.

Federer squandered a 3–0 lead in the first set, plus a 6–3 lead in the tiebreak, before taking the shootout 9–7. Nadal should have broken at 3–3 in the second – Federer bounced back to save two break points, but Nadal did break in the tenth game to level the match. Federer had to save break points midway through the third set as Nadal upped his level. The Spaniard was making very few errors, but he played a poor tiebreak as Federer took it 7–3 to claim a two-sets-to-one led.

Nadal was ruthless at the start of the fourth set, reeling off four games as Federer looked lost. But then at 4–1, Nadal needed treatment for a niggle in his right knee. It didn't appear to hinder his movement, but the time it took to get the knee strapped allowed Federer to regroup, and the match was more competitive after that.

Nadal was far enough ahead in the fourth set for the match to go to a fifth and, when he had Federer at 15–40 at both 1–1 and 2–2 in the final set, the champion was wobbling. But Federer weathered the storm, played a superb sixth game to break Nadal, and from then on the Spaniard was broken. Another break made the final score 7–6, 4–6, 7–6, 2–6, 6–2.

A roving microphone caught snippets of Federer's conversation with Borg as the two met in the lobby of the Wimbledon clubhouse after the trophy presentation ceremony. While it may have been a meeting of equals in terms of their Wimbledon achievements, it was decidedly unequal in terms of the conversation. Borg seemed limited in what he felt he should say – his normally easy-going demeanour with contemporaries such as John McEnroe, Mats Wilander and Yannick Noah was constrained in the company of his modern-day equivalent. By contrast, Federer was masterful in his ease of conversation, asking Borg plenty of questions and not getting deterred by the constricted answers he was getting. It was almost as if Borg was in awe of Federer.

Federer was also partly in awe of Nadal. In a formal interview after the match, he said, 'He's a fantastic player and he's going to be around so much longer so I'm happy with every one I get before he takes them all!' There was no doubt an element of politeness in that comment, but it proved remarkably prophetic over the subsequent eighteen months; in fact that 2007 Wimbledon final was the last time Federer was to beat Nadal in a Slam for nearly ten years.

The final had been a great contest. It had ended a very wet Wimbledon on a real high, and it had put Nadal firmly on the map as a grass-courter of quality. Indeed there were many who wondered that Sunday night whether it was possibly the greatest Wimbledon final ever. Such musings lasted precisely one year.

As the world number one in a sport with as high a profile as tennis, Roger Federer has been asked to do his fair share of odd stunts. The set with Agassi on the helipad of Dubai's Burj al-Arab hotel was one such (see pages 209–10) and, when the ATP rebranded its tour at the start of 2009, he and Nadal were asked to hit some balls on a mini-court built on an Arabian dhow boat. But in May 2007 came probably the oddest of all stunts, staged to celebrate the rivalry between the king of grass and the king of clay.

With Nadal on his unbeaten clay streak and Federer unbeaten for four years on grass, the International Management Group got them to play a 'Battle of the Surfaces' – a match with one half of the court grass, the other half clay. The city tourism office of the Mallorcan capital Palma agreed to host and sponsor the event in the Palma Arena, and half a grass court was installed at an astonishing cost of $1.63 million. Even more astonishing, after nineteen days bedding down, it had to be ripped up again and re-laid (the original grass had suffered an infestation of worms!).

As for the match, it went to the wire, Nadal winning it on a 12–10 third-set tiebreak. With the players changing shoes at every change of ends, it was hard not to think of it as a gimmick, but both seemed to want to win the decider. Both men will have been handsomely paid for their efforts, so none of their comments about it can be taken to be a complete picture of what they really felt, but Federer is always open to new ideas, especially those that are fun, while Nadal had the chance to play on his home island against his principal rival, so everyone got something. And they never repeated it.

Despite Nadal's achievement in the Wimbledon final, he again proved to have shot his bolt by mid-season. As he faded in the second half of the year, Novak Djokovic emerged as the leading challenger to Federer on hard courts.

The Serb had risen to third in the rankings on the back of semi-final showings at the French Open and Wimbledon, and a superb run in the Masters Series. That run continued when he beat Federer for the first time in the final of the Montreal Masters, and, with a superior hard court record to Nadal, he seemed a bigger threat to Federer for the US Open than the Spaniard. Despite his aversion to back-to-back Masters Series tournaments, Federer nevertheless went to and won Cincinnati, which made him still very much the man to beat at Flushing Meadows.

After surviving a marathon second-round match against Radek Stepanek, Djokovic looked set to face Nadal in the semi-finals for the third successive major. But Nadal was beaten by Spain's number-two player David Ferrer in the fourth round, leaving Djokovic with a clear run to his first Grand Slam final. With Federer looking slightly below his best, this was Djokovic's chance. But he wasn't able to seize it.

Portents of Federer's drop in form in the first half of 2008 were very much in evidence in a final that was Djokovic's for the taking. In particular, the champion's big forehand was misfiring far too often, and he looked nervous in the early stages. The erratic forehand contributed to Djokovic leading 6–5 and 40–0, but the Serbian player couldn't close out the set. Five set points went begging, before a double fault allowed Federer to break back, and he won the set on a 7–4 tiebreak, Djokovic double-faulting on set point.

Djokovic should have won the second set 7–5, but he missed another two set points in the twelfth game, and then saw Federer play his best tennis of the match to take the tiebreak 7–2. Djokovic again had break points at 2–2 in the third, but he was looking increasingly tired and frustrated, and, when Federer saved them, he was almost home and dry. A break in the tenth game of the set gave him a 7–6, 7–6, 6–4 victory that was as much attributable to his reputation as to the way he played on the day. It took him to twelve Grand Slam titles, and made him the first man ever to win the Wimbledon and US Open titles in the same year four times in a row.

The fact that Djokovic beat Federer in the Australian Open semi-final four months later suggests it was just inexperience that deprived the Serb of his maiden Grand Slam in September 2007. He joked afterwards that 'my next book will be called *Seven Set Points*', and it could well be that, in processing the defeat, the Serb worked out that he lost the match in his own head rather than on the court, and the only thing he needed to improve was his fear of the great man's reputation. Yet there is an equally compelling argument that Djokovic's success in Melbourne in 2008 was more down to Federer's ill-health than Djokovic being genuinely on the same level. Indeed, if one looks back through the head-to-head between the two men, that Australian defeat was the only one that Djokovic won that really mattered to Federer until Djokovic beat him in the 2010 US Open semi-finals and at the same stage of the 2011 Australian Open, by which time the Serb had learned to play as the Swiss's equal.

Two defeats to David Nalbandian meant Federer didn't add to his Masters Series haul, but he did defend his titles in Basel and the Tennis Masters Cup, the latter featuring another semi-final victory over Nadal. It was the pair's eleventh match, and Federer's easiest victory, though one that didn't mean a lot. Federer's 6–4, 6–1 victory meant the head-to-head with Nadal read 8–6 for Nadal, as narrow a gap as Federer had enjoyed since early 2006, but one that was to expand again in 2008. The following day he beat the likeable and honest toiler David Ferrer comfortably in the final to win his fourth Tennis Masters Cup title.

As well as the usual rush of awards, the year ended with Federer playing three exhibition matches in Asia against Pete Sampras, the man he had played only once at tour level: Federer's fourth-round Wimbledon victory in 2001. They took place in Seoul, Kuala Lumpur and Macau. Federer won the first two and Sampras the third, a sequence that fuelled the thought that maybe Federer deliberately lost the third to keep interest alive for another – and bigger – match against Sampras scheduled for New York four months later. Although meaningless in historical terms, the matches seemed a harmless way of earning some extra pocket money, except that they came at the end of a long season that had seen Federer's dominance in the Grand Slams become less pronounced. And it more than likely contributed to Federer's hitherto reliable health suddenly rebelling at the start of 2008.

THE BIG FOUR 4

14

THERE COMES A period in any top athlete's career when their form dips. It happened to Tiger Woods in golf, it happened to Muhammad Ali in boxing (though with a more dramatic backdrop given his political activities), and it happened to Roger Federer in tennis in 2008. He recovered from it, but, by the time he did, the tennis landscape had changed. The years of Federer as the dominant top dog, the pack leader who could win matches on reputation because the enormity of beating him was too much for many opponents to handle, were over. Not that he was no longer a factor – over the subsequent twelve years he won another eight major titles, an Olympic singles silver medal and the Davis Cup, and he twice returned to the top of the rankings. But from the mid-point of 2008 onwards, he was not the sole elite player but a member of the elite group in world tennis, a group that gradually became known as 'the big four'.

There are many who question whether it was a 'big three' or a 'big four'. There's no question Rafael Nadal and Novak Djokovic caught and overtook Federer at various junctures, but does Andy Murray really count in the same company as his three contemporaries? And if he does, should Stan Wawrinka be included to make it a 'big five'? Federer finished his career on twenty major titles, a mark since eclipsed by both Nadal and Djokovic; they are streets ahead of the rest. Yet in an era when hardly any other players got near the finals of the Slams because of the dominance of the other three, Murray reached the semi-finals or better twenty-one times, advancing to eleven finals, and winning three of them amid phenomenal weight of expectation from the British public. In addition, he so dominated the circuit from May 2016 to the end of that year that he spent thirty-seven weeks at the top of the world rankings. He also beat Djokovic to the number-two ranking by more than five months, so at the end of 2009 a 'big three' in men's tennis might have included Murray and not Djokovic. By any reasonable assessment, Murray is worth his place. By contrast, Wawrinka reached just three finals (the three he won) and was a semi-finalist just six other times, suggesting he is well behind Murray in achievements at the majors.

Federer, Nadal, Djokovic and Murray form a remarkable generation, not just in tennis terms but as four admirable human beings who, in their different ways, understood their responsibilities to their sport and the wider community, and became genuine role models in the way many of their predecessors hadn't. They also proved remarkably durable. It was easy to assume in 2013 and 2014 that their hold on the top echelons was weakening, especially when Wawrinka,

Cilic, Nishikori and Raonic made significant advances, yet at the start of 2015 the top four places in the world rankings were still occupied by the big four. Even after a chronic hip injury caused Murray to fall away in 2017, the continued dominance of Federer, Nadal and Djokovic makes them by far the most remarkable generation in the almost 150-year history of modern tennis. Apart from Cilic's US Open title in 2014 and Wawrinka's three majors 2014–6, no one outside the big four won a major in the 2010s, and the four also dominated the nine Masters-1000 events and ATP Finals played each year.

The four form a backdrop to Federer's achievements in the period from 2008 onwards: he was still a member of the elite, but the days of him picking up three Slams a year had gone.

The dip in form he suffered in the early part of 2008 was in some ways a totally natural phenomenon. A player at the top will inevitably find that the constant drag of having to be at one's best the whole time eventually loses its attractiveness, especially after a great run of success. The hunger then goes, and the defeats – particularly those of a hitherto unexpected nature – follow.

There are then two ways to go: back up, or on down. The likes of Björn Borg and Mats Wilander hit that wall in their mid-twenties – both decided it wasn't worth the effort and gave up. They both made minor comebacks, but their best years were gone. By contrast, Jimmy Connors bounced back after seemingly losing his lustre as Borg and John McEnroe reached their respective peaks. The same can be said for Andre Agassi, who was down to 141 in the rankings in November

1997 but returned to become French Open champion eighteen months later. In other sports, Muhummad Ali's regaining of the world heavyweight title against George Foreman in 1973 is one of boxing's defining moments; and Tiger Woods rebounded from a loss of form to add to his haul of major titles; knee surgery and some high-profile sexual infidelity caused a second watershed in his career, from which he bounced back spectacularly to win the 2019 US Masters.

Roger Federer hit that watershed in the first months of 2008. There were extenuating circumstances, such as his health, but his air of invincibility disappeared. Viewed with the benefit of hindsight, it was hardly a disastrous period – in the first six months of the year, he reached two Grand Slam finals and one semi-final – and the fact that he went on to regain his number-one ranking and beat Pete Sampras's record of Grand Slam singles titles in 2009 makes it seem like a blip. But after his exploits in 2006 and 2007, every defeat was treated as a sensation, and, in the fiercely competitive world of top-level sport, Federer went from being the untouchable at the top of the game to the wounded beast everyone was gunning for. And that spawned all sorts of theories about whether these were the early signs of a permanent decline, and whether there was some discontent in his private life.

The first indication that Federer might be a lesser force than he had been in 2006 and 2007 came in the third round of the Australian Open when it took him four hours to beat the likeably studious but unremarkable Janko Tipsarevic. He eventually won the match 10–8 in the final set. When a listless display against another Serb, Novak Djokovic, in the semi-finals resulted in Federer's first defeat in Melbourne since the dramatic Safin semi-final of 2005, there were plenty ready to hail a decline in the great man's fortunes.

But there had been mitigating circumstances for these uncharacteristic performances. A week before the Australian Open, Federer had spent a night in a Sydney hospital with an upset stomach, which the doctors had initially thought was due to food poisoning. When his condition improved, the initial diagnosis appeared to have been confirmed. However, it seems few people knew then that Federer had come very close to missing his first Grand Slam tournament since the 1999 US Open, or that he was actually suffering from much more than just tummy trouble.

By the time he arrived at the French Open, he was something of a marked man. His form on the tour had been well below the level of the previous few years, and he had just one title to his name, the modest Estoril tournament in the Portuguese capital, Lisbon. He had also been outpsyched by Nadal in the Hamburg final. Federer's preparation for the one major still to elude him was not looking good, and yet, ironically, the French Open was the tournament he was supposed to be best prepared for.

At the end of 2007, Federer's fitness coach Pierre Paganini had made a few changes to the December practice schedule and to the regular regime in the early part of 2008, with the intention of having Federer in optimum shape by the time he arrived in Paris. However, those efforts were being undermined at the very time they were being undertaken. Unbeknown to all of Federer's entourage, the player was suffering from the strength-sapping mononucleosis, often known as glandular fever. He says he had it during the Australian Open, which, if that is the case, makes his victory over Tipsarevic and run to the semi-finals a remarkable achievement. He also says he had it very lightly, which explains why he missed very little time on the tour. But the nature of glandular fever is that, while the illness itself may be short-lived, the after-effect of fatigue can linger for several months, and doctors generally advise sufferers to give up sport for at least four weeks after 'mono' is diagnosed. He may well have had a very mild dose, but, looking back on Federer's 2008, the fact that he played on through it means it is medically quite plausible that it robbed him of strength for the first half of the year.

In retrospect, Federer's decision to play the three exhibition matches against Pete Sampras in Asia after the 2007 Tennis Masters Cup looks somewhat misguided. After a long and hard season, surely he should have rested, rather than played three interesting but ultimately meaningless matches against a man no longer in his prime. He was clearly handsomely rewarded for his efforts (some reports claimed he received $1 million per match, although fees for exhibition matches are seldom made public and are highly susceptible to exaggeration), and which of us would turn down such an offer, especially for an attractive assignment? By playing in Seoul, Kuala Lumpur and Macau, he could also claim to be doing his bit to spread the tennis gospel in places that are by-passed by the global tennis tours. But, even with the benefit of hindsight, he still chose to play three more exhibition matches in Asia at the end of 2008. Perhaps he figured the exhibitions would do nothing to undermine his general health. Interestingly, although his IMG agent Tony Godsick was on the record as saying Federer was cutting down on his exhibition matches,

Federer began 2009 with two different exhibitions in the run-up to the Australian Open.

That having been said, it would be wrong to view his fourth exhibition with Sampras in March 2008 in the same light as the three in Asia three months earlier. The two met in a massively hyped occasion in Madison Square Garden, New York, in a match aimed at raising money for a programme to make vaccines available to people in poorer parts of the world. It was sponsored by the NetJets company, which hires out private jets and which counted Federer as one of its best clients. It was also Federer's chance to play at the prestigious Madison Square Garden, a venue he was happy to describe as 'the greatest arena in the world'. Wearing an outfit all in black, to contrast with the angelic white of Sampras (very deliberately, as the two were clad by the same clothing company), Federer won the match on a final-set tiebreak in front of 19,000 spectators. Taken as a sporting comparison of the two greats, it told the world little or nothing it didn't already know, but as a one-off competitive match, chance to experience playing in a historic venue and fundraising opportunity, it had some value.

Despite the spirited challenges of six players, Federer still made it to the Roland Garros final, to set up a third successive decider with Nadal. If Federer had done enough to get through the early stages without too much turbulence, Nadal had looked positively imperious in his run to the final, which involved no dropped sets and some crushing defeats for accomplished players, such as Nicolas Almagro and the Australian Open champion Novak Djokovic. To the sanguine observer, it appeared Nadal was in a class of his own and Federer was a step slower to the ball.

All that was overlooked on the morning of the final, as people got psyched up for what, for the third year running, was set to be Federer's moment of history. There were suggestions that he hadn't played well up to the final because he was saving everything for an assault on Nadal, and that a new Federer would turn up for the title decider. With the wily Spanish coach José Higueras in his corner, Federer clearly had a game plan based around attacking Nadal with his big forehand at the first opportunity.

The plan made sense, but the gun misfired. Federer was broken in the opening game as he made three forehand errors, and the writing was on the wall. He seemed to be making a match of it in the second set but, once he missed a chance to go 4–3 up, he didn't win another game, and Nadal handed out a humiliating 6–1, 6–3, 6–0 drubbing.

As Federer climbed on to the rostrum at the prize-giving ceremony to the sound of polite applause, he took the microphone and said, 'Oui, c'est moi' (yes, it's me) to the crowd. It was a neat encapsulation of how the man everyone had come to respect as arguably the greatest player of all time could look so unlike himself.

How much that defeat undermined his confidence and played a part in the outcome of the magnificent Wimbledon final they played four weeks later is difficult to gauge. A feature of the following four weeks was the number of times he was to say that the severity of the loss wouldn't affect him if he met Nadal at Wimbledon. To a certain extent, one must sympathise with players who get asked the same question over and over again, each journalist thinking he or she is the first to ask it. But there were times when

Federer was volunteering the information unbidden, and it did tend to evoke a paraphrased line from Shakespeare: 'Methinks he doth protest too much.'

Whether Federer's sense of belief against Nadal had indeed been undermined by his crushing defeat in Paris, or whether Nadal was simply doing what he does best – moving his game relentlessly to a level few previously considered him capable of – what followed twenty-eight days after the Paris massacre was a contest that surely has to make it into anyone's list of the ten greatest tennis matches of all time: the Wimbledon final of 2008.

In the run-up to the final, it seemed plenty of people were wondering whether the crushing defeat in Paris indicated that Federer was still suffering from the continuing after-effects of the glandular fever, although Federer denied that he was in any way below peak health. After winning his fifth Halle title with a level of play that rose steadily during his five matches, he said, 'People tell me when they saw my matches in Paris that I still have it in my system. I honestly don't feel it. I'm happy when people worry for me, but I don't wake up a single day any more feeling sick or tired or anything, so I'm not feeling the after-effects any more.'

Federer also claimed – with some justification – that his defeat by Nadal in the Roland Garros final should not make people think he had had a poor French Open. And, when he stormed into the semi-finals at Wimbledon, it did seem to be a case of a few warm-up matches before his now customary meeting with Nadal in the final. The way he dismissed Lleyton Hewitt in the fourth round and the potentially more dangerous Mario Ancic in the quarter-finals was clinical. However, he faced a class act in the semis in the form of

Marat Safin, the mercurial Muscovite who had dumped the third-seeded Novak Djokovic out of the tournament in the second round and gone further at Wimbledon than he had ever gone before.

Safin had taken a set off Federer in a superb Halle final in 2005. Now back in a Grand Slam semi-final for the first time since his Australian Open triumph in January 2005, all seemed set for a superb contest. Yet Federer snuffed it out with a three-set victory, which left some doubting how much Safin really believed he could win; it may also have eroded Safin's confidence for their meeting at the 2009 Australian Open, which Federer also won in straight sets despite Safin playing a very good match. More importantly, it established Federer as the champion who had finally rediscovered his best form. With Nadal demolishing Andy Murray and Rainer Schüttler to set up a third successive Federer–Nadal final, Wimbledon had the showdown it wanted, with both players seemingly in great form. Yet few could have expected the contest the two men delivered on a damp Sunday, 6 July.

As discussed elsewhere in this book (see pages 201–3), what makes a match one of the all-time great contests is difficult to define. Obviously, a high level of tennis is an essential ingredient, as is the presence of at least one great player. But there are many great matches between great players, so many, in fact, that only a few stand out after the short-term memory has faded.

There is normally an extra component, a certain element that heightens the tension. It could be festering animosity between the players, or even extraneous circumstances that have nothing to do with tennis. Neither factor applies to

Federer and Nadal; the two men are, in their different ways, so charming and inherently generous that their rivalry is based on a strict demarcation between intense competition on court and mutual respect bordering on friendship off it.

But there were two extra components in the 2008 Wimbledon final. The first was the historic nature of the moment, which would have been significant whatever the result. On one side of the net was Federer, looking to become the first man since William Renshaw in 1886 to win six Wimbledon titles in a row, and to go one better than Björn Borg, who in 1981 had fallen to a rising upstart of a left-hander in the match that would have given him six titles (a man he had beaten in five sets in the previous year's final). On the other side was Nadal, the undisputed king of clay who had set his heart on doing something that would really impress his countryfolk: winning Wimbledon. The second was the fact that the final finished in near darkness. There are many who say the most prestigious tournament on the global tennis calendar should never have been allowed to end in such gloom, and it's a powerful argument, but it unquestionably added to the drama.

The first set had tennis of an extrememly high quality. After his slow starts in the previous two finals, Nadal was quick off the mark, and broke Federer in the third game, a strike that sufficed for the first set. When Federer led 4–1 in the second, the match looked set for parity, but, with Nadal reeling off five straight games to take a 6–4, 6–4 lead, the champion was suddenly facing an uphill battle. Although he was to rally, those five games probably cost him the match.

When Federer trailed 0–40 at 3–3 in the third set, Nadal

looked like repeating his drubbing of the champion in Paris. But Federer found some of his best serves just when he needed them, and, with rain then forcing an eighty-minute interruption as the third set neared its conclusion, he had the chance to regroup. He came out looking more positive, and played by far the better tiebreak as the match went into a fourth set.

Nadal kept up his level, and, when he had Federer at 4–5, 0–30, the Spaniard was just two points from the title. Federer survived that storm but then found himself in deep trouble as Nadal led 5–2 in the tiebreak, again just two points from victory. The lead involved a double-minibreak, but Nadal – looking strangely unconfident for possibly the only time in his career – then played two of his worst service points to allow Federer back on-serve. Federer blew a set point at 6–5, and at 7–6 Nadal had championship point. Federer saved it with an unreturnable serve, but a stunning forehand passing shot gave Nadal a second championship point, this time on his own serve. Nadal followed his serve with a crosscourt forehand that seemed to push Federer hopelessly out of court, yet he calmly moved into position and stroked the most sublime backhand into the corner of Nadal's court.

'It was one of my first backhand passing shots all match,' Federer said afterwards. 'With his forehand, I thought it was all over, so for me to come out with that one was a great feeling. I really thought, with winning last year in five and getting the momentum, that would be enough.'

With the tiebreak recalling the epic Borg–McEnroe tiebreak from the 1980 final – when McEnroe too saved one of six championship points with a stunning backhand winner – the tide ebbed and flowed. At 9–8, Federer had his second set point, this time on his own serve; Nadal's backhand went long, and the match was into a final set.

With the clock approaching eight in the evening, and the skies still leaden, the first fears that the final might not be completed that day began to surface. When rain interrupted play at 2–2 in the final set, those fears intensified. Wimbledon was desperately keen to get the match finished – going into a 'third Monday' is a logistical nightmare, and it rather wrecks the glitz of its official champions dinner on the Sunday night if one of the two singles champions hasn't been decided. The rain break proved short-lived; the players returned to the court at 8.20pm, with the meteorologists giving them 45–60 minutes of dry weather, and about the same in daylight.

If Federer had profited from the first rain break, the second break favoured Nadal. Although Federer served first and therefore had Nadal frequently just two points from defeat, Nadal never looked seriously threatened on his serve, while Federer seemed to have lost some of the bite from his fourth-set triumph. At 6–6 the players glanced up at the umpire, Pascal Maria, who himself glanced at the referee Andrew Jarrett. The signal was to play two more games. At 7–7, Federer looked for the signal to come off, but they were again told to play two more games. Nadal then broke Federer, and, despite losing the first point of the sixteenth game, held on to claim his first Wimbledon title as a Federer forehand went into the net.

The television footage of that match point, Nadal's fourth, is no guide to just how dark it was, as the cameras make it seem lighter than in reality. If Pete Sampras had beaten

Pat Rafter in the gloaming in 2000, at least that was on an evening with relatively clear skies, and pretty much on the stroke of nine o'clock. This was an overcast day, with the final ball struck at 9.17pm. The brightness of the flashbulbs that illuminated Nadal's ecstatic fall to the turf, followed by his precarious walk up to his entourage and then over the fragile roof of NBC's commentary box to greet Crown Prince Felipe and Princess Letizia, and his holding of the trophy, testify to just how dark it had become.

Nadal admitted as much when, on the stroke of one o'clock in the morning, he strode, immaculately dressed and coiffed, into London's Intercontinental hotel to attend the champions dinner. His few words to the guests included the line: 'I couldn't see nothing at the end!'

In his post-match comments, Federer agreed, but he was in a more difficult position about saying so when he faced the media in his post-final press conference. He was well aware that, if he had said anything that could be remotely construed as complaining about the match conditions, there were members of the British media who would be only too happy to write 'Federer loses the final, and the ability to lose with dignity'. Therefore, he declined to comment in English about the light, saying merely, 'What can I say? It's over, so. What's the point in arguing about it? It's the way it is.' But in French and German, he was more forthcoming, saying, 'I could hardly see what I was playing at the end. The most important tournament in the world is decided in a light that isn't playable.'

Federer clearly felt that he and Nadal should have come back to finish the match the next day, but there are two important points to be made about this that are not readily appreciated. Firstly, the following day it drizzled at Wimbledon until mid-afternoon, which meant that, had they stopped at 6–6, 7–7 or 8–8, one of the great Wimbledon finals would have dragged on through a mist of cloud gazing and weather forecasting, before possibly being decided in a few anticlimactic minutes late on Monday afternoon. Such a final was surely worth more than that, and Andrew Jarrett showed good judgement in trying to get the match finished on the Sunday night. Secondly, over the whole match, Nadal had clearly been the better player. Federer looked slow in the first set, he seemed to have no answer to Nadal's surge in the second, he missed countless break points, and he was even slightly fortunate in the timing of the first rain break near the end of the third set. Even after his escapology in the fourth-set tiebreak, he never really looked like using that momentum to turn the screw on Nadal, and the Spaniard always seemed the more likely player to break serve as dusk set in. The triumph for Federer was that it was a rearguard action that very nearly succeeded in spite of his overall level – admirable though the champion's fighting qualities were, it was not a match he deserved to win more than Nadal did.

Apart from setting a new record (since surpassed) for the longest final in Wimbledon's history – at four hours forty-eight minutes it was more than half an hour longer than the McEnroe–Connors final of 1982 – Nadal had done what Federer had until then always failed to do: win the French Open and Wimbledon in the same year. In fact, he became the first person to do it since Borg in 1980, another indication that Nadal was matching Borg's achievements as much as Federer was.

A feature of Federer's general disposition is the dignified

way he is able to deal with defeat. However, after that final, his body language and tone of voice in his post-match press conference were most uncharacteristic. At the start, he was as dismissive as he has ever been and he only warmed up a little as the cathartic effect of talking about the match seemed to take hold. When asked what he was feeling, he replied, 'Nothing, it's over, I'm not feeling much, I'm disappointed. It's a disaster, I'm not joking. I'd prefer to lose the way I did in Paris than the way I did here.'

The media were keen to know whether he thought it was the greatest match ever, an understandable question, but one Federer was understandably keen not to get into. 'It's not up to us to judge whether it was the best ever,' he said, 'it's up to fans and media to debate. I'm happy Rafa and I put in a great effort, it was a fair battle which was tough with the rain delays. We both played tough till the very end, but in tennis there are no draws, there has to be a winner and a loser.'

Without resorting excessively to cliché or purple prose, there were actually two winners and one loser that day. Nadal won the match, Federer lost it, and the whole of tennis, if not the whole of sport, won through the sheer quality and drama of one of the best pieces of sporting theatre tennis has ever produced. Federer can be forgiven for not seeing that in the immediate aftermath of defeat, but he has since realised what a very special day it was.

In March 2008, a seemingly minor development took place in Federer's life that is worth noting. It was no more than a house move, but there was a little more to it than merely quitting one building for another.

In the spring of 2008, it emerged that Federer no longer

lived in Basel. And the news did 'emerge' – 'the Basel press heard about it after it had happened, almost as if he didn't want people to know about it,' says Beat Caspar, then of the *Basler Zeitung* newspaper. 'One can only assume he was embarrassed about it.'

Federer and Mirka swapped their flat in the Oberwil suburb of Basel for a palatial residence on the banks of the Zurich Lake in Wollerau, in the canton of Schwyz. In space and scenery terms it was a vast improvement, but the reason Caspar talks of 'embarrassment' is that Canton Schwyz has a markedly lower level of taxation than Basel-Land, the canton in which Federer had lived all his life. And given the magnitude of Federer's annual earnings, even a small variation in tax rates could make a significant difference to his take-home pay. The counter-argument is that at least he was still paying tax in Switzerland, and had not relocated to Monte Carlo (which has no income tax), so his home country was still benefiting from his income.

The other reason for potential embarrassment is that Federer genuinely likes his home city and would not have wanted his move to be seen as a slight. Interestingly, even after the move to Wollerau, Federer continued for several years to list Bottmingen, the Basel suburb where his parents live, as his residence for media biography purposes, before opting to say simply 'Switzerland' without listing a specific city. (The ATP website has since stopped listing where players live, giving only their birthplace.)

One thing the move to Wollerau allowed for was a bigger room to house his growing collection of trophy replicas. And that extra space prompted Federer to make use of an opportunity that Wimbledon offered him in 2008.

Up to and including the 2006 championships, Wimbledon awarded all its champions half-sized replicas of the trophies they had won. In 2007, it decided to make the replicas three-quarter-sized, so Federer's fifth replica was 50 per cent bigger than the other four. Because he is so proud of his Wimbledon record and because the place means so much to him, in 2008, Federer bought three-quarter-sized replicas for the first four years he won the title, in order to make up the full set. The All England Lawn Tennis and Croquet Club doesn't like talking about money, so it is not known how much Federer had to fork out, but, as the replicas are gold plated, or 'silver gilt' to use the correct term, they would not have come cheap.

It's easy to forget just how low Federer's standing had fallen by mid-2008, and that fall needs to be understood to appreciate how well he bounced back. With the Olympics forcing the two hard-court Masters Series tournaments, Toronto and Cincinnati, to begin just two weeks after the end of Wimbledon, Federer was still in his fug when he lost his first match in one and limped through just one match in the other. And his tone appeared to be that of a broken man.

After losing to Gilles Simon in Toronto from 3–1 up in the final set, Federer described the defeat as 'one of those matches I think I should never have lost' but, when asked about the four unforced errors he made in the final game, he replied, 'It's all a blur right now.'

When asked sympathetically, 'It seems you were mentally and physically drained since Wimbledon. Is that fair?' he replied, 'You wouldn't have asked me that if I'd have won, right?' and offered no more. And when a journalist asked,

'Do you agree with Justine Henin's decision to retire at the peak of her career?' (referring to Henin's sudden retirement two months earlier while well ahead at the top of the women's rankings), Federer retorted, 'Do I agree with that? Not today. Ask me another day, please. Don't kill me with questions like this.'

A week later, after he just scraped home in Cincinnati against Robby Ginepri, he talked about a 'one-match winning streak'. Ginepri had summed up the mood in the locker room by saying it was a good time to play Federer because 'he used to be a little more confident with his forehand and could win points more quickly, now he's a little more hesitant – I think guys have seen that he's human.'

Federer dismissed this, but two days later he lost again, this time to Ivo Karlovic on two tiebreaks.

With Nadal reaching the semi-finals at a time of Federer's abject form, the Spaniard had guaranteed himself the number-one ranking. Because of the intricacies of the generally logical 52-week rolling ranking system, the actual ascent to the top was to be delayed by two weeks, but the crown prince had acceded to the throne, and Federer's run at the top came to an end after a record 237 consecutive weeks.

He was gracious in his demotion. 'When I got to number one, I said I hoped I would keep it until someone else came along and took it from me,' he said. 'I didn't want to lose it because I was playing badly and it just slipped to someone else, so I'm pleased with what Rafa had to achieve to get it. If I'd lost first round in Paris and Wimbledon, I wouldn't be so nonchalant, but Rafa deserves it for sure.'

An interesting footnote to this period came in the offices of a Swiss newspaper. After Wimbledon, the sports editor told his long-standing tennis correspondent that he wasn't sending him to the US Open 'because Federer was finished'. No doubt financial considerations also played a part in the decision – the dollar was strengthening against the Swiss franc and the world economy was about to go into convulsions – but it seemed an easy decision to justify on sporting grounds.

The correspondent concerned asked not to be identified, nor his paper named, to save his boss from embarrassment. For, however much the boss in question saved financially, it was to prove a major sporting misjudgement.

What tennis has got from its return to the Olympic fold in the 1980s was always clear: the Olympic cachet that allowed all sorts of money to flow into the coffers of tennis-development projects that almost certainly would have gone to other sports if tennis had remained non-Olympic. What the Olympics got in return was never quite so clear. Until the first days of August 2008, that is.

When Federer and Nadal arrived at Beijing's new international airport, they attracted all the attention. Nadal arrived at the same time as Michael Phelps, the American swimmer who was a sensation even before the eight gold medals he won in China, but it was Nadal who garnered most of the publicity. In fact, most of the tennis players were captured on camera by the official television feed during the spectacular opening ceremony. Tennis's big names were enhancing the Olympics' credibility as the greatest spectacle involving the world's biggest sports stars.

Federer had long since decided that, for his third Olympics, he would not live in the Olympic village because he had been pestered so much in Athens by other athletes wanting their photo taken with him that he had had no privacy. In fact, his hotel room in Beijing had been booked as early as 2005. While some criticised Federer's decision to avoid the village, two separate incidents emphatically justified his reason for it.

On his twenty-seventh birthday, Federer did what few athletes have ever achieved – he carried his country's flag in an Olympic opening ceremony for the second time. He entered the arena and led the Swiss team around the stadium to their allotted space inside the parade track. No sooner had the Swiss reached their destination than a whole horde of other athletes descended on Federer, asking to have their photo taken with him. Federer obliged for as long as the structure of the ceremony allowed.

Two days later, he went to visit some friends in the Olympic village. In total, he spent forty-five minutes signing autographs and being photographed. As one whose romance began in the Olympic village in Sydney eight years earlier, it had not been an easy decision to stay outside the village in Beijing, but for practical reasons it had proved to be totally justified.

In the tennis event, he was blessed with a reasonable draw; in fact, in his second-round match the greatest threat seemed to come from his opponent's name. He faced Rafael Arevalo, ranked 447, the first player of note to come from El Salvador (his brother, Marcelo, went on to win the men's doubles at Roland Garros). Arevalo's support team went out chanting, 'Come on, Rafa,' in the hope of unsettling Federer, but Arevalo was no Nadal, and Federer beat the Olympic wildcard 6–2, 6–4.

But then calamity struck. On day five of the eight-day tennis event, Federer came up against James Blake, and again looked diffident on the crucial points. Blake played a great match, but it was another of those that Federer would have won over the previous five years. Federer was ahead early in the second-set tiebreak, but, after squandering his advantage with a ridiculously tame volley that seemed to sum up his fragile confidence, he went on to lose 6–4, 7–6.

He was looking jinxed at the Olympics. His missed bronze in Sydney, his defeat to Berdych in Athens, and now this. Maybe Federer was fated never to get an Olympic medal, or so it seemed that Thursday night. But then the all-round skills of the man earned him the gold he had craved, and turned round his year.

It's a fact that few specialist doubles players like to admit, but most of them can only earn a living out of doubles because the leading singles players seldom play doubles. And the Olympic doubles event is arguably the highest-quality doubles tournament in world tennis, simply because it attracts the top singles players (there were even three occasions in Beijing where a player pulled out of the singles to improve their chances of a doubles medal – something virtually unthinkable on the regular tour).

Federer had a choice of partners, between his former flatmate Yves Allegro and the much higher-ranked Stan Wawrinka. He had played with Allegro in Athens and in Davis Cup ties, whereas he had played just twice with Wawrinka and lost in the first round on both occasions. But Wawrinka was enjoying the best year of his career at the time and had given Switzerland two players in the men's top ten for the first time ever, so Federer opted for Stan.

After routine wins in the first two rounds, the competition suddenly got very stiff. The pair had to beat the Indians Mahesh Bhupathi and Leander Paes in the quarter-finals, and then the same day the Bryan brothers. In bright sunshine after lots of rain, they beat Bhupathi and Paes 6–2, 6–4, after which they indulged in a strange routine. Wawrinka lay down on his back, and Federer held his hands over him as if warming them over a hot fire. 'It's a private joke,' Wawrinka explained. 'It comes from cards, the story of fire, the story of being on fire. It developed naturally after we beat the world number-one pair.'

It actually developed after the Bhupathi–Paes victory, but there was no doubt both men were on fire against the top-ranked Bryan brothers. This was the match that would guarantee Federer a medal if the Swiss won, but would leave him still to win a playoff if they lost. And, when the Californian twins had break points in the opening game, it appeared that the opposition was going to be just too tough.

But that was the one chance the Bryans had. The Swiss came through, and were never broken after that, winning 7–6, 6–4, thanks to breaking Mike Bryan's serve in the seventh game of the second set, the only break of the match.

The danger then was to take the final too easily. In the bottom half of the draw, the fancied pairs had gradually tumbled, leaving the veteran Swedes Simon Aspelin and Thomas Johansson standing between Federer and gold. The score in the gold-medal match reads 6–3, 6–4, 6–7, 6–3, but, with no disrespect to the Swedes, who had won a very long three-set match to reach the final, there was only one pair in it, and Aspelin and Johansson did well to win the third set.

As Federer stood on the rostrum listening to the strains of the Swiss national anthem, while the white cross on its red background was raised, a gold medal round his neck, his year had been 'saved'. All the talk about his decline had suddenly been eclipsed, not because the decline was in some way fictitious – it was very real – but because he had filled one of the few remaining gaps in his impressive collection of titles.

'Right now this is quite a surreal moment,' he said after winning gold, his voice just starting to crack with emotion. 'The joy of sharing this victory with somebody else who I like very much, who we had a great two weeks with, it's quite different to anything I've ever gone through. I could only maybe compare it a little bit to some incredible Davis Cup victories I've ever had.'

That was the change in Federer, or at least appeared to be. He had won his much-longed-for Olympic medal, and it had come not by himself but with the help of a partner. It had not been The Roger Federer Show with a little help from Stan Wawrinka; in fact, if anything Wawrinka had played better in the final, showing a confidence that betrayed no sense of being cowed by the presence of his more illustrious partner. And Federer seemed to appreciate that. 'I think I'm definitely going to play the [Davis Cup] first round next year,' he told the media after the doubles final, although other issues ultimately prevented him from fulfilling that pledge.

A team competition had helped save Federer's year, and he promised to be a more committed team player after that. No doubt he meant it at the time, but his actions in the five years that followed severely undermined the authenticity of that statement. Only in 2014 was he a fully committed team player again.

Initial indications at the US Open suggested that nothing had changed for Federer as a singles player. In the second round he laboured to a 6–3, 7–5, 6–4 victory over the 137th-ranked Brazilian Thiago Alves. And his language after the match gave no indication that he had turned a corner. Asked about some easy shots he had missed, he replied, 'Well, I guess we're talking about it today and if I win the title you forget about it again. That's usually how it goes.'

Given that he did win the title, such comments are justified in hindsight, but, on the day itself, talk of winning the title seemed fanciful. In fact, there were numerous members of the tennis media family – including this one – who were convinced on that Friday night that Federer was in denial. He was beginning to sound like a former champion trying to convince himself despite all evidence to the contrary that he could still win the major titles. With a third-round match against Radek Stepanek, one of the players to have beaten him earlier in the year, coming up, it seemed Federer was in for a reality check.

Perhaps the quality of the opponent helped focus Federer's mind. Whatever his public utterances, he must have known he could not have got past Stepanek with the quality of play he showed against Alves. Whatever went on in his mind and his camp, he came out against the talented Czech with a new sense of purpose. Not only did he win 6–3, 6–3, 6–2, but the whole performance was that of a reborn man. Where in recent months his forehand had broken down on him, this time it worked to perfection, and, while previously he had shuffled around his backhand to hit the big forehand, this time he danced boxer-like, creating the impression of a man allowing his talent to overwhelm his opponent. Federer was back.

Not that he breezed through the rest of the tournament. He needed five sets in windy conditions to beat Igor Andreev, an immensely likeable Russian with a massive forehand, and there was only one break of serve in his straight-sets win over Gilles Müller. That took him into a semi-final line-up that reflected the new elite in men's tennis, the first Grand Slam semis to feature the 'big four' – Federer facing Novak Djokovic in the bottom half of the draw, with Nadal facing the rising Andy Murray in the top half. All looked set for the first Federer–Nadal final on hard courts in a Grand Slam event.

Federer did his bit. On a day when the imminent arrival of a hurricane forced an uncharacteristically prompt start of play at Flushing Meadows, Federer gained revenge for his Australian Open defeat against Djokovic by beating the Serb in four sets. It was a popular win; Djokovic had been booed off court following his win over Andy Roddick in the quarter-finals after receiving treatment for an injury. Then Murray did much of Federer's spadework for him, beating Nadal in four sets to reach his first Grand Slam final.

If Murray had beaten Nadal, he was surely a match for Federer. But not this time. While Murray had beaten Federer in lesser matches, this was a Grand Slam final, and Federer, in his seventeenth, would make Murray pay for his lack of experience. But, even more than that, Nadal's game provided problems for Federer, in particular the left-hander's use of the full width of the court and the heavy topspin that Federer found hard to counter at that stage. Murray, while no easy player, was more within Federer's reach, and the Swiss was suddenly a red-hot favourite.

Using the dancing footwork to crunch his big forehand, Federer made his statement early, opening with an ace and breaking Murray in the sixth and eighth games. A little lucky with some line calls in the second set, Federer again knew when to press home his advantage, breaking in the twelfth game for a two-set lead and, with it, effectively the match. His twelfth Grand Slam title was achieved with a 6–2, 7–5, 6–2 scoreline and his celebration at the end smacked of vindication following eight months of people writing him off.

He was quick to acknowledge the role his Olympic gold medal had played in his US Open triumph. 'I think that's what really made the big difference,' he said after beating Murray. 'If I wouldn't have played doubles at the Olympics, I would have come here with three tough losses. But with the Olympic gold in doubles, it really sort of made me forget about it, and just come in here and enjoy this tournament.' He also said he felt the Andreev five-setter was the key to the tournament. Although that may be how it felt to him, to the watching tennis world it was the Stepanek match that got him back on track, as it sent out a signal to the world that the old Federer was back.

But was it the old Federer? The US Open title was certainly a vindication, but was it a total rehabilitation? Well, of sorts, yes. But events four months later were to suggest that Nadal had moved on to a different level.

*

Federer won just one more tournament in the rest of 2008 to finish the year with four – his lowest total since 2002. It was only a poor year compared with the magnitude of his achievements in 2004-7, and he had still won a major, as well as an Olympic gold medal.

And yet, even allowing for relativity (Albert Einstein was after all Swiss), there was a clear dip in success rate for Roger Federer in the first eight months of 2008. This unleashed a torrent of theories – with associated rumour mill – about why this was so, and whether the great man was on the way down. The fact that he was still in the top four in early 2020 when the tour was put into cold storage for the Covid-19 pandemic renders all the speculation a lot of hot air, but there is no benefit of hindsight in the present. And the Federer legend feeds at least in part off the number of times he was written off and bounced back.

The theories included the mononucleosis, the improved competition (notably the rise of Djokovic and Murray), perhaps losing a bit of competitive edge after several years of unadulterated dominance, and other people's propaganda – after Djokovic beat Federer in the 2008 Australian Open, Dijana Djokovic, Novak's mother, was quoted as saying 'the king is dead', which, if accurate, can best be put down to wishful thinking. There were also rumours that something might be awry in Federer's private life that was costing him energy and focus. Such speculation was roundly quashed in March 2009 when he announced that Mirka was pregnant, and the two got married in a small and (well-kept) secret wedding in Basel on 11 April. The desire for journalists to write the first draft of history is understandable, but it leads to premature judgements about the end of an athlete's career, and with great champions that can be a very dangerous activity.

Seldom have expectations at a Grand Slam tournament centred on a quartet of players as much as they did on the big four at the 2009 Australian Open. At an event known at the time for producing an unexpected finalist, if not champion, almost all serious tipping for the men's singles title centred on Nadal, Federer, Djokovic and Murray. If anything, Murray was the favourite after a sparkling second half of 2008 and victory in two events at the start of January 2009: the Qatar Open and an exhibition event in Abu Dhabi, both of which featured Nadal and Federer.

But Murray fell in the fourth round in Melbourne to the breakthrough player of the fortnight, Fernando Verdasco, while Djokovic lost in the quarter-finals to Andy Roddick, a result that owed as much to Djokovic's physical frailties as to Roddick's revival in form. Meanwhile, Federer was outstanding against Marat Safin in the third round, merciless against Juan Martin del Potro in the quarter-finals, and just too good for Roddick in the semis.

With Nadal looking every bit the world number one in the top half of the draw, the great rivals had set up their first match since the epic Wimbledon final seven months earlier and casual polling of players, ex-players and journalists showed that a clear majority expected Federer to win. The tournament was desperate for a good contest after a women's final that proved as disappointing in the 6–0, 6–3 scoreline with which Serena Williams beat Dinara Safina as it was in its paltry duration of fifty-nine minutes.

Nadal and Federer certainly made up for the women's

final in both time and quality of play, but the result was a crushing blow for Federer. It may be no disgrace to lose a five-set match, especially to a player of Nadal's quality, but it was the way in which Federer lost that was so damaging. He was 4–2 up in the first set but lost two of his next three service games to lose the set. He had six break points in successive Nadal service games at 4–4 and 5–5 in the third set but, just as in past finals, he simply couldn't convert them into service breaks. And, after rallying back in the second and fourth sets, he crumbled in the fifth, his backhand deserting him as Nadal won the four-hour-and-twenty-three-minute match 7–5, 3–6, 7–6, 3–6, 6–2.

His assessment that he 'had many chances but missed them' and 'didn't serve particularly well' is fair. But the psychological damage to Federer came in the fact that the dice were loaded so favourably for him. His previous two matches had been straight-sets affairs, while Nadal's semi-final on the Friday night had been a record-breaking five-hour-and-fourteen-minute battle against Verdasco. And yet Nadal always looked the stronger player, with Federer's best chance appearing to be that the Spaniard might run out of gas having played so much tennis in the previous two days. Nadal played a good match, but it wasn't his best tennis and he could have played better too.

The following morning, the Melbourne daily *The Age*'s front page declared: 'The king no longer holds court. Long live the king'. And another Australian daily, *The Australian*, continued the metaphor in its front-page story, which included the line 'Federer's kingdom, slowly but surely, is crumbling.'

Commentators on radio and television were similarly

dismissive, using phrases such as 'the Federer era is over' and 'it seems like Federer's best chance of beating Nadal is if Nadal falls over and breaks his ankle'.

Needless to say, journalists and commentators are prone to hyperbole, and historical analysis is never at its best in the heat of the moment; after all, if Federer could take the world number one to five sets in his fourth consecutive Grand Slam singles final, it was hardly a sign that he was finished. But what the 2009 Australian Open had shown was that Federer was clearly the world number two – undoubtedly still ahead of the chasing pack led by Djokovic and Murray, but just as unmistakably behind the undisputed best in the world, Rafael Nadal.

Although he didn't mention it at the time, Federer was also bothered by his back, at least in his mind. 'I don't actually remember whether the back was really bothering me,' he said a year later, 'but I was worried that it could come back, so I was playing with a bit of doubt.'

As Federer stepped up on to the Rod Laver Arena's podium to receive his runner-up salver, there was another outbreak of what the Australians – with characteristic wit and very little sympathy – call 'the waterworks'. As the warmth of the ovation for him showed no signs of dying down, he stammered into the microphone, 'God, this is killing me,' and was ushered away in tears by the master of ceremonies to 'settle down' before speaking again a few minutes later.

As was the case three years earlier when he had cried on the podium, what caused the emotions to flow is not entirely clear. The presence of five of the legends of the game might have had something to do with it. On the fortieth anniversary of Rod Laver's 'open' Grand Slam, Tennis Australia had invited Laver plus the four men he had beaten in the 1969 finals (Andres Gimeno, Ken Rosewall, John Newcombe and Tony Roche) to attend the final, and Federer is always moved by the presence of tennis's great names. The warmth of the ovation may also have contributed, as could the fact that Federer has always had a soft spot for Australia that could be traceable to Peter Carter's role in his life, as could the fact that Federer put so much discipline into his tennis that his emotions did seep out, sometimes when he least intended them to.

Later in the year, Federer made light of the tears, and on the first anniversary it was he who was consoling a tearful Andy Murray, who felt he had let down the over-expectant British public after losing to Federer in the 2010 final. 'I've been crying after losing matches since I was five years old,' Federer said, 'so to cry after the loss of a Grand Slam final was normal for me, but there was this big fuss that I didn't understand. The thing that was killing me was having to talk while crying. What I meant was "I wish I could stop crying and could talk normally and give Rafa the stage he deserves". The last thing I wanted was for people to feel bad for me. I wish I would have won, but I had to accept – and did accept without a problem – that Rafa was better on that day.' Federer also explained that the atmosphere at the Australian Open is more likely to bring out tears because there is less noise during the ceremonies than at other events, so it creates a more reverential environment.

All that makes sense with hindsight, but there may have been another reason for the tears – a tiny fear that his era of domination might now be over. His defeat to Nadal in the

Wimbledon final could have been put down to his poor start to the year and the mononucleosis, and he had redeemed himself in the US Open final. But here was apparently conclusive proof that Federer had been surpassed by his greatest rival, that there was now someone on the other side of the net against whom Federer's best was no longer necessarily enough. And the possibility of him being left stranded on thirteen Grand Slam titles, one short of Pete Sampras's record of fourteen, was becoming a real one.

Because Federer went on to win another seven Grand Slam singles titles, it's tempting to gloss over just how vulnerable the tennis world thought he was in the first five months of 2009. He pulled out of both Dubai and his much-vaunted return to the Davis Cup first round, citing his back. It was clearly a problem, if only the fear of a problem. He later admitted he also had concerns over Mirka's pregnancy, though as it wasn't public at the time he couldn't mention that.

When he lost to Andy Murray in Indian Wells and Novak Djokovic in Miami, headlines heralding a changing of the guard were easy to write. His defeat to Djokovic in the Miami semi-finals also created headlines. After winning the first set, Federer lost his way in the second, and, as the third set began, it seemed a crucial moment to the tennis world. It was no doubt highly charged for Federer too, for, after dropping serve early in the third set, he smashed his racket tempestuously on the concrete court in full view of all spectators and the world's television. It made headlines for its rarity value, and the incident became one of the most popular YouTube videos for several weeks.

Federer refused to engage in discussion about the incident after the match, a contest he lost 3–6, 6–2, 6–3 thanks to that one break in the final set. He said only that he broke his racket 'and felt good about it', a slightly odd way to dismiss a matter that was so out of character. He seemed to want to dismiss it as a minor aberration, but the tennis world read more into it than that. Taken in the context of the hold Nadal had on him, it was easy to see it as another step in a slow but inexorable decline in his on-court fortunes.

The Greek dramatist Euripides observed that 'whom the gods would destroy, they first make mad'. The tennis gods, it seemed, were making Federer mad by leaving him stranded on thirteen Grand Slam singles titles as his powers began to wane.

15

AND YET THE tennis gods had another twist in the tale. Instead of destroying him, they reprieved him.

As Federer arrived for the 2009 French Open, he seemed as vulnerable as ever. He had beaten Rafael Nadal in the final of the Madrid Masters (only his second win over Nadal on clay), but the biggest story from that tournament had yet to come out. Had it been known, the first week of the 2009 French Open could have been very different.

Nadal had followed his usual clay season routine by winning in Monte Carlo, Barcelona and Rome. But after beating Novak Djokovic in the Rome final to leave him with just one set dropped in fifteen matches, Nadal returned home with increasing pain in his kneecaps. He was diagnosed as suffering from patellar tendinitis in both knees and was advised to rest. The problem with top-level sports stars is that they invariably have an insatiable appetite for competition, and with the next event on the calendar being the Madrid Masters, to be played for the first time in the Spanish capital's brand new state-of-the-art Caja Mágica tennis centre, Spain's tennis icon felt he just couldn't pull out. So he showed up, and played arguably the match of the year in the semi-finals to beat Djokovic 3–6, 7–6, 7–6 in over four hours. But that left him with little in the tank when he faced Federer in the final the following day.

Federer's 6–4, 6–4 win announced that he was still capable of beating Nadal on clay, but no one took it particularly seriously as a result – Nadal at Roland Garros would be a different proposition. Only he wouldn't be. His knees were even worse at the end of the Madrid week than at the beginning, and he was able to do very little court work in the remaining week before the tennis world gathered in Paris. It's just that the world didn't know it, so Nadal was as strong a favourite for the French Open as he had ever been.

Federer went to Paris to play his first Grand Slam tournament as a married man. He and Mirka had announced in March that they were expecting their first child, and, when they married on 11 April in Basel in a ceremony attended by thirty-nine people sworn to secrecy, plenty of tennis watchers wondered whether Federer's priorities were now shifting to the domestic arena and away from tennis.

Everyone assumed it would be 'baby' – singular. Roger and Mirka knew as early as the end of January that it was twins, but such is the leak-proof nature of Team Federer that only when Mirka delivered twin daughters on 23 July was the secret out. Federer actually learned that it was twins on the day he played Juan Martin del Potro in the Australian Open quarter-finals, and promptly went out and beat him for the loss of just three games in a magnificent display of tennis. If people had known at the time that he could play like that after receiving such life-changing news, they might have feared less for his chances as a parent. The only crisis in Mirka's pregnancy came shortly after that, and was part of the reason for Federer missing the Davis Cup first-round tie against the USA that he had promised to play after winning his Olympic gold medal. Again showing a remarkable ability to keep the lid on information about his private life, he kept quiet about the pregnancy and blamed his Davis Cup absence on his back.

The French Open didn't really get going until the middle Sunday. Nadal, parading a striking pink shirt, won his first three rounds confidently, leaving his fitness unquestioned. But then on the last day of May, he came up against Robin Söderling in a match that was to change Federer's fortunes.

Söderling had been a promising Swede who, like many promising youngsters, had never known how to make the transition from player of great tennis to great tennis player. Now aged twenty-four, he began to see that his career wasn't infinite and, if he was going to make something of his ability, he had to start soon. He came out crunching his big forehand, and his relative height – he is 1.93 metres or six foot four – meant Nadal's heavily topspun shots came into his optimum hitting zone. After Nadal won the second set on a nervy tiebreak to level the match, Söderling's challenge could have collapsed, but the combination of his determination to seize the moment and Nadal's knee problem allowed Söderling to reassert himself in the third set. And when he won the fourth to defeat the champion, he had inflicted Nadal's first-ever defeat at Roland Garros.

Nadal was typically gracious in defeat. Asked about an injury he neither denied it, nor blamed his defeat on it. But the medical advice he received after he left Paris was unequivocal – he would not do himself any good playing on through patellar tendinitis. He quickly pulled out of the following week's tournament at London's Queen's Club, and, while it took him another two weeks to withdraw from Wimbledon, that decision hardly came as a surprise.

Suddenly the way was open for Federer. His nemesis had been felled and the gods were smiling on the Swiss once more. The number-two seed became the new tournament favourite – only Nadal had stopped him in the previous four years. But it very nearly went wrong the following day.

Federer has subsequently admitted that he was desperately nervous when he came out to play Tommy Haas, the German enjoying an Indian summer at the age of thirty-one with three shoulder operations behind him. The fact that Nadal's defeat had removed his only insurmountable obstacle was preying on his mind. 'That was the only time in my life I think I went out feeling the pressure,' he said several months later. 'It had a huge effect on me when Rafa lost at the French, just knowing the opportunities I had and being already occupied with my own game and opponents.' When Haas led by two sets and 4–3 in the fourth against a strangely subdued Federer, the German had a break point on Federer's serve – he was just five points from victory, and only one from serving for the match. But a moment of genius (or was it luck? The line separating the two can be very fine) turned the match around. Federer played an in-to-out forehand that just clipped Haas' sideline, he went on to hold serve, and that was the first of nine straight games that put Federer back in charge. He won the final set 6–2 to complete his fifth comeback from two sets down.

Not that the draw got any easier after that. In the quarter-finals he faced Gaël Monfils, the flamboyant Frenchman he had beaten in the previous year's semis, and then Juan Martin del Potro took Federer to five sets in the semis. But by then it was a somewhat different Federer, and it had little to do with Nadal. He had added a new weapon to his armoury, the drop shot. For years he had largely shunned the shot, but a slow-burning campaign by José Higueras to get him to use it more often, together with his four defeats to Nadal, had woken him up to the potential of the well-disguised short ball, especially on clay where the bounce is lower than on hard courts.

The drop shot played an important part in all Federer's matches, but it deserted him a little in his win over del Potro, in which he started slowly and was twice a set down. Federer admitted he got a little lucky as del Potro ran out of gas in the fourth and fifth sets, though those watching the match felt he won it on a greater sense of belief, and del Potro was not to make the same mistake when the two men met in the US Open final three months later.

So, for the fourth year running, Federer walked out onto the Court Philippe Chatrier looking to complete his set of major titles. If some people had been saying in 2006 that victory then would have made him the greatest-ever tennis player, surely victory in his fourth successive French Open final would guarantee him that unofficial epithet? But it wasn't going to be easy on a day when rain was forecast.

Federer profited from a desperately nervous start from Söderling, who won just one game in the first set. The Swede got his game together in the second, a set characterised by an intruder who ran onto the court in the fourth game and approached Federer – it was not the Roland Garros security guards' finest moment. As the rain got heavier, Söderling got stronger, but the rain eased and the set went into the tiebreak. Despite the heavy conditions, Federer served perfectly, racking up four aces as he took the tiebreak 7–1.

The momentum of that tiebreak allowed Federer to break in the opening game of the third set. The title was in Federer's own control, albeit with another five games to serve out. Söderling's level picked up. He had a break point at 1–2 but missed it. At 5–4, Federer was serving for his moment of glory – but then the nerves set in big-time.

The forehand he hit to go 15–30 down was a howler, as the great man looked visibly nervous for the first time in years. Söderling then had a second break point at 30–40. Was it all going to go horribly wrong on the verge of triumph? No it wasn't. Söderling missed his break point chance, and two points later his backhand return went into the net on Federer's first match point. Federer's light blue shirt was suddenly at one with the clashing orange-red clay, as he collapsed with the relief of victory amid tears of joy.

He told the crowd it was his 'greatest victory', though he also admitted he had been hugely nervous. But then the stakes were as high as they could possibly be – this was his best chance, perhaps his last realistic chance, of completing his set of major titles, an achievement completed by only six other men at the time in the history of tennis. He received the Coupe des Mousquetaires from the fifth man to achieve the full set, Andre Agassi, who had been asked to present the trophy on the tenth anniversary of his own accomplishment.

The skies thundered, the rain really did get heavier after being incredibly kind to the players, but tennis history had been made under the grey Parisian skies.

The word Federer used several times in the subsequent months to describe his French Open triumph was 'relief'. Seven months later, in front of 15,000 spectators in Melbourne's Rod Laver Arena, he was asked for his highlight of 2009. Despite having won Wimbledon several weeks after Paris, he put his triumph at the home of clay at the top of his list.

'It feels a relief to be able to go back to Paris knowing they won't be asking me if I'll ever do it,' he said, a rich seam of truth hidden in a slightly jocular answer. It had been the last monkey off his back – the next target to achieve was at least one more Grand Slam title to take him past Sampras's mark of fourteen.

Despite the contract tying him to play in Halle, Federer knew playing in northern Germany the week after such an emotional triumph made no sense (the third week between the French and Wimbledon was only added in 2015), and duly pulled out, saying he felt 'emotionally overwhelmed and exhausted' after Paris. So his next appearance was to open the Centre Court programme on day one of Wimbledon, a role that, by tradition, should have been Nadal's as defending champion, but he was absent nursing his sore knees. And Federer continued a tradition of his own that his clothing supplier, Nike, was happy to fuel – the unveiling of a new Wimbledon fashion line.

Some like it, others don't. In the words of one of the British media's correspondents, 'He sauntered on to Centre

Court, resembling a cross between a Sergeant Pepper figure and something out of *An Officer and a Gentleman*, before he put down his glittering kit bag, stripped off his embossed white jacket and started practising in a waistcoat ... Federer departed his second home two hours later, having proved conclusively that he has the game to carry off such preposterously dandy apparel.'

Once the waistcoat – really a cardigan – had been safely packed away, Federer beat Hewitt, Söderling and Haas en route to a final that the British had hoped would be against Andy Murray. It was against an Andy, but not the one the home fans wanted. Murray had been out-thought in his first Wimbledon semi-final by Andy Roddick, who was displaying the fruits of his coaching relationship with Larry Stefanki, with whom he had been working since the start of the year. Roddick's four-sets win over Murray was arguably the single best tactical performance of his career, certainly since winning the US Open in 2003, and this still prickly character had the considerable class and sensitivity to mouth the words 'I'm sorry' to the crowd after acknowledging the applause, recognising he had spoiled the home nation's party.

But could Roddick overcome Federer, the man who had defeated him in his two previous finals? He proved that he could, but he let his fish off the hook. Playing in a crowd that featured Rod Laver, Björn Borg and the travel-shy Pete Sampras, Roddick took the first set 7–5; when he led the second-set tiebreak 6–2 he had Federer on the ropes. But at 6–5, a moment of indecision cost Roddick the set and probably the match. Having been driven into his forehand corner, Federer responded with a lob over Roddick's backhand side. It was a good shot, yet Roddick still had time to guide the ball into the open court and claim the set. But his first thought was that the ball was going out, and when he realised he had to play it he was too late, and put the volley wide. It was the let-off Federer needed, and he took the tiebreak 8–6 with six points on the run.

Roddick wasn't going to lie down, but the significance of the second-set tiebreak was that from then he was chasing the game. Federer took the third set on the tiebreak, but Roddick bounced back to take the fourth. For the third year running the Wimbledon final was into a fifth set.

Statistically, the final set in 2009 reads more spectacularly than its equivalent a year earlier, but in truth it lacked the drama of Nadal's victory. Roddick maintained his level as 4–4 became 5–5, and 6–6 became 7–7. But he was always serving second, and, while his serve kept up, he never got close to breaking Federer. For his part, Federer was happy to play a waiting game. As 8–8 became 9–9, 10–10 became 11–11, there was never the sense that he was looking to put his foot on the gas pedal, only to slice his backhand into the last half-metre of Roddick's court and wait for his opponent to play a lax game. He had to wait a long time, as 12–12 became 13–13, and then 14–14. Eventually the moment came. Serving for the eleventh time to stay in the final, Roddick mis-hit a forehand, the ball went into the stands, and Federer had won his fifteenth Grand Slam title in four hours sixteen minutes, the ninety-five-minute fifth set notching up a new record for a Wimbledon final.

Ten years after that final, Roddick explained in an interview how his assessment of Federer as a person rose after the match. Devastated at his defeat, Roddick first apologised to Pete Sampras that he was unable to prevent Federer from passing the American's record of fourteen major titles. Then he retreated to the locker room, an elegant, carpeted open-plan changing room with a range of mahogany-door members' lockers offering background décor. As Roddick sat there nursing his sorrows, Federer and his support team entered in high spirits. 'They should have been celebrating, absolutely,' Roddick told CNN Sport. 'I saw him [Roger] out of the corner of my eye, he kind of gave them one of these "Be quiet" [signs] and pointed to me, and they walked out and went about their business in another part of the All England Club. I thought that was considerate.'

In the space of four weeks, Federer had equalled and overtaken Pete Sampras's record of fourteen Grand Slam titles, and he was able to pose for photographs alongside the three other greats whose achievements he had largely surpassed. He had also recaptured the number-one ranking. Nadal's absence from Paris and Wimbledon had made it somewhat easier for him, but no one wanted to hold that against the Swiss. On the tennis tour, it was widely acknowledged that Nadal's ability to match and out-do Federer was based on his phenomenally energy-intensive game, which eventually took its toll on the Spaniard's body. By keeping his level and staying in great shape, Federer had bided his time and been in the ideal position to cash in when Nadal's body rebelled. Federer had made it to twenty Grand Slam singles finals, and won fifteen. The other five had all been won by Nadal. That speaks as much for Nadal as for Federer.

*

The Federers had not only kept the fact that Mirka was expecting twins secret; they had also jealously guarded the due date. Boris Becker was thought to have let the cat out of the bag when he said while commentating on British television that the baby (singular, and male) was due in the first week of August. But maybe that was just a bluff. Federer himself had talked about 'the baby'.

The twin girls (non-identical) arrived on 23 July in the Bethanien private hospital in Zurich. Although born sixteen days before their father's birthday, like him they are also Leos in the zodiac star sign system, and one British bookmaker was offering somewhat gimmicky odds of 100–1 that, with such impressive genetic inheritance from father and mother, the girls would make it as professional tennis players. They were named Charlene Riva and Myla Rose – Myla is a Czech name derived from the diminutive of Ludmilla, which in ancient Slav means 'the precious' or 'the lovely one', while Charlene is one of several female versions of Charles and is popular in South Africa. In a statement issued on his website, Federer said he and Mirka felt this was 'the best day of our lives'.

Much is made of the difficulty of winning tennis tournaments as a parent. The difficulty is self-evident for women who have put their bodies through the rigours of pregnancy, but very few men win the leading tournaments when they have the next generation in tow. No doubt many a night's sleep is disrupted by a crying baby, and, in a close match the following day, sleep deprivation could make a difference. But it's largely a statistical thing – most men on the tennis tour don't become dads until they're well past their playing peak, and those dads who have won majors, the likes of Federer, Becker, Andre Agassi and Jimmy Connors, had earned enough money to afford a team of nannies to protect their beauty sleep.

The Federers didn't so much try to manage having kids – they truly embraced it. They set about being a Swiss Family Federer on semi-permanent tour, although a disciplined *Familia Rodante* is probably a more apt cinematic metaphor. Legend has it that, when Federer had spent several months off the circuit in 2020, his kids asked when they were going travelling again. And indeed, with the girls barely three weeks old, he beat Murray and Djokovic to claim his first title as a father at the Cincinnati Masters.

Ironically, the US Open in 2009 was won by a mother but not by a father. Like Federer, Kim Clijsters was playing her third tournament since becoming a parent, but in her case it followed a 'retirement' of twenty-seven months. Her triumph created the news story of the year in the women's game, especially as it involved Serena Williams being disqualified in the semi-finals for directing a torrent of abuse at a line umpire who had foot-faulted her. How Federer didn't join Clijsters in making it a first mother-and-father double in the open era is still baffling.

After wins over Söderling and Djokovic (the latter featuring an eye-wateringly perfect 'tweener' shot on the penultimate point), Federer faced Juan Martin del Potro in the final. Federer had won all their previous six matches, and if he could beat the tall Argentinian on clay, surely he would beat him on hard courts – so the logic went. And so it should have been, as he moved to within two points of victory in the fourth set.

Yet there was something edgy about Federer during that

US Open. No one is quite sure why, and he himself denies he was in any way irritable, but he came across that way, both behind the scenes and in another five-set Grand Slam final. With Federer serving at 5–4 in the second set for a two-sets lead, del Potro took a long time to request a challenge. When the challenge led to an overrule and del Potro then broke for 5–5, it began to rankle with Federer. Later in the match, when del Potro was again slow to challenge, Federer let the umpire, Jake Garner, know exactly what he thought, using the F-word within clear range of the television effects microphones and refusing to accept anything Garner said in response. There are many people in the tennis world who felt that Federer had a point over challenges – if an umpire can only overrule if he or she instantly sees an error, why should a player be allowed to wander across the court to see a mark, glance up to their coach, and then challenge several seconds after the ball has landed? It's a legitimate point that the officiating branch of the sport took a while to get a grip on. Yet it was uncharacteristic for Federer to be so high-handed and abusive about it. He was later awarded a rare fine – $1500, which will hardly have troubled his accountant – but, more importantly, he went on to lose the match.

He should still have won it in the fourth set, but, once del Potro had taken the final into a decider, Federer looked a spent force, and del Potro won 3–6, 7–6, 4–6, 7–6, 6–2 in four hours and six minutes. In sets, it was a mirror image of Federer's victory in the French Open semi-finals.

In his post-match remarks, he seemed almost a little fatalistic. 'That's the way it goes sometimes,' he said. Perhaps he had a sense that this final just wasn't meant to go his way. He has been equally fatalistic about the Wimbledon final he lost to Nadal, saying, 'I believe things happen for a reason, and maybe that sixth Wimbledon in 2008 was not meant to be.' But despite his otherwise great year, this was another major that got away, and del Potro became the first player other than Nadal to beat Federer in a Grand Slam final.

Like most players who beat Federer, del Potro found it easy to be magnanimous. 'I had two dreams this week,' he said at the trophy ceremony, glancing towards his beaten opponent. 'One was to win the US Open, and the other was to be like Roger. One is done, but I need to improve a lot to be like you.'

It had been a remarkable turnaround. Federer had begun the Grand Slam year with his game disintegrating as he lost the final set of the Australian Open 6–2. It ended with his game disintegrating again for him to lose the final set of the US Open 6–2. But he had once more reached the finals of all four majors, and had won two of them. Even in his moment of defeat in New York, he could see the big picture. 'I was two points from the match today, but I've had an unbelievable run this year, being in all major finals and winning two of those. Sure I would have loved to win those two as well, but the year has been amazing already – got married and had kids, don't know how much more I could want.'

And, in reality, he didn't want much more. It would be wrong to suggest he didn't take the rest of the season seriously – such was his wish to remain at the top of the rankings at least until 7 June 2010, when he would surpass

Pete Sampras's record of 286 weeks in the number-one slot, that he was keen to pick up ranking points wherever possible. But Grand Slams clearly meant more to him than tour events, and it was only when the Australian Open came around at the start of 2010 that his level really picked up.

Six days before the Australian Open began, a massive earthquake hit the central American state of Haiti. Already very poor and ravaged by decades of questionable government, the country suffered a humanitarian catastrophe on a scale few people had ever seen. The United Nations described it as the worst disaster it had ever had to deal with.

On the Saturday morning, two days before the start of the tournament, Roger Federer phoned Craig Tiley, the Australian Open's tournament director, and asked whether he and a group of other top players could play a charity match to raise money for Haiti. 'My initial reaction was to say no,' Tiley says, 'because it would be a logistical and safety nightmare.' But he agreed to explore the idea, while Federer went off to sound out his top-level colleagues about their willingness.

At five o'clock that afternoon, barely seven hours after his call to Tiley, Federer gave a pre-tournament press conference in which he announced the 'Hit for Haiti'. He had secured Lleyton Hewitt, Rafael Nadal, Andy Roddick, Novak Djokovic, Serena Williams, Kim Clijsters and Australia's top women's player Samantha Stosur to play a mixed doubles in which substitutions were allowed and all players would play with a headset-microphone so the crowd would hear everything they said. For his part, Tiley had mobilised the massed ranks of the Melbourne Park temporary staff, notably security and catering, to work an extra day, in some cases for free.

In explaining the rationale, Federer used the term 'the tennis family', a phrase often used by administrators trying to get various warring factions to pull in the same direction. 'I think it's something as a tennis family that we're very happy to do,' he said. 'I know it's on the eve of the first Grand Slam of the season, so it's for some not so easy to separate mentally, but I think it's a great initiative. I'm happy we can go through with it, we hope to have some fun tomorrow, maybe also make it a nice day for families to come and see some top players play.'

Less than thirty hours after his initial phone call to Craig Tiley, Federer and the other seven players stepped out into the Rod Laver Arena for what was to prove a magical experience. Charity days on the eve of the French and US Opens were by then commonplace, but it was new in Australia. A briefing sheet handed out on the morning of the event to staff and some broadcasters said a crowd of between two and five thousand was expected. That was to be a hopeless underestimate of Federer's pulling power. The 15,000-seater stadium was full, and many Melburnians who had queued couldn't get in and had to make do with watching the event on the big screen in Garden Square, Melbourne Park's equivalent to Henman Hill at Wimbledon. Everyone paid ten Australian dollars admission (children under twelve were allowed in for free but many parents paid for them), and bucket collections went from row to row. Even journalists had to pay the entry fee if they wanted to watch the event from the stands. Nearly A$200,000 was raised, a sum that was quadrupled thanks to contributions from the ATP, WTA, ITF, Grand Slam Committee and individual players.

But it was more than just an exercise in raising money for a humanitarian disaster. It showed the public a different side to the players. If Federer always had his 'game face' on when he played matches, this was a chance for the joking personality to shine through. All players entered into the spirit, and the result was ninety minutes of wonderful artistry and great fun. Roddick captured the spirit of the occasion when he told a line judge who had foot-faulted him that he ought to be careful as Serena Williams was on his team – after Williams's outburst at the US Open, it was a wonderful way of defusing tension, and Serena roared with laughter at the joke at her expense.

It was a great success all round, and it also showed the role Federer played as a statesman and de facto leader of tennis players. He spoke to the crowd after the event, he held a couple of extra press conferences, and took a commanding role. There will be many in Haiti who have reason to be grateful to him, even though most will not know who he is.

There was one other act of statesmanship that Federer was required to perform at that tournament.

On the first Thursday, Melbourne received a visit from Prince William, at the time the second-in-line to the British throne and son of the late Princess Diana, who had been a great tennis fan and frequent visitor to Wimbledon. The prince was in Melbourne to meet survivors of some horrendous bush fires that had ravaged the state of Victoria eleven months earlier, and his evening entertainment at the Australian Open had been kept out of the public domain until he took his seat during Federer's match against Victor Hanescu.

Federer had, however, been privately briefed. The briefing included informing him about the way he should address someone of Prince William's status. When told that the correct way to address him was 'Your Royal Highness', Federer at first thought this was a joke. When told that it wasn't, he is said to have replied, 'All right, I'll call him "Your Royal Highness" if he calls me "king of the court"!'

All that was behind closed doors and no doubt meant as a harmless private joke. When Federer had beaten Hanescu, he did his on-court interview with the former world number one Jim Courier, at the end of which Courier invited Federer to formally welcome the prince. Federer took the microphone and uttered the words, 'Your Royal Highness, welcome to the world of tennis – thanks for coming!' But he did so with a barely suppressed giggle that betrayed his apparent belief that having to address a twenty-seven-year-old spectator as 'Your Royal Highness' was all rather silly. As a genuine fan of England and the English, Federer can easily be allowed his snigger at the pomposity of British royal protocol.

If one dismisses the first part of Federer's opening match of the 2010 Australian Open against Igor Andreev, there is a case to be made that his sixteenth Grand Slam title was the one in which he played his best tennis ever. 'I think this has been one of my finest performances,' he said after beating Andy Murray in the final, 'certainly in a long time, maybe for ever.'

It had seemed such an open Open. Federer was the

bookmakers' favourite, but it was plausible to see any one of about eight players lifting the Norman Brookes trophy. In hindsight, perhaps the greatest threat to Federer was Nikolay Davydenko, who came to Melbourne having won the ATP World Tour Finals at the end of 2009 and who won the biggest tour event before the Australian Open, the Qatar Open in Doha. And it was Davydenko who gave Federer his greatest test.

For an hour of their quarter-final, Davydenko seemed destined for a major upset. In a match starting late because of two long previous matches, Federer seemed bothered by the setting sun that caused a two-tone effect on the court. Rallies were frequently played with one player in the sun and the other in the shade, the ball passing between the two. It happens at a lot of tournaments, but the combination of Davydenko's precision hitting and Federer allowing himself to become unsettled by the tricky light led to an hour of total dominance by the Russian. Federer even admitted he took his time over a bathroom break at the end of the first set, to allow the sun a little longer to disappear behind the roof of the arena.

Yet there is a pattern to many of Federer's matches that challengers gradually became aware of. They frequently worked themselves into a commanding position, but, if they then didn't seize their opportunity, they found the full force of Federer's talent unleashed upon them. So it proved with Davydenko. When the Russian led 6–2, 3–1 and had Federer at 15–40, the top seed was looking so frail that some wondered if he was ill. But then at 30–40, Davydenko dumped a fairly simple backhand into the net. That was the let-off that Federer needed, and he surged into a run of twelve successive games that effectively won him the match.

The Australian and British media were convinced Federer engaged in a form of psychological warfare before the final against Andy Murray. After beating Jo-Wilfried Tsonga in the semi-finals, Federer joked with Jim Courier in an on-court post-match interview that poor Murray was carrying the pressure that the British hadn't had a Grand Slam champion 'for 150,000 years or whatever it is'. He also mentioned in his post-match press conference that Murray had yet to win his first Grand Slam title, and that the Scot was 'playing me who's won many Grand Slams and has won three times here'.

Federer and the Swiss press saw it very differently. When asked about the 'psychological warfare' in a question that specifically mentioned that term, Federer replied, 'It got exaggerated. You ask me a question, I'll give you a straight answer. That's what happened after the Tsonga match. It's not an easy thing to win your first Grand Slam. That's not mental, trying to screw with his head. It's just a tough thing.'

It would be disingenuous for Federer to claim he always gives straight answers – there are always nuances in what he says that indicate to those who can read the runes what he thinks about someone. But it is fair to say that the media are often so keenly on the lookout for a different news angle that they can read more into something than was ever intended, and miss an unloaded straight answer. If Federer made a tactical error, it was to rile Murray – Murray is always competitive but finds an extra layer of zeal when riled; by contrast, Rafael Nadal always talked in the most respectful tones about Murray, and Murray never seemed to have quite the same determination to beat Nadal as he had when facing Federer.

Whatever Federer may or may not have intended, he let his tennis win the war in a final that saw him outclass Murray. The Briton's consistent play from the baseline wears down most opponents, but against an aggressive and creative player at the top of his form it was never going to be enough, and Federer notched up his sixteenth Grand Slam title with a 6–3, 6–4, 7–6 win. The tiebreak had lots of drama, before eventually going to Federer 13–11, but there was always a sense that, even if Murray had converted one of his five set points, Federer would have bounced back to take the fourth set. And let's face it, if you've got the greatest player of all time playing pretty much at his peak, it would take a very special performance to beat him.

A year earlier, it had been Federer in tears on the podium – this time it was Murray. And the normally taciturn Scotsman came out with one of the quotes of the tournament when he composed himself to utter, 'I can cry as well as Roger, it's just a shame I can't play as well as him.'

But then with the form he showed at the 2010 Australian Open, who could play as well as Roger? Federer had raised his level to a new degree of sublimity, spurred on by the new generation of players who hit powerfully and seldom miss. 'When I came on the tour, matches were played very differently,' he said. 'It was more of a bluff game – guys served well, but there was always a weakness you could go to. Today that doesn't exist any more, and that's thanks to guys like Murray. They've made me a better player.'

As the competition got hotter, the best got better, and

the greatest was becoming even greater. In an ominous postscript to the Australian Open, Federer said, 'I believe I can always improve.'

There was an improvement, but it was to require another setback – or twin setbacks – before it materialised.

Federer always knew his streak of Grand Slam semi-finals would come to an end, but few expected it to end in the quarter-finals of the 2010 French Open. True, he was up against a quality opponent in Robin Söderling, the Swede whose victory over Nadal in the previous year's tournament had paved the way for Federer to win his missing French title. But Federer had played imperiously in four rounds, and was thought to have too much all-court ability against the big-hitting but slightly limited Swede.

When Federer took the first set 6–3, he looked set for a semi-final against Tomas Berdych, but then the clouds rolled in and intermittent drizzle started. The court soaked up more moisture, the balls got heavier, and Söderling's greater weight of shot became more of a factor. On a damp and dank Parisian evening, Federer's confidence on the big points was gradually eroded, and his twenty-three-tournament semi-final streak was snapped with the Swede's 3–6, 6–3, 7–5, 6–4 win.

No one seriously expected him to declare that such a defeat was the end of the world, but Federer once again endeared himself to the tennis community with his comment, 'Well at least I still have the quarter-final streak!' And he did – his run to the last eight in Paris meant it was twenty-four straight quarter-finals, a total he took to thirty-six before his shock second-round defeat to Sergiy Stakhovsky at

Wimbledon in 2013. Those two statistics – the twenty-three successive Grand Slam semi-finals and thirty-six quarter-finals – should always be quoted in discussions about who is the greatest-ever tennis player, as they denote a consistency at the highest level that no other player has matched.

While Söderling was completing his win over Federer, the great and the good of the tennis world were gathering a few kilometres away for the annual ITF World Champions' Dinner. Federer was expected to attend to be honoured as men's singles world champion for 2009, but, as news filtered through that Söderling was beating him, everyone at the dinner knew that the chances of seeing Federer at the gala event were virtually nil. And yet, just as no one should ever write off Federer on a tennis court, nor should they ever assume he won't turn up. After discharging his media obligations at Roland Garros, Federer spruced himself up and turned up for a good hour at the dinner, earning the undying respect and gratitude of all those there. It was clearly a mark of great class, though perhaps it was also a very smart psychological move – after losing a match that must have seriously hurt, what better way to pick yourself up than to go to a dinner where everyone is pleasantly shocked to see you and some of your greatest recent achievements are honoured? It was one of those win/win situations that left everyone feeling happy.

The one lasting irritant from the Söderling defeat was that it meant Federer would lose his number-one ranking the week after Roland Garros. Nadal would take over, leaving Federer on an aggregate of 285 weeks in the top slot, just one short of equalling the record of 286 held by Pete Sampras. Had Federer beaten Söderling and then lost to Berdych in the semi-finals, he would have held the number-one ranking until after Wimbledon and therefore broken Sampras's record then rather than two years later. It meant that getting back to the top remained a goal for Federer, when one more win in Paris might have reduced its attractiveness.

However, not all was well in the Federer body. He had been troubled again by some back strains and, when he picked up a groin injury in the final of the grass-court event in Halle, a match he went on to lose to Lleyton Hewitt, it meant he arrived at Wimbledon in much worse shape than usual. And he was nearly caught out at the very first hurdle.

The reigning champion's traditional opener on Centre Court is normally a formality, but after two hours there was a serious chance that the title holder's defence could be ended on the first afternoon for the second time in seven years. Federer dropped the first two sets to the unheralded Alejandro Falla from Colombia, a player he had beaten twice in the previous four weeks without dropping a set, and came within five points of losing in the third set. Federer averted the danger, but another set dropped against Ilija Bozoljac in the second round sent the message through the player lounge that the great man's invincibility was cracking, and in the quarter-finals his ability to play around the back and groin problems met too big a challenge.

Tomas Berdych had announced his presence to the tennis world by beating Federer at the Athens Olympics in 2004. Since then he had become a great prospect but had never taken the final step into the top category. Playing a near-faultless game based around his massive forehand, the Czech beat Federer in four sets, and followed it up with a win over Novak Djokovic in the semis to reach his first Grand Slam final. He was taken apart by the irrepressible Nadal, who was playing so well that Federer could have been humiliated had the two met that year.

After losing to Berdych, Federer tried to find the right balance of admitting to his injuries without detracting from his opponent's great success. The admission of back and groin injuries made sense to those who couldn't work out why Federer should have looked so defenceless against Berdych, but it did little to dampen the journalistic line being peddled that evening: that maybe there was a changing of the guard and the great man's best days were behind him.

The defeats in Paris and Wimbledon prompted Federer to bring in some new tactical advice. He hired Paul Annacone, a former touring professional whose best achievements were in doubles, but who had still reached number twelve in singles on the back of a net-rushing game. Annacone had surfaced as a coach while a member of Pete Sampras's entourage; when Sampras's coach Tim Gullikson died of brain cancer in 1996, Annacone slipped easily into Gullikson's shoes, and he went on to coach Tim Henman after Sampras's retirement. Federer said he wanted to hear 'a fresh, different voice' and incorporated Annacone into his team alongside Severin Lüthi.

It was certainly a more aggressive Federer who reached the semi-finals of the US Open. Facing Djokovic with everyone expecting the result to set up a first-ever Federer–Nadal clash at Flushing Meadows, Federer came within a point of winning, but for the fourth time that year he lost a match from match point up. With Djokovic serving at 4–5 15–40 in the fifth set, Federer had two second serves but did nothing with his returns, and Djokovic was rewarded for taking the bigger risks. When Djokovic broke Federer at 5–5, the match had turned in an instant, and the Serb won the set 7–5.

Astonishingly for a man of his experience, Federer got distracted by the thought of the final. 'I was playing the second semi-final,' he said several weeks later, 'Rafa had already made it to the final, and I was conscious that I needed to win without using up too much energy if I was to have a realistic chance in the final. So I stopped playing with the same intensity and I let him back into the match.' Ironically, the final was to be delayed until Monday night because of rain, so Federer would have had an extra day to recover.

Nadal beat Djokovic in four sets in the final to complete his career Grand Slam, and the Spaniard could well have done the same – or worse – to Federer. Either way, it was another wake-up call for the twenty-nine-year-old legend that his aura of invincibility had been seriously dented.

By the time Federer faced Djokovic in another major, four months later in Melbourne, he had at least regained his confidence. A programme of exercises to strengthen his abdominal muscles had given his body a greater cushioning to soak up some of the pounding his back was taking from hard-court tennis, with the result that he was playing pretty much pain-free by the start of 2011. And he had beaten Djokovic three times in tour matches since the US Open for the loss of just one set, so was feeling good when the two squared up in the Australian Open semis, with a place in the final against Andy Murray or David Ferrer at stake (Ferrer had beaten Nadal in the quarters, though a torn Nadal hamstring had played a big part).

Yet what nobody knew at the time was that Djokovic was in the early stages of a forty-five-match winning streak that would see him totally dominate world tennis in 2011. In the middle of 2010 he had met an alternative health practitioner who had identified gluten and dairy intolerances as the major cause of so many of Djokovic's medical issues (not the news the son of pizzeria owners wants to hear), so he had switched to a different diet. He had won the Davis Cup for Serbia on home soil in December 2010, and in January 2011 he was playing with a freedom and confidence not everyone had thought him capable of.

The result was a trouncing for Federer, Djokovic winning 7–6, 7–5, 6–4 with a display of footwork that was at times breathtaking. Federer's aggressive tactics proved a little too inflexible faced with a guy whose ability to counterpunch was sublime on the day. Federer played much of the match close to his baseline, but Djokovic's great depth of defensive shot meant Federer could seldom get to the net, and he had less time to adjust when countless balls from the Serb cleaned his baseline. Djokovic was the better player by a distance, and went on to claim his second Australian Open title with an even more clinical demolition of Andy Murray in the final.

The semi-final defeat left the tournament with only the second Grand Slam final in six years to feature neither Federer nor Nadal. Inevitably, the world's tennis media were again wondering whether the torch was being handed on to a new generation. The thought was entirely legitimate, but journalists seldom ask themselves what it must be like for a player to receive a question such as 'Do you think this result means the torch is being passed to a new generation?' Someone asked that of Federer, immediately after he had lost to Djokovic, to which the quietly irritated Swiss replied, 'Don't know, ask me in six months.'

Great champions are invariably written off too soon, and most add to their legend by bouncing back when the world thinks their time has passed. It was too soon to write off Federer after a defeat that meant he didn't hold a Grand Slam title for the first time since mid-2003. But the Federer–Nadal duopoly had ended, and, while few were yet talking about the big four, it was clear there was at least a trio at the top of the men's game.

16

I T IS A TRUTH universally acknowledged that a sportsman
or sportswoman with a three at the start of their age is
generally reckoned to be in the twilight of their career. In
some sports that is less applicable than others – golf, for
example, and other disciplines that require less physicality
or offer greater scope to recover from exertions. But for
sports like tennis that demand a level of sustained physical
fitness, thirty has become a milestone beyond which
popular instinct assumes a player is inevitably battling
against nature's decline.

The fact that Federer was still in the world's top four
just five months short of his thirty-ninth birthday when the
pro tour was mothballed in March 2020 requires a rethink
of what being a thirty-something means in tennis. There
has been a tendency to view the longevity of Ken Rosewall,
Rod Laver and Jimmy Connors as a reflection of an era
of less depth of competition. But Federer's achievements –
indeed the fact that most recent major titles have been won

by thirty-somethings – mean the tennis watcher will need in future to give greater credence to the role of experience and on-court cunning and somewhat less regard to age, even after the current remarkable generation have hung up their rackets.

This context is important to remember when assessing Federer's achievements after his thirtieth birthday in August 2011. There was an assumption on the tour that he was now the grand old man defying age, and, as the hairline began gradually to recede (visible when the carefully tied bandanna came off), the image of the granddad who still had a thing or two to teach the youngsters took root. Thus it was that his seventeenth Grand Slam title and seventh Wimbledon, won in July 2012 just four weeks before he turned thirty-one, were put down as a triumph of age over youth.

Speaking after winning that title, which took him back to the top of the rankings, Federer said the build-up to it began more than a year earlier at the French Open in 2011. That had been something of a milestone Grand Slam tournament, because it was the first one for eight years in which no one seemed to be talking about Federer as a realistic contender. Despite being the third seed, he slipped under the radar. There were good reasons for this: Djokovic had carried his momentum from winning the Davis Cup and the Australian Open into the two early-year hard-court tournaments and the three clay-court tournaments. He was playing outstanding tennis, and came to Paris having not lost a match all year. In fact the last man to beat him was Federer in November 2010 in the semi-finals of the ATP Finals in London, a match Djokovic seemed mildly uninterested in, perhaps because of the impending Davis

Cup final that meant so much to his country, and thus to him as a proud patriot.

Apart from his impressive streak, Djokovic had done something few considered possible – he had beaten Nadal on clay, twice, both in meaningful matches, both in straight sets. Having beaten Nadal in the hard-court finals in Indian Wells and Miami, the Serb shocked the tennis world by beating him in the final of the Madrid Masters. Nadal's defenders could just about put that down to the fact that the Mallorcan has never played his best in Madrid. But what did shock Nadal was Djokovic's 6-4, 6-4 win in the Rome final. This meant that the anticipated Roland Garros final between the Spaniard and the Serb was what everyone was talking about, and Federer barely warranted a mention.

But Federer hadn't exactly had a bad year. Apart from defeats to Jürgen Melzer and Richard Gasquet, the only players who had beaten him in the run-up to Paris were Djokovic and Nadal. And he reached the semi-finals without dropping a set against some handy opposition. That set up a Federer–Djokovic clash that Rafael Nadal, the defending champion who beat Murray in the other semi-final on another 'big four' day, described as 'the best of the moment against the best of the history'.

It was Federer's best match of the year, one of the greatest of his career, and arguably the match of 2011. He was Djokovic's equal throughout the first set and, after taking it on the tiebreak, he forged ahead to open up a two-sets lead. Djokovic won the third set, and, when he served for the fourth in fading light, it looked as if the two men would have to come back for a one-set shootout the following day. But some well-timed moments of brilliance allowed Federer to break back and take the match on the tiebreak at 9.40pm. He had done what no one else had done all year – beaten Djokovic, the Serb's streak snapping at forty-five consecutive victories.

He couldn't repeat the performance against Nadal. Tennis is a sport where match-ups are crucial, and, while Djokovic's game allows Federer to play to his strengths, Nadal's wears him down, especially on clay, and so it proved in their fourth Roland Garros final. Had Federer converted the set point he had at 5–2 in the first set, things might have been different, but his attempted drop shot fell just wide, Nadal won the set, and by the time Federer found his best tennis Nadal had taken control. But Federer had announced that he was still a factor, and had started the process that would lead to his seventeenth Grand Slam title thirteen months later.

Despite losing to Nadal, Federer was well placed to live up to the 'ask me in six months' riposte he had given to the journalist in Australia who wanted to know if he was finished. If he could beat Djokovic and push Nadal hard on clay, surely he had a great chance at Wimbledon? Yet that theory was never tested, because against Jo-Wilfried Tsonga in the Wimbledon quarter-finals, Federer had one of his increasingly common lapses from a commanding position, and on this occasion was made to pay for it. After going two sets down, Tsonga broke early in the third set, and, once he had broken early in the fourth, Federer looked to be fighting an irrepressible tide. Not that the Swiss played badly, but he had let the genie out of the bottle, and Tsonga went on to inflict Federer's first-ever defeat from two sets up in a Grand Slam match.

Then came a crushing blow – a near-identical defeat against Djokovic at the US Open from a year earlier. Meeting again in the semi-finals, Federer looked the better player for three sets, and reached two match points in the fifth, only for Djokovic to save them both and go on to win. The way Djokovic saved the match points was also familiar – while Federer played a little safe, Djokovic was willing to tee off on a half-chance, and the forehand winning return with which he saved the first match point has lasted in the memory, perhaps because it seemed to outpsyche Federer; once Federer had dumped a forehand into the net on his second match point, Djokovic grew while Federer shrank, and Federer was uncharacteristically ungenerous in the press conference afterwards. But then Djokovic had the irresistible force with him, and he beat Nadal in the final in near-identical fashion to the way he had beaten him in the Wimbledon final. At the end of the 2011 Grand Slam year, Djokovic's only defeat was Federer's win in the French Open semi-finals. But having contested the last three finals, Djokovic and Nadal were clearly the leading pair, with Federer an increasingly distant third.

After that US Open defeat, Federer did a lot of thinking and discussing with his team. 'I'd played an amazing French Open,' he said. 'I was very close against Rafa in the final, and I actually think I played very well at Wimbledon against Jo – things just didn't turn out well for me. Then I played great as well at the US Open, but again I was unlucky, or Djokovic played well – whatever you want to call it. But things were tough for me there. It was a time when I just had to believe that things were going to turn around for me, but I couldn't wait for it to happen naturally, I had to work at something. I'd played a lot of tennis, good tennis, but I wanted to win titles, not just lose in quarters and semis. So I decided to look differently at my schedule, play some tournaments that I hadn't played for a while, and try to get back to number one. But the first thing I needed was a long break from tennis.'

To many tennis watchers, the idea that Federer might win another couple of Slams was entirely plausible; indeed very few were willing to say the thirty-year-old wouldn't add to his total of sixteen. But the idea of him getting back to being world number one seemed fanciful. Reaching the top of the rankings requires phenomenal consistency over fifty-two weeks, and the feeling was that Federer was no longer up for that, for all his ability to peak at the big tournaments.

When Federer won his two singles on a grass court of dubious quality in a Davis Cup tie in Sydney in September, it was the start of a run that was to see him unbeaten for the rest of the year. He picked up a fifth Basel title, a first Paris Masters 'tree' (the tournament has a distinctive if odd trophy), and then stormed through the ATP Finals, including a 6–3, 6–0 thrashing of a strangely uninterested Nadal in the group stages. It meant he finished the year on seventeen straight wins, and the unusual achievement of beating the same player, Jo-Wilfried Tsonga, in three successive finals on three successive Sundays. There was almost a sense that the end of the year had come too early for the Swiss. 'The confidence rose as I went to Paris and also to London,' said Federer eight months later. 'I think this is when I realised that a lot was possible in 2012.'

*

Federer's winning streak lasted until Rafael Nadal beat him in the Australian Open semi-finals, but another seventeen straight victories saw him take the titles in Rotterdam, Dubai and Indian Wells. He had a reasonable clay-court season, winning on the blue clay of Madrid when all around him were moaning that the colour had added to the slipperiness (it hadn't, but the colour proved a one-year experiment), and he was beaten in the Rome semi-finals by Djokovic.

Djokovic again awaited him in the semi-finals in Paris, and everyone was keen to see whether Federer could produce the same vintage display from a year earlier. He couldn't; indeed it was a massive disappointment, though perhaps a blessing in disguise. Federer never got going, indeed never gave the impression of caring that much, and Djokovic beat him in straight sets.

The blessing was that Federer was no more than third-favourite for Wimbledon. But then came the boost that his Wimbledon campaign needed – Nadal crashed out on the first Thursday to the little-known Czech Lukas Rosol, the world number 100 beating the world number two in five sets with a combination of blistering tennis, a stroke of luck as the roof had to be closed just as Nadal had got into his stride, and probably a little outpsyching of Nadal.

Just as Federer had nearly lost to Tommy Haas the day after Nadal had crashed out of the 2009 French Open, so he wobbled again the day after Nadal's defeat to Rosol. He went two sets down, this time to Julien Benneteau, and came within two points of losing in the fourth-set tiebreak. He eventually came through what was to prove his final wobble of the tournament, although he did have back problems during his fourth-round match against Xavier Malisse, a match that saw the rare spectacle of Federer calling for the trainer mid-match.

With Nadal gone, everyone believed Federer could win the final, whoever he played. The big question was whether he could beat Djokovic in the semi-finals. They had played twenty-six times before but never on grass. Most tennis followers felt Djokovic had the edge, but the absence of previous experience on grass made it hard to call. Whether grass-court prowess made the difference is hard to say. Djokovic was clearly not at his best (and something was afflicting him that he refused to talk about afterwards), but Federer was inspired, and he ended Djokovic's reign as Wimbledon champion in four sets. It was to prove his last ever win against Djokovic at a major.

That should have been the title wrapped up, but there was an extra dimension to the final. Federer's opponent was Andy Murray, the first British men's singles finalist at Wimbledon for seventy-four years. It ought to have been an away match for Federer, but such is his popularity that even against a Brit at Wimbledon he had plenty of fans. For nearly two sets, Federer looked unsteady, as Murray threw everything at him. Murray was clearly on top, but the consolation for Federer was that he always had something in reserve – the question was whether he could find it in time. With Murray serving at 5–6 30–30, he did. He ended two long baseline rallies with exquisite drop shots, the second of them a volley with sidespin that had even the Murray fans purring. Federer had levelled the match and, when the players came back after a rain break at 1–1 in the third set, he was vastly more aggressive on Murray's second serve. Murray kept up his level, but the tide had turned, and, when Federer broke in the fifth game of the fourth set, the Wimbledon title was his.

The presentation ceremony will be remembered by the home nation for Murray's tearful attempt to explain his defeat and acknowledge that he had once again come up against a better player in a Grand Slam final (his fourth). But for Federer it was also emotional, even if he held back the tears on this occasion. It wasn't quite his first major title as a father – that had come in Australia when his twins were six months old. But this one was the first with the twins able to sit for the presentation ceremony in Federer's enclosure. The girls recognised their dad on the grass, but probably did not appreciate why he was there. To them he was just their dad. To the man himself, he was both a proud champion and a proud father in the same moment.

One thing being a thirty-something enhanced was Federer's gravitas as a statesman of the sport, and in 2011 and 2012 his 'political' career in tennis was gaining a momentum of its own in parallel with his playing career. As president of the ATP Player Council he began to play a very big behind-the-scenes role over the question of prize money at the four Grand Slam tournaments.

There were two things Federer recognised that suggest he has a very good political brain. The first was that asking for more prize money was likely to go down badly with the world at large, whereas asking for a greater percentage of the tournaments' income from television rights sounded much more reasonable (even if it amounts to the same thing). After all, it was the players' attractiveness that elicited the big bucks from the television companies, so, Federer argued, the players should get their fair share of that income. The second was to concentrate the distribution of the increased prize money on the lower end of the tour players, to reduce (a little) the large discrepancies in earnings between the big names at the top and those who are committed to the tennis tour but even at their peak will seldom if ever break into the world's top sixty. Together with this political awareness came a resolute refusal to reveal any details of discussions with players to the media. Every now and then a question would arise at a press conference and, while Federer would try to answer it, he would never do so at the cost of revealing what had been said in a Player Council meeting. This created a climate of trust with his fellow professionals.

At one stage, the hive of political activity extended to the rumour that the players might boycott the Australian Open. This was never going to happen, if only because the players have contracts for rackets, clothing and other accessories based on them being seen in the biggest tournaments, so a refusal to play in a major would have cost them dearly. But Federer – aided by Nadal, Djokovic and Murray, who all had various meetings with leading figures of the four Grand Slams – achieved significant results. The Wimbledon prize money in 2012 included considerable increases in the rewards for first-round losers, while the Australian Open hiked its prize money pool in 2013, also with a massive boost for the early-round losers.

Yet such successes didn't mean Federer was immune to getting himself into hot water, and, at the start of 2012, he got himself embroiled in two minor controversies. One was of his own making, the other was not, and he showed great statesmanship in defusing a potentially explosive situation.

At the end of 2011, the idea was mooted of basing the tennis ranking system on two years' worth of results. The model used in tennis since computer rankings were introduced in 1973 is for a player's results over the previous fifty-two weeks to determine his or her ranking. That means that players who do well at a specific tournament can use their results to qualify for the following year's staging of that event. By contrast, golf uses a two-year ranking – in other words, results taken over the preceding 104 weeks – and when the idea of a two-year ranking was put forward for tennis, it gained the voluble support of Nadal, who at the time was vice-president of the ATP Player Council.

But one person strongly opposed to it was Federer, the president of the council. He said it might serve him very well, but it would make it a lot harder for players lower down the rankings to break into the top 100. The media enjoyed playing up the dispute between the two rivals who had seemed such good friends off-court. There was certainly a disagreement, but Federer defused any suggestion of nastiness between the two men by saying at the Australian Open, 'Rafa always used to agree with me, he'd always say that he was happy with what I said. Now he's developing more of his own opinions and that means he sometimes disagrees with me. That's good.' Nadal was equally respectful of Federer's position, saying the two men were entitled to disagree and it was up to both of them to justify their positions. The media read a lot into it when, in March 2012, Nadal resigned from the Player Council. The speculation was that Nadal felt he could no longer work with Federer; with hindsight the reason Nadal gave for his move – that he couldn't devote enough time to his duties as a council member – is entirely plausible, especially with a physique that required increasing amounts of work to keep match-fit.

Federer was re-elected to the ATP Player Council in June 2012 for his third two-year term, this time without Nadal and Djokovic as fellow council members.

The other controversy arose over the weekend Switzerland played the USA in the Davis Cup first round in February 2012. The Swiss were expected to win, so when Mardy Fish beat Stan Wawrinka in a five-set opening match, it at least looked like being a contest, as Federer was expected to win both his singles. But Federer was beaten in four sets by John Isner, and a defeat for Federer and Wawrinka in the doubles against the makeshift pair of Fish and Mike Bryan left the Americans victorious inside two days. Federer's first appearance in a Davis Cup first-round tie for eight years had suggested a new dawn for the Swiss, yet it had ended in a disaster that was to become a debacle.

When asked for his assessment of Switzerland's shock defeat, Federer seemed to throw the blame on Wawrinka. 'If Stan had won his singles, it would have been very different,' he said, 'but he didn't play very well.' It seemed a strange thing to say about a teammate ranked outside the top twenty who had taken a top-tenner to five sets, when Federer himself, ranked three, had just lost to the seventeenth-ranked Isner. Wawrinka took it very personally and declined to turn up for Sunday's dead rubbers, leaving a three-man Swiss team to face the press at the end of a hugely disappointing weekend for the Alpine nation. Fences with Wawrinka were never likely to stay broken for long, but it was a remarkably undiplomatic thing for a generally diplomatic man to say. Maybe the world underestimated how strongly the emotions still burn beneath Federer's normally dignified exterior?

The off-court decision Federer made at this time that was to have long-term implications was the foundation of his own player management agency. In the spring of 2012 he severed his ties with the International Management Group (IMG), which had represented him since the summer of 2005. Federer's contract with IMG ran out at the end of May 2012, and was simply not renewed. At the same time, his personal manager Tony Godsick also left IMG, ostensibly because his contract was up for renewal and he wanted a new challenge. Godsick was known to be frustrated at persistent attacks from the media levelled against both him and his wife Mary-Joe Fernandez for alleged conflicts of interest as an IMG employee (IMG has so many interests across world sport and media that many see it as a by-word for conflicts of interest, whether real or imagined), but speculation was rife that Godsick and Federer were working on a new enterprise, perhaps with the partial intention of setting up a post-playing-career role for Federer.

This enterprise saw the light of day eighteen months later, when Federer, Godsick and two American investors launched 'Team8', a new agency that from day one had Federer and Juan Martin del Potro on its books, and shortly afterwards signed up the Bulgarian Grigor Dimitrov, whose playing style is strikingly similar to Federer's. Godsick made it clear that Team8 would not become a big agency in the style of IMG but would remain a 'boutique' agency representing just a handful of players. 'Small is the new big,' he told the media at Team8's launch, and the proliferation of boutique player management agencies did seem to reflect the Zeitgeist of a move away from the big three management companies.

However, a brand that has Roger Federer as its figurehead means the Ohio-based agency is unlikely to struggle for clients. It has one of the hottest prospects on the women's tour, Coco Gauff, on its books, and in 2019 Alexander Zverev switched to Team8, although he parted company with them a year later after being embroiled in serious but unsubstantiated allegations by a former girlfriend. In addition, Team8 runs the Laver Cup team competition and staged Federer's 'Match in Africa' against Rafael Nadal in February 2020.

After winning Wimbledon in 2012 and returning to the top of the rankings, there were really only two meaningful gaps left in Federer's trophy cabinet: a Davis Cup winner's medal and an Olympic singles title. If the Olympic singles gap could be filled by any medal, then he had achieved that within four weeks of his Wimbledon triumph, but a singles gold medal was never achieved.

From the moment in 2005 when London secured the 2012 Olympics, it was clear the Olympic tennis event would be played at Wimbledon. It was a very different-looking Wimbledon, with players allowed to wear coloured clothing, striking fuchsia-pink backdrops at each end, different camera positions for television, and a very different type of crowd made up of off-the-street Olympic tennis fans and lacking the traditional Wimbledon 'blazerati' (the corporate tickets and debenture holders).

Federer had the opportunity to carry the Swiss flag in

the opening ceremony for the third Olympics running, but declined this time, and the honour fell to his doubles partner Stan Wawrinka. The pair lost their Olympic title in the second round of the doubles, but that just freed Federer up for his assault on the singles title, for which he was the favourite with Nadal absent due to knee problems. After wins over Alejandro Falla, Julien Benneteau, Denis Istomin and John Isner, he faced Juan Martin del Potro in the semi-finals in what proved to be the longest-ever three-set match in history. They were over the two-hour mark by the time Federer had taken the second-set tiebreak 7–5, and, with no tiebreak in the final set, it always looked destined to be a long one. Federer should have won it 11–9, but was broken to love when serving for the match at 10–9. He served thirteen times to stay in the match, and at one stage was 0–30, but he broke at 17–17 and served out the victory in four hours twenty-six minutes.

Whether that affected him for the final may never be known. He was thought to be the favourite against Andy Murray in a repeat of the Wimbledon final from four weeks earlier; Murray had put out Djokovic in the other semi-final. But this was a different Murray. Some people thrive in a team environment, and Murray had discovered the joys of being a member of 'Team GB'. What's more, the host nation had enjoyed a stunning day on the eve of the gold medal match, winning six golds, three of them in athletics in the space of forty-five minutes. It was a force Murray tapped into by crushing Federer 6–2, 6–1, 6–4 in less than two hours. Seldom has Federer looked so out-of-touch – it was not a humiliation the way his defeat to Nadal in the 2008 French Open final had been, but it was a case of the greatest tennis player having no answer to an irresistible onslaught.

It was also a popular onslaught, and perhaps that had something to do with Federer's lacklustre display. The great respect and esteem in which he is held around the world means he seldom experiences the hostility of an 'away' crowd. The Olympic tennis crowd wasn't hostile, but the fans were riding the crest of the British success wave, and Federer's brisk rhythm was frequently interrupted by noise from boisterous spectators, something that clearly irritated him.

Federer declined to use that as an excuse for his defeat. He admitted making 'one or two bad decisions', and added 'I came here for a medal and I've got one, and I'm very happy with the silver'. Even several months later he was admitting that he might have lacked Murray's motivation, since he had achieved his aim of a singles medal before walking out for the final. But whatever Federer's real level of motivation, it was a remarkable turnaround for Murray from the Wimbledon final four weeks earlier, and, while the colour scheme of Federer's bulging trophy cabinet will be enhanced by medals of different metals, the absence of an Olympic singles gold does stand out.

From the vantage point of the second half of 2013, the idea that he might add to his seventeen Grand Slam titles seemed fanciful. But after a pretty disastrous year by his standards, one that saw his ranking fall to a most un-Federeseque eighth, he reinvented himself at the age of thirty-two. All the evidence in the peak months of 2013 suggested that the decline in Federer's fortunes had begun. If a defeat to

Andy Murray in the semi-finals of the Australian Open was no disgrace, it was nonetheless a match that showed Federer a clear second-best. In fact if ever there was a five-set drubbing, this was it. That sounds like a contradiction in terms, and it is, but the facts are that Murray dominated the first, third and fifth sets, and was arguably the better player in the second and fourth, only to lose them on tiebreaks. The match went the distance, but the result never seemed in doubt.

Yet that proved the high point of Federer's year. He reached the final in Rome, only to suffer another heavy defeat to Nadal; and then, at the French Open, he was roundly beaten in the quarter-finals by Jo-Wilfried Tsonga when his route to the final seemed open thanks to Andy Murray's withdrawal and a favourable draw. He led Tsonga by a break in the first set, only to crumble as the Frenchman outplayed him in front of his own public.

If that was disappointing, Wimbledon was a disaster. After winning his sixth title in Halle, Federer went to London feeling moderately optimistic, and his biggest problem of the first week looked like being a mild ticking-off for violating Wimbledon's all-white clothing rule with some orange-soled shoes. But his pattern of winning the first set, losing the second and then failing to find his way back struck in the second round against Sergiy Stakhovsky. Once Stakhovsky had taken the second set on a 7–5 tiebreak he was effectively in charge, and, while Federer had the chance to turn the match around right to the end, he never seriously looked like doing so.

After thirty-six consecutive Grand Slam quarter-finals, Federer had lost in the second round. It was a crushing way to come crashing down to earth. In fairness, it was a seriously strange day, with carnage among the top names that left both the men's and women's singles shorn of most of their big names through defeat or injury. But Stakhovsky's win was without question the upset of the year.

Federer knew he was going to face questions from the media about his declining fortunes, so he had his answer ready when he walked into his post-match press conference. 'The twenty-four-hour rule applies,' he said. 'Don't panic at this point. Go back to work and come back stronger. It doesn't feel like the end of an era for me because I still have plans to play for many more years to come. Some finals haven't hurt this much. At least having lost I didn't have to go through a trophy ceremony with this one.'

Playing a couple of low-ranked clay-court tournaments after Wimbledon might have been a good way to rediscover the confidence, but Federer's back was playing up again, and he was experimenting with a new racket. The result was a poor run-in to the US Open. At least that diminished expectations and, with him projected to meet Nadal in the quarter-finals, that looked the realistic limit of how far he could go. But he didn't even get that far. With everything set for his first-ever US Open match against his Spanish nemesis, he lost in the fourth round to another Spaniard, Tommy Robredo. Robredo was on an impressive comeback after a long absence, and had reached the quarter-finals of the French Open with three successive five-set matches. And he played well against Federer, but it was a lame display by the great man. He had sixteen break points but converted just two of them, both in the first set, and it left some commentators saying he ought to end his career there and then before too much of the gloss of his reputation came off in an inglorious descent into mediocrity.

Federer himself said he 'self-destructed' and 'I beat myself'. It was a fair assessment but, at thirty-two, who was to say this was not henceforth to be the norm?

17

THE JOURNALISTS, COMMENTATORS and fans who said Federer was finished midway through 2013 were proved spectacularly wrong by subsequent events, yet it seemed a perfectly reasonable view to take at the time. Here was a player who had worked his way into the hearts of pretty much all tennis lovers through what can only be described as tennis artistry, yet he was faced with a slow, painful and possibly embarrassing decline into the status of a has-been, putting him in a position where he would have to talk publicly about still being capable of winning the biggest prizes but whom the world would see as someone failing to acknowledge the fading of his powers.

The fact that Federer bounced back, or rather reinvented himself, and went on to reach three major finals in the subsequent two years – and then reinvented himself a second time to pick up three more Grand Slam titles – adds to the legend. Yet anyone watching him squander all his opportunities against Robredo would have been entitled to scoff at the suggestion that, within a year, Federer would be on the verge of an eighth Wimbledon title, and, within four, he would be the reigning Wimbledon and Australian Open champion. Yet he was, and his willingness to seek new stimulus and add new elements to his game in his early thirties was to pay handsome dividends over the next six years.

After a reasonable end to 2013, Federer made a shock announcement: he was to start working with the six-time Grand Slam singles champion Stefan Edberg in 2014. The choice of coach was not inconsistent – Edberg was a natural serve-volleyer, the kind of game Federer needed to work on if he was to hold his own at a time when his physical powers might be starting to wane, but so was Paul Annacone, the American coach from whom he had parted just a few weeks earlier. What could Edberg do that Annacone couldn't? Then again, Federer was right in with the fashion – the announcement of his partnership with Edberg coincided with Kei Nishikori's decision to work with Michael Chang, Marin Cilic's partnership with Goran Ivanisevic, and, most surprising of all, Novak Djokovic's recruitment of Boris Becker. With Ivan Lendl already working with Andy Murray, it had become almost *de rigueur* for the greats of 2014 to team up with one of the greats from the 1980s and 90s.

The first signs that Federer was reinventing himself under Edberg's tutelage didn't come until late February 2014. After an impressive Australian Open that saw Federer beat Tsonga and a still ring-rusty Murray en route to a semi-final defeat to Nadal, he won his seventy-eighth career title in Dubai, thanks to successive come-from-behind wins against

Djokovic and Tomas Berdych. Both followed a similar pattern – he went a set down, and then started coming to the net so much more. Some might have criticised him for leaving it so late, but, with both Djokovic and Berdych, the switch in tactics fazed them. It was almost as if Federer was learning to trust his volleys. Not that that they have ever been anything other than very good, but his reluctance to come forward had left him unsure of optimum positioning at the net, which is an underestimated part of good volleying. Suddenly he was trusting himself to cut off shots from the front of the court. They were exciting wins.

That seemed to give him confidence. He reached the finals in Indian Wells and Monte Carlo, losing both in three sets, and he did so by coming to the net much more. He hadn't become a pure net-rusher in the way Edberg, Becker, Rafter and co had been, but he mixed up baseline battles with net play, and, as his results improved, so his confidence in his volleys grew. In many ways this should have happened under Annacone, who had been a great net player; in fact Annacone had a much better coaching CV than Edberg, having worked with Sampras and Henman, while Federer was Edberg's first coaching assignment on the pro tour. Maybe Federer had more respect for Edberg, having admired him as a kid? Maybe the characters meshed better? Or maybe it was simply that Edberg had won six Grand Slam singles titles, while Annacone had never broken into the top ten? Such are the vagaries of player/coach relationships – you never know why one coach clicks with a player and another doesn't.

It also seemed the best way for Federer to be playing in the run-up to his thirty-third birthday. The days of him being able to battle it out from the baseline with younger men would surely be numbered, so an effective way of shortening the points would be welcome. Yet, speaking in January 2015, Federer didn't see it that way. 'It was just to try something different,' he said of his greater willingness to go to the net. 'I don't feel any different to, let's say, four years ago. I really don't. You maybe listen to the signs of your body a bit more, and by now I know my body even better. And as the years go by I want to try new things, but that's not necessarily always down to age. It's simple to say I did something because of such-and-such, but actually it was just to make it different, make it fresh, make it new, try something else. Clearly you have to listen to your body, but I think the mind is also important. You have to ask yourself how badly do you want to be out there, how badly do you want to play and win, why are you still doing it, are you doing it for the right reasons? I think that becomes more important than the whole body talk that everybody puts emphasis on.'

Despite his run to the Monte Carlo final, where he lost to the man who had finally taken over as Swiss number one, the Australian Open champion Stan Wawrinka, Federer didn't have a great clay-court season – largely because his focus was more on domestic matters. In early May, Mirka gave birth to a second set of twins, this time boys, named Leo and Lenny. Bookmakers tried to work out the odds on a couple having two sets of twins, and all sorts of well-wishing messages were sent, many referring to the possibility of family doubles and mixed doubles pairings.

His clay season ended with a defeat to the mercurial Ernests Gulbis at Roland Garros. Federer seemed to be cruising and had set points for a two-set lead. But once Gulbis had ridden his luck to win the second set, Federer faded and lost the match in five sets.

But then came the grass, and the chance for the new net game to shine most brightly. He won a seventh title in Halle, and then went to Wimbledon, where the only players he seriously feared were the other members of the big four. Nadal lost in the fourth round to the big-hitting Australian teenager Nick Kyrgios, while Murray had a bad day in the quarter-finals against Grigor Dimitrov. That just left Djokovic, who Federer played in a glorious five-set final. It was not just that the sun shone and Centre Court was at its picturesque best, a combination that has left us with galleries and albums of gloriously lit photos of this final. There was also the added frisson caused by Wimbledon's primary rivals of the late 1980s and early 1990s, Boris Becker and Stefan Edberg, coaching the opposing players. And it highlighted the absurdity of all those comments that had recommended Federer should retire after the Stakhovsky and Robredo defeats in 2013.

The standard of tennis was very high. The winners count for both players vastly exceeded the unforced error count, and Federer served superbly, hitting four successive aces in one game. Djokovic seemed to have the better of the first set, but Federer won it on a 9–7 tiebreak. Djokovic won the second, and, when he took the third on a second tiebreak and broke for 3–1 in the fourth, Federer was fading. With Djokovic leading 5–2, it was looking like a standard straight-sets victory for the Serb if one were to discount the aberration of losing the first set. But Federer staged a fightback. He broke for 4–5, then saved a match point with an ace before levelling at 5–5. Another break allowed him to serve out for two sets all.

Having been struggling to keep up for much of the match, Federer looked the likelier winner for the first seven games of the final set, especially with Djokovic having to have some medical attention for a leg problem. At 3–3, Federer had a break point for 4–3, but fluffed it with a sliced backhand. As the ball hit the net and dropped back Federer's side, Djokovic let out his animalistic roar, and, when he held serve moments later for 4–3, he had seen off the danger. Federer saved three break points in holding for 4–4, but, serving to stay in the match at 4–5, he was broken, Djokovic picking up his seventh major title instead of Federer collecting his eighteenth.

Although defeated, the match added to the Federer legend. At the start of the match he had stood to become the oldest man in the 'open' era to lift the Wimbledon singles title, and at the start of the final set he stood to become the first since 1949 to win a final having saved a match point. But despite failing on both counts, the quality of the match made it one of the great Wimbledon finals – not quite in the same league as the Federer–Nadal final of 2008, but not far behind.

Djokovic himself said, 'This has been the best quality Grand Slam final that I've ever been a part of. I played in the longest ever final against Nadal at the Australian Open in 2012, but in terms of the quality of the tennis from the very first point this was definitely the best match.'

While the Wimbledon final stands out as the pick of Federer's 2014 Grand Slam year, he came remarkably close to the elusive eighteenth title nine weeks later. In retrospect he should have won the US Open. He came to New York as the runner-up in Toronto and the champion in Cincinnati, Nadal was missing through injury, and Murray was beaten by Djokovic in the quarter-finals. Federer's quarter-final was a classic, in which he saved two match points before beating Gael Monfils in five sets. That left a semi-final line-up of Djokovic facing the Japanese player Kei Nishikori, with Federer up against Croatia's Marin Cilic. And it was in that order, so, when Nishikori beat a strangely subdued Djokovic in the first semi, Federer was the clear favourite to win the title.

But a thunderstorm delayed the start of his semi-final against Cilic, which gave him too much time to think. He came out a little flat, and was made to pay for it as the tall Croat played one of the matches of his life to beat Federer in straight sets. Federer might have lost even if he had played better, such was the ferocity and accuracy of Cilic's game that day, but it was another case of a weak match after his biggest obstacle had been removed – he'd got away with it against Haas at the 2009 French and Benneteau at the 2012 Wimbledon, but he didn't get away with it this time. And the result meant tennis had a major final not involving a member of the big four for the first time in thirty-eight Grand Slam tournaments.

Off-court Federer was tested twice during the latter weeks of the 2014 season. One test he passed with admirable statesmanship, the other involved him having to mediate in a totally unexpected rumpus.

After he lost in the final of the 2012 staging of the Swiss Indoors, Federer let it be known that it was far from certain that he would reappear in Basel in 2013. The issue appeared to be the payment of an appearance fee, one the impresario behind the Basel tournament, Roger Brennwald, was reported to be refusing to pay. For a while Federer suggested he might not play the tournament at all, then that he might play only doubles. In the end, he chose to play without an appearance fee, a decision taken because Basel was his home tournament and he opted to overrule the money issue and play.

It's important to stress that the exact details of such contractual negotiations are by definition confidential, and therefore it is largely pointless to speculate on the whys and wherefores of what deals are actually struck (or not struck). But given that the people of Basel feel they helped create the great Roger Federer and didn't just spawn him, it was a smart decision of Federer's to put the money issue to one side and show up, especially as his refusal to commit to the Davis Cup hadn't endeared him to everyone in the Swiss sporting public. He did the same in 2014, even though by then he had committed to attempting to win the Davis Cup for Switzerland. His gesture went down well, helped no doubt by comparison with Brennwald's local reputation as being a difficult man to deal with. From 2015, Federer did receive an appearance fee for playing the Swiss Indoors, Brennwald and his team no doubt recognising that Federer was so in demand that the absence of a fee for Basel could make him susceptible to a rival offer he simply couldn't refuse.

The other test came out of the blue on the penultimate night of the individual tennis season. With Switzerland due to play France in the Davis Cup final, Switzerland's two stalwarts, Federer and Wawrinka, faced each other in the second semi-final of the ATP World Tour Finals in London the weekend before. They played an outstanding match, Federer winning on a final-set tiebreak after saving four match points, three of them on the Wawrinka serve. It was one of the matches of the year, probably second behind the Djokovic–Federer Wimbledon final, but it had a sinister overtone.

Throughout the middle to latter stages of the match, Federer's wife Mirka was shouting things from Federer's box to Wawrinka. When Wawrinka complained to the umpire Cédric Mourier that she had done the same thing at Wimbledon when the two Swiss had met in the quarter-finals four months earlier, Mirka shouted in French, 'You're a cry baby'. Mourier said, 'Not now, Stan' several times to try to defuse the situation, but it left tremendous bad feeling between the two players after the match.

The first thing Federer did was have a four-way conference between himself, Wawrinka, Mirka and the Swiss Davis Cup captain Severin Lüthi (who had been sitting in Federer's box for the match so was right next to Mirka). That helped defuse some of the tension, though it meant Federer did not get immediate treatment for an irritation to his back he said he sustained during the final-set tiebreak of the two-and-three-quarter-hour match. He was also reported to have had a major row with Mirka later that night – such marital tiffs are thought to be rare, but this one was allegedly heard by people through the door, and is thought to have involved Federer exasperatedly telling his wife that, irrespective of the rights and wrongs of what she was saying, her timing a week before the Davis

Cup final was quite awful, that this was a week when he really needed to get on with Wawrinka.

The notable thing about this incident is that Federer's entourage is remarkably leak-proof, and his image as a nice guy, class act and phenomenal tennis player is carefully crafted in a very slick PR operation. Yet this was the first time the mask really slipped. The fact that Federer pulled out of the following day's final against Djokovic with a slightly half-hearted on-court apology didn't go down well, nor did the fact that he didn't turn up to a press conference to take questions from the world's tennis media. His efforts to patch things up with Wawrinka clearly worked, and a week later they were all smiles, but the incident left something of a scar on the Federer image. It also left questions about why Mirka did what she did. Was it a sign that she was becoming tired of being the woman in the background? Was she condemning another aspect of Wawrinka's life? – Wawrinka's relationship with the mother of his child ended shortly afterwards, so was Mirka having a dig at some of Wawrinka's off-court activities? It certainly left a number of questions that Federer wasn't going to answer in a hurry.

From the moment Switzerland lost its Davis Cup first-round tie at home to the USA in early 2012, with Wawrinka taking offence at Federer's insensitive comments, the general assumption in the tennis world was that the Davis Cup would be the one meaningful historical trophy to elude the great man. And Federer did nothing to challenge that assumption in the subsequent two years.

Following the debacle in Fribourg, he at least made himself available for Switzerland's playoff-round tie against the Netherlands in September 2012. That meant the Swiss kept their place in the world group and were rewarded with a home tie in February 2013 against the Czech Republic. The initial suggestions were that Federer would play, and Swiss Tennis announced the tie would take place in Basel, the first one in Federer's home city for twelve years. But then Federer started to indicate that he might not play, so the tie was moved to Geneva, where a reasonable crowd could still be expected even if Federer didn't show. When Federer made it clear his truncated schedule did not include the Davis Cup first round, Wawrinka was moved to say, 'I really don't understand him at all.' Wawrinka, who never declined an invitation to play for his country until the Davis Cup was won, left everything on the court in a three-day personal marathon against a weakened Czech team, including a record-breaking seven-hour doubles, and left the stadium in tears on the Sunday afternoon after losing the crucial singles to Tomas Berdych.

After losing to Tommy Robredo at the US Open, Federer declined to play Switzerland's 2013 playoff-round tie at home to Ecuador. The decision was partly motivated by a feeling that he wasn't needed, as the Ecuadorians have not had a team to seriously challenge for a place in the world group since the Lapentti brothers left the tour. And it was perhaps significant that the Swiss proved they could win a playoff tie without their talisman, whatever the opposition. Not that their victory seemed to provide much hope for 2014, as the draw for the first round dispatched Switzerland to an away tie against the 2013 finalists Serbia, with Federer still not committing to play. Yet that all changed, largely behind the scenes, at the start of 2014.

Wawrinka's maiden Grand Slam title at the 2014 Australian Open – a deserved title despite Nadal's back problems in the final – meant he overtook Federer in the rankings for the first time. To the tennis world, still digesting Federer's defeats to Stakhovsky and Robredo in the previous seven months, the only realistic thing left for Federer to do was to prioritise the one competition missing from his trophy cabinet, the Davis Cup. As it happens, Federer had done exactly that even before Wawrinka's triumph in Melbourne. He had told Swiss Tennis before the Australian Open that he would travel to Novi Sad for Switzerland's first-round tie against Serbia, though he didn't want it announced until the very last minute. The Swiss were up against a Serbian team that was always going to be weak even if Djokovic had played; without Djokovic and up against Federer and Wawrinka, it was a sitting duck. But symbolically, the Swiss won without Federer having to play doubles – for many years he said Switzerland never won without him playing on all three days but, with Wawrinka playing equally well in early 2014, the pressure on Federer had lessened (and as Switzerland's number-two player, Federer would be up for any decisive fifth matches rather than having to sit idly by while a teammate held the Swiss fate).

And Federer did have to play a decisive fifth match in the quarter-finals. With Wawrinka struggling to sustain his level after his high in Melbourne, he was beaten on the opening day by Kazakhstan's Andrey Golubev, which dumped the pressure on Federer. Federer came through against Mikhail Kukushkin, but Federer and Wawrinka then lost to Golubev and Aleksandr Nedovyesov in the doubles as Wawrinka played a howler. That left the Swiss 2–1 down going into the final day, but, roared on by a passionate 14,000 crowd in Geneva's Palexpo hall, Wawrinka came back from a set down to beat Kukushkin, and Federer then beat Golubev in straight sets to see the Swiss through.

Federer's reaction at the very end was interesting. He got noticeably more pumped as he neared victory, and on hitting the winning shot he bounced up and down like a small boy. There was no hiding what the victory meant to him, but a few minutes later he seemed to be doing his best to be underwhelmed in his on-court interviews. He wouldn't even look forward to the semi-finals, despite it being known by then that the Swiss would again be at home, this time to Italy; in fact Federer wouldn't even confirm that he'd be available, saying only that 'there's a lot of time between now and then'. That was true – five months is a long gap between the quarters and semis of a tournament, and he had three of the year's four majors in those five months. But it was as if he was determined not to show anyone that the Davis Cup was important for him.

There was a similar scenario against Italy, also in the Palexpo, but this time with the capacity expanded to more than 18,000. By September, Federer was back as Swiss number one thanks to a better few months than Wawrinka had had, so he played the fourth rubber of the five. This time the Swiss were 2–1 up, the two stars having won their opening day singles but Wawrinka and Chiudinelli going down in the doubles. So Federer was playing the mercurial Fabio Fognini for Switzerland's place in the final. Fognini got better as the match went on, and there was a lot of tension in the third-set tiebreak. Again Federer was geeing himself up for the final push, again he bounced with delight after winning the tiebreak 7–4, and again he played down the victory in his post-match interviews. This time there was no denying that he would be playing the final, but instead of any enthusiasm it was just going to be 'a nice way to end the year', and in his on-court interview he described his feelings in the moment of victory as 'nice sharing emotions with your fans and your close ones, especially sharing it with my team members'.

Federer's attitude to the Davis Cup came up at a chat he had with the Swiss press between the semi-final and final during the Swiss Indoors in Basel. He explained to them that he wasn't half-hearted about the competition, that he really did want to win it for Switzerland and for his teammates, but that he was reluctant for people to see it as another of his own achievements. 'I want it for the team,' he said. All of which is very admirable but doesn't sit easily with all his years of not playing in the early rounds. He could have been forgiven for not playing in 2005–7, because he really was a one-man team, but from 2008, when Wawrinka was regularly in the top twenty, Federer gave the impression that the Davis Cup was an optional extra to be slotted in around his main commitments if the urge took him. That was not a message his teammates and countryfolk heard with any joy, however much they were dependent on him if they ever wanted to lift the trophy.

By the time the final came, there was no question Federer was prioritising the Davis Cup. Whatever the damage to his back that resulted from his two-and-three-quarter-hour semi in London six days before the final, the likelihood is that he would have attempted to play the ATP Finals' decider if he hadn't had his one shot at the Davis Cup looming. His apology to the crowd for being unable to take to the court against Djokovic was polite but didn't give the impression of a serious injury. He had clearly decided that he wasn't going to risk the chance of Switzerland winning the Davis Cup, even if the ATP's showpiece final was the one to suffer on this occasion.

That led to speculation about whether his back was bad enough to threaten Switzerland's chances, and, when he was roundly beaten by Gael Monfils on the opening day of the final in front of 27,000 spectators in Lille, there were many who were worried for him and his country. He did indeed move gingerly around the court, but Monfils was in excellent form and might have won anyway. And Switzerland were already one-up following Wawrinka's four-sets win over the ailing Jo-Wilfried Tsonga in the opening rubber of the final, so it was a match the Swiss could afford to lose.

The real work towards Switzerland's triumph was done not so much by the physios working on Federer's back but by the doubles coaching brought in especially for the final. Mindful of the fact that Federer and Wawrinka had lost their last five Davis Cup doubles, the Swiss captain Severin Lüthi brought in David Macpherson, the Australian who had coached the Bryan twins to greatness and kept them at the top of the game. This was the masterstroke with which the thirty-eight-year-old Lüthi showed just how much he had grown into the role of captain. Federer and Wawrinka may have won an Olympic gold medal but, based on subsequent results, they were not a great doubles team. Macpherson made them into one, if only for that one vital day.

France were expected to field Tsonga and Richard

Gasquet, their captain Arnaud Clément's pair of choice. But on the morning of the doubles, Tsonga came off his practice saying he couldn't play, which threw the French into a makeshift pairing of Gasquet and Julien Benneteau. With Wawrinka taking the initiative with some mighty hitting, the French were cowed into dropping three crucial service games, which gave the Swiss a straight-sets win.

That left the destiny of the cup in Federer's hands. Facing him was not Tsonga but Gasquet, the one-time French prodigy who had been thought to be the equal of Federer as a junior, but who had buckled in his biggest moments. As he walked into the Pierre Mauroy Stadium, boasting a record crowd for an official tennis match of 27,448, Gasquet looked petrified. By contrast, Federer walked in imperiously. France's tennis fans, who had been encouraged by the players in the weeks leading up to the final not to succumb to the temptation to cheer for the great Federer but instead to support their own players, must have feared the worst. And it wasn't long in coming.

Federer won the match comfortably, without ever seeming in danger. Gasquet had nothing to hurt him with, and the crowd seemed to know it. As Federer played an exquisite, heavily undercut backhand drop shot to win the match, he briefly spread his arms before sinking to the ground, his bright red shirt almost merging with the red clay. There was no doubt this meant something big to him, even if he persisted in saying, 'this is one for the boys' in most of his post-match interviews.

The one big title to elude him had been captured. No longer could anyone say his comparison with the greats was affected by the fact that they all had at least one Davis Cup title to their name and he didn't. No longer was he the most successful male player never to have won the Davis Cup.

And yet his relationship with the competition still left questions. His decision not to play against Belgium in the 2015 first round was entirely understandable but, asked about it during the tournament in Dubai two weeks beforehand, Federer said, 'I think by winning the Davis Cup, I can finally do whatever I please. It's been a big burden for me throughout my career, and one of the things that has caused more difficulties in my life than many other things, because I always feel there is so much guilt put on you from the federation, or from the ITF, more so than anybody else. So I'm happy I was able to finally tick that off and do it all together.'

Does this leave us any clearer about Federer's relationship with the Davis Cup? Not really. It's interesting to pursue the line about his attitude towards a team ethic. His comment that an aspect of football he didn't like was that he could play a blinder but the team might lose because of a goalkeeping error (see Chapter 2) may be revealing here. In a sport where everything stands or falls on the individual, Federer may have struggled with being a team player. It's clear he also got immense satisfaction out of it when the team worked – not just the Davis Cup winning team of 2014 but also the Olympic gold medal in doubles from 2008, which really meant a lot to him. It's easy to forget that, for all his eloquence, this is a fundamentally shy person who had a lot of conflicting emotions that he had to keep under control in early adulthood because they were threatening to undermine his tennis career. Maybe he relinquished too much control for his own comfort when he hooked up with the Swiss team? If true, this would explain the stress he obviously felt about having to juggle what he thought was right with what he felt most comfortable with. It would also explain why he tended to view Davis Cup weekends for many years as standalone periods in which the main priority was to have fun with his mates for a few days, rather than a year-long campaign to lift the trophy. While he may never admit this, he is probably grateful to have won the Davis Cup in its 1981–2018 format as a year-long endeavour, because the changes that altered the competition in 2019 (essentially cramming it into one long week in late November) have taken away some of the prestige of tennis's most venerable team event. We may learn more as he reminisces on his playing career in retirement, but it's possible this will remain a Federer enigma.

His line that he did it 'for the boys' does ring true from his teammates' perspective. The success meant Stan Wawrinka finally got the Davis Cup winners medal that his dedication to the Swiss team merited. His career would have been notable even without the Davis Cup, in fact more than that if Wawrinka had been around at any other time he would have been a Swiss legend, the standout Swiss player of his generation. So in one way, the Davis Cup was a reward for him for having had to stand in Federer's shadow for so much of his career. It also meant that Marco Chiudinelli and Michael Lammer could retire having captured one of tennis's most significant prizes, a Davis Cup winner's replica and medal. They were honest professionals, like so many unsung toilers on the tour, and their reward for always picking up the pieces when Federer was absent was their moment of glory and the enduring silverware. When

Lammer announced he would retire after Switzerland lost to Belgium in the 2015 first round, Federer agreed to play doubles with him at his final tournament in Dubai, so Lammer could go out in a quality match.

Federer's final Davis Cup appearance, in Switzerland's home playoff-round tie against the Netherlands in September 2015, gave him a homecoming with Wawrinka and Chiudinelli after Switzerland's 2014 triumph. He even played doubles with Chiudinelli; they lost their match, but it's still a nice story that the two schoolboy friends played a Davis Cup doubles together.

Federer's irritation with the Davis Cup, and with the emotional blackmail he feels he was subjected to, is understandable. It would just be nice if he were a little more enthusiastic and gracious about having finally lifted a trophy that meant so much to so many of the tennis greats he has always professed to admire.

Given Federer's heroics in 2017–9, it's easy to look back on 2015 as a fallow period in his career. He won no significant titles that year, but, with Nadal suffering an uncharacteristic drop in confidence and Murray still struggling for match toughness after serious back surgery at the end of 2013, Federer was the principal challenger to the year's undisputed world number one, Novak Djokovic.

Federer and Djokovic played eight times in 2015, and Federer was to beat Djokovic in three of them, but in all their important matches Djokovic got the better of him. In fact the three successive Grand Slam finals they played – Wimbledon 2014, Wimbledon 2015 and the US Open 2015 – all made the same point: that Federer's best was enough to stick with Djokovic but, the moment his level dropped, Djokovic was in like a rapier.

Djokovic's victory in the Wimbledon final of 2015 was perhaps the most demoralising for Federer and his legion of fans.

Wimbledon was the one tournament where Federer was still fancied to make most impact, and he went to London having won an eighth title in Halle. When he took Murray apart in the semi-finals to set up another final against Djokovic, everything seemed set for his eighteenth major. The display against Murray was vintage Federer – it was vintage grass-court tennis, as well, with Federer's bird-like swoops to the net and use of sumptuous volleys causing even the most hardened British Murray fans to doff their caps in appreciation.

But two days later, under slightly cloudier skies in which the ball flew fractionally more slowly through the air, Federer couldn't reproduce the form – or Djokovic didn't let him. Federer led 4–2 in the first set, but the moment that lead was wiped out he was on the back foot, and, when Djokovic took a one-sided tiebreak to take the first set, the match was effectively decided. Federer somehow eked out the second set on a marathon 12–10 tiebreak, but the effort made him easy prey at the start of the third, and there was only one winner after Djokovic had seized an early break.

It was a similar story eight weeks later at the US Open. Federer beat Djokovic in the final of Cincinnati, but lost to him in the US Open final on a similar scoreline to the one at Wimbledon. And there was a third successive four-sets victory for Djokovic in the majors, when he beat Federer in the semi-finals of the 2016 Australian Open.

This time Federer was slow starting, and was brutally punished, Djokovic almost wrapping up the first two sets in forty-five minutes. Somehow you knew he'd get himself into the match, and he did so sufficiently to take the third set, but once again it was a case of Federer's best just about matching Djokovic, and at the first let-up Djokovic sprinted away. (The same happened to Murray in the final – he was crushed in the first set, before matching Djokovic for two sets, yet both went to the Serb as he wrapped up a sixth Australian title.)

Djokovic's dominance of Federer was starting to threaten Federer's widely held status as the greatest player of all time. Federer was not only streets ahead of most people on the tour, but in some tennis watchers' eyes he was playing the best tennis of his career. He won most of his matches with ease, he generally got the better of Murray, and even beat Nadal to win the 2015 Basel title. His all-court game with drop shots, exquisite slices and above all volleys made him arguably a better player than in his golden years of 2004–7, yet he couldn't touch Djokovic in the big matches. Was Djokovic, though far less pretty to watch, now the better player? Had he reached a higher level than Federer's best?

It's important to remember the context in which such questions were being asked: for much of 2016, Federer's fortunes continued to decline, and his age made it natural to assume this was the beginning of the end. In February, he underwent surgery for the first time in his career, but not for an injury incurred on a tennis court. Federer says he was running a bath for his twin daughters while still in

Melbourne, the day after his defeat to Djokovic, when he turned and heard a click in his left knee. 'It was a very simple movement, probably a movement I've done a million times in my life,' he said. At first he thought nothing of it, but walking round Melbourne Zoo the following day it was clear he had a problem. It required arthroscopic surgery to repair torn cartilage. He had hoped to come back to the tour in Miami, in fact even travelled to Florida, but then withdrew as a precautionary measure and didn't play until Monte Carlo. Even then he pulled out of the French Open with a minor back problem, and also to concentrate on the grass.

Meanwhile, Djokovic was further cementing his own legend. Having faltered in the Paris finals of 2012, 2014 and 2015, the Serb finally completed his set of majors by winning the French Open in 2016. He could have been forgiven a drop-off in form after completing such a sought-after milestone, but the cracks were beginning to show even before his triumph at Roland Garros. There were tensions in his home life, there were tensions in his team, and there was wear and tear on his body. He just about held it together to win the French, but after that he hit the wall, lost early at Wimbledon and was a tame runner-up to Wawrinka at the US Open.

Djokovic's defeat at Wimbledon seemed to clear Federer's passage to the final and, when he beat Marin Cilic in five sets to reach the semis, he was on course for another final against Andy Murray. Federer led Milos Raonic by two sets to one, but a poor game at the end of the fourth set allowed Raonic to level the match. Serving in the fourth game of the final set, Federer's left leg gave way as he lunged for a volley, leaving him face-down on the turf. He called the trainer and was able to play on (he never once retired mid-match in his tour-level career), but lost the final set 6–3.

Two and a half weeks later, Federer announced that he wouldn't play again in 2016. In a statement on his Facebook page, he said, 'The doctors advised that if I want to play on the ATP World Tour injury-free for another few years, as I intend to do, I must give both my knee and body the proper time to fully recover.' As usual, he was talking an optimistic game, adding, 'I am as motivated as ever and plan to put all my energy towards coming back strong, healthy and in shape to play attacking tennis in 2017.'

But how realistic was that, only a few days before his thirty-fifth birthday? He had just finished his first year without a tour title since 2001, and his body was starting to creak after nearly two decades on the pro tour. He had defied the doubters once by bouncing back from his slump of form in 2008. He had defied them a second time by winning Wimbledon in 2012 after a two-and-a-half-year gap dominated by Nadal and Djokovic. And he had defied them a third time by rebounding from the Stakhovsky and Robredo defeats in 2013 to come so close to winning Wimbledon in 2014 and 2015. But at thirty-five and with a rebelling body, there was no way he was going to bounce back to be a contender for the major prizes again.

Was there?

THE GLORIOUS TWILIGHT

5

18

THE FRIGHTENING EASE with which a player gets forgotten the moment they're not on the tour happened with Roger Federer in the second half of 2016. Despite him being the biggest marquee name for the previous decade, the tour just went on without him. His name was often quoted as a past champion of a certain tournament or a participant in a memorable match, but he was off the scene and no longer a factor. There certainly wasn't any sense that results were somewhat false because a major player was temporarily absent.

Not that Federer was alone in taking a break. Nadal ended his 2016 season several weeks early after an unexpected defeat in Shanghai. Djokovic played on until the end but looked a shadow of the player who had dominated the circuit up to his French Open triumph. All of which left the way clear for Andy Murray to enjoy the best run of his career. The fact that Federer, Nadal and Djokovic were all in various states of disrepair could be held against Murray, but the fourth man in the big four got himself into supreme shape and was a deserved year-end number one. His problem was that the effort wiped him out, and he was a spent force early in 2017.

Off court, Federer gave himself the break he needed and which he had never had before. His ranking slipped to seventeen by the end of the year, as low as it had been since June 2001, but that was never going to bother him. Once he felt the knee was strong, he started building up the practice blocks. The aim was always to be ready to play five sets, and then if necessary to play five sets two days later, and again two days after that, so some practice sessions were over three hours. He was in fact sufficiently ready by October that he toyed with playing Basel and the Paris Masters, and possibly even the ATP Finals (as a semi-finalist in Australia and at Wimbledon he was close to qualifying), but decided that his original intention to take the rest of the year off should stand, a decision that meant that, by the time he did take to the match court, he had stopped thinking about the knee. The final bout of training took place in Dubai to acclimatise to the heat, before three gentle warm-up matches and three mixed doubles at the Hopman Cup in Perth.

A crucial figure in Federer's off period was Ivan Ljubicic. The two had started working together at the start of 2016, alongside Severin Lüthi, who remained a constant feature of Team Federer, after Ljubicic ended his coaching arrangement with Milos Raonic in December 2015. Federer's knee and back injuries meant there wasn't a lot the genial Croat could influence, but in the second half of the year Ljubicic came into his own. The biggest thing he did was encourage Federer to be more aggressive with his backhand, in particular not to fear having to hit the ball hard when an opponent's topspin caused it to rear up, but also to take the ball early. Both areas are generally thought of as weaknesses for the one-handed backhand compared with the two-hander, but, having had a one-hander himself, Ljubicic had every confidence that the shot needn't be a weakness.

The five months off the tour meant Federer was raring to go when he and Belinda Bencic represented Switzerland at the twenty-ninth Hopman Cup in Perth, starting symbolically on the first day of 2017. In his eagerly anticipated first match back, he dismissed Dan Evans in sixty-one minutes; he then lost to Alexander Zverev in a match of three tiebreaks, before easily beating Richard Gasquet. It was exactly the preparation he needed, but expectations were understandably not high as the Federer circus decamped and pitched its tents in Melbourne.

The story of the 2017 Australian Open reads like a film script, and a rather corny one. In fact, if people hadn't seen it happen, they would probably never believe it. That didn't just relate to Federer – for the tournament to have singles finals of Venus against Serena Williams followed by Roger Federer facing Rafael Nadal was like a dream sequence or a staged legends' exhibition. And yet they were two wholly legitimate, fully fledged Grand Slam singles finals.

Coming in as the number-seventeen seed in the draw meant Federer was likely to have two winnable matches, but then face a potential run-in of Berdych, Nishikori, Murray, Wawrinka and Djokovic. With that line-up, reaching the fourth round or quarter-finals would be a respectable result, but the initial task was to get through the first round. Facing him as he walked out into the Rod Laver Arena for the opening day's night session was the veteran Austrian Jürgen Melzer, who had come through qualifying. Federer admitted to being nervous, and his belief that he had to really focus and concentrate to get himself back into the groove of matches meant he framed and mis-hit a number of shots. He scraped through the first set, but then lost the second. Yet those two sets were enough to blow away the cobwebs, and a shift to a more relaxed mindset in the third set – the excess focus was 'just consuming me, like it was too much already' was how he described it later – allowed him to cruise through sets three and four for a comfortable victory.

A slightly stuttering straight-sets win over Noah Rubin brought on the third-round clash with Tomas Berdych. This was the first real test, but it brought out the best in Federer. He danced around his baseline, played 'worlds better than in the first couple of rounds', and never faced a single break point. This was the match where the world was forced to sit up and take notice – sustaining that level was still not proven, but at least Federer could still produce it.

With Novak Djokovic having lost a second-round five-setter to Denis Istomin, one of the big challengers was suddenly out of the way. But after beating the tenth seed Berdych, the stakes were raised again, as Federer faced the fifth seed Kei Nishikori in the round of the last sixteen. He came through it, but in a manner that many felt had killed off his chances of going much further. Having lost the first set on the tiebreak, Federer won the second and third 6–4, 6–1, but then lost the thread in the fourth set and ended up having to go three hours twenty-four minutes to win. Yet two things that day worked heavily in Federer's favour. One was the fact that Nishikori was merciless in targeting the Federer backhand, and the backhand passed the test – he even remarked with casual sarcasm after the match 'I thought actually I hit my backhand very well tonight, which probably won me the match for once. My backhand – who'd have known!' The other was Andy Murray's defeat to Mischa Zverev. Federer had come through his tests with Berdych and Nishikori, and was now into a quarter-final line-up that featured him and Nadal, but no Murray and no Djokovic.

The elder Zverev brother had peaked with his win over an ailing Murray, and Federer picked him off easily in an hour and thirty-two minutes. Asked what had pleased him most just eight matches into his resumption following a six-month break, Federer said, 'Winning back-to-back matches in best-of-five sets against quality, great players. That was for me the big question mark, if I could do that so early in my comeback. I felt I was always going to be dangerous on any given day in a match situation, but obviously, as the tournament would progress, maybe I would fade away with energy.'

He had thought a run to the semi-finals so unrealistic that he hadn't bothered to keep tabs on who he might face, and it was only when he came to play his quarter-final that he realised his old mate Stan Wawrinka was likely to face him; with Wawrinka posting an impressive straight-sets win over Jo-Wilfried Tsonga in his quarter-final, the younger Swiss was the favourite going into their semi-final. Federer took the first two sets, but Wawrinka bounced back to take the third and fourth as Federer's energy levels dropped. When he called for the trainer at the start of the fifth set, the fear that lack of matches had finally caught up with him was very strong. He admitted later that the physio's work on his leg hadn't helped much; in fact the language he used suggested he had called the medic just to break up Wawrinka's rhythm and had felt legitimised to do so by the injury timeout Wawrinka had taken after the second set. It was close to a confession from the saintly Federer that he too was not averse to using the rules to his full advantage. And just chatting to the physio may have made the difference, because Federer had his energy back in the fifth set. He held serve in a marathon fifth game, broke in the sixth, and served out the victory in a comparatively quick time for a five-set match: just four minutes over three hours.

Regardless of the final, he had delivered a remarkable comeback. He was into his twenty-eighth major decider, and was the oldest finalist since Ken Rosewall reached the US Open final at the age of thirty-nine (Rosewall had written to Federer at the start of the Australian Open wishing him well). 'I never ever in my wildest dreams thought I'd come this far in Australia,' Federer said in his on-court interview, 'it's beautiful, I'm so happy.' And regardless as to whether it would be Grigor Dimitrov or Rafael Nadal in the final, Federer simply said of the match, 'The comeback is so great already. Let it fly off your racket and just see what happens!'

Having played two five-setters in his six matches in Melbourne, Federer clearly profited from the extra day that the winner of the first semi-final at the Australian Open enjoyed at that time. Having won on Thursday night, he had all of Friday and Saturday, plus most of Sunday, to prepare. On the Friday night, his cause was further aided by Nadal and Dimitrov playing four minutes short of five hours in their semi, Nadal edging it as Dimitrov's belief failed him in the crucial moments after looking the better player for much of the match. The thirty-fifth match between the old rivals was on, their first for fifteen months, and, despite Nadal's 23–11 lead in their previous thirty-four, this seemed a fifty-fifty as they were back in a Grand Slam final for the first time in six and a half years. It was fairy-tale stuff, especially with the Williams sisters playing the women's singles final (although their match once again failed to engage emotionally).

In the run-up to the final, Ivan Ljubicic proved his worth as a coach. In essence he gave Federer two pieces of advice. Firstly, not to go into the match thinking he had to win quickly. He impressed on Federer that, despite his two five-setters, if the final went to five sets he could still win, and that therefore there was no need to rush things from the start. Secondly, Ljubicic had noticed that Federer had been netting a number of backhands off the slice. Federer had one of the best sliced backhands in the game, mainly because the damage his forehand could do meant most opponents peppered his backhand, and therefore Federer developed a varied and effective slice that both soaked up pressure and could be an attacking weapon. But Ljubicic felt Nadal would be expecting the slice, and therefore Federer had more to gain by throwing caution to the wind and countering Nadal's topspin with bags of his own on his high backhands. He was basically saying: if you're going to miss, miss with ambition; if you're going to miss, go long, not into the net! It would be hard to think of two pieces of advice that bore greater fruit.

It started to come into its own in the second set. After a first set characterised by a break of the Nadal serve in the seventh game, Nadal bounced back in the second to lead 4–0. This was surely the time for Federer to kiss the set goodbye and regroup for the third, but no – he battled to retrieve one of the breaks, before the Spaniard levelled the match. The first two sets had taken an hour and a quarter, not the longest of sets despite the amount of time Nadal took between points in those pre-shotclock days.

Federer's hold of serve in the ten-minute opening game of the third set was crucial, and it unleashed his best period of the match, as he raced to take the third set. But Nadal upped his level in the fourth game of the fourth set, broke Federer, and, after just under three hours, the match was all-square at two sets all.

At that point, most people in the Rod Laver Arena assumed it was Nadal's match. The pattern was classic Nadal, especially against Federer: soak up all the early pressure, refuse to lie down, and prove indefatigably stronger at the end. That model gained further credence when Federer called for the trainer at the end of the fourth set for attention to his thigh problem, and when Nadal broke in the first game of the decider, and then saved four break-back points en route to a 3–1 lead, Federer's fairy tale was falling at the final fence. But then Ljubicic's second piece of advice became gold-plated.

The final five games of the 2017 Australian Open final have become the stuff of tennis folklore. If they come to be seen as the defining passage of play in Federer's entire career, it will not be a unfair reflection, however much one solitary chunk of twenty minutes should never define a career as rich in varied artistry as Roger Federer's. As a combination of skill, good decision-making, boldness, trust, a bit of luck, and sheer cussed unwillingness to concede, those twenty minutes were arguably his finest hour.

With Nadal serving at 2–3, Federer hit five aggressive backhands on the first point of the game, the first four fizzing with topspin, the fifth flattened out to create a fiery crosscourt winner. After the second point, he uttered his *Chumm jetzt* rallying cry (Swiss German for 'Come on now') which was always a sign that his juices were flowing. Despite the 0–30 lead, and a subsequent break point, Nadal still fought back, and Federer seemed to have no answer. But on Federer's sixth break point of the set, Nadal overhit an in-to-out forehand, one of three forehand errors from the Spaniard in that game, and suddenly the set was level.

That was the break Federer needed. He held serve to love for 4–3. When Nadal double-faulted to go 0–40 down in the next game, Federer was flying and Nadal looked to be feeling the pressure. But Nadal is never beaten until the final point is lost, and he played three superb points to get back to deuce. Then, after a mere three and a half hours of play, the two men delivered a point for the ages, a twenty-six-stroke rally in which at least half the shots would have been a winner against most other opponents, and which was eventually ended by Federer hitting a sublime forehand down the line at full stretch. Nadal saved the fourth break point in that game, but on the fifth Federer teed off on a backhand crosscourt return, and suddenly he had turned a 1–3 deficit into a 5–3 lead. He had promised to 'let the ball fly off the racket', he was doing that to remarkable effect, and he was serving for the title.

Still there was to be no let-up in the drama. Nadal played two topspin-heavy points to lead 0–30. Federer fired down an ace for 15–30. Nadal then thundered a backhand up the line to give him an easy volley winner: 15–40. Federer served an ace: 30–40. He then hit a high forehand for a winner to get back to deuce and was now just two points from the title.

Though it barely seemed possible, the drama then went up yet another notch. On championship point, Federer's second serve was called long – a double fault. Or was it? He challenged, and was proved right. That gave him a retaken serve, which he thought he'd hit for a service winner, but Nadal challenged – if Nadal's challenge was wrong, the title was Federer's. But Nadal had got it right; this time the serve was long, and, on the third stroke of the ensuing rally, Federer overhit a forehand to squander his opportunity. Federer's twentieth ace of the match gave him a second championship point, and again the electronic review was called for. Federer served down the centre, Nadal could only slice the return at full stretch, it landed mid-court, Federer took a swing at a crosscourt forehand, but didn't catch it cleanly in the centre of his strings. Both players seemed to think the ball had gone out. But the line umpire's call was 'in'. Nadal challenged, but this time the screen favoured Federer – about a third of the ball had caught the line. As the big screens produced the evidence, Federer bounced up and down, embraced Nadal, and dissolved into ecstatic tears in the centre of the court. The most phenomenal of remarkable comebacks was complete.

The superlatives used by the world's tennis media that night could never do justice to the sheer sporting drama of the three-hour-thirty-eight-minute match. There was much talk of the 'greatest of all time', and several commentators talked about Federer having done to Nadal what Nadal does to most other players. In terms of historical significance, it established in the record books that Federer could beat a fully fledged Nadal on one of the big stages – not since the Wimbledon final of 2007, when Nadal wasn't quite the finished article, had Federer beaten him in a major. Now he had.

Among the many things Federer said that night was one addressed to Nadal at the trophy ceremony. 'I'm happy for you,' he said. 'I would have been happy to lose, to be honest. The comeback was perfect as it was.' That was the practised diplomat, but no one should take that at face value for one moment. The comeback would have been superb without him winning the final set, but the magic of the story needed him to win it, and he is so competitive he would have been speaking through gritted teeth if he'd ended up with the runner-up's plate on the podium. Federer was out there to win, his champion's qualities had shone through, and without that indomitable spirit – and Ljubicic's wise words – he wouldn't have got near the final in the first place.

Roger Federer could have retired there and then. He was never going to, in fact his whole approach to his calendar planning from the knee injury at Wimbledon six months earlier was aimed at prolonging his longevity. He had three tournaments on his schedule before the circuit moved to clay, and only then was he going to assess where he was.

When he lost his first tour match, it didn't augur well. He was beaten by the world number 116, Evgeny Donskoy, from match point up in the second round in Dubai, but how much that really bothered him was open to question. The next big test came when, after two easy matches, he faced Nadal again in the fourth round in Indian Wells. Had Nadal taken an easy revenge for the defeat in Melbourne, Federer would still have won the more important match. But if anything the reverse happened – Federer used the springboard of his Melbourne win to blitz the Spaniard in the California desert, winning for the loss of just five games. He went on to win the title without dropping another set.

As chance would have it, he faced Nadal for the third time in just over two months when the two met in the Miami final, twelve years after they had done the same in 2005. This time Federer had more tennis under his belt from the previous days – he needed a final-set tiebreak to beat Tomas Berdych after saving two match points, and he played three tiebreaks in beating Nick Kyrgios – so this was a better chance for Nadal. Nonetheless, while the Spaniard posted two more games than in Indian Wells, Federer still ran out a comfortable winner playing some of the best tennis of his life.

Not only had Federer beaten Nadal at a major, but he had beaten his old nemesis four times on the run, if you go back to their Basel final of 2015. That was by far his longest winning streak against Nadal, and he was to take it to five with another straight-sets victory in the Shanghai final six months later. It was almost as if Nadal had developed the complex against Federer that Federer had had for years against Nadal. History records that Nadal won more of their matches, but that streak nullifies the argument that, even at his best, Federer could never beat Nadal. He even posted another win over Nadal at Wimbledon in 2019 when Nadal was back to his very best form and won two of that year's four major titles.

Federer skipped the clay-court season to focus on the grass, and, as with Donskoy in Dubai, came a cropper against a player thought unlikely to trouble him. Playing the grass-court tournament in Stuttgart for the first time, he faced Tommy Haas in his first match, Haas profiting from a sentimental wildcard, and thanking the tournament organisers by sending their top attraction packing.

A ninth title in Halle meant Federer went to Wimbledon having won four titles from the six tournaments he had played, with his only two defeats coming to players ranked outside the world's top 100. And while his eighth Wimbledon title and nineteenth major lacked the excitement and drama of the Australian Open five months earlier, the fact that he won another Grand Slam title without dropping a single set is yet one more phenomenal achievement.

He had his fair share of luck. He profited from a retirement in the first round against Alexandr Dolgopolov, Marin Cilic clearly had a knee problem in the final, which caused the Croat to seek medical advice through tears of realisation that, in his first Wimbledon final, he couldn't put up a plausible challenge, and his biggest rivals all fell away. Murray was clearly feeling the hip that was disintegrating after his stupendous efforts of 2016 and did well to reach the quarter-finals, where he lost to Sam Querrey; Djokovic retired with a shoulder problem in his quarter-final against Tomas Berdych and that proved the end of his year; and Nadal lost a marathon final set in his fourth-round match against Gilles Müller. But Federer had kept his head while all around him were losing theirs, and that sufficed for the title. He was even able to joke afterwards that he wasn't even a full-timer on the tour – 'I feel like I'm working part-time these days,' he said of his truncated tournament schedule. Maybe he had worked out something that the rest of the tennis world had yet to.

If 2017 was turning into an annus mirabilis for Roger Federer the tennis player, it also included an important milestone for Roger Federer the entrepreneur. For in September that year, Federer celebrated the culmination of several years of efforts to emulate golf's Ryder Cup, with the inaugural staging of tennis's Laver Cup.

An exact mirroring of the Europe v America Ryder Cup format was not going to create a balanced sporting spectacle, as Europe is too dominant in men's tennis, but the best Europeans taking on the rest of the world would be far more of a contest, and would bring some colourful players into contention for selection. The competition should really be called the Federer Cup – indeed some people jokingly refer to it as that – because it is very much Federer's baby. But as one of his motivations is to keep some of the great names of tennis's heritage prominent in today's game, he wanted to name the event after a true legend whom he and his contemporaries have always admired, and Rod Laver, the first (and so far only) man to win all four major titles in the same year with everyone eligible to play, was an obvious name. It also made it easier for Federer to persuade Rafael Nadal to play, and Novak Djokovic in 2018 and 2022.

Federer also signed up Björn Borg and John McEnroe to captain the two teams, and Laver himself was ever-present in the crowd, along with other champions from tennis's past. The venture itself is run by Federer's own management agency Team8, jointly with the Australian national association Tennis Australia and a Brazilian businessman. For the first staging of the cup in Prague, it's hard to believe there was anyone left in Tennis Australia's Melbourne offices, as everyone who was anyone seemed to have decamped to the Czech capital.

Federer couldn't have wished for a better opening event. With a format that keeps the competition alive until the final day (unlike the Davis Cup at that stage), it was still alive right up to the final rubber. But perhaps his biggest act of marketing nous came when he played a seventy-nine-minute doubles, partnering Nadal for the first time in their careers.

As Federer said afterwards, he and Nadal 'just had to win', because everyone expected it of them, but in Jack Sock and Sam Querrey, they were up against a resilient pair; Sock had a Wimbledon doubles title to his name by then and Querrey was an experienced doubles operator. Another problem is that both Federer and Nadal prefer returning in the deuce court, so one of them had to accept the advantage court; they eventually adopted the traditional default position in righty-lefty combinations of the left-hander taking the ad court. But it was on one of Federer's serves that their unfamiliarity with each other as doubles partners almost came to calamity. Federer served down the centre, Querrey lobbed the return at full stretch, and both Federer and Nadal went for the smash. It was only Federer's last-second decision to withdraw that avoided an embarrassing accident ('too much energy' was Nadal's explanation afterwards; Federer had clearly called 'me' so the excess energy was, perhaps unsurprisingly, on Nadal's part). The legends won the first set on a single break, but then fell victim to Sock's mighty forehand to concede the second 6–1. But they regrouped to take the super-tiebreak played instead of a final set 10–5 to give the cameo the ending everyone wanted.

Federer himself was involved in the final match of the weekend. He needed to beat Nick Kyrgios to give Europe a 15–9 win, but, with three points resting on final-day rubbers, Kyrgios was playing to level the contest at 12–12 and take it into a deciding doubles shootout. It was also a weekend on which Kyrgios, so often the wild child of the pro tour, showed that, when he's playing for an entity bigger than himself, his dedication to the cause is faultless. It was the match of the weekend and, when Federer took the second set on an 8–6 tiebreak, having been two points from defeat, it was Nadal who was playing the role of captain, tactical adviser and motivator-in-chief, as the introverted Borg resembled a fish out of water. When Kyrgios had match point at 9–8 in the super-tiebreak, he was on the verge of spoiling another Federer party, but he overhit a forehand, and two more errors on the subsequent two points saw Federer home to an ecstatic victory.

Federer played a part in Europe's win the following year in Chicago – a contest notable for him playing doubles with Novak Djokovic and being struck on the back of the head by a Djokovic serve – and again in Geneva in 2019. But perhaps his biggest victory was in getting the Laver Cup to be an officially recognised event on the ATP tour, which means a player's results in the Laver Cup are now listed among the rest of his official matches in a tennis year.

The Laver Cup also provided the perfect final curtain for the Federer career (see page 421), though how long it will survive now Federer is no longer a player remains to be seen. There is an obvious role for him as Borg's eventual successor as Team Europe captain, but the ultimate success of the event is more likely to depend on how much it means to the players, and in the long term that is impossible to predict.

There was no way Federer's phenomenal year could continue at the level he had sustained to the end of Wimbledon, and it didn't. If anything, he was made to pay in the second half of the year for his supreme efforts in the first half.

His first meaningful defeat came in the final of his first tournament after Wimbledon, when he lost in straight sets to Alexander Zverev in Montreal. At face value that was no disgrace, but he was laboured in his movement against Zverev, and came off court with a back problem. That caused him to skip the following week's tournament in Cincinnati, and in his first-week matches at the US Open he was clearly not moving well. He eked out five-set wins against Frances Tiafoe and Mikhail Youzhny, but found something of his movement in the third and fourth rounds, which set up a quarter-final against Juan Martin del Potro. Of greater interest to most tennis watchers was the prospect of the first-ever Federer v Nadal match at the US Open, and their potential meeting in the semi-finals would have been for the number-one ranking as well. But while Nadal honoured his part of the deal by beating Andrey Rublev, Federer faltered.

In some ways it was always asking a lot of a man with a back problem to overcome one of the biggest hitters on the tour, and at that tournament del Potro played arguably his best tennis since winning the title in 2009. But had Federer converted one of the four set points he had in the third set, he might have made it. Once he lost that tiebreak 10–8, the game was up, and the Argentinian wrapped up victory in four sets. It was Federer's first defeat in a Slam that year.

His back problems threatened his involvement in the Laver Cup, but he found time for singles wins over Querrey and Kyrgios, and his doubles cameo with Nadal. He then inflicted a fifth straight defeat over Nadal in the Shanghai final, and added an eighth Basel title to his growing list. He had won seven of the eleven tournaments he had played in 2017 as he went into his final event, the ATP Finals in London.

After winning his three group matches, he was the one quality name left in the last four, alongside David Goffin, Grigor Dimitrov and Jack Sock. It was Federer's title for the taking, but then came another of those Federer match patterns where he plays sublimely early on but loses the thread and can't get it back. In the semi-finals, he blew David Goffin away in the first set, comfortable in the knowledge that he had never lost to the Belgian in six previous matches. But Goffin, who had told the media the previous day that he didn't know how to beat Federer, got himself back into the match, and, by the time he won the second set, Federer was looking edgy. A break for the Belgian allowed him to take the final set 6–4 and bring a slightly premature close to one of the most remarkable years of Federer's career.

It had been the kind of year few could have imagined when he announced at the end of July 2016 that he was taking the rest of the season off. He finished the year with two of the four major titles, sharing the four with Nadal, and the two war horses – who had both ended 2016 early because of injury – were one and two in the world. Eventually Old Father Time finally caught up with Federer, but, until it became clear in September 2022 that the game was up, 2017 was always there to give succour to the hope that he might still prove the doubters hopelessly wrong.

19

DESPITE THE REMARKABLE body of work Federer put together in 2017, there was still one tiny piece of the comeback missing.

Even those who considered Federer capable of adding to his seventeen Grand Slam titles when he returned to the tour at the start of 2017 never considered it likely that he would get back to the top of the rankings. Playing just twelve tournaments a year made that a tough ask, given that a male player's ranking is made up of his best eighteen events, of which twelve are mandatory (the four Slams plus eight of the nine Masters-1000s). He came within two wins of the number-one ranking at the US Open, even if del Potro and Nadal were severe obstacles, but having failed to pick up maximum points at the ATP Finals, and going into the start of 2018 as the defending champion in the first three significant tournaments, the chances of him reclaiming the top spot were slim.

And yet he defended his title in Melbourne. Just as at Wimbledon six months earlier, he didn't have to face any of the other three members of the big four. When the quarter-final line-up was complete, it looked like he might have to face Djokovic in the semis and Nadal in the final. But Djokovic was still in the early stages of a comeback after taking the kind of break in 2017 that Federer had taken in 2016, and he was 'outDjokovic'd' by Hyeon Chung, a young Korean for whom that was his breakout tournament. But Chung had done so much running in his five matches that he started his semi-final against Federer with severe blisters, and gave up a hopeless cause in the second set.

Nadal came unstuck in the quarter-finals when Marin Cilic halted an early onslaught, and Nadal then felt something go in his upper thigh in the fourth set. Treatment didn't make it any better, and he retired early in the fifth. So just as at Wimbledon, it was the tall Croat standing between Federer and another major title. The final saw another lightning-fast Federer start, but, just as against Goffin and numerous other players, he couldn't sustain it, and the potential derailing as Cilic got into the match was very real. Winning the third set was crucial for Federer, because he faded badly in the fourth, and looked like he was fading rapidly at the start of the fifth. But a combination of a new lease of life, and Cilic easing off when he had the upper hand, allowed Federer to reclaim the initiative, and in the end the final set was not close.

With Nadal having lost two rounds earlier than the previous year, and Federer defending his ranking points, suddenly the number-one ranking was within reach. He had not intended to play the tournament in Rotterdam two weeks later, but, needing only to reach the semi-finals to retake the top spot, he changed his plans. That gave a buzz to his quarter-final against the home player Robin Haase, and many of the world's tennis media gathered in the Dutch port city to witness the ascent. When Haase took the first set, the moment of theatre could have fallen flat, but Federer got his act together in the second set, and lost just two more games after that to assure himself of being ranked number one again. And for good measure, he won his ninety-seventh title by emphatically beating Grigor Dimitrov in the final.

He was to remain at the top for only five weeks, but that was immaterial. He had made it back there, he was the oldest player – man or woman – to occupy the top spot, and it completed a phenomenal comeback over the previous fourteen months. In the early part of his career he would often play down the world number-one ranking, saying that if you won enough matches the ranking would take care of itself. This time there was more respect for the numerical accolade: 'When you're older you maybe have to put double the work in,' he said after beating Haase. 'This maybe means the most to me in my career.' When he looks back, the achievement will probably pale in comparison with beating Nadal in the previous year's Australian Open final, but, as proof of a sustained level of performance few had considered him capable of, it is a remarkably strong piece of evidence.

Throughout his career, Federer has been associated with two tennis brands: Wilson and Nike. His lifetime racket contract means that, short of the Wilson Sporting Goods company going bust, he will always have a Wilson racket in his hand, even long after his tour days are over. But Nike never signed him up for life, and the brash Oregon apparel company has a record of letting names firmly associated with the Nike swoosh disappear in the final years of their career. Perhaps the most surprising was Andre Agassi, one of the iconic names who had helped establish the Nike brand, who played his final years in Adidas clothes, but Lleyton Hewitt, Amélie Mauresmo and others were also let go by Nike before their sell-by date.

As Federer's Nike contract came up for renewal at the end of June 2018, after more than twenty years with the brand, his agents picked up a reticence on Nike's part to push the boat out. The company, founded by the indestructibly confident Phil Knight and named after the Greek goddess of victory, would have preferred Federer to stay, but they were not going out of their way to make him feel wanted, or so Federer's people felt. And when the Japanese high-street label Uniqlo offered a sum generally thought to have been astronomical, Federer signed with them. The actual amount was reported as $30 million a year, but serious tennis watchers should never take such numbers too seriously, as the amount a player ultimately gets is almost always based on results, so exact figures are impossible to give. The news was so well guarded that it was only made public at one o'clock London time at the precise moment Federer was due to walk out on Wimbledon's Centre Court to start the champion's traditional title defence. As a result, there were tennis insiders who wondered what was going on when they saw Federer emerge from the clubhouse wearing Uniqlo's red patches where the Nike swoosh was thought to be a fixture.

However, one thing that was missing from the Uniqlo shirts was the distinctive 'RF' logo; Nike retained control over that until early 2020, though it hardly mattered as many fans use it liberally on pro-Federer banners seen in stands and outside tennis stadiums. (In his book *The Master*, the American writer Christopher Clarey devotes a lot of space to Federer's business dealings, including a fair bit about what went on behind the scenes over the Nike negotiations. The Uniqlo deal, together with a parallel deal Federer did with the Swiss sports shoe company On, allowed him to become the first tennis player to top the Forbes sports rich list in 2020, although Clarey rightly points out that such lists are based largely on income estimates that are often far from reliable.)

The way Federer had won the Australian Open suggested that, at thirty-six, his only realistic option for adding to his twenty Grand Slam titles was to ensure he got through his early rounds with sufficient ease that he had a full tank left for the closing stages. That model was working to perfection at Wimbledon in 2018, when he suddenly fell victim to that Federer pattern of losing the thread and never getting it back.

Once again he missed the clay-court season, and warmed up for Wimbledon with nine matches on German grass. It was probably a couple too many, for having won in Stuttgart he seemed a little listless in his Halle final against Borna Coric, which he lost in three sets. But he raced through his first four matches at Wimbledon without dropping serve or having to face even a tiebreak, to set up a quarter-final against Kevin Anderson.

An embarrassment of riches on men's quarter-finals day meant Federer was scheduled for a rare appearance on

Court 1 to play Anderson. For the first two hours, the riches came from Federer's racket, as he blitzed the South African 6–2 in the first set and then took the second on a 7–5 tiebreak. He stood at match point two minutes short of the two-hour mark, but he framed a backhand with Anderson bearing down on the net. In the next game Anderson broke, and the match turned. Although Federer discovered more energy in the final set and had the advantage of serving first, he never looked like breaking the South African, and a break in the twenty-third game allowed Anderson to serve out a 13–11 set to seal an unlikely victory in four-and-a-quarter hours.

That match, followed by Anderson's 26–24 final-set victory over John Isner in the semi-finals two days later, helped seal the fate of the open-ended final set at Wimbledon, and also at the Australian and French Opens. By the start of 2019, Wimbledon and the Australian had made arrangements for final-set tiebreaks, and the French followed suit in 2022. While Anderson's victory was a surprise, it cannot be said to have effectively denied Federer a twenty-first major title. Even if he'd won, and had beaten Isner in the semis, he would have had to face either Nadal or Djokovic in the final, and both were in blistering form. As it happened, Djokovic edged out Nadal in a high-quality semi-final, and was much fresher than Anderson in the final, but either legend would have been a tough nut for Federer to crack.

Djokovic's hold on Federer was reasserted in the Cincinnati final, when the Serb beat Federer to an accomplishment Federer never achieved – a complete set of all nine Masters-1000 titles. Still, it left Federer in good shape going into the US Open, but, on a brutally humid night, he lost to the likeable Australian John Millman in the third round. Again he got off to a fast start, but, after dropping the second set from 5–3 up, Federer faded badly, and another major slipped out of his grasp.

A ninth title in Basel was his also ninety-ninth tour title. That set him up for a good end-of-year run-in in Paris and London, either of which would have been a worthy venue for the 100th title, but he lost both in the semi-finals. The Paris semi was one of the matches of the year, Djokovic winning 7–6, 5–7, 7–6 in three hours of brilliant tennis from both men. This time Federer was able to sustain his level, but Djokovic was still a notch better. The effort drained the Serb, and he was picked off in the final by Karen Khachanov. And then at the ATP Finals Federer lost to an inspired Alexander Zverev in the semis, the German going on to beat Djokovic in the final.

The Australian Open would also have been a fitting setting for his 100th title, but a coming-of-age performance by Stefanos Tsitsipas extinguished that dream in the fourth round. By the time the two men – separated by seventeen years – faced each other again, Tsitsipas was the last man standing between Federer and his century. They met in the Dubai final, where a 6–4, 6–4 win took Federer to his magic 100. Only Jimmy Connors, who finished his career with 109 titles, has won more, and, while Federer finished six short on 103, he was winning his titles at a greater age than Connors.

Ever up for a change in routine to keep his hunger fresh, Federer opted in 2019 to go back to the clay. He never harboured specific hopes of winning a second French Open title, and there were inevitably those who saw his decision to go back to Madrid, Rome and Paris as a pre-retirement valedictory tour, but then Federer has been used to people asking about his impending retirement since he was twenty-eight. The plan worked. True, he was foiled by the rain in Rome, which required him to play two matches in a day, and, after taking two and a half hours to beat Borna Coric on a final-set tiebreak, he decided not to risk an ailing body against Tsitsipas in the quarter-finals. He won five matches at Roland Garros, and was only stopped in the semi-finals by the irrepressible Nadal. It would have been interesting to see if Federer could have given Nadal a run for his money in normal conditions, but a stupendously gusting wind rendered the contest a farce, and Nadal won comfortably.

Despite the defeat, Federer was perfectly set for a ninth Wimbledon and twenty-first major. He won Halle for the tenth time, the first tournament to bring him ten titles, and dropped just two sets en route to the Wimbledon semi-finals. From there, the run-in suddenly got a lot harder, for facing him in the semis was Nadal, with the likelihood that he would face Djokovic in the final.

His four-sets win over Nadal was notable for its reflection of how much the two men had changed on grass since their three Wimbledon finals of 2006–8. Then they were a veritable contrast in styles, now they were still players with striking differences but playing a much more similar game. It's as if they had both worked out what they had to do, and had met much closer to the middle than in the early parts of their careers. It was an absorbing match, but Nadal seemed to lack his usual intensity, and only won the second of the four sets they played.

That set up a third Djokovic–Federer Wimbledon final in six years. Three weeks off his thirty-eighth birthday, Federer was thought to have his best chance if the match was short. Once again, that proved misguided thinking – the match set a new record for a Wimbledon final of four hours fifty-seven minutes, and Federer was in it right until the end, which featured the first final-set tiebreak in the history of Wimbledon singles finals. By then, though, Federer had missed his chance.

As a display of sustained high-quality tennis, it could not be beaten, but what made the 2019 Wimbledon final especially memorable was the drama of the final set. Having opted for a first-to-seven tiebreak at 12–12, Wimbledon had kept open the chance of a cliff-hanging final set (just not an endless one), and in its first year, the title was decided on a 12–12 tiebreak. Federer should perhaps have won the match in four sets. Having lost the first set after leading the tiebreak 5–3, he won the second comfortably and then had a set point at 5–4 in the third. But Djokovic took that on a second tiebreak, before Federer bounced back to take the fourth 6–4. Djokovic broke for 4–2 in the decider, but Federer came straight back. With the spectators almost exclusively barracking for Federer, his winners were celebrated with elation resembling New York razzmatazz rather than sedate Wimbledon appreciation.

At 7–7 Federer broke, and earned the chance to serve out the match. After two nervous forehands, he fired down two aces to give himself two championship points. They had played four hours eleven minutes. On the first, Federer missed his first serve, and saw Djokovic thunder the second back to his feet, forcing a forehand error. On the second championship point, Federer got a first serve in. Djokovic's return dropped short. Here was Federer's chance – he charged into the net behind a forehand approach shot, but he didn't swing quite freely enough and the ball landed short, offering Djokovic a small but clear gap. The Serb still had to make it, but his accuracy on the most tension-laden of points is legendary, and he found the gap with a precision crosscourt winner.

That was Federer's opportunity. In fact it proved his last opportunity to win another major. He dropped serve two points later and, while he had a break point in a marathon game at 11–11, Djokovic by then was playing like a man released from jail. In the third tiebreak of the afternoon, Djokovic made it three out of three, the crucial point coming at 5–3 when he picked the perfect moment to unleash a backhand down the line that caught Federer off-guard. On the next point, Federer didn't get his feet quickly enough into position for a forehand, the ball flew off the frame of his racket, and the match was over.

So near and yet so far. Once again he had proved that you write him off at your peril, but once again he had lost a match from match point up – the twenty-second of his career, and the third against Djokovic in a major from two match points up. He was typically gracious in defeat, but, when asked to give it some perspective in his post-match press conference, he said, 'Like similar to '08 maybe, I will look back at it and think, "Well, it's not that bad after all." For now it hurts, and it should, like every loss does here at Wimbledon.'

Of all the near-misses in his career, this was the nearest. But one of the pitfalls of setting new standards is that you encourage others to match you and ultimately overtake you. Federer had brought the best out of Djokovic, from the man-to-man talk in October 2007 about too many injury timeouts, to just being a class act on court. Now for the third time in a Wimbledon final, Djokovic had shown greater nerve than Federer, and, while he was a less popular champion, few can say he didn't deserve to lift the trophy.

In mid-2019, Federer finally succeeded in a softly-softly lobbying campaign that had been going on behind the scenes for a couple of years.

Since 2010, Federer had staged a 'Match for Africa' at roughly two-yearly intervals to raise money for the Roger Federer Foundation. The first staging was in Zurich and involved Federer and Rafael Nadal playing an exhibition match, and the following day they played another exhibition in Madrid for Nadal's foundation. For the sixth staging of Federer's event, he asked Nadal to play an exhibition with him, but this time, and for the first time, a 'Match *in* Africa'. Nadal took his time to accept, but eventually agreed to play Federer in the Cape Town Stadium on 7 February 2020. The two warmed up for their match with a gentle doubles involving the computer magnate Bill Gates and the South African comedian turned American satire television host Trevor Noah. Federer and Nadal played a three-set match, which Federer won, though few players talk about the result of exhibition matches given that entertainment and their sheer presence is what they're there for.

The exhibition raised $3.5 million for the Roger Federer Foundation, specifically to be spent on creating educational opportunities in rural South Africa. Publicity put out by Federer's agency Team8 said the match set a new world record for the largest attendance at a tennis match – well, perhaps for an exhibition match, but exhibitions have routinely gone well beyond the figure for an official tour-level match. Federer played in front of 42,517 in a Mexico City bullring for an exhibition against Alexander Zverev at the end of 2019, while the Match in Africa is reported to have sold 51,945 tickets. Both were hailed as world records and, while there are unconfirmed reports of one-off matches in Peru involving Alex Olmedo in the early 1960s that are reported to have attracted around 45,000 spectators, the 51,945 attendance – if accurate – is likely to be a record. Either way, Federer's popularity is such that it should surprise no one that he can claim to have been on court for both the best-attended exhibition match and the best-attended official match (27,448 at the 2014 Davis Cup final) in tennis's history.

In other off-court matters, thirteen years after having his face on a postage stamp, Federer became the first living Swiss person to have his image on a coin. The Swiss federal currency issuer Swissmint announced that Federer's image (playing a backhand) would appear on a 20-franc commemorative silver coin to be released in January 2020. The silver coin proved so popular that Swissmint issued a 50-franc gold coin in September 2020 bearing the same Federer image.

And with Switzerland and the rest of the world in lockdown to fight the Covid-19 pandemic, Federer gave one million Swiss francs in March 2020 to help vulnerable families during the country's fight against the coronavirus. Switzerland was one of the worst affected states in the early days of the virus in terms of numbers of citizens with the disease.

Fate clearly didn't want Roger Federer and Rafael Nadal to play each other at the US Open. A Nadal–Federer match was on in September 2019, but again Federer didn't make it to the appointed round. After two stuttering matches, he hit good form against Dan Evans and David Goffin in the third and fourth rounds, and in the quarter-finals faced Grigor Dimitrov, whom he hadn't lost to in their seven previous matches. Yet once again the fluent Federer of the previous two rounds gave way to a laboured Federer, and the Bulgarian sensed his chance.

Federer won the first and third sets, but even in the second it was clear this would be no walk in the park, as his movement was not what it is when everything is flowing, and when he lost the fourth set he looked spent. He called for the trainer and, while he played out the match, he never looked like putting up a fight in the fifth set. In retrospect, it was a sign that seven matches in fourteen days on an unforgiving surface was becoming increasingly hard for Federer to handle.

The 103rd – and ultimately last – title of his career came, fittingly, in Basel, his tenth triumph in the home city where he had such difficulty early on. He was never tested, and only had to play four matches because of a walkover. But again he lost in the semis of the ATP Finals, this time to Stefanos Tsitsipas, who went on to take the title in a high-quality final against Dominic Thiem the following day. After lots of false dawns, a new generation behind Federer, Nadal, Djokovic and Murray finally seemed to be emerging.

The strain on Federer's body was again apparent at the 2020 Australian Open. He hurt a thigh muscle in his third-round match against John Millman, but had enough experience and courtcraft to fashion a victory from the jaws of defeat. Millman led the final-set super-tiebreak 8–4, but Federer won six points on the run to take it 10–8 and a somewhat unlikely place in the fourth round. Four days later he saved six match points against Tennys Sandgren. It was a remarkable display of 'come on, I dare you' by Federer, who could barely move, and on Sandgren's match points just kept getting the ball back with no pace, which eventually undermined the American's confidence and he duly imploded. Federer went for a scan on his thigh after that, but there was no serious damage, so he was able to take to the court against Djokovic in the semi-finals. No serious damage perhaps, but after two five-setters and all the treatment, few thought he had any chance; indeed Federer said after his straight-sets defeat that he had 'a three per cent chance to win', adding 'You've got to go for it, you never know, but once you can see it coming, that it's not going to work any more, it's tough.' Federer did make a fist of it in the first set, breaking early and taking the set to the tiebreak, but ultimately the 7–6, 6–4, 6–3 score reflects a respectability that was a relief to Federer fans, as it could have been so much worse.

Federer was initially worried that he might not be able to play his 'Match in Africa' with Nadal. The worry proved groundless and the match went ahead, but that experience confirmed that there was once again something wrong with his right knee. With the benefit of hindsight, this was the beginning of the end; the knee never recovered. He opted for arthroscopic surgery, the results of which he said confirmed that it was the right thing to do, but the recovery would take at least three months. He therefore put out a statement saying he would be missing Indian Wells, Miami and the whole of the clay-court season, and would return on the grass in June.

Yet by June, there was no grass. There was no Indian Wells either, no Miami, no clay-court tennis, and no Wimbledon. In some ways Federer got his timing for the knee surgery spot-on, because the advance of the Covid-19 pandemic would wreak so much havoc on global life that he didn't miss any tournaments he had planned to play: they simply didn't take place. Yet even if the grass-court season had taken place as planned, he would have missed it too. He suffered a setback in his rehabilitation, and in May he had to have 'an additional quick arthroscopic procedure' on the knee. Mindful of the benefits he gained from granting himself time for a complete recovery in 2016, he announced in early June that he would be taking the rest of 2020 off, in order to be 'one hundred per cent ready to play at my highest level' at the start of 2021. So the chance to pick up another major title in the truncated tour schedule of the second half of 2020, when he might have been quicker out of the blocks than his principal rivals, went begging.

Federer's first opportunity to pick up a racket after his two knee operations made for a very touching internet video that once again saw him hitting tennis balls in a most unlikely setting.

In June 2020, two tennis-playing girls from Finale Ligure on Italy's north-west coast found themselves bored, so began hitting balls from one girl's rooftop to the other. A friend filmed thirteen-year-old Vittoria and eleven-year-old Carola hitting across some steep drops; the film went viral, and touched a lot of people – including Federer. 'When I saw the video on social media from the girls, I just thought: what a wonderful idea,' he said. 'The passion doesn't go away just because of a lockdown, and I think that video really resonated with a lot of people. And with me too.' With the Italian pasta company Barilla as one of his sponsors, he was invited to Finale Ligure, and on 10 July he played out a cute ambush. The success of the original video gave excellent cover for a film crew to interview the two girls on one of their rooftops, but, unbeknown to them, Federer himself was on the roof. So after they had told the camera that he was their favourite player – and that one of them would 'jump on him' if she ever met him – the two were astonished to see the real Roger Federer standing alongside them with a big childlike grin on his face. 'He's not a mannequin,' Vittoria said, once she'd got over her shock at having her hero on her own roof.

The whole thing could have been very cheesy, especially as it culminated in a pasta lunch that created great advertising material for Barilla. But the delight Federer and the two girls had both in hitting balls and meeting each other trumped the fact that the whole thing was staged, and the video of 'The Rooftop Match' has been viewed over 35 million times. 'It was an extraordinary place to play, on the rooftop with them,' he said. 'The passion you have about the game doesn't have to be in front of a full crowd – it just has to be for fun with no expectations, just having a good time.'

The announcement that the 2021 Australian Open would be put back by three weeks to mid-February, as the Sars-Cov2 virus continued to wreak havoc with global schedules, seemed to indicate a definitive comeback date for Federer, but in December 2020 he announced he would miss it. He said the knee still wasn't right; but there was an equally plausible secondary explanation: that Australia's strict quarantine regulations meant it simply wasn't viable for the Federer family to travel together. The travelling circus that the Federers had become had survived all sorts of privations and haphazard modes of accommodation, but with the girls eleven and the boys seven, and the rules offering no scope for them to leave their designated hotel room for fourteen consecutive days, Roger and Mirka decided not to inflict this on the energetic twins and called off the trip.

By the time Federer returned to the court, he had been off the tour for well over a year, and was just five months short of his fortieth birthday. The memory of his brilliant comeback in 2017 allowed the believers to believe, and, when the flashing blade of his racket conjured up a three-sets win over Dan Evans in Doha in his first match back, the magic seemed still within reach. But what was he hoping to achieve? Even if the knee had completely healed – which it hadn't – what was he playing for?

In his biography of the 1920s champion Bill Tilden, who was tennis's first male superstar, Frank Deford quotes observers as saying that, at the age of forty, Tilden was still the best in the world over one set, but couldn't sustain it for longer. When Jimmy Connors made a brief return to tour tennis at the age of forty-two, he declined to play Grand Slam tournaments because he said he couldn't do it over five sets any more. Could Federer really win seven best-of-five matches in a fortnight, or even five best-of-three matches in a week? And would he really be happy playing on if a couple of tour titles or the odd glory match at a major were all he could realistically hope for?

In the end, the decision was made for him, and his final comeback lasted just thirteen matches.

In his third tournament back, he reached the fourth round at the French Open, beating Dominik Koepfer in his first ever night-session match at Roland Garros. But he didn't take to the court for his next match to protect his knee for the grass. When he lost to Félix Auger-Aliassime in the second round in Halle, he was in tears: he realised the knee just wasn't up to the rigours of the pro tennis tour. Having come this far, he played Wimbledon and somehow scraped through four rounds. But in the quarter-finals, his match against Hubert Hurkacz disintegrated into a nightmare. He was beaten in straight sets, the last of them 6–0, which many found excruciating to watch.

A year later he was back at Wimbledon, but in a sharp navy suit, not his tennis whites; he had undergone two more operations on the troublesome knee and hadn't played a single official match. He received by far the biggest cheer and applause in a parade of past champions to celebrate the centenary of Wimbledon's Centre Court. In a brief interview on court, he said, 'I hope I can come back one more time,' and he meant it. The Swiss Indoors was holding a wildcard for him to play once more in his home city, but it didn't take long for the last hopes to be extinguished. A few days later he was playing a practice match, and it dawned on him that he would never again be able to move the way a tour-level singles player needs to. He went through a few days of agonising, and then made the decision that his time had come to stop.

He chose to communicate it by writing a letter to his fans, which he then read and disseminated on social media. His last tournament would be at the Laver Cup in London at the end of September, and that would bring the curtain down on his career.

The one match he played in London, a doubles partnering Rafael Nadal against Jack Sock and Frances Tiafoe, was the perfect way to finish. It was clear he didn't have the movement. One point in the fourth game graphically showed it: Tiafoe mis-hit a volley that Federer would normally have run down, but he just couldn't take off. Federer and Nadal had a match point at 9–8 in the match tiebreak, but Federer couldn't make it to a very makeable forehand, and two points later the Americans sealed victory. The beautiful shots that had characterised the Federer career were still working, but the body couldn't carry him any more. After a dozen years of the world wondering how Federer's career would end and him promising he would go out on his own terms, the evidence in front of the 17,000 crowd in London's O2 Arena was unequivocal: Federer had not called time too early, he was physically unable to compete any more.

One of the most glorious eras in tennis, indeed in world sport, had come to an end. Because of an earlier match between Andy Murray and Alex de Minaur that went very long, Federer didn't start his final doubles until after 10pm, and it ended well after midnight. It meant that some very tearful scenes were played out in the small hours of a Saturday morning, with a history book of tennis greats present: Federer, Nadal, Djokovic, Murray, Borg, McEnroe and younger contemporaries all in tears in the blue and red uniforms of Team Europe and Team World; they had all turned out for Federer's farewell, Nadal somewhat nervously as he awaited the birth of his first child. Rod Laver, Stefan Edberg and others watched from the VIP seats. Jim Courier conducted the on-court interview, seemingly with a brief to get Federer to cry as much as possible, and at quarter to one in the morning the English singer-songwriter Ellie Goulding came out for one of the more bizarre gigs of her career, singing her hits 'Still Falling For You' and 'Burn' as a still nearly full arena decided it would rather trust the through-the-night Underground trains to get home than miss Federer's final farewell. It was a surreal moment, but how else could the Federer career have ended?

'I'm not sad, I'm happy,' Federer told the crowd through another burst of tears. 'I wanted a celebration, and it's been a great night.' And with that he was gone.

20

DISCUSSIONS ABOUT ROGER Federer's place in history inevitably centre on whether he is the greatest-ever exponent of the game of tennis. It's a topic with endless scope for theories and counter-theories, not least because the definition of what 'the greatest' actually means is so open to interpretation. Is it the player who played the highest-ever level of tennis, even if for only one match? Is it the player with the greatest sustained level of dominance? Is it defined purely by results and statistics, or is there something else that goes with it? And should it be limited solely to tennis, or does an ability to transcend the sport come into play?

There will never be a definitive answer, and, with players like Rafael Nadal and Novak Djokovic still at the top, the landscape is forever changing. This final chapter therefore pulls together some of the strands that should feature in any discussion about Federer's place in history, and leaves it to the reader to decide which side of the imaginary fence to come down on.

The history of modern tennis – or 'lawn tennis' to be strictly accurate; the word 'lawn' does not mean 'grass' in this sense – is still less than 150 years old. Tennis historians now generally agree that 1874, the date Walter Wingfield marketed his boxes of rackets, nets, balls and instructions, marks the birth of the tennis we know today. As such, it is a much younger sport than many others such as football (soccer), golf, cricket, baseball, Olympic track and field disciplines, and even American football. It therefore ought to be easier to work out the greatest tennis player, as there is a certain amount of documentary evidence on everyone who has played at the highest level in the sport's past. But there's a problem.

From the 1930s until tennis went 'open' in 1968, the sport was divided into amateur and professional circuits. It meant the greatest players of an era remained amateurs until they had won two or three of the Grand Slam titles (in which only amateurs were allowed to compete), which then made them sufficiently marketable on the professional circuits for them to turn pro and make a living out of tennis, playing never-ending series of exhibition matches in a motley collection of arenas. Many of the amateurs weren't truly amateur anyway – tales abounded of under-the-table payments from national associations who wanted to collect more major titles, and the word 'shamateurism' came into use, and is still used to describe this less than glorious period of tennis's history.

So how can one say how good Fred Perry was in the 1930s? He may have won eight major titles, but by then the big-serving Ellsworth Vines and the wily Bill Tilden had turned professional so were out of Perry's way. Similarly, would Don Budge have done the first pure Grand Slam in 1938 if Perry and others had been in the starting line-up? And what of the great Aussies of the 1960s? Would Rod Laver have won a pure Grand Slam in 1962 if Ken Rosewall, Lew Hoad, Ashley Cooper, Pancho Gonzalez and others had been in all four draws? Would Roy Emerson have won twelve Grand Slam titles if Laver hadn't turned pro after his Slam year of 1962? All impossible to answer.

There's another element that makes defining the greatest tennis player hazardous. For years, the sport was the preserve of a certain affluent social elite, and only in the past forty years or so has it become more accessible to a wider social spectrum (albeit still often very dependent on affluent and committed parents who can ferry their talented offspring to practice and tournaments). As such, fewer people played tennis in earlier eras, so the strength and depth of competition among the top one hundred or so players was nowhere near as great as it is today.

It's therefore possible to make the case that any one of Bill Tilden, Don Budge, Jack Kramer, Lew Hoad, Ken Rosewall, Rod Laver, Björn Borg, John McEnroe, Pete Sampras, Andre Agassi, Roger Federer, Rafael Nadal and Novak Djokovic is the greatest male player of all time. It certainly makes for good discussion, especially when you take into consideration factors such as Hoad regularly beating Laver on the professional circuit. All were men who, like Federer, combined immense natural talent with a work ethic that is frequently missing in the intensely gifted.

The one way of slicing through the inability to compare one great champion with another was always going to be if a player emerged who was just so good and so dominant that he elevated himself above all the variables in the equation. Did Federer do that? Has he become, as some sections of the American media tastelessly call it, the 'Goat' (Greatest Of All Time)?

The case for Federer being the greatest has many elements, but the one most often cited, rightly or wrongly, is a numerical one: the number of Grand Slam singles titles he has won. Until 2000, the most major titles any man had ever won was twelve. For many years the record was held by Roy Emerson, the Australian who declined to turn professional as quickly as many of his contemporaries had done, and picked up twelve titles in the 1960s. When Pete Sampras equalled Emerson's record by winning Wimbledon in 1999, the general feeling was that he had effectively exceeded Emerson's mark because Sampras had had to face the best in world tennis to win his titles, something Emerson could not claim. Sampras went on to beat Emerson's record by winning a seventh Wimbledon in 2000, and took it to fourteen with his last major title, the 2002 US Open.

Federer not only surpassed Sampras's mark, he took it up by six to twenty. He also has a full set of majors, having won all four at least once. Sampras never won the French Open – his best was one semi-final – whereas Federer reached five Roland Garros finals, winning one of them. Remarkable though a total of twenty is, it has already been passed by both Nadal and Djokovic. Given that the tennis circuit revolves around the four Grand Slam tournaments, it is a powerful criterion, but should it on its own measure who is the greatest-ever tennis player?

There is more statistical evidence, even allowing for the fact that you can make any case with numbers if you try hard enough. Until early 2021, Federer held the record for the number of weeks spent at the top of the world rankings with 310, achieved in four periods ranging from February 2004 to March 2018. Djokovic has since beaten that mark, but there is something remarkable in the fact that Federer reached the semi-finals or better at every Grand Slam tournament from Wimbledon 2004 to the 2010 Australian Open, and thirty-six consecutive quarter-finals: that record of twenty-three successive semis may well never be beaten. This is a consistency that no one in tennis history can compete with. True, one must always acknowledge that the 'shamateur' era meant the likes of Perry, Budge, Bobby Riggs, Kramer and the Aussie greats never had the chance to play twenty-three consecutive Slams at their peak, but neither did they face the depth of competition that Federer saw off.

The biggest rival claims to be the greatest come not so much from Sampras, Agassi, Borg, McEnroe or Laver, but from his contemporaries Nadal and Djokovic. At the time of writing, Nadal and Djokovic each has twenty-two Slams. Both also enjoy a vastly superior head-to-head record against Federer, and, without the latter's five successive wins over Nadal between October 2015 and October 2017 plus his Wimbledon semi-final victory in 2019, that head-to-head might exert more influence. But in a sport where the match-up between two players' games can throw spanners into the works of expected results, a player's entire body of work should probably count for more than his record against any one opponent, and in that respect Federer's achievements are spread more evenly than Nadal's.

One could argue that in Federer's most prolific years

(2004–7) he didn't face the quality of opposition that he faced later. A look at the players in the top five around that time shows a lot of who were either beyond their best (Roddick, Safin, Hewitt, Moya) or who never made it to a major final (Henman, Davydenko, Ljubicic, Blake). But the argument can equally be reversed – Nadal is arguably the greatest clay-court player ever, certainly one of the top three, and if he had not been around from the mid-2000s Federer would have won two or three more French titles. Pointless though it is to speculate, if Federer had been born two years earlier, he would have cashed in on the 2001–3 period when no one dominated, and he could have picked up the titles that Hewitt, Ferrero and Roddick won and finished in the mid-twenties. All he could do was beat whoever was on the other side of the net.

As for Djokovic, his dominance in the period from 2014 to the coronavirus interruption in early 2020 makes for arguably the greater challenge to Federer's unofficial status as the greatest of all time. After Federer beat Djokovic in the Wimbledon semi-finals of 2012, Djokovic won every significant match they played, and, despite being deprived of the chance to compete at two majors in 2022 (because he declined to take a Covid-19 vaccine) for which he was a strong favourite, he will finish his career with more major titles and a body of work that will look more impressive than Federer's after he has hung up his racket.

Yet however many Grand Slam titles Nadal and Djokovic end their careers with, there are other factors than mere statistics that add to the argument that Federer is the greatest ever.

*

An unquantifiable factor that sways opinion is that Federer has played with an elegance that attracts people sometimes ambivalent about tennis, and his eloquence in three languages gives him a statesmanlike quality that McEnroe, Agassi and Sampras could never approach. That shouldn't be held against those brought up without a workable second language, but there's no doubt Federer has a radiance that only McEnroe's volatility and Borg's and Agassi's sex appeal could eclipse in the public consciousness.

The elegance with which Federer played his tennis stems from the fact that his strokes were a modern version of the classic technique that evolved in the era of wooden rackets (he has described his playing style as 'modern retro'), and despite the back and knee injuries it might well have protected his body from the punishment endured by some players with modern technique. One can never be sure, but the pounding that his hips and lower back took while playing his groundstrokes might well have been reduced by the much lesser degree of exaggerated body rotation that normally comes with the two-handed backhands and heavily topspun, wristy forehands that characterise modern top-level tennis. Having said that, it's possible the whip that made his forehand such a big weapon took a greater toll on his physique than a truly conventional forehand would have done.

And then there's his backhand. By and large, the one-handed backhand meets with more aesthetic approval from tennis watchers than the utilitarian two-hander, largely because the absence of the second hand makes it a more fluent stroke. The fact that the two-hander is a more recent habit, dating largely from the 1970s (although the Australian

Vivian McGrath won the Australian title with a two-handed backhand in the 1930s), means traditionalists find it easier on the eye, and that enhanced Federer's on-court attractiveness. Throughout his career his backhand was thought of as the 'go-to' wing for opponents, but such was the improvement he made to his topspin backhand during his months off the tour in 2016 that later opponents had to question that strategy. He is on record as saying he would encourage children to hit with a two-hander, because it is a more reliable shot, but he has also expressed frustration that his backhand is the subject of so much discussion, his general line being that whether one hits a backhand with one hand or two is just a minor detail. He did experiment with a two-hander at the age of twelve, but found 'it hurt me everywhere, my chest and my wrist' and is relieved he stuck to his one-hander, which he said 'feels very free'. In an era where the one-handed backhand is something of an endangered species, Federer's ability to use it – both slice and topspin – as part of an arsenal that has won twenty major titles adds further mystique to his legend.

He also seemed to have effortless movement. Commentators often talked about him 'gliding' across the court. Sometimes it's just a bit of flowery language, but Federer did seem to float around a tennis court. It may be simply an optical illusion, but maybe he really did put less pressure on his soles than the average player, and that would explain both the visual spectacle of his graceful movement and the lack of pounding taken by his body.

And he made it look so easy. In *Moments '05*, the Swiss journalist Freddy Widmer writes, 'Federer's game makes it look as if his side of the court is smaller and the opponent's side is bigger, and that he has more time to play his shots than his opponent. You're almost tempted to tear up the rulebook and give the opponent two bounces of the ball to Federer's one, just to be fair. In many situations, Federer seems to know what his opponent should be doing well before his opponent realises this for himself.'

This broader mix of achievement, style and general demeanour was neatly encapsulated by John McEnroe, who for years said that Rod Laver was the greatest tennis player and that the era in which he, Borg and Connors played was the greatest. While much of what McEnroe says can carry a slightly self-serving element (when he and Borg were playing on the oldies' circuit, it suited him very well to push the line that their era was the golden one!), he has mellowed his view about 2000s and 2010s tennis compared with the late 1970s and early 1980s, and is increasingly effusive about Federer.

'Roger is just the greatest player of all time,' McEnroe said in an interview ahead of an ATP Champions Tour event in Zurich in early 2010. 'He is the most beautiful player I've ever seen and I don't ever get tired of watching him. Rod Laver is my idol, Pete Sampras is the greatest grass court player ever, but Roger is just the greatest player of all. I think we can all appreciate how incredible he is even more lately, because he's shown a bit more emotion on court, and he's become a father, so he seems a bit more human, more relatable. That makes what he's doing seem even more amazing.'

It is therefore statistically, stylistically and emotionally plausible to make the case that Federer is the greatest tennis player in the history of the sport, if only because, on the complete package of all attributes, no one can really match him.

So much for the tennis legend – what of the man himself?

There's no question that Federer is a quite remarkable man – a superb international diplomat in the literal (rather than governmental) sense of the word. Talk to anyone who has dealt with him face-to-face, even if only for a few seconds, and they will testify to how he makes them feel valued for the duration of his time with them. He has the politician's knack of giving the person he's talking to the impression that, at that moment, they are the only person in the world who matters, but, while politicians generally invest in personal contact in the hope of garnering votes, Federer believes everyone he meets has something worth listening to.

The American tennis journalist Christopher Clarey quotes Andy Roddick telling the story of how Federer came to Roddick's home city of Austin, Texas, to help with an event for his charitable foundation. Roddick had expected to be Federer's escort for a time-limited period of glad-handing, but Federer took the initiative, introduced himself to numerous people, and made everyone feel cherished. 'The thing I'm most jealous of,' Roddick said, 'is not the skill and not the titles, it's the ease of operation within which Roger exists. There are people who are as great as Roger in different sports, but there's no chance that [Michael] Jordan or Tiger [Woods] had the ease of operation Roger has day to day.'

This makes him a dream to the business community. You can put him in any situation and he will charm the people with him. No one should be surprised that his business ventures have been highly successful – of course, they have to be fundamentally sound as projects, but such a superb front man gives everything he invests in an immense lift. Despite his listening skills and ability to make decisions, he is not someone who is particularly comfortable in deep and meaningful discussions, and he's not massively into books or philosophical ideas. He presents a very impressive front, but then that is who he is – what you see is really what you get. His former flatmate and doubles partner Yves Allegro says Federer 'is not playing a role. It's not a game he's playing – it's just the way he is. He looks relaxed because he is relaxed. That's just him.'

In spite of his openness, he has a very strong sense of demarcation. He guards his private life jealously, and is polite but firm if anyone asks him something he feels is out of bounds. From the moment he won the first of his twenty Grand Slam titles in July 2003, he knew life would change, but he has adapted himself to keep the essence of a decent human being, even though he has to manage situations where a bit of judicious deafness comes into play, and he has people around him who make sure he can be extricated from situations that might become troublesome.

In assessing Federer's character, or – to be cynical – to ask whether he's really as good as he seems, one has to keep in mind what economists call the 'business as usual scenario' – a comparison of what would have happened if nothing had changed. This is important, because, while Federer is not quite the same affable, easy-going character he was when he first won Wimbledon, who wouldn't be in some way affected by the strange cocktail he has to deal with in his everyday life? It's a mixture of athletic rigour, public pressure, large sums of money and massive adulation, adoration and fawning from those with whom he comes into contact – a cocktail that would influence the character of a saint, and would drive many of us to despotism. While the not-so-positive attributes of his personality should not be glossed over, there are surprisingly few, and any realistic assessment of Roger Federer the person comes out very favourably.

This raises the question about whether there is something special about him that goes beyond normal human characteristics. There are those on the tennis tour who jocularly referred to 'Saint Roger', often in a slightly sarcastic way, but let's pose the question: is there something saintly about Roger Federer? Does he justify any comparison with modern-day figures who have been talked about in reverent tones, people like Mohandas Gandhi or Nelson Mandela, even if they haven't been beatified? While it would be wrong to draw too many comparisons with the likes of Gandhi and Mandela (how can hitting tennis balls compare with seeing off a long-standing colonial power or ending apartheid?), there's no doubt Federer has the calming charisma that was a big part of those men's ability to appeal as unifying leaders of oppressed peoples. Just as they were known to be difficult men in their private life, so Federer can be, but in public he has a magnetism that reassures. The counter-argument is that the Federer personality is all a simple calculation that he needs to be like that to achieve his goals – that the real Federer has been subverted in the pursuit of sporting greatness. That would be too harsh, as Federer stands for greatness with humanity, which cannot be said for many who achieve greatness in sport. But it's worth noting the words of the very thoughtful Andre Agassi, who, in an interview with the veteran American tennis journalist Bill Simons in 2009, said of Federer's serenity, 'I never knew if I believed it. And if it is believable, it's certainly a different life than I've had. When you see those moments, like when he lost to Nadal and he just broke down, you wonder what he's suppressing.'

Roger Federer is not a saint. If nothing else, it would be putting too onerous a responsibility on him to label him as such. But, at risk of getting dangerously into the realms of the spiritual or the philosophical, he is an example of someone who has worked out how to process setbacks and grow from them, and to use a positive approach to deal with the obstacles in his way. And the fact that he has emerged as a thoroughly decent individual can serve as an inspiration to all of us who struggle to find the right way to deal with our demons.

Essentially, Federer is a positive person. In an interview with Paul Kimmage for the *Sunday Times* in November 2009, he explained that, when he and Tiger Woods came to do an advert for their clothing provider, the script involved the lines 'I love winning' and 'I hate losing'. Roger said he was keen to take the 'I love winning' line – and said Tiger was happy to take 'I hate losing' – because he (Federer) felt his love of winning characterised him much more than a fear of losing. 'I'm a positive person, a very positive thinker,' he said. 'To me, to hate losing is a bit negative. I dreamed about doing what I'm doing now, but it's so difficult to keep winning and to keep your love for the game because of all the travelling and the sacrifices. So I just said, "I'm not going to let that happen to me. I'm going to take a positive approach that travelling is great and that I'm going to see different cultures and places I would never see if I wasn't a tennis player." My wife loves it, I love it, so let's have a good time because it's not going to last until I'm seventy.'

Part of this positive approach includes an appreciation of the path trodden by the greats of the game that has allowed him to harvest rich pickings from his ability as a tennis player, and an awareness of his responsibilities to the sport in general. 'I try to be good for the game,' he says, 'to leave it better off than when I arrived, even though that's hard. Of course, the Grand Slams are important, but I try to respect every tournament that invites me. There are the fans who pay for tickets, and I want to live up to my expectations too.' His gratitude towards the groundwork done by past champions was a big factor in his motivation for founding the Laver Cup.

The requirements of getting to the top in a highly competitive sport like professional tennis make it highly unlikely that the leading exponents will be down-to-earth people, at least in their playing days (many a great champion has developed a sense of the bigger picture when the need for single-minded dedication has gone). That is what makes the generation of Federer, Nadal, Djokovic and Murray so remarkable – they are all driven, no doubt a nightmare at times for the people who have to deal with them behind the scenes, but with great presentational skills. Tennis has been phenomenally lucky in the first two decades of the twenty-first century to have four icons who genuinely understand how tennis fits into the world and what the obligations of the top players are. As the eldest of the quartet by almost five years, Federer has set the tone, but Nadal, Djokovic and Murray have all been big enough as people to follow the signals.

The role of 'world number one' is thought of as just a statistic, a number to signify the person whose results have been the best over the previous twelve months. But there's more to it than that. It is a genuine role, albeit an indefinable one. Whether they are aware of it or not, world number ones set the tone of the locker rooms and player lounges. When Federer became world number one in 2004, the tone he set was an outgoing but responsible and respectful one, and Nadal, Djokovic and Murray have continued that tone, to the point where the players behind them have taken their cue.

Nadal is as much of a humanitarian as Federer but in a very different way. He was brought up to believe that children in Africa and other parts of the world would love to have just one of his rackets, so in no way should he abuse his racket on court. As a result, he seldom if ever does. Nadal is also scrupulously polite, thanking journalists at the end of interviews even if he may have felt the interview was a pain he could happily have done without. And there is the story from September 2008 of Nadal eating a meal on a café terrace in Madrid with his Davis Cup colleagues when the sound of a boy's voice came down from a balcony above: 'Rafa, can I have your autograph?' it said.

'Come down here and I'll give it to you,' replied Nadal.

'OK, but it may take a few minutes because I'm in a wheelchair,' came the boy's voice.

At which point, Nadal shouted, 'Wait there,' then scaled the outside of the building, climbed up the balcony, gave the boy his autograph and sat chatting with him for ten minutes.

Djokovic is in some ways the biggest statesman of the four, having lived through the 1999 Nato bombing of Belgrade and had to represent a country with a severe image problem. He not only cut out the early on-court ailments, but he learned to manage the sense of irritation he felt at being viewed as, effectively, the third man in a two-man show, and he suppressed his understandable irritation at getting less recognition for a greater body of work than Federer and Nadal. Nadal took his sense of responsibility to the level where he hardly ever blamed an injury when he lost a match, even if he was clearly affected by one, for fear of detracting from his opponent's victory. And Murray was almost too respectful of Nadal, never quite turning on the competitive juices the way he did against other players. To some observers, this is all a bit too clean for an ultra-competitive sport, but, in an era when sport and business are massively intertwined, having tennis's image defined by a cluster of thoroughly decent individuals is of inestimable value. This could be Federer's greatest legacy to his sport.

For most of his career, he benefited from a quite remarkable popularity that was almost stateless. He seemed always to be the crowd favourite, even playing against a home opponent, and plenty of Australian, French, British and American players have cursed the fact that they received less of a welcome walking on court in their home Grand Slam to face Federer. (The one exception was in the Olympic Gold Medal match at Wimbledon in 2012, when the British crowd were so pro-Murray that it seemed to faze Federer a little.) He also seemed to defy that aspect of popularity whereby a player at the peak of their fortunes loses popularity simply because every opponent is a plucky underdog. When he lost to Nadal in the 2008 Wimbledon final, there almost seemed more sadness that he had missed out on a sixth consecutive title than that a new champion was crowned for the first time in a while.

A feature of Federer that the Swiss and international communities don't always appreciate is that Federer comes across somewhat differently in Switzerland than abroad; or, more specifically, he comes over differently when speaking Swiss German than when speaking English, French or High German. It's not really the comfort of his mother tongue, as there's nothing he can't say in any of his learned languages, but rather that he's more the unaffected boy-next-door when speaking his Basel German, compared with the international ambassador in the other three languages. This was particularly apparent when, a week after winning the French Open in 2009, he went on a live sports talk show with the experienced Swiss television interviewer Matthias Hüppi. In tennis terms, it wasn't the greatest interview ever, but, by catching Federer back on home soil and in his mother tongue, Hüppi extracted more of the personality of Roger Federer than emerged from many a dignified international interview. Federer regularly admitted to aspects of self-doubt when speaking Swiss German, something he seldom did in English (or French or High German).

He was also universally respected by his fellow professionals, and was very influential during his six years as president of the ATP Player Council (2008–14). He decided to run for election because he felt the players' voice wasn't being sufficiently heard, but he was also not averse to countering the prevailing view of his fellow competitors if he felt it was not in the best interests of the sport.

For example, at a general players' meeting in Melbourne in 2009, players expressed their horror at a decision by the World Anti-Doping Agency (Wada) to introduce what became known as the 'whereabouts rule'. Wada insisted that, to allow it to randomly test athletes without warning, it required players to give their whereabouts for one hour every day up to three months in advance. Because no one can say for certain where they will be three months hence, there was scope for players to update the information they had given, but the players were still in a severe state of uproar, with one after another standing up and voicing their disgust. What should have been a ninety-minute meeting lasted for nearly four hours, and experienced players said the level of indignation was pretty much unprecedented.

Eventually Federer stood up and calmly said that while the indignation was understandable, everyone wanted a clean sport and this was the price they would have to pay. He suggested they all fill in '5am player hotel or home' for the next three months and make amendments as their plans changed. The doubles player Ashley Fisher, who himself later served on the Player Council, said, 'To me, this showed what a class act and practical guy Roger Federer is. In the back of the room one player after another ranked 30–100 in the world was arguing, yet the guy who probably gets tested the most and has less time than anyone was able to calmly rationalise the actions of Wada. I found it inspirational, and it was one of the factors that made me agree to join the council when a vacancy came up shortly after that meeting.'

*

Federer seems to inspire remarkable loyalty in those immediately around him: the group of friends, family and service providers known loosely as Team Federer. One could argue this is pure self-interest – after all, when you have a mate who's earning millions and is happy to provide a bedroom for you in his luxury apartment in Dubai, you're unlikely to do anything to rock the boat. Yet by modern media standards, the good ship Federer is phenomenally leak-proof. All thirty-nine people invited to Roger and Mirka's wedding in April 2009 kept the secret to the point where the press only heard about it after the event, no one spilled the beans about Mirka expecting twins (twice!), and, when Federer had to undergo arthroscopic surgery on a meniscus problem sustained the day after the 2016 Australian Open, no one could get their hands on further information in the days after despite the news release from Team8 prompting as many questions as it answered.

Perhaps in some respects the art of remaining the nice guy lies in keeping your own nose clean while all around are dirtying theirs. In 2008, Federer appeared in a television commercial for Gillette razors alongside two other clean-cut sporting heroes, the golfer Tiger Woods and the French footballer Thierry Henry. By the end of 2009, both Woods' and Henry's reputations were in tatters, Woods' after the revelation of a series of affairs, Henry's following a double-handball that allowed France unfairly into the 2010 soccer World Cup finals. Simply by doing nothing, Federer's stock had risen. It's also worth adding that Federer's attitude to his Gillette contract was scrupulously professional – he never turned out anything less than smoothly shaven during his years as an ambassador for the razor company, which perhaps explains the rumpus that greeted the pirate beard he allowed to grow during the 2015 ATP Finals (by which time he was out of contract).

He is not into alcohol or fast cars. In his bachelor days he preferred to play cards or computer games. Quality time with his four children has rather taken over his leisure pursuits, but he still enjoys time with his mates where he can have the odd game of PlayStation. He's willing to try out new things, but isn't a great risk-taker. He's scared of bungee jumping and sky diving, and says he was only able to play on the helipad of the Burj al-Arab hotel in Dubai 'because it wasn't moving'.

An attribute that goes hand-in-hand with his affable personality is a strong sense of fairness and responsibility. He himself has said, 'I think there's a lot of fair play involved when I play the game, respect for the game, respect for the opponent, being polite to everyone you meet. I think those are key things my parents have taught me.' That is true up to a point, but it would be wrong to deny the subtle advantages Federer enjoyed just because of who he is. Because of his name, he always got star billing on the main courts, which in places like Melbourne and New York meant he often played when the worst of the heat had gone out of the day. And just by being Roger Federer, he had a magnetism that meant the playing field was never totally level; the opponent was playing the reputation as well as the player. And in the latter years of his career, he was not averse to making occasional use of injury timeouts in situations where one could be forgiven for wondering whether it was tactical.

He's not massively materialistic, at least not ostentatiously so. The Swiss tennis journalist René Stauffer tells a delightful story about how Federer's aspirations as a teenager were different to those of many aspiring tennis players, and how people hear what they want or expect to hear rather than what is actually said. In an interview for a youth magazine, Federer was asked what he would buy when he received his first prize-money cheque. When Lynette read the published article, she was surprised to see her son quoted as saying he'd buy a Mercedes. After further reflection, she was so sure this was a mistake that she called the magazine's office and asked to listen to the recording of the interview. It transpired that Federer had said, 'mehr CDs', the German for 'more CDs', which is pronounced almost identically to the German pronunciation of the luxury car.

Federer himself hasn't changed much in this respect, and his own materialism has remained very low-key. But it would be wrong to think he is immune to either material goods or maximising his income. He has lived in some seriously luxury residences, notably the three-storey glass palace he built in Wollerau overlooking the Zurich Lake, reported to be worth around $10 million, though it would be unfair to say he is ostentatious about his wealth. In 2018 he sold the palatial glass house in Wollerau after the family had moved into a house he had built in Valbella, a ski resort just south of Chur in the most eastern of Switzerland's cantons, Graubünden. Intended originally as a holiday home, the house has a practice wall that Federer used in March 2020 for a video that went viral of him practising trick shots in sub-zero temperatures while snow lay all around. That was his official residence for a few years, but then the family moved to another self-built house on the north side of the

Zurich Lake in Rapperswil-Jona, diagonally across the water from Wollerau.

Rapperswil-Jona is in the canton of St Gallen, which has a higher tax level than Graubünden, but whether the tax levels mean anything in terms of Federer's take-home pay is questionable. Income from prize money is taxed in the country in which it is earned, so where he lives is irrelevant. However, his endorsement income exceeds by some margin his prize money, and where he lives then does become relevant for tax. He clearly pays some of his income into the Roger Federer Foundation, but how his finances are structured can be difficult to assess. He doesn't talk about it, and annual reports in the public domain from companies in Switzerland don't leave the observer much wiser. There are three iterations of a company called 'Tenro' (thought to be assembled from Tennis Roger), one of which is a significant contributor to the Roger Federer Foundation with which it shares the same address in Basel (the Federers' address). Publicly available credit information somewhat mysteriously describes Tenro AG as being part of the asset management industry, with a total of ten employees 'across all of its locations' and 'generating $1.31 million in sales'.

To what extent are Federer's personal financial arrangements relevant to the Federer story? They would be relevant if the outward appearance is of a generous, socially aware individual who then manages his finances according to a different set of ethics. But while he is clearly maximising his income – to the point where he will never have to earn another cent if he doesn't want to – it is a big leap to say that this indicates a discrepancy between his financial management and his outward moral compass.

The fact that he has stayed in Switzerland, where he pays considerably more in taxes than he would if he moved to Monaco, the Bahamas or another tax haven, suggests either that he has a moderately favourable arrangement with the Swiss tax authorities or he is paying a lot of money for the right to live in his home country and bring up his four kids in the country of his and Mirka's choosing. And while no one outside the inner circle knows how the Federer millions are managed, it is hard to make any sort of claim that his outward generosity is some sort of charade.

Having said all that, it would probably be fairer to say that Federer is not ostentatiously materialistic than that he isn't materialistic at all.

Federer's management constantly receives offers for him to advertise certain products and services, and the number they turn down massively outweighs the number they can accept, or even consider. To those walking the streets of Basel, it is sometimes hard to avoid the impression that he advertises everything that exists, from luxury coffee makers to new lines of running shoes. But while his earning potential is fully exploited, his endorsements are limited.

There are three core ones: his racket, his clothing and his wristwatch. The racket contract with Wilson Sporting Goods guarantees that we will never see Federer using a rival manufacturer's racket – in fact, if he turned up at an event without a racket and someone asked him to hit a few balls, he would be contractually obliged to decline unless the racket was a Wilson. His clothing is now established as Uniqlo, after he played the vast majority of his career in Nike apparel. The fact that Uniqlo doesn't seem that keen on getting quantities of Federer tennis shirts into the world's sports shops and online stores suggests the Japanese company is not looking to become a big name in tennis but is merely using Federer's profile to enhance the global recognition of the Uniqlo brand.

In 2004, Federer signed a five-year deal with a Swiss luxury watchmaker, Maurice Lacroix, following the end of a contract with another Swiss watchmaker, Rolex. After switching back to IMG's representation in 2005, Rolex brought back Federer in 2006 by buying him out of his Lacroix contract. Federer is now very much associated with the Rolex brand, which has a neat tie-up with Wimbledon, where Rolex sponsors the on-court clocks.

And endorsements are important if you want to get into the somewhat dubious territory of comparing one athlete's worth against others'. The most recognised global vehicle for sports income comparisons is the list of the world's highest-paid athletes published annually by the American magazine *Forbes*. This is a ranking of the world's leading athletes according to the aggregate of their prize money or officially published earnings, and *estimates* of their endorsements. For stars of individual sports like tennis and golf, the endorsements massively exceed the prize money, whereas for team sports income from salaries normally dwarfs individual endorsements. For most of the 2010s Federer was between fourth and seventh overall, but in 2020 he became the first tennis player to top the overall list (he was regularly the biggest earner from *Forbes*' endorsement estimates alone), at least in part because team sports had missed several months due to Covid-19 while Federer could continue earning from endorsements even when the tennis tour was suspended. In both 2021 and

2022, when he barely played any tennis, he still managed to finish seventh. That testifies to how well he and his advisers are maximising his name.

Although he was always happy to expound on a number of aspects of tennis in his post-match interviews, Federer has proved generally reticent about giving opinions about the world at large. While Martina Navratilova used to enjoy giving her take on social and environmental issues (she once turned up for a press conference at Wimbledon wearing a T-shirt with the slogan 'It happens in the best families' emblazoned on it, referring to homosexuality), Federer generally limits himself to tennis matters. Such reticence should not be taken for a lack of interest, merely a decision to concentrate on those areas where he is clearly qualified to speak. 'There's no doubt that Roger is a highly intelligent young man!' his former school head teacher Theresa Fischbacher said. 'Nobody thinks about asking a prominent scientist to explain the word "deuce", because his main concern is his special field of sciences, and an active tennis player's main concern must be tennis.'

On a personal note, I recall being pleasantly struck by Federer's composure as a teenager with issues he didn't feel competent to comment on. In June 2001, I conducted a lengthy interview with him in Halle for an article for a British newspaper and, after I'd asked my main questions, the interview developed partly into a casual chat. At one stage, the topic got onto South Africa and, in the course of the conversation, I asked him what he thought about the political situation there. He stopped in his tracks and said that, at nineteen, he couldn't be expected to make judgements about the politics of South Africa. For me, the most interesting aspect of that brief exchange wasn't that he didn't know enough about the subject to have an opinion (to admit you don't know something can be as much a sign of strength as of ignorance), but that I'd assumed he would have an opinion. Something about the assurance with which he talked about the country of his mother's childhood made me feel it was entirely logical to ask him about the political situation there. From my brief exchange with him, I suspect it won't be difficult for Federer to take an intelligent interest in something more meaningful than tennis when he decides to put his mind to it. Then again, not every athlete with statesmanlike qualities can carry them beyond the confines of being primarily a player of their sport and into their post-playing life. Federer certainly starts from a position of being greatly admired, and he has generally come across as more measured than the man who is closest to him temperamentally, the equally intelligent but more warrior-like Novak Djokovic (Djokovic proved a more divisive president of the ATP Player Council than the conciliatory Federer), but who knows whether that will still hold true thirty years from now?

People close to Federer say he will never fundamentally change, that his basic humanity is strong enough to withstand any temptation. That will probably only be tested when his playing days are well behind him and he returns to a lower-profile existence. He himself has said it would be unrealistic for anyone to expect him to have remained unchanged by his achievements. In an interview in June 2004 in the run-up to Wimbledon, when he was the defending champion for the first time and still a relatively new world number one, he said, 'I feel like I had to change

– or adapt to the situation, I'd rather call it. There are a lot of demands from press, media, very important people I've met in the past, and it's a different life I'm living now. It has changed me a little bit because I'm more careful, but at the same time, now that I've reached my dreams, it's more of an enjoyment playing on the tour.'

He has remained remarkably popular. He won the ATP's 'Fan Favourite' award nineteen times running, and only surrendered it to Nadal after he had retired. But needless to say, in today's world you cannot be an exemplary role model and a legend without someone making fun of you.

Federer has been remarkably free from mockery and parody. There's an impersonation of him on YouTube done by a young Novak Djokovic in the Flushing Meadows locker room in 2007, which really emphasises Federer's effeminate gestures, a bit the way a cartoonist exaggerates various facial features. And there's @PseudoFed, the Twitter handle and blog that parades under the name 'Not Roger Federer'. This is a parody that plays on Federer's sartorial awareness in particular, his effeminate gestures in general, and his willingness to shun conventional modesty when he thinks he has done something well. The tone of the tweets and the blog is very consistent, and anyone with limited knowledge of Federer would assume from PseudoFed that he is a rather arrogant, upper-crust dandy. 'He' is forever #humble, he puts capital letters on all references to 'me' and 'my', his mythical staff earn regular mentions, and he frequently talks about goats, a veiled reference to his unofficial status as the Greatest Of All Time. Of course Federer himself doesn't write it, and one of the attributes that makes the feature enduring (apart from it being very funny) is that the tennis world is not quite sure who does. It is effectively a social media version of a long-running cartoon. Federer has kept his counsel on it but, if PseudoFed is the worst thing that happens to him, he will have got off quite lightly.

Much as it is admirable to note how Federer overcame the wild side of his personality as a child to become a highly disciplined and focused tennis player, the other side of that coin is that few people have witnessed his deep-rooted sense of fun. If one talks to those who knew him as a junior, the picture painted is one of a fun-loving, happy, joking person who was always into practical jokes.

Talk to players on the tour, and they will testify that the mischief is still alive and kicking. It occasionally shines at a charity exhibition event, such as the 'Hit for Haiti' and 'Rally for Relief' that he initiated at the 2012 and 2013 Australian Opens, but for most of Federer's matches it remained firmly hidden from view. The doubles player Ashley Fisher tells the story of the time he was lying face-down on a massage table and couldn't work out why his back kept feeling slightly damp. A day after his massage, someone who had been in the room at the time revealed that the dampness had come from Roger Federer, who was squirting water from a kid's water pistol over the privacy screens in the treatment room.

He has a stubborn streak, but few champions in any sport don't. His long-time coach Severin Lüthi told the ATP podcast, 'Sometimes you say something to your player and he only does it a year later,' which is a diplomatic way of describing Federer's stubbornness – his reluctance to play drop shots in the early part of his career and his slowness in embracing a bigger racket frame could be put down to that trait.

For many years, some tennis watchers wondered how Federer would handle the inevitable decline of playing level in his twilight years. The short answer is that he hasn't had to, because the decline never really happened. In February 2014 his ranking had fallen to eighth, at the start of 2017 it was down at seventeenth, and there were plenty on both occasions who were sure they could see signs of an irreversible downward trend. Yet, until his right knee proved too damaged for him to compete as a singles player, he always bounced back, and his belief that he could return to the top has meant he has shielded himself from that loss of dignity that afflicts many in sport and the arts when their star begins to wane and they struggle to deal with their status as potentially vulnerable prey. And he was blessed with that slice of luck that all top athletes seek but few find: the chance to go out with dignity in front of an adoring public, as his Laver Cup finale in September 2022 provided the perfect stage.

If he is the greatest in tennis – or certainly one of the greatest – where does that leave him in the wider sporting world, and indeed the wider world in general?

There is no question that he is recognised as one of the sporting greats of our time. His obvious contemporary rivals would be Tiger Woods, Michael Jordan, Lionel Messi, Usain Bolt , LeBron James and possibly the German Formula One drivers Michael Schumacher and Sebastian Vettel (until his fall from grace in 2012 Lance Armstrong would have been in that group, perhaps topping it). There might be other individuals in a given year, like Michael Phelps in 2008 or Mo Farah in 2012, but we are talking here mainly of enduring presence at the top. Woods had the same period of dominance that Federer had, but his career faded badly the way Federer's didn't, and even his emotional triumph at the US Masters in 2019 was a blip in the twilight of Woods' career rather than a sustained comeback. Jordan captured the imagination of a sporting nation with his ability to apparently hang bird-like in the air, but are Woods and Jordan (and even Armstrong before his meltdown) greater sportsmen than Federer? Greater sports personalities, perhaps, but that is a slightly different matter.

And, as for comparison with Woods and Jordan, James Blake offered this assessment after losing to Federer in the quarter-finals of the 2006 US Open: 'I heard something on television about two weeks ago saying Tiger Woods is going to pass Michael Jordan as the best athlete of our time. I think that's a joke. I'd make a case for Roger Federer being the best athlete of our time. Not tennis player, athlete. No offence to Tiger, he's an incredible golfer, but his record in matchplay events, the events where you're out if you have a bad day, isn't particularly impressive. We tennis players have that every single week. Roger wins every Grand Slam title except the French Open, and he wins every Masters Series tournament. That means he can't allow himself a single bad day. That's incredible.' By Blake's logic, you'd now have to include Djokovic in the same bracket as Federer, but not necessarily Nadal as the Spaniard has not posted the same consistency of results that the Swiss and the Serb have.

Where Federer scores less well than some of the great names in sport is on personality. That doesn't mean he is dull – tennis fans are well aware of his personality, even if it was often hidden behind a very focused calm exterior until a match was won. But, as a sports personality, he cannot be said to have transcended the boundaries of sport as much as some have done.

Martina Navratilova was known beyond both tennis and sport thanks to her forthright social views, in particular those on sexual orientation and the environment. It made her a household name, even in households whose members knew little or nothing about tennis. The same went for John McEnroe at the height of his volatility in the early 1980s. At that time, the British satirical television programme *Not the Nine O'Clock News* performed a sketch that seemed to sum up McEnroe, then at the peak of his playing career. Entitled 'Breakfast in the McEnroe household', it portrayed McEnroe coming down to breakfast, hyperactively gulping down some orange juice, and being ticked off by his mother for slurping. 'What did I do?' pleaded the McEnroe character incredulously, thereby triggering a domestic row that mirrored his rages at umpires. Even the dancer Wayne Sleep had a routine that portrayed McEnroe's anger in balletic form.

Such instances reflect players becoming bigger than just the tennis or other sporting world in which they have made their name, and it's hard to think of Federer in that context. He has suffered the compliment of being mocked, notably by the PseudoFed Twitter feed, which enhances his status somewhat, but that has been a phenomenon largely contained within the tennis world. The opinions he has expressed publicly are generally within the realms of tennis. It is very much his style to keep his opinions low-key, a character trait that works against building up a high profile in a celebrity-driven world. Perhaps in the future he might venture an opinion on, say, the unacceptability of severe poverty in the twenty-first century, based on the work in Africa undertaken by his foundation. That could raise his broader profile, and might lead to some diplomatic role as a quiet but persuasive voice for social justice in the developing world.

His standing in Switzerland is a little different. Obviously he is a household name there, having become an unofficial ambassador for the country and carried the Swiss flag at two Olympic Games. Yet the Swiss don't go overboard about him, at least not compared with sports fans in most other countries, and non-Swiss sports fans who have been in Switzerland when Federer was winning Grand Slam titles testify to a people pleased with his success but a long way from ecstatic about it.

A lot of this may be to do with Switzerland as a land-locked country with few natural resources, a combination of economic circumstances that has spawned in the Swiss a powerful land-based work ethic that underlies all Switzerland's big exports (from cuckoo clocks and luxury watches to cheese and chocolate). Against that background, a player achieving fame and fortune through sporting prowess doesn't cut as much ice as in other countries. 'There isn't the adulation and adoration for him here,' says, Theresa Fischbacher. 'Perhaps that's why he can still afford to live in Switzerland.'

The Basel journalist Thomas Wirz goes further: 'The Swiss don't like top stars. When the first Roger Federer fan club was opened in Allschwil [a suburb of Basel], I thought there would be a storm of fans but it was very intimate. I think it has less to do with Basel and more to do with Switzerland.'

There are certainly no plaques around Federer's old childhood haunts, and it wasn't until he'd won three Grand Slam titles that the Old Boys club put up a portrait of him in the clubhouse and renamed Court 1 the Roger Federer Court. They also named the neighbouring court the Marco Chiudinelli Court in honour of Federer's contemporary, who also won a Davis Cup winner's medal (Lynette Federer attended the naming ceremony, but Roger didn't). That somehow sums up how the Swiss view the two – Federer has won incomparably more than Chiudinelli, yet the club they grew up at honours them both equally. There is talk of having a street in Basel named the 'Roger Federer Weg' (Roger Federer Way), but it hasn't happened yet. The only commemorative acknowledgements are Federer's appearances on a postage stamp and a coin.

'It hangs together with the reticence of the Swiss to respect people who make their living from sport,' says Niki von Vary, the former teammate of Federer's at Old Boys who went on to become a political adviser. 'You saw it with Marc Rosset. Whatever you may think of him, he won an Olympic gold medal, but there's no monument or plaque to him. The same with [top-level skier] Bernhard Russi. However much sportsmen and -women achieve at the highest level, they don't earn the same reputation that they do in America or Australia or other European nations. The typical Swiss citizen is so grounded, so connected to the land, he doesn't want to stand out from the crowd; he just wants to come through life without creating a scene. That's the history of Switzerland. It's always been that way and, to a large extent, will always be that way. You see it in politics, with Switzerland's attitude to the EU. We don't have a star culture and as a result we haven't had a boom like Boris Becker created in Germany. The Swiss are probably too low-key for that.'

All the coaches interviewed for this book were asked if they thought the Federer factor had increased interest in tennis in the Basel area. All could point to the enthusiasm that many youngsters there today have for Federer and their wish to play like him, but few have much evidence that youngsters gifted in several sports are being attracted to tennis because of the inspiration of Roger Federer.

As one of three Swiss gold medallists at the 2008 Beijing Olympics, he clearly enhanced his reputation among his compatriots, his steering Switzerland to the Davis Cup in 2014 really didn't do anything more for his profile. He is liked and well respected, but he is not hero-worshipped the way someone of his achievements would be if he had grown up in most other developed countries. A survey in 2014 showed he had a recognition rating among the German-speaking Swiss of ninety per cent, with eighty per cent favourably disposed towards him. In other words, there were still ten per cent of Swiss Germans who didn't know who he was, and, of those who did, just over ten per cent didn't like him. (It should also be assumed that, among those who like him, there is a small group who do actually worship him and who see even the slightest hint of criticism as blasphemy.)

Asked by his editor to write a piece in the *Aargauer Zeitung* newspaper in March 2015 about whether Federer should retire, the Swiss tennis journalist Michael Wehrle wrote, 'The question is as daft as it is irrelevant. Federer is by a mile the best-known Swiss citizen; abroad he's quite simply the face of Switzerland. He is always under discussion, and because he is without scandal there is only the sport to go on. But sporting triumphs don't last very long in the news, so people start speculating about how he managed to conceive twins, whether he's planning more children, or when he's going to retire. That question is as relevant as whether he's wearing white socks or black socks. For some, it seems that Federer's only value is as a topic into which they can stick their oar.'

Having retired as a tennis player at forty-one, Federer has the world at his fingertips. There are plenty of things he could do in tennis, in social activities, in business, and in any number of other fields. He is likely to maintain an eclectic mix of activities, with his role as father to four children taking up a large share of his time.

Within tennis, the list of possibilities is almost endless. He has said he wants to keep playing, if only occasionally, and he would be a tremendous asset on the seniors tour, both as a legend in his own right and for his ability to be creative with a tennis ball in an arena where entertainment value counts for far more than results. He could be a TV commentator or pundit, he is an obvious captain for both Team Europe in the Laver Cup and Switzerland in the Davis Cup. And if ever the alphabet soup of tennis's seven governing bodies decide to appoint a commissioner of tennis to unite the sport (an idea that has been mooted for several decades but without ever getting off first base), Federer would be an obvious target, though he would have to call more on leadership and visionary skills than the conciliation skills he deployed so successfully as president of the ATP Player Council.

He would be a dream catch for any business, and he already has connections with numerous blue-chip companies. His work for the less privileged of the world's citizens – especially in Africa – is likely to continue to occupy a sizeable chunk of his interest. And there is always the chance he could take on a role few people expect of him, simply because it offers him a direction he had never thought of and that would therefore keep his mind active.

A role that has been suggested for him that is unlikely ever to happen is president of Switzerland. He has never been a particularly political animal, and has preferred to conciliate and make his own decisions rather than play the give-and-take games that are essential to political achievement. His sense of ethics might also prevent him from embracing the cut-throat nature of political survival. Switzerland's system of government means the president is always one of the seven members of the ruling cabinet, which in turn is made up of representatives of four parties, making for continuous consensus. The consensus would suit Federer well, but to jockey for position within a political party for a route into the cabinet seems something alien to his character.

Where he might have a semi-political role is in the diplomatic sphere, not as a career diplomat or ambassador, but as a representative of a cause. A job with international disaster efforts or refugees might be well suited to him, as could one-off troubleshooting missions (like the one in 1980 when the US president Jimmy Carter asked the former world heavyweight boxing champion Muhammad Ali to be a one-time envoy to Africa).

Through this chapter, and indeed throughout this book, I've tried to identify the flaws in Federer's personality in order to paint a realistic picture of him. In truth, there are precious few, and there's no doubt he's a remarkable man and a great benefit to his sport. He exudes a calmness both on and off the court that gives the impression of wisdom beyond his years, almost of an old soul who has an innate sense of what's really important and what can be discarded. And while the journalist Marco Mordasini might be correct in saying, 'You can't be as successful as he is without creating some envy,' it's astonishing how little envy Federer has created and how few enemies he has.

When I asked Seppli Kacovski, Federer's first coach and a man who's seen his fair share of real life and suffering, what he thought Federer's less attractive attributes might be, he replied, 'He must have his shadow sides, but I don't know them. I think he has everything he needs. He needs to be physical and competitive, so tennis gives him that. He has a sense of fun, and that is satisfied by people around him. He likes to make contact with people, so he gets them talking. He is basically fulfilled, and that is why he's the man he is.' Kacovski spoke those words in December 2005 when Federer's professional career was still in its early stages, but they seem to be as valid now as they were then. It's hard to think of any stage in his glorious career when they were not equally valid.

BIBLIOGRAPHY

THIS BOOK IS a development of a book first researched and written in 2005–6 that has gone through ten incarnations: two editions of *Fantastic Federer*, one edition of *Roger Federer: Spirit of a Champion*, two of *Roger Federer: The Greatest*, three of *Federer* and two of this one, *Roger Federer: The Definitive Biography*. At the time the first *Fantastic Federer* was published in May 2006, it was the first full-length biography of Roger Federer, and as such there was no obvious bibliography or recommendation for further reading. Much of the information for this book and all its predecessor editions has come from my own personal experience, articles I have written for various publications, and recordings of interviews and press conferences. Obviously, I cannot be everywhere, so a lot of other information has come from newspaper cuttings, especially those of fellow tennis journalists I have worked with and respect. I have tried to credit them at least once within the text. I also gained useful insights in the course of researching and writing my own *The Sporting Statesman: Novak Djokovic and the Rise of Serbia* (John Blake Publishing, 2014), now *Novak Djokovic: The Biography*.

Since the first edition of *Fantastic Federer* came out, there have been two other full-length biographies. The first, and more recognised, was written by the leading Swiss tennis journalist, René Stauffer. It was originally published under the title *Das Tennisgenie*, and it was published in German by the Swiss publishing house Pendo. The title translates as 'The Tennis Genius', but when it came out in English, published by the American firm New Chapter Press in 2007, it was under the name *Quest for Perfection: The Roger Federer Story*. Stauffer has since updated his book under the title *Roger Federer: die Biografie* (no translation necessary). That book was written under the same circumstances as this one, namely without the direct co-operation of Roger but with no serious obstacles put in the way. As a result, it covers similar ground to this one. It is stronger than this book in some ways and weaker in others; as the tennis correspondent of the *Tages-Anzeiger* newspaper of Zurich, René has been at more Federer events than I have, though inevitably I have been at some he was not at. As a result, his book is more Swiss and mine more international.

I have tremendous respect for René, believing him to have been the most knowledgeable of the Swiss tennis writers until his retirement at the end of 2022; I am pleased that his book now forms part of the database of public information from which a biography of Roger Federer can be drawn; and it's good that his work is available to the English-speaking world. I would, however, encourage anyone who has the ability to read German to opt for the original Stauffer book rather than the English. Translations never feel quite as authentic as the original, and René's smooth-flowing German prose hasn't always survived the journey into English with its meter intact!

The other full-length biography came fifteen years after Stauffer's and my books. With Federer having always declined any interviews for the purposes of a book, any subsequent biographies could only come from journalists who had access to him for their daily work, and in 2021 the *New York Times* tennis correspondent Christopher Clarey brought out *The Master*. Given that the American market is high up the priority list in the promotion strategy Federer and Tony Godsick worked out and followed, Clarey has had immense access to Federer and his entourage, so he has more material to draw on than most. I count Chris as a friend and enjoyed reading his book, yet I found *The Master* not that different from Stauffer's and my biographies. It goes into greater technical analysis of Federer's game, and is largely driven by first-person tales of Clarey's own experiences with Federer (and a lot of detail on Nadal, Djokovic and others that one might argue is not strictly relevant). Clarey is arguably the most elegant writer on today's tennis, and the narrative flows beautifully off the page (the way Stauffer's does in German), but the flow is slightly undermined by his irritating use of 'told me' after nearly every quote that emanates from his own interviews, suggesting he's trying a little too hard to say what access he got. The book was overhyped by the publisher before it came out, so Clarey may have been under pressure to imply he was closer to Federer than any author is in reality.

It may be worth noting that my biography is the only one

of the main three that acknowledges the other two. Where I feel Stauffer and Clarey have some interesting information, I quote from their biographies, citing my source as appropriate.

Alongside these three biographies are two other books worth a mention in the bibliography of Roger Federer, and both involve Stauffer's long-time colleague as a tennis writer on the *Tages-Anzeiger*, Simon Graf. Graf's own book, *Roger Federer: Phenomenon. Enthusiast. Philanthropist*, published in 2019, is a collection of fifteen short chapters looking at different aspects of Federer's life. And in 2022, Graf teamed up with the British writer Simon Cambers to compile *The Roger Federer Effect*, which focuses on how Federer's career has affected various friends, fans, rivals and artists. I have not read either so cannot offer any comment.

The database of public information on Roger Federer also includes two short books that were of considerable help to me. Roger Jaunin's French-language book *Roger Federer* (Favre/Le Matin, 2004, updated 2006) was very useful, particularly for stories from the French-speaking part of Switzerland, while Freddy Widmer's *Moments '05: Augenblicke mit Roger Federer* (Basler Zeitung, 2005) provided some of the details about Federer's background in Basel.

Matthew Syed's book *Bounce: The Myth of Talent and the Power of Practice*, mentioned on page 137, is published by HarperCollins (2010).